SELECTED READINGS IN

CRIMINAL

JUSTICE

SELECTED READINGS IN

CRIMINAL

JUSTICE

David L. Bender, *Publisher*

Bruno Leone, *Executive Editor*

Bonnie Szumski, *Editorial Director*

Stephen E. Schonebaum, *Series Editor*

Philip L. Reichel, Professor of Sociology and Criminal Justice, University of Northern Colorado, *Book Editor*

Editorial Advisory Board
  Mary Ann Farkas, Marquette University
  Devereaux Kennedy, State University of New York College at Cortland
  Al Miranne, Gonzaga University
  N. Prabha Unnithan, Colorado State University

Contemporary
Perspectives

GREENHAVEN PRESS, INC., SAN DIEGO, CA

Every effort has been made to trace the owners of copyrighted material. The articles in this volume may have been edited for content, length, and/or reading level. Those interested in locating the original source will find the complete citation on the first page of each article.

Library of Congress Cataloging-in-Publication Data

Selected readings in criminal justice / Philip L. Reichel, book editor.
p.   cm. — (Contemporary perspectives)
Includes bibliographical references and index.
ISBN 1-56510-901-5 (lib.). — ISBN 1-56510-900-7 (pbk.)
1. Criminal justice, Administration of. 2. Crime. 3. Criminal justice, Administration of—United States. 4. Crime—United States. I. Reichel, Philip L. II. Series.
HV7419.S45   1998
364—dc21
98-4874
CIP

Copyright ©1998 by Greenhaven Press, Inc.
P.O. Box 289009
San Diego, CA 92198-9009

CONTENTS

PART II: LAW ENFORCEMENT

PART III: COURTS

PART IV: CORRECTIONS

PART V: OTHER ISSUES

FOREWORD

The purpose of the Contemporary Perspectives series is to provide college students with a convenient collection of readings with various points of view from a variety of sources. The readings are chosen with care for depth and breadth and presented in a low-cost format to introduce students to the subject discipline. Each anthology is organized to reflect the standard course, and each book is indexed.

The information explosion of recent years has made special demands of instructors. It has become difficult to remain informed about one's own specialty, let alone wade through the enormous amounts of material (in journals, magazines, books, and on-line) not directly related to one's research but relevant to students and teaching. Searching for useful readings in all forms of media (including the Internet—a tremendous resource, but often of suspect quality) and preparing a cohesive collection is a time-consuming exercise.

Each Contemporary Perspectives reading is selected to emphasize representative points of view in the discipline and expand on high-interest areas often slighted in texts. The editor of each volume is an expert in the subject area and has taught the course for many years. The advice and guidance of an editorial board ensures the usefulness of these high-quality selections. An instructor's manual with test bank, written by the editors, is available for busy instructors.

Each Contemporary Perspectives editor believes that exposure to diverse opinions effectively leads students to read critically and generates class discussion. To encourage students to become more discerning readers, the editor has prepared helpful pedagogy, including insightful introductions to each chapter's readings, discussion questions, and descriptions of pertinent websites to encourage further exploration.

Thoughtful examination of these readings can help students bridge the gap between theory and application and broaden their understanding of key issues in the discipline. Contemporary Perspectives anthologies also serve as an introduction to the range of material that students can expect to navigate in the course of their school career.

The editors of this series hope that it will serve the needs of instructors by instilling in students a desire for investigation. We value your opinions and experience and welcome your comments.

EDITOR'S PREFACE

To the Student

The study of crime and justice is inherently fascinating because it touches on the range of human experience—from the "dark side" of human behavior to the enlightened philosophical underpinnings of a society's system of social control. In addition, many of us have had indirect or direct experiences with crime and justice either through the media or, unfortunately, as offender or victim, which adds to our interest. But these experiences are insufficient to make us informed citizens; that understanding requires a familiarity with the theories, research, policies, and practices linked to the general topic of criminal justice. For the student of criminal justice, an introductory text often does not supply the detail that bridges the gap between theory and application or reflect the diversity of opinion in the discipline. As a thought-provoking basis for class discussion or to spur research for papers or projects, *Selected Readings in Criminal Justice* well serves instructors and students of our criminal justice system.

The Criminal Justice System

Some of you are planning, or currently enjoying, a career in the criminal justice field, perhaps as a police officer, lawyer, or correctional officer, or in less well known vocations as a mediator or an investigator for the public defender's office. If so, a rudimentary understanding of the entire criminal justice process from the varied perspectives of the contributors to this book—police officers, prisoners, academics, and others—offers insight into the field and assists future practitioners in making the system work properly.

Those who are not, and will not become, criminal justice practitioners must also be well informed about crime and justice issues. Though most of us might never set foot in a police station, courthouse, probation office, jail, or prison, their operations affect our daily lives. Our ability to feel safe and secure as we move about our neighborhood, the purchases we make whose prices include the costs of shoplifting and employee theft, and the taxes we pay each year are only a few examples of how the policy, practices, and procedures implemented in the name of criminal justice influence our lives. When we elect sheriffs, district attorneys, and judges, we should know something about patrol tactics, plea negotiations, and sentencing options. When we assess the reports of the civil servant police chief, supervising probation officer, or prison warden to the city council, chief judge, mayor, or legislator, we need to be familiar with issues related to community policing, intensive supervision probation, and work release. The criminal justice system works best, in other words, when all those it involves—that is, all of us—understand key issues affecting the process. The readings in this book provide some of that understanding.

Equally important in understanding criminal justice issues as an informed citizen is the need to be an intelligent consumer of information. Whatever the source of information—government agency, nonprofit organization, business corporation, criminal justice employee, or academic researcher—we must view it critically. The intelligent consumer is able to sort opinion from fact and evaluate conclusions. It is not necessary to know everything about a topic to accomplish this task. Instead, the intelligent consumer anticipates alternate explanations, appreciates the complexity of issues, realizes the right questions to ask, and knows where to find additional information about a topic. Becoming both an informed citizen and an intelligent consumer is the outcome of education that provides not only factual information about a topic but also the skills to critically evaluate that and other information. This reader is one of many aids in that education process, providing additional information about criminal justice, presenting points of view that are often neglected in the mass media or in standard criminal justice textbooks, and supplying a starting point for discussion. It is, in other words, a portion—and only a portion—of the material needed to become an informed citizen and intelligent consumer on the topic of criminal justice.

What There Is to Learn

Learning about criminal justice can be a daunting task. An introductory course typically covers law, crime, victimization, police, courts, corrections, and more. The U.S. criminal justice system can be an especially challenging subject because each state is allowed to write its own laws and set its own punishments. With fifty-two jurisdictions (the fifty states, the District of Columbia, and the federal system) providing twists to the criminal justice process (to say nothing of the military system), you might wonder how anyone can discuss an "American" system of criminal justice. Fortunately, for textbook writers and for students, there is enough similarity among the jurisdictions to allow for generalized discussion of theory and practice. But though authors of introductory criminal justice textbooks make valiant efforts to provide students with a basic understanding of the key agencies, procedures, personnel, and issues linked to contemporary criminal justice in the United States, the detail and the diversity of opinion that make this such an interesting discipline are often lost. The readings in this book have been selected to (1) provide specific examples to supplement the general content of survey courses or textbooks and (2) reflect the variation in opinions that exist regarding the most appropriate way for society to accomplish its social control goals.

The selections come from many types of sources. The growth in academic and public interest in criminal justice over the last thirty years has resulted in a host of professional journals, books, magazines, news segments, television shows, movies, and official reports covering almost every imaginable aspect of criminal justice. Selections are taken from mass-distribution periodicals like the *New Yorker* and *Psychology Today*, specialized professional publications (e.g., *Police*, from the International Association of Chiefs of Police, and the *Keepers' Voice*, published by the International Association of Correctional Officers), the writings of prison inmates (see chapter 11 on "How I Became a Convict"), the publications of organizations that approach criminal justice with a wary eye (e.g., Human Rights Watch), and perspectives from other countries (see the *CJ International* readings in chapters 3 and 9). The readings were selected to provide information relevant to the main components of criminal justice. Specifically, chapters 1 through 13 highlight the system as a whole, law enforcement, the courts, corrections, and juvenile justice. The remaining chapters remind us that today's procedures may not be tomorrow's (chapter 14) and that countries may be able to learn from each other about new ways to achieve social control (chapter 15). By the end of the book you will gain an understanding of many key issues confronting criminal justice practitioners and policy makers, whether you eventually work in the justice system or simply use your understanding to be a better-informed citizen.

To the Instructor

Each reading in this book meets at least one of three criteria. First, I searched for articles outside the mainstream press and journals. Because even smaller college and university libraries are likely to have most mass-distribution periodicals and to subscribe to the primary criminal justice journals, I sought articles that might be harder to find. Instructors can assign readings from magazines like *Time* and *Newsweek* and important journals like *Justice Quarterly*, *Criminology*, and *Crime and Delinquency*, then use this collection to provide students with interesting and informative readings from less well known publications.

A second goal was to include nontraditional perspectives on common topics. Where possible, I have used articles written from a different point of view than might typically be provided. For example, the second reading in chapter 2 provides an explanation of crime from the perspective of inmates and correction officers rather than from sociologists or psychologists. Similarly, the second reading in chapter 8 provides a former police officer's version of jury duty. These types of readings provide the student with a broader perspective of the field of criminal justice.

Finally, some articles were selected to expand on topics that are often given less coverage in introductory criminal justice textbooks. So much information is included in standard textbooks that in-depth coverage of some topics is not possible. Twenty years of teaching experience has given me a good understanding of issues that are both of interest to students and valuable pedagogically. I hope I have provided a selection that will provide students with more important supplemental information on key topics that will help instructors initiate stimulating discussion and debate.

This reader follows the organization of topics of standard introductory criminal justice textbooks. Fifteen general categories appear in most of these texts; these categories comprise the fifteen chapters of this reader, divided into five parts with three chapters per part. Two or three readings are used in each chapter, and although the readings may be of different lengths, the total words per part are similar. This allows instructors to make part assignments with the confidence that each part will require a similar amount of reading time by the student.

Several pedagogical tools have been incorporated to help the student learn. Introductory comments precede each chapter, tie the readings together, and focus the student on essential issues. Chapters conclude with discussion questions and World Wide Web addresses that allow students to gather more information from the Internet.

Instructor's Manual

To facilitate teaching, the author has prepared an instructor's manual with teaching tips and helpful references and a test bank with multiple-choice and essay questions. Please contact Greenhaven Press or your Greenhaven Press sales representative for more information.

Acknowledgments

I am very grateful to Dan Leone and Greenhaven Press for the opportunity to participate in this project. Steve Schonebaum, who proposed the project and brought me on board, continues to teach me about the publishing process. His mentoring is greatly appreciated.

Philip L. Reichel
Department of Sociology
University of Northern Colorado
Greeley, CO 80639
plreich@unco.edu

PART I

CRIMINAL JUSTICE, CRIME, AND LAW

CONTENTS

PART I. CRIMINAL JUSTICE, CRIME, AND LAW

CHAPTER 1: SYSTEM OVERVIEW

Some people argue it is no mistake that we refer to a "criminal justice system" rather than a "victim justice system," that the omission of victims from the label is simply a reflection of society's disregard for victims in the process. Others argue that when society assumed responsibility for social control, crime became a social harm more than an individual harm. As a result, the criminal justice system appropriately emphasizes the offender and society as a whole rather than the wronged individual. The two readings in this chapter represent these perspectives.

Charles S. Clark's article examines the growing victims' rights movement in the United States. The participation of victims and their families throughout the criminal justice process—especially during plea negotiations, sentencing, and parole board hearings—has raised important questions. Do the rights of victims infringe upon the rights of defendants? Should type, severity, or duration of punishment be influenced by the wishes of victims or their survivors? What role do you think victims and their families should have in the criminal justice process?

Since most users of this reader already have, or are simultaneously getting, information about the American justice system from an American author, a contrasting view may be beneficial. Alison Gomme wrote the article excerpted here for employees of the Prison Service of England and Wales. Her goal was to describe and make recommendations about the management of HIV disease in a correctional setting based on her visit to prisons in the United States. Gomme believed that her readers would best appreciate her suggestions if they understood the cultural context in which they were practiced. This approach provides the American audience with a unique opportunity to see how our system is viewed by a person from a different cultural background.

Of particular interest are Gomme's perceptions of American cultural values. For example, her impression is that the United States is a more punitive society than are England and Wales. Further, in her opinion America is a "quick fix" society that prefers politically fashionable responses to problems to longer-term commitments that tackle root causes. Rather than dismissing Gomme's impressions as inappropriately critical, approach them in an attempt to gain self-insight. For example, if you believe her impressions are mistaken, what circumstances in the United States do you think have led her to form these impressions? Or, even if you believe her impressions are basically accurate, how might her characterization of American values be criticized as overly simplistic?

CRIME VICTIMS' RIGHTS

Charles S. Clark

Long ignored as the "forgotten people" of the criminal justice system, victims of crime are now organized and vocal. The families of crime victims, and the victims themselves, are seeking new laws and state constitutional amendments guaranteeing victims the right to participate in legal proceedings. Opponents warn that such rights threaten a defendant's traditional presumption of innocence. Judges are wary of allowing emotionalism in their courtrooms, while prosecutors and police raise concerns about costs added to their heavy caseloads. Still, victims say that giving them an active role provides a needed catharsis and a chance to help in reducing crime. Charles S. Clark is a staff writer for CQ Researcher.

In late January 1988, 21-year-old Kelly Rudiger received the news that changed her life: Her 16-year-old brother Jeffrey had been found beaten and stabbed to death not far from the San Diego, Calif., pizza restaurant where he worked. Within hours, a co-worker was arrested and charged with the murder.

Three months later, however, the 23-year-old suspect was released on bond. For the next two years, Kelly and her family felt like victims of the judicial system as a series of appeals considered the legality of the man's arrest and whether the evidence against him should be suppressed. As

the matter wound its way to the U.S. Supreme Court, Rudiger's family, schoolmates and neighbors organized community meetings and a letter-writing campaign to protest the man's release and to keep her brother's case alive.

In July 1990, the case finally went to trial, and within three weeks defendant Mark Radke was convicted of first-degree murder in what police described as a sexual attack. He was sentenced to the maximum—25 years to life.

Her brother's death turned Rudiger into a victims' rights activist. Emotionally, she says, "I've been able to talk about the case only since I took this job" as director of the Doris Tate Crime Victims' Bureau in Sacramento.* "I don't put a sign on my forehead saying I'm a crime victim, but when I go into the state Legislature and mention the case, everyone remembers."

The Justice System's "Forgotten People"

Rudiger is one of thousands of Americans who have turned a grim experience with crime into a springboard for action in one of the fastest-growing civil rights movements. Crime victims, because they lacked legal standing under state law and the U.S. Constitution, have long been known as the justice system's "forgotten people."

For years, "victims were treated as if they were no different from a bloody shirt or a sperm

---

Reprinted from Charles S. Clark, "Crime Victims' Rights," *CQ Researcher*, July 22, 1994, courtesy of the *CQ Researcher*.

*The bureau was named for the mother of actress Sharon Tate, who was murdered by followers of Charles Manson in 1969.

sample in a vial," says Deborah P. Kelly, a Washington attorney who chairs the Victims Committee of the American Bar Association (ABA). "Because of the myth that only the state has a case against the defendant, [crime victims] were kept outside the court so they couldn't find out what was happening. The result was they felt twice victimized."

Beckie Brown, the president of Dallas-based Mothers Against Drunk Driving (MADD), recalls that after a drunken driver killed her son in 1979, she had to depend on newspapers to follow the proceedings, suffering the further "indignity of having to pay $1 a page for a transcript of the trial."

Today, the legal landscape is vastly different. The number of local victims' rights organizations has exploded from 200 in 1980 to more than 8,000, according to the National Organization for Victim Assistance, a Washington nonprofit. All 50 states have crime victims' statutes, and 14 have enacted constitutional amendments to guarantee those rights. All 50 states now have victim compensation programs covering counseling, funerals and medical expenses, compared with only 27 states in 1980. And more than a third of the country's major police departments have their own victim assistance programs, according to the International Association of Chiefs of Police.

Most dramatically, at criminal sentencings it is now common for family members of victims to stand and deliver "victim impact statements," as the nation saw in May of 1994 when an emotional widower told a New York City court how his life was shattered when his pregnant wife died in the 1993 World Trade Center bombing.[1]

"The movement has finally come to the forefront because of the incredible increase in crime— 18,000 homicides, 40 million victims a year," says activist John Walsh, host of the Fox Network TV show "America's Most Wanted." His 6-year-old son Adam was abducted and murdered in a case that became nationally famous in the early 1980s. "People from Beverly Hills to Watts are realizing that anyone can be a crime victim," he says.

What motivates many victims' advocates is a sense that the many recently passed laws affecting victims and criminals too often go unenforced. They want *assurances* that busy police, prosecutors, judges and parole officials will keep victims and families informed of progress through each stage of the criminal justice process. They want speedy trials for defendants. (In Arizona, an appeal by a rapist 15 years after his conviction required his victims to repeat their age-old testimony and, in some cases, discuss the rape with their spouses and children for the first time.)[2]

Rape victims, in particular, are seeking to keep the news media from publishing their names and to require mandatory HIV testing for people accused of sex offenses.[3] And the survivors of homicide victims are seeking to prevent criminals from profiting from movie or book contracts, as many families feared might happen in the 1991 case of Milwaukee, Wis., serial killer Jeffrey L. Dahmer.

An Unusual Coalition

Politically, the movement is a hodgepodge of feminists and law-and-order purists, "a coalition of bleeding-heart conservatives and hard-nosed liberals," as one observer put it. Some groups, such as the Doris Tate Crime Victims' Bureau, actively lobby for tougher criminal sentencing. Others, such as the 300-chapter, 40,000-member group Parents of Murdered Children, based in Cincinnati, Ohio, counsel grieving families and help them navigate the legal system, monitor parole hearings and protest products that are offensive to crime victims, such as kids' trading cards featuring serial killers.

Crime victims are a vulnerable constituency. Psychologists have long noted how the violent death of a loved one can wreak emotional havoc for years and even destroy the survivors' marriage. The tendency to dwell on a crime gives victims a fear that friends will find them boring and self-pitying. "As a society, we do little to help victims to make them whole," notes George Kendall, assistant counsel at the NAACP Legal Defense Fund. "When we see a recent victim, we cross the street because we don't want to deal with them."

The public, however, appears solidly behind the victims' rights movement. A 1991 poll commissioned by the Arlington, Va.-based National Victim Center showed that 84 percent of the respondents supported a victim's right to be notified about dates and places of trials while 82 percent backed the victim's right to attend a trial and 72 percent backed the opportunity for a victim to discuss a case with the prosecutor during plea bargaining.

Critics, however, worry that the presence—and emotionalism—of victims and their families in court may jeopardize defendants' rights to a fair trial, particularly in death penalty cases where racial prejudice can affect sentencing. They argue that judges and juries alone are competent to dispense justice and charge, moreover, that guarantees and programs for victims are expensive.

"Victims have been victimized, and we don't want to sound like we don't care," says Nancy Hollander, an Albuquerque, N.M., attorney and former president of the National Association of Criminal Defense Lawyers. "But if you start a case and say, 'This is the defendant and this is the victim,' there's a presumption of guilt, and you decrease the public understanding of the presumption of innocence."

What's more, Hollander adds, "getting a victim involved with a trial won't solve crime in America. It's eye-for-an-eye retribution that risks institutionalizing vigilante justice. If we're concerned about preventing crime, let's use our resources for that."

Victims' rights advocates are fond of quoting Supreme Court Justice Benjamin N. Cardozo's phrase: "Justice, though due the accused, is due the accuser also."

Whether victims' advocates can transform the criminal justice system will hinge on the following questions:

Do Victims' Rights Infringe on the Rights of Defendants?

Roberta Roper is a Maryland victims' rights advocate who was stirred to action after the rape and murder of her daughter, Stephanie, in 1982. She recalls the vitriol that critics heaped on her and her allies when they first got involved with the case.

"We were barred from the guilt-innocence phase of the trial," she says. And, as the family of the deceased, they were blocked from offering testimony about Stephanie's life even as the defense attorneys raised questions about how many drinks she'd had on the night she died and why she had been driving alone at 3 a.m.

"The testimony I was offering was called emotional, irrelevant and probably cause for a mistrial," says Roper.

"We were labeled a vigilante mob with blood dripping from our hands simply because we wrote letters saying we would be there."

Washington Post columnist Richard Cohen questioned whether the Stephanie Roper Committee, founded by Roper, her husband and some friends, was seeking justice or revenge. From the legislation they propose," Cohen wrote, "it's hard to tell."[4]

Judges have traditionally sought to keep their courtrooms focused on facts rather than ruled by passion, and even the passage of victims' rights laws has not prevented defense attorneys from trying to exclude murder victims' family members from trials. (Indeed, a Maryland defense lawyer in 1991 tried to call as a witness the widow of the state highway patrolman his client was charged with killing, despite the fact that she had been at home asleep when the killing occurred. The reason? So the widow, under court rules, could be barred from the courtroom along with the other witnesses, who are not supposed to hear each other's testimony for fear they might coordinate their stories.)[5]

The victims' rights movement has sought to get around this roadblock through laws specifically permitting relatives of crime victims to sit in on trials after they've given testimony, to meet with prosecutors and to deliver, either orally or in writing, a victim impact statement before a sentencing or plea bargain (the so-called right of allocution). "The courts require that we treat defendants decently, but should not this be extended to victims?" asks Roper. "We trust juries to sift and weigh all information, and without the victims' input, they can't."

Ann Reed, the associate director of Parents of Murdered Children, complains that courtroom efforts to eliminate displays of emotion show that "the criminal justice system is all geared to justice for the criminal. The parent of the murderer can flop all over the court and scream, but if you're the parent of the murder victim, you can't even blow your nose without the judge calling you into his chamber," she says. (Reed's 18-year-old daughter Becky was raped and beaten to death in 1980.)

"Prisoners are guaranteed rights all at the expense of taxpayers," argues Walsh. "And not one victim I've met has said that criminals should be denied legal counsel and medical treatment or a parole hearing. All we're asking is to be treated the same."

The ABA's Kelly says that victims who don't know their rights under new victims' laws often leave the courtroom when the order is routinely given for all witnesses to leave. "Defense attorneys don't want the human presence," she says, "not because there's a risk of tainting testimony but because a real person who's present makes the jury realize the human consequences of crimes. Removing the victim makes it easier for the defense to turn the case into a clash between a real person and the impersonal bureaucratic machinery of the state."

John Stein, deputy director of the National Organization for Victim Assistance, says "There is always the potential for prejudicing a jury when a relative of one party is present. That's true if it's the mother of the defendant or of the victim. But the message is only that this person has family and friends who love him," and the defense should be concerned with more important lines of argument.

David Price, president for litigation affairs at the Washington Legal Foundation, which sues on behalf of violent-crime victims, says the presence of victims "helps the triers of fact. They are part of the facts, you can't isolate them, just as the defendant's background prior to the crime is part of the facts." Price, however, believes the decision to include victims in a courtroom should be left to the prosecutor's discretion, based on whether it helps make the case.

Victim Impact Statements Controversial for a different set of reasons are victim impact statements, which are allowed only after guilty verdicts have been rendered. Introduced in Fresno, Calif., in 1974, they were originally prepared by probation officers as part of pre-sentence investigations. Nowadays, they are often prepared by victims themselves and can be cited at sentencings, plea bargainings and in limited ways at bail hearings, often at the discretion of the judge.

"They're an important rite, a forum for an expression of passion," says Stein. "The victims frequently express rage against the offender, but just because it's discomforting for us doesn't mean they shouldn't be allowed to speak."

The victim's statement "gives the court complete information for use in parole, plea bargaining and the need for restitution," says Roper. It isn't inflammatory, it's not prejudicial to any sentence and it doesn't take away from defendants' rights. It is limited to the crime's consequences emotionally, physically and financially. But it does help to sensitize the criminal justice system to the reality that the state is not the only victim, that it's human lives that are devastated.

To underscore their point, backers of victim impact statements cite the case of two youths convicted of the savage 1980s murder of a 79-year-old woman. Before their arrest for repeatedly stabbing the woman at the small store she operated, the boys were seen giving each other "high fives" and bragging about the crime.

Initially, prosecutors and defense attorneys agreed on a plea bargain to second-degree murder, carrying sentences of at least 38 years in prison. But the judge refused to accept the plea, noting the savagery of the crime and reading into the record a statement about the crime's impact from the victim's daughter and son-in-law. The defendants later switched to guilty pleas to first-degree murder and received sentences of 50 years to life.[6]

Impact statements are opposed, however, by many judges and prosecutors. A survey of their use in California commissioned by the National

Institute of Justice in the mid-1980s showed that 69 percent of judges, 48 percent of prosecutors and 81 percent of probation officers said victim impact statements were not effective.[7]

Judge Vincent Femia of Maryland's 7th Judicial Circuit says that both victims and defendants have the right to allocution, but "neither side can get emotional in my court." He points to a recent case in which a victims' rights advocate asked to address the court. "I asked the lawyer, 'to what end?'" the judge recalls. "He said, 'Your honor should know how the family feels about the loss of a loved one.' I asked him what will that do for my judgment, make me more severe?

"There are only two reasons for victim statements: to increase the sentence and provide catharsis. I'm not competent in catharsis, that's for doctors and clergymen. But I'm competent in sentencing, and I don't need a victim to tell me how to do that. Being a judge isn't doing what's emotionally satisfying to the loudest of the multitude."

Douglas Spencer, a retired circuit judge in Eugene, Ore., disagrees. "Technically, a criminal trial is between a sovereign state and the defendants, and the victim is not a party," he acknowledges. "But having said that, I can understand why the victims' rights people are saying, 'We've got all these people wringing their hands over the defendant, saying what a good boy he was, how he loves his mother, how we don't know why he cut that guy's throat except that he fell in with evil companions.'

"You can't necessarily trust the district attorney to present the victims' information, because he's busy. So we passed legislation saying that the D.A. must notify the family of the time and place for sentencing. I like to have the family there to balance things out. I can't think of one case in which I had one sentence in mind and made it harsher after hearing the victim's family. But it feels good, even if I don't change the sentence, that the victims had their chance to be heard."

A major objection to victim impact statements, one that has been the focus of three recent Supreme Court cases, is the fear that their use in capital trials increases the risk of racially biased applications of the death penalty.

"Yes, victim impact statements are often the only opportunity a victim has to make a point," says the NAACP's Kendall. "But because race has always influenced the imposition of the death penalty, the statements become one more temptation for prosecutors in deciding in which cases to ask for capital punishment. Consciously or unconsciously, juries that are overwhelmingly white will identify with white victims, so we will have more death sentences applied to blacks."

On the contrary, counters Price, "The victim impact statement is a potentially valuable way to overcome racial bias in the criminal justice system. We all have preconceptions about race, and if the victim is a young black male, a juror may feel he had it coming. That's why a statement from people we don't rub shoulders with every day can bring a [victim] to life in the jury's mind and bridge the emotional distance."

In general, says Walsh, "When a person is convicted and sentencing recommendations are made, the defense can bring in 50 character witnesses including his clergyman. Why shouldn't the victim make a statement? Why can't a father hold a picture of his dead child to show that this child existed and now will never graduate from high school and will never get married? Since when is the law unemotional? Isn't somebody's life worth 10 minutes? If the judge is so smart, he will afford the victim this dignity and then go in his chambers and make a wise decision."

Morton Bard, a longtime victims' rights activist and professor of psychology emeritus at the City University of New York, says: "The rights of defendants can be protected to the nth degree without sacrificing the victim. What's really involved is a turf battle among the players—the judges, prosecutors and the cops—who like to run the system. They don't want another system making problems. But we have a moral obligation to victims."

Are Victims' Rights a Drain on the Justice System?

In their psychological study *The Crime Victim's Book*, Bard and his co-author recount a woman's experience after her husband was murdered. A year after his death, when the killer had been sentenced and the woman was emerging from the grieving process, an envelope was delivered to her door. Inside, with no letter of explanation, was her husband's wallet, which the police had been keeping as evidence. It was still stained with blood.[8]

Doubtless, the harried evidence clerk who returned the wallet never meant to traumatize a widow but was acting out of habit dictated by the realities of short-handed staffs and tight budgets.

Victims' rights advocates say it doesn't have to be that way. "I don't see that being sensitive to the needs of people in extreme situations requires lots of money," says Bard. "But police are often like doctors who deal only with physical illnesses—it seems that people themselves count the least."

Victims' services, however, do cost money. State victim compensation funds, which are financed largely through fines levied against convicted criminals, "are facing financial pressure and some are delaying payments," says Dan Eddy, executive director of the National Association of Crime Victim Compensation Boards.

In many states, claims have doubled or quadrupled in recent years, partly because the victims' rights movement has lent the programs new visibility. "I don't know of one that's not either facing a problem or nervous about the future," Eddy says. "Some states like New Jersey and Texas have tried boosting the fines, but there's a point of diminishing returns."

What's more, police departments and agencies that provide services for victims would be even more strapped if everyone who is eligible for the services were actually served. A January 1994 poll by the *Los Angeles Times* showed that 84 percent of U.S. crime victims in the previous 12 months had not received assistance from a victims' group or social service agency.

Prosecutors argue that victims' rights laws come with a price tag because they reduce prosecutors' discretion. "The victims' rights movement doesn't often consider the practicality of requiring us to give services that decency requires, but

that when made mandatory become onerous," says Andrew L. Sonner, the Maryland state's attorney in Montgomery County. For example, "most people think victims are people like us. But many times they're not the people a prosecutor would want to talk and consult with, because, say, in a shootout in a drug war, the person who died may have been worse than the shooter."

Sonner also sees an unworkable costliness in cases with multiple victims, such as nationwide mail order fraud cases committed with television advertisements. If all the victims had the right to be kept informed throughout the trial, he says, the costs would be substantial.

Sonner recalls the 1981 case of Washington, D.C.-area burglar Bernard Welch, who had broken into at least 40 homes when he was arrested after shooting and killing a prominent doctor outside his house. In conducting the burglary prosecution, "we chose four cases, because it would have been ridiculous to go to trial 40 times. But several other victims still complained, even though it didn't affect their getting restitution."*

Victims' rights advocates counter that it's a matter of priorities. "If our government can spend billions for the Hubble telescope," says activist Walsh, "we can come up with money for a letter or a phone call from a D.A. saying that a parole hearing is next week."

Cost is a fair issue to debate, concedes Roper, but "look at the money we spend on incarcerating offenders vs. what we spend on their victims. Even if we could prove that victims' services were a financial drain, which they're not, it would be money well spent because it would preserve the system of justice by instilling faith and cooperation."

People who are concerned about costs too often see the problem "as a zero sum game, with the victims' rights coming at the expense of the offender," says David Beatty, director of public affairs for the National Victim Center. "But the relative amounts spent come to millions for defendants and pennies for victims. Nobody ever

---

*Bernard Welch was convicted of first-degree murder in the death of physician Michael Halberstam and sentenced to 143 years in federal prison. He was later sentenced to an additional 30 years for robbery.

discussed costs during the civil rights movement or when the *Miranda* decision was made."*

Price of the Washington Legal Foundation says that whatever small costs occur are "outweighed by the value of having the victim's family as watch dogs, involved every step of the way to help the system avoid errors. Police are well-intentioned, but they are overwhelmed by the magnitude of their caseload, so there should be outside encouragement or pressure to maintain the human element."

The National Victim Center poll indicated that 70 percent of Americans would pay higher taxes to improve services to crime victims.

Movement's Birth

The notion that individuals wronged by crime should take it upon themselves to seek redress goes back at least 3,500 years, to ancient Babylon, where the famous Code of Hammurabi required thieves to make restitution.

In England since Norman times, and later in Colonial America, it was common for victimized private citizens to take action themselves. In 18th-century Boston, for example, a victim could arrest a suspected wrongdoer assisted by a night watchman or constable, then pay for any warrants, conduct the investigation himself and hire an attorney to write the indictment and prosecute. Punishment was often servitude, since a jail sentence would require the victim to repay the government for incarceration costs.[9]

All this changed with adoption of the Constitution's Bill of Rights, which laid out the rights of defendants—but not victims—in its Fourth, Fifth, Sixth, Seventh and Eighth Amendments. By the 1830s, the nation's system of homemade criminal justice had been replaced by salaried police and prosecutors.

Victims' rights advocates, however, cite the earlier system of private justice as a key precedent. "In light of this history," said the Washington Legal Foundation in a 1991 Supreme Court brief, "it would be hard to say that the Framers

thought that victim participation in criminal prosecution raised a constitutional doubt. Nor can it be said that the move to public prosecution reflected a desire to eliminate any role for the victim."[10]

Feminists and Rape Victims Spur Initiatives
The U.S. victims' rights movement had its first stirrings in the early 1960s, after Great Britain, New Zealand and other nations enacted the first victim compensation programs. (In the U.S., in 1964, Sen. Ralph W. Yarborough, D-Texas, introduced the first bill to create a federal victim compensation program, but it did not pass.) It was also in 1964, in New York City, that the murder of a woman named Kitty Genovese, whose screams for help were largely ignored by dozens of neighbors, dramatized for many the discomfort people feel when confronted with victimizations.

By the early 1970s, feminists and rape victims became the first victims' rights organizers when they staged urban rallies against rapists, often under the theme "Take back the night."

Law review articles began appearing at the same time proposing court reforms showing more respect for the needs of victims and witnesses. An academic publication, the journal of *Victimology* was launched while rape crisis centers, clearinghouses for information on missing children and telephone hotlines for battered women were set up. The first victim assistance programs were created in St. Louis, Mo., San Francisco, Calif., and Washington, D.C., and by 1974 the Law Enforcement Assistance Administration (LEAA) had spent $3 million to set up 19 victim assistance centers.

California, which had enacted the first state crime victimization fund in 1965, again led the way in 1978 with the nation's first law permitting crime victims to deliver impact statements at sentencings.

Reagan Takes Lead

It was the Reagan administration, in the early 1980s, that took the lead in bringing victims' rights reforms at the federal level, thanks largely to lobbying by Frank Carrington, a civic-minded Virginia Beach lawyer. In a 1982 White House Rose Garden ceremony announcing a new Presi-

---

*The Supreme Court's 1966 ruling in *Miranda v. Arizona* requires police to inform people being arrested of their rights to remain silent and to be represented by an attorney.

dent's Task Force on Victims of Crime, President Ronald Reagan said: "The innocent victims of crime have frequently been overlooked by our criminal justice system. Too often their pleas have gone unheeded and the wounds—personal, emotional and financial—have gone unattended. They are entitled to better treatment, and it is time to do something about it."[11]

The task force's final report contained strong language. "Victims have discovered that they are treated as appendages of a system appallingly out of balance," it said. "They have learned that somewhere along the way, the system has lost track of the simple truth that it is supposed to be fair and protect those who obey the law while punishing those who break it. Somewhere along the way, the system began to serve lawyers and judges and defendants, treating the victim with institutionalized disinterest."[12]

Most important, the task force made 68 recommendations, among them a proposal that the Constitution's Sixth Amendment, which enumerates a defendant's rights to counsel and a speedy trial by jury, be amended as follows: "Likewise, the victim, in every criminal prosecution, shall have the right to be present and to be heard at all critical stages of judicial proceedings."[13]

Federal Fund for Crime Victims The result was not a constitutional amendment, however, but a bipartisan movement in Congress led by Sens. Strom Thurmond, R-S.C., and Joseph R. Biden Jr., D-Del., to pass the 1984 Victims of Crime Act. The act set up a federal crime victims fund. Financed through fines paid by federal criminals, the fund sends grants ($137 million in 1992) to states to replenish their victim compensation funds and support some 2,500 victim assistance programs nationwide.[14]

Victims' funds cover a wide range of expenses incurred as a direct result of a crime, including medical bills, mental health counseling, funeral and burial costs, wage loss, loss of alimony or child support and job retraining. Such expenses are covered only if insurance and other sources aren't available. Property loss, including loss of cash, is not covered.

A state might finance its fund by assessing $25 from each felon, or $3 from each traffic violator, notes Eddy of the compensation board association. States differ in their generosity toward victims, with maximum benefits generally ranging from $10,000 to $25,000.

In recent years, there has been a shift in the types of services in demand, Eddy says. "The funds used to be just for physical injuries, and they'd patch you up and you'd get back on the job. But over the past 5–10 years, there has been more attention to mental health counseling for victims of child abuse, sexual assault and domestic violence. It's a big victory for the victims' rights movement."[15]

Unlikely Allies

The victims' rights movement that emerged in the past two decades is "an interesting marriage" of liberals and conservatives, notes Beatty of the National Victim Center, uniting such groups as the National Organization for Women (NOW) and the Heritage Foundation.

The conservatives got involved after activist Carrington convinced the Reagan administration of its importance, notes Stein of the National Organization for Victim Assistance, "but [the fact that Reagan was then president] was just an accident." In the Clinton administration, he says, Attorney General "Janet Reno is equally persuasive with today's White House."

"Most people forget that the movement has [liberal] elements," says the ABA's Kelly. "They assume we must be to the right of Attila the Hun. But I'm a feminist who wrote a Ph.D. on rape victims. What's more, the left should be involved because crime victims are disproportionately minorities and the poor."

The right wing, says Bard, emphasizes "how we can make sure the victim feels better by punishing criminals more and depriving defendants of rights. The left emphasizes what services we can perform to help victims manage trauma, and sensitize the system to see the victim as a legitimate player."

The National Rifle Association (NRA), which conducts a victims' rights advocacy program called CrimeStrike, is involved "because of its long-standing commitment to criminal justice reform and mandatory sentences for armed offenders," says program director Steve Twist. "Our 3.4 million members are affected by crime, and frankly, if policies controlling crime are more effective, there will be less calls for attacks on the right to bear arms."

Crime doesn't discriminate between Republicans and Democrats, not by gender or economic status, says Roper, who before being pulled into activism by the murder of her daughter was a "full-time wife, mother and art teacher who had never even been in traffic court. We organized quickly, naively," she says. "I don't know if I would have preserved my sanity if we hadn't."

NOTES

1. *The New York Times,* May 25, 1994.

2. National Rifle Association, "CrimeStrike Special Report: Elements for an Effective Criminal Justice System" (undated), p. 10.

3. For a discussion of whether the news media should use rape victims' names, see *Time*, April 29, 1991, p. 28.

4. *The Washington Post,* Jan. 25, 1983.

5. *The (Baltimore) Sun,* June 23, 1991.

6. Robert C. Wells, "Victim Impact: How Much Consideration Is It Really Given?" *The Police Chief,* February 1991, p. 44. Wells is victim/witness coordinator at the Federal Law Enforcement Training Center, Glynco, Ga. For background, see "Juvenile Justice," *The CQ Researcher,* Feb. 25, 1994, pp. 169–192.

7. Edwin Villmoare and Virginia V. Neto, "Victim Appearances at Sentencing Under California's Victims' Bill of Rights," National Institute of Justice, August 1987.

8. Morton Bard and Dawn Sangrey, *The Crime Victim's Book* (1986), p. 153.

9. James Stark and Howard W. Goldstein, *The Rights of Crime Victims* (1985), p. 20.

10. Washington Legal Foundation, *amicus curiae* brief in *Payne v. Tennessee,* 1991.

11. Office of Victims of Crime, *Report to Congress,* April 1990, p. 2.

12. Bard and Sangrey, *op. cit.,* p. 212.

13. Stark and Goldstein, *op. cit.,* p. 21.

14. Justice Department, "Office of Justice Programs Annual Report for Fiscal Year 1992," p. 72.

15. For background, see "Child Sexual Abuse," *The CQ Researcher,* Jan. 15, 1993, pp. 25–48, and "Violence Against Women," *The CQ Researcher,* Feb. 28, 1993, pp. 169–192.

READING 2
A BRITISH VIEW OF AMERICAN JUSTICE

Alison Gomme

A British researcher explains the American system of justice. Alison Gomme works for the Prison Service of England and Wales.

The United States ranks first in the world in imprisoning the highest number of its citizens on a per capita basis. This is partially attributable to the levels of violent crime, particularly crime involving the use of firearms. An extreme example of this is the homicide rate in Washington, D.C.; 483 persons were killed in 1990.* The proportion of homicides relating to the drug trade have reduced from 60 per cent in 1988 to 42 per cent in 1990, and are shifting towards the common disputes of daily life, particularly with young men taking the law into their own hands.[1]

With so many persons incarcerated, there is plenty of choice for the researcher. I decided at an early stage to compare state prisons. This would allow me to study several jurisdictions' management of, and approach to, the same disease [HIV] under similar conditions. All of the states have a prison system, funded by the state, which holds their sentenced populations in accordance with state law. Thus there is potential for diverse approaches to any particular problem whether it be overcrowding, sentence calculation, the death penalty, or HIV disease.

After reviewing the literature, I decided to visit male and female prisons in New York, California, Colorado, Kentucky, Florida, Texas, Mississippi, Massachusetts and Illinois. I also had an opportunity to visit the city jails of New York (Riker's Island) and Chicago Cook County Jail. . . .

The visits were all easy to arrange and I met with great courtesy, kindness, generosity and hospitality. Individuals were easily accessible and their information unrestricted and readily available. I received candid replies to my direct questioning of issues which were often very sensitive and I found people willing to share their failures as well as successes. . . .

Imprisonment in the USA

In 1990, approximately 1.2 million adult and juvenile prisoners were held in public and private correctional centres (Federal Bureau of Prisons, State Prisons, Jails, Youth Centers) in the USA.[2] Of a total national population of approximately 248 million, this figure equates to 0.4 per cent of the population.

By comparison, in the same period in England and Wales the total adult and juvenile prison pop-

---

* Since 1990, the homicide rate in Washington, D.C., has declined, with 454 reported homicides in 1993 and 360 in 1995. 1. Castaneda R. (1991) 'Revenge as a catalyst for killing'. Lead article in *Washington Post*, August 4, 1991.

Reprinted from Alison Gomme, "The Management of HIV Disease in the Correctional Setting," in *Prison Policy and Practice: Selected Papers from Thirty-five Years of the "Prison Service Journal,"* edited by Jack Reynolds and Ursula Smartt (Leyhill, England: Prison Service Journal, 1996), by permission of the publishers.

2. US Department of Justice, Bureau of Justice Statistics: *Jail Inmates 1990*, June 1991.

ulation was approximately 45,000 from a general population of approximately 50 million. This equates to 0.09 per cent of the population.

The US prisoner population has increased dramatically over the past decade and this has called for innovative measures to house the excess numbers which have included the use of tents in Louisiana and barges in New York City, in addition to massive building programmes embarked upon by many states. By contrast, the prison population of England and Wales has declined by some 2,500 since 1989, largely as a result of legislative changes which have impacted the juvenile population in particular.

Correctional Systems

There are three main systems of imprisonment in the United States which operate autonomously. The unconvicted, those sentenced to less than one year, and in some states those awaiting a vacancy in overcrowded state prisons, are held in city and county jails. These establishments are funded by the county or city in which they are located, and tend to have limited facilities, few programmes and experience the most severe overcrowding.

Prisoners convicted and sentenced of federal crimes are held in a nationwide network of Federal Prisons according to the security requirement of the prisoner. Allocation near to home is not necessarily a priority. The Federal Bureau of Prisons is funded through the federal government.

Those sentenced to state terms, usually of more than one year, are held in the state prisons of the state in which the term was ordered. The states operate independently of each other through rules and policy decided by the state legislature and Department of Corrections (DOC). Therefore the approach may vary widely between states on such diverse issues as the death penalty, compassionate release strategies, sentence calculation and programming. State prisons are funded by the state, although they may be supplemented with federal funds for specific programmes.

Corrections and the Political Picture

The state legislature establishes the laws of the state in accordance with the broad outline of the state and federal constitutions. This may impact state prisons in terms of policy and procedure. The Constitution of the United States (the federal constitution) sets minimum standards for the civil and procedural rights of all prisoners, but the state constitutions may provide for additional civil and procedural rights for prisoners within that state. However, state constitutions may not set civil or procedural rights *less* than those embodied in the Constitution of the United States.

Each state, as well as the federal government, maintains a system of courts to administer justice and interpret the law. Appeals on questions of state law are heard in the state court system up to the state's highest court. Appeals on federal law are heard in the federal court system up to the Supreme Court of the United States. In a limited number of cases, appeals on questions of state law also raise issues affecting federal law and may be appealed beyond a state's highest court to the Supreme Court.

A state legislature is to a Governor what Congress is to the President of the United States (checks and balances). A Governor's term of office is for two to four years dependent upon the state constitution. The maximum number of terms a person may be elected to serve as Governor is determined by the constitution of that state. Individuals who hold ministerial or cabinet positions in state government, including the state's correctional administrator, are appointed by the Governor and serve at his or her pleasure. A state's correctional programmes are likely to be impacted by this, particularly when there has been a change of political party. If a Governor has won the election on a 'get tough on crime and criminals' ticket, a current popular opinion, then state correctional policy and practice is likely to be affected.

State correctional policy and practice is also affected by national politics. For example, during the 1988 Presidential campaign, candidate George Bush used the case of Willie Horton, a prisoner who committed several violent crimes whilst on furlough from the Massachusetts correctional system, to raise doubts about the managerial competence of his chief opponent, then Governor of

Massachusetts, Michael Dukakis. As a result of the successful Bush campaign and the equation of prison furlough programmes with managerial incompetence or foolhardiness, the use of prison furlough programmes has substantially reduced across the USA.

Impressions

During the course of my visits the most dominant impression I have gained is that the US is a more punitive society with the emphasis being on punishment rather than rehabilitation. This is exemplified by the huge numbers imprisoned in the US, the availability of the death penalty in the majority of states,[3] the paucity of furlough programmes and in some states the unavailability of compassionate release for terminal medical cases.[4] I have been shocked to see mechanical restraints and an extensive use of shackles; especially to see young offenders in medium security shackled in Illinois; and surprised to see an enthusiastic interest and adoption of rigorous shock incarceration programmes across the country.

The secure perimeter, which is always armed, has allowed reduced staffing levels and enhanced prisoner movement within the facilities. I have been surprised at the amount of prisoner activity which is not directed by a staff member, especially sports activity, and wonder whether reduced staffing levels have resulted in 'no-go' areas for staff, but have been pleased to see positive interactions between staff and prisoners and staff of either sex carrying out their duties efficiently and effectively in singleton-post housing units.

Another surprise in some jurisdictions has been the number of transvestites in male establishments which was open, and presumably tacitly approved of by the authorities. This was especially marked in Vacaville, California. It has seemed to me that there is a much higher level of homosexual activity among male prisoners in the US, although it may be that this behaviour is simply more open. I have gained the impression that the

amount of homosexual activity is related to the regime: where there is a limited regime or a lack of direction then there seems to be more homosexual activity. High levels of sexual activity may also be related to a lack of legitimate income— unavailability of work, low incomes or enforced work without remuneration: in those situations, sex becomes a method of earning income.

The Private Sector

The increase in the prisoner population and consequent cost to the states has led some to believe that the private sector may be able to operate parts or all of the process of imprisonment more effectively, efficiently and cheaply, thus absolving the state of some of the responsibility whilst simultaneously saving money. Not all of the states have adopted private prisons, and there are states that have passed specific legislation forbidding the use of private prisons. Illinois is such a state.

Particular aspects of the imprisonment process may be contracted out, such as the delivery of health care, food service, prison building, and prison industries. The last is widely vaunted as a way to introduce meaningful work with realistic wages for prisoners; part of this wage is paid to the prison as 'Room and Board', part sent to family, and part sent to the victim. In this way, the prisoner funds his own imprisonment and makes restitution.[5]

Influence of Litigation

As a result of successful litigation in 1976, prisoners have become the only group in the United States who have an enforceable right to health care. Subsequently, class action suits were taken out by individual prisoners in several states and partially as a result of their success, the amount spent on prisoner medical services has increased dramatically over the last decade.

Litigation is big business in the United States. All state prisons must provide law libraries and in the event of dissatisfaction prisoners take out law

3. US Department of Justice, Bureau of Justice Statistics: *Capital Punishment 1989*, October 1990. 4. Criminal Justice Institute Inc., The Corrections Yearbook: 'Adult Prison and Jails', 'Probation and Parole', *Juvenile Corrections 1991*.

5. US Department of Justice, National Institute of Justice: *Recovering Correctional Costs through Offender Fees*, June 1990.

suits. It is unfortunate that it appears to the casual observer that the major catalyst to positive change or development in corrections is successful litigation. This is obviously not the absolute position; I have seen excellent programming and regimes being pushed forward by initiative at local level in spite of a paucity of resources.

American Cultural Values

Any prison system will reflect the culture and values of the country/state/area in which it is located; therefore it is not surprising to find that Mississippi decided to establish a plantation prison whereas Minnesota with its Scandinavian legacy has created Oak Park Heights—a maximum security prison with a good regime and freedom of movement which is so highly regarded in the UK.[6] For precisely the reasons of regional diversity and cultural influence, concepts, methods, policy and procedure do not always readily translate either between states or internationally. Although there will be regional variations dependent upon history and tradition, there are some broad statements to be made about the United States in general which may be helpful as background information.

The Quick Fix Society

Firstly, it appears that America is a quick fix society. In the face of a state or national problem, the legislature looks for a quick fix solution as a response to public pressure. The solution may impact all or part of the symptom of the problem but not necessarily the root cause. The solution will be adopted with vigour, especially if it is endorsed by the Administration and is politically fashionable. An example of this is the strategy known as the 'War on Drugs'; whilst the symptoms of the problem (drug trafficking, drug dealing) are being energetically pursued, there is less emphasis on, or research into, the root causes of drug taking.

This quick fix approach receives good press as it gives the impression that the Administration is responding to the problems presented to it and thus serving the demands of the public who elected them.

The USA is also a society with an abundance of data. In order to understand any problematic issue there must be data produced and in order to measure the effectiveness of a solution there must be out-turn data. These data are available for all who would care to study them.

Punishment and Programmes

There is a move away from the prisoner and rehabilitation and a move toward punishment and retribution with the offender being expected to pay restitution and in some cases pay towards his/her imprisonment rather than being a burden on society. In today's climate of fiscal restraint and budget deficit for many states, difficult decisions have to be made as to whether the limited funds available should go towards the construction and staffing of new prisons, or state education, or welfare programs, or the provision of health care for the indigent of the state. Corrections will usually find themselves low on the list of priorities. Corrections budgets have been cut to the extent that some states with severe financial problems have temporarily laid off corrections employees.

Whilst the American public want people locked up, they want this done as cheaply as possible.

In spite of the above rather than as a function of it, programmes continue to exist in corrections, and innovative ways are found to enhance the regime by the staff at local level. In most of the prisons I visited, the local mission was much more than simply warehousing the prisoner population.

6. King R.D. (1991) 'Maximum-security custody in Britain and the USA—a study of Gartree and Oak Park Heights', *British Journal of Criminology*, Vol. 31, Number 2, Spring 1991.

DISCUSSION QUESTIONS

1. Although individuals certainly are harmed by both property and violent crime, crime is also injurious to society as a whole. Accordingly, society, rather than the individual, takes action against the offender. If society takes the role of the victim, is it either desirable or necessary to provide the individual victim with a significant role in the justice process? Why or why not?

2. Assuming that victims or their families should not have significant influence over an offender's type, severity, or duration of punishment, what other types of "victim's rights" might still be desirable?

3. Should the U.S. Constitution be amended to include a Victims' Bill of Rights? Why or why not?

4. Alison Gomme applies her impressions of American values to issues of corrections. Assume, for the sake of argument, that she has correctly identified some basic values. How do a reliance on the private sector, a desire for the "quick fix," and a preference for punishment over rehabilitation influence America's policing and court systems?

5. "To the casual observer," Gomme laments, "the major catalyst to positive change or development in corrections is successful litigation." Offer arguments that support or dispute that statement.

6. At the end of her article, Gomme notes that she found plentiful and innovative programs for prisoners in the United States in spite of the values she identifies as orienting Americans' view of the proper role of corrections. Develop an argument that shows how the values Gomme highlights are not necessarily inconsistent with plentiful and innovative programs.

WEBSITES

www.musc.edu/cvc (National Crime Victims Research and Treatment Center)
www.access.digex.net/~nova/ (National Organization for Victim Assistance)
www.nvc.org (National Victim Center)
These three websites offer an abundance of information about victim assistance and about research on victimology.
www.ncjrs.org/victrght.htm
The National Criminal Justice Reference Service provides documents on victim's rights at this web page and suggests links to other websites concerned with victim's rights.
www.penlex.org.uk
The Penal Lexicon website provides several opportunities to delve into both good and bad aspects of corrections in Britain and other European countries.
www.open.gov.uk/home_off/rsdhome.htm
This is the home page for the British Home Office's research and statistics division. Here you will find interesting studies and statistical reports about all aspects of criminal justice in Great Britain.

CHAPTER 2: CAUSES OF CRIME

In the United States, criminology is primarily the province of the social sciences. Typically, college courses on criminology and juvenile delinquency are taught in sociology departments by professors knowledgeable in how the structure of society affects behavior. They use textbooks that devote extensive coverage to sociological and social-psychological explanations for crime. Alternate explanations, such as biological abnormality, are given less attention. That is not necessarily because the professors and textbook authors discredit non–social science explanations. More often it is because their own academic background has not provided them with, for example, a biological perspective. The first reading in this chapter was chosen specifically because it highlights explanations for crime that are not sociological or social-psychological in nature.

Malcolm Gladwell's article challenges us to consider the possibility that some violent criminals are responding to neurological, rather than societal, conditions. As he explains the work of psychiatrist Dorothy Otnow Lewis and neurologist Jonathan Pincus, Gladwell takes us on a sometimes distressful tour of the brain in serial killers and other violent offenders. While reading this selection, you should search for possible links between biological and sociological explanations for violent crime. For example, pay special attention to Gladwell's explanation of how child abuse might affect the abused person's brain. However, think about how abusers might be influenced by social conditions. If their abusive behavior results in neurological damage to their victim, the abuse victim may turn to violent behavior because of neurological, more than societal, conditions. In this way, both biology and sociology/psychology may make important and necessary contributions to our understanding of criminal behavior.

The reading by Robert Kelly shows how sociological and psychological factors, just like biological ones, might "force" people down a path of crime—at least from the perspective of inmates. Reporting on his study of New York inmates, Kelly suggests that some believe their criminal acts were the result of circumstances beyond their control and are therefore not responsible for those acts. As you read Kelly's report consider how *any* explanation of crime can be used by those who are misbehaving to absolve themselves of responsibility for their actions.

READING 3

WHY SOME PEOPLE TURN INTO VIOLENT CRIMINALS

Malcolm Gladwell

New studies of the brain suggest that violent criminals may suffer from a combination of child abuse, brain injuries, and psychotic symptoms. Malcolm Gladwell is New York bureau chief of the Washington Post.

On the morning of November 18, 1996, Joseph Paul Franklin was led into Division 15 of the St. Louis County Courthouse, in Clayton, Missouri. He was wearing a pair of black high-top sneakers, an orange jumpsuit with short sleeves that showed off his prison biceps, and a pair of thick black-rimmed glasses. There were two guards behind him, two guards in front of him, and four more guards stationed around the courtroom, and as he walked into the room—or, rather, shuffled, since his feet were manacled—Franklin turned to one of them and said "Wassup?" in a loud, Southern-accented voice. Then he sat down between his attorneys and stared straight ahead at the judge, completely still except for his left leg, which bounced up and down in an unceasing nervous motion.

Joseph Franklin takes credit for shooting and paralyzing Larry Flynt, the publisher of *Hustler,*

Reprinted from Malcolm Gladwell, "Damaged," *The New Yorker*, Crime and Punishment Issue, February 24 and March 3, 1997, by permission of the author.

outside a Lawrenceville, Georgia, courthouse in March of 1978, apparently because Flynt had printed photographs of a racially mixed couple. Two years later, he says, he gunned down the civil-rights leader Vernon Jordan outside a Marriott in Fort Wayne, Indiana, tearing a hole in Jordan's back the size of a fist. In the same period in the late seventies, as part of what he later described as a "mission" to rid America of blacks and Jews and of whites who like blacks and Jews, Franklin says that he robbed several banks, bombed a synagogue in Tennessee, killed two black men jogging with white women in Utah, shot a black man and a white woman coming out of a Pizza Hut in a suburb of Chattanooga, Tennessee, and on and on—a violent spree that may have spanned ten states and claimed close to twenty lives, and, following Franklin's arrest, in 1980, earned him six consecutive life sentences.

While Franklin was imprisoned in Marion Federal Penitentiary, in Illinois, he confessed to another crime. He was the one, he said, who had hidden in the bushes outside a synagogue in suburban St. Louis in the fall of 1977 and opened fire on a group of worshippers, killing forty-two-year-old Gerald Gordon. After the confession, the State of Missouri indicted him on one count of capital murder and two counts of assault. He was moved from Marion to the St. Louis County jail, and from there, on a sunny November morning, he was brought before Judge Robert Campbell, of the St. Louis County Circuit Court, so that it could be determined whether he was fit to stand trial—whether, in other words, embarking on a campaign to rid America of Jews and blacks was an act of evil or an act of illness.

The Prosecution's Case

The prosecution went first. On a television set at one side of the courtroom, two videotapes were shown—one of an interview with Franklin by a local news crew and the other of Franklin's formal confession to the police. In both, he seems lucid and calm, patiently retracing how he planned and executed his attack on the synagogue. He explains that he bought the gun in a suburb of Dallas, answering a classified ad, so the purchase couldn't be traced. He drove to the St. Louis area and registered at a Holiday Inn. He looked through the Yellow Pages to find the names of synagogues. He filed the serial number off his rifle and bought a guitar case to carry the rifle in. He bought a bicycle. He scouted out a spot near his chosen synagogue from which he could shoot without being seen. He parked his car in a nearby parking lot and rode his bicycle to the synagogue. He lay in wait in the bushes for several hours, until congregants started to emerge. He fired five shots. He rode the bicycle back to the parking lot, climbed into his car, pulled out of the lot, checked his police scanner to see if he was being chased, then drove south, down I-55, back home toward Memphis.

In the interview with the news crew, Franklin answered every question, soberly and directly. He talked about his tattoos ("This one is the Grim Reaper. I got it in Dallas") and his heroes ("One person I like is Howard Stern. I like his honesty"), and he respectfully disagreed with the media's description of racially motivated crimes as "hate crimes," since, he said, "every murder is committed out of hate." In his confession to the police, after he detailed every step of the synagogue attack, Franklin was asked if there was anything he'd like to say. He stared thoughtfully

over the top of his glasses. There was a long silence. "I can't think of anything," he answered. Then he was asked if he felt any remorse. There was another silence. "I can't say that I do," he said. He paused again, then added, "The only thing I'm sorry about is that it's not legal."

"What's not legal?"

Franklin answered as if he'd just been asked the time of day: "Killing Jews."

The Defense Argument

After a break for lunch, the defense called Dorothy Otnow Lewis, a psychiatrist at New York's Bellevue Hospital and a professor at New York University School of Medicine. Over the past twenty years, Lewis has examined, by her own rough estimate, somewhere between a hundred and fifty and two hundred murderers. She was the defense's only expert witness in the trial of Arthur Shawcross, the Rochester serial killer who strangled eleven prostitutes in the late eighties. She examined Joel Rifkin, the Long Island serial killer, and Mark David Chapman, who shot John Lennon—both for the defense. Once, in a Florida prison, she sat for hours talking with Ted Bundy. It was the day before his execution, and when they had finished Bundy bent down and kissed her cheek. "Bundy thought I was the only person who didn't *want* something from him," Lewis says. Frequently, Lewis works with Jonathan Pincus, a neurologist at Georgetown University. Lewis does the psychiatric examination; Pincus does the neurological examination. But Franklin put his foot down. He could tolerate being examined by a Jewish woman, evidently, but not by a Jewish man. Lewis testified alone.

Lewis is a petite woman in her late fifties, with short dark hair and large, liquid brown eyes. She was wearing a green blazer and a black skirt with a gold necklace, and she was so dwarfed by the witness stand that from the back of the courtroom only her head was visible. Under direct examination she said that she had spoken with Franklin twice—once for six hours and once for less than half an hour—and had concluded that he was a paranoid schizophrenic: a psychotic whose thinking was delusional and confused, a man wholly unfit to stand trial at this time. She talked of brutal physical abuse he had suffered as a child. She mentioned scars on his scalp from blows Franklin had told her were inflicted by his mother. She talked about his obsessive desire to be castrated, his grandiosity, his belief that he may have been Jewish in an earlier life, his other bizarre statements and beliefs. At times, Lewis seemed nervous, her voice barely audible, but perhaps that was because Franklin was staring at her unblinkingly, his leg bouncing faster and faster under the table. After an hour, Lewis stepped down. She paused in front of Franklin and, ever the psychiatrist, suggested that when everything was over they should *talk*. Then she walked slowly through the courtroom, past the defense table and the guards, and out the door.

Later that day, on the plane home to New York City, Lewis worried aloud that she hadn't got her point across. Franklin, at least as he sat there in the courtroom, didn't *seem* insane. The following day, Franklin took the stand himself for two hours, during which he did his own psychiatric diagnosis, confessing to a few "minor neuroses," but not to being "stark raving mad," as he put it. Of the insanity defense, he told the court, "I think it is hogwash, to tell you the truth. I knew exactly what I was doing." During his testimony, Franklin called Lewis "a well-intentioned lady" who "seems to embellish her statements somewhat." Lewis seemed to sense that that was the impression she'd left: that she was overreaching, that she was some kind of caricature—liberal Jewish New York psychiatrist comes to Middle America to tell the locals to feel *sorry* for a murderer. Sure enough, a week later the Judge rejected Lewis's arguments and held Franklin competent to stand trial. But, flying back to New York, Lewis insisted that she wasn't making an ideological point of Franklin; rather, she was saying that she didn't feel that Franklin's brain worked the way brains are supposed to work—that he had identifiable biological and psychiatric problems that diminished his responsibility for his actions. "I just don't believe people are born evil," she said. "To my mind, that is mindless. Forensic psychiatrists tend to buy into the notion of evil. I

felt that that's no explanation. The deed itself is bizarre, grotesque. But it's not evil. To my mind, evil bespeaks conscious control over something. Serial murderers are not in that category. They are driven by forces beyond their control."

The plane was in the air now. By some happy set of circumstances, Lewis had been bumped up to first class. She was sipping champagne. Her shoes were off. "You know, when I was leaving our last interview, he sniffed me right here," she said, and she touched the back of her neck and flared her nostrils in mimicry of Franklin's gesture. "He'd said to his attorney, 'You know, if you weren't here, I'd make a play for her.'" She had talked for six hours to this guy who hated Jews so much that he hid in the bushes and shot at them with a rifle, and he had come on to her, just like that. She shivered at the memory. "He said he wanted some *pussy*."

The Criminal as Victim

When Dorothy Lewis graduated from Yale School of Medicine, in 1963, neurology, the study of the brain and the rest of the nervous system, and psychiatry, the study of behavior and personality, were entirely separate fields. This was still the Freudian era. Little attempt was made to search for organic causes of criminality. When, after medical school, she began working with juvenile delinquents in New Haven, the theory was that these boys were robust, healthy. According to the prevailing wisdom, a delinquent was simply an ordinary kid who had been led astray by a troubled home life—by parents who were too irresponsible or too addled by drugs and alcohol to provide proper discipline. Lewis came from the archetypal do-gooding background . . . and she accepted this dogma. Criminals were just like us, only they had been given bad ideas about how to behave. The trouble was that when she began working with delinquents they didn't seem like that at all. They didn't lack for discipline. If anything, she felt, they were being disciplined too much. And these teen-agers weren't robust and rowdy; on the contrary, they seemed to be damaged and impaired. "I was studying for my boards in psychiatry, and in order to do a good job you wanted to do a careful medical history and a careful mental-status exam," she says. "I discovered that many of these kids had had serious accidents, injuries, or illnesses that seemed to have affected the central nervous system and that hadn't been identified previously."

In 1976, she was given a grant by the State of Connecticut to study a group of nearly a hundred juvenile delinquents. She immediately went to see Pincus, then a young professor of neurology at Yale. They had worked together once before. "Dorothy came along and said she wanted to do this project with me," Pincus says. "She wanted to look at violence. She had this hunch that there was something physically wrong with these kids. I said, 'That's ridiculous. Everyone knows violence has nothing to do with neurology.'" At that point, Pincus recalls, he went to his bookshelf and began reading out loud from what was then the definitive work in the field: "Criminality and Psychiatric Disorders," by Samuel Guze, the chairman of the psychiatry department of Washington University, in St. Louis. "Sociopathy, alcoholism, and drug dependence are the psychiatric disorders characteristically associated with serious crime," he read. "Schizophrenia, primary affective disorders, anxiety neurosis, obsessional neurosis, phobic neurosis, and"—and there he paused—"brain syndromes are not." But Lewis would have none of it. "She said, 'We should do it anyway.' I said, 'I don't have the time.' She said, 'Jonathan, I can *pay* you.' So I would go up on Sunday, and I would examine three or four youths, just give them a standard neurological examination." But, after seeing the kids for himself, Pincus, too, became convinced that the prevailing wisdom about juvenile delinquents—and, by extension, about adult criminals—was wrong, and that Lewis was right. "Almost *all* the violent ones were damaged," Pincus recalls, shaking his head.

Over the past twenty years, Lewis and Pincus have testified for the defense in more than a dozen criminal cases, most of them death-penalty appeals. Together, they have published a series of groundbreaking studies on murderers and delinquents, painstakingly outlining the medical and psychiatric histories of the very violent; one of their studies has been cited twice in United States Supreme Court opinions. Of the two, Pincus is more conservative. He doesn't have doubts about evil the way Lewis does, and sharply disagrees with her on some of the implications of their work. On the core conclusions, however, they are in agreement. They believe that the most vicious criminals are, overwhelmingly, people with some combination of abusive childhoods, brain injuries, and psychotic symptoms (in particular, paranoia), and that while each of these problems individually has no connection to criminality (most people who have been abused or have brain injuries or psychotic symptoms never end up harming anyone else), somehow these factors together create such terrifying synergy as to impede these individuals' ability to play by the rules of society.

Trying to determine the causes of human behavior is, of course, a notoriously tricky process. Lewis and Pincus haven't done the kind of huge, population-wide studies that could definitively answer just how predictive of criminality these factors are. Their findings are, however, sufficiently tantalizing that their ideas have steadily gained ground in recent years. Other researchers have now done some larger studies supporting their ideas. Meanwhile, a wave of new findings in the fields of experimental psychiatry and neurology has begun to explain why it is that brain dysfunction and child abuse can have such dire effects. The virtue of this theory is that it sidesteps all the topics that so cripple contemporary discussions of violence—genetics, biological determinism, and, of course, race. In a sense, it's a return to the old liberal idea that environment counts, and that it is possible to do something significant about crime by changing the material conditions of people's lives. Only, this time the maddening imprecision of the old idea (what, exactly, was it about bad housing, say, that supposedly led to violent crime?) has been left behind. Lewis and Pincus and other neurologists and psychiatrists working in the field of criminal behavior think they are beginning to understand what it is that helps to turn some people into violent criminals—right down to which functions of the brain are damaged by abuse and injury. That's what Lewis means when she says she doesn't think that people are intrinsically evil. She thinks that some criminals simply suffer from a dysfunction of the brain, the way cardiac patients suffer from a dysfunction of the heart, and this is the central and in some ways disquieting thing about her. When she talks about criminals as victims, she doesn't use the word in the standard liberal metaphorical sense. She means it literally. . . .

Testing for Brain Damage

The human brain comprises, in the simplest terms, four interrelated regions, stacked up in ascending order of complexity. At the bottom is the brain stem, which governs the most basic and primitive functions—breathing, blood pressure, and body temperature. Above that is the diencephalon, the seat of sleep and appetite. Then comes the limbic region, the seat of sexual behavior and instinctual emotions. And on top, covering the entire outside of the brain in a thick carpet of gray matter, is the cortex, the seat of both concrete and abstract thought. It is the function of the cortex—and, in particular, those parts of the cortex beneath the forehead, known as the frontal lobes—to modify the impulses that surge up from within the brain, to provide judgment, to organize behavior and decision-making, to learn and adhere to rules of everyday life. It is the dominance of the cortex and the frontal lobes, in other words, that is responsible for making us human; and the central argument of the school to which Lewis and Pincus belong is that what largely distinguishes many violent criminals from the rest of us is that something has happened inside their brains to throw the functioning of the cortex and the frontal lobes out of whack. "We are a highly socialized animal. We can sit in theatres with strangers and not fight with each other," Stuart Yudofsky, the chairman of psychiatry at Baylor College of Medicine, in Houston, told me. "Many other mammals could never crowd that closely together. Our cortex helps us figure out when we are and are not in danger. Our memory tells us what we should be frightened of and angry with and what we shouldn't. But if there are

problems there—if it's impaired—one can understand how that would lead to confusion, to problems with disinhibition, to violence." One of the most important things that Lewis and Pincus have to do, then, when they evaluate a murderer is check for signs of frontal-lobe impairment. This, the neurological exam, is Pincus's task.

Pincus begins by taking a medical history: he asks about car accidents and falls from trees and sports injuries and physical abuse and problems at birth and any blows to the head of a kind that might have caused damage to the frontal lobes. He asks about headaches, tests for reflexes and sensorimotor functions, and compares people's right and left sides and observes gait. "I measure the head circumference—if it's more than two standard deviations below the normal brain circumference, there may be some degree of mental retardation, and, if it's more than two standard deviations above, there may be hydrocephalus," Pincus told me. "I also check gross motor coördination. I ask people to spread their fingers and hold their hands apart and look for choreiform movements—discontinuous little jerky movements of the fingers and arms." We were in Pincus's cluttered office at Georgetown University Medical Center, in Washington, D.C., and Pincus, properly professorial in a gray Glen-plaid suit, held out his hand to demonstrate. "Then I ask them to skip, to hop," he went on, and he hopped up and down in a small space on the floor between papers and books. . . .

"Then I check for mixed dominance, to see if the person is, say, right-eyed, left-footed," he said. "If he is, it might mean that his central nervous system hasn't differentiated the way it should." He was sitting back down now. "No one of these by itself means he is damaged. But they can tell us something in aggregate."

At this point, Pincus held up a finger forty-five degrees to my left and moved it slowly to the right. "Now we're checking for frontal functions," he said. "A person should be able to look at the examiner's finger and follow it smoothly with his eyes. If he can only follow it jerkily, the frontal eye fields are not working properly. Then there's upward gaze." He asked me to direct my eyes to the ceiling. "The eye should go up five millimetres and a person should also be able to direct his gaze laterally and maintain it for twenty seconds. If he can't, that's motor impersistence." Ideally, Pincus will attempt to amplify his results with neuropsychological testing, an EEG (an electroencephalogram, which measures electrical patterns in the brain), and an M.R.I. scan (that's magnetic resonance imaging), to see if he can spot scarring or lesions in any of the frontal regions which might contribute to impairment.

Pincus is also interested in measuring judgment. But since there is no objective standard for judgment, he tries to pick up evidence of an inability to cope with complexity, a lack of connection between experience and decision-making which is characteristic of cortical dysfunction. Now he walked behind me, reached over the top of my head, and tapped the bridge of my nose in a steady rhythm. I blinked once, then stopped. That, he told me, was normal.

"When you tap somebody on the bridge of the nose, it's reasonable for a person to blink a couple of times, because there is a threat from the outside," Pincus said. "When it's clear there is no threat, the subject should be able to accommodate that. But, if the subject blinks more than three times, that's 'insufficiency of suppression,' which may reflect frontal-lobe dysfunction. The inability to accommodate means you can't adapt to a new situation. There's a certain rigidity there."

Arthur Shawcross, who had a cyst pressing on one temporal lobe and scarring in both frontal lobes (probably from, among other things, being hit on the head with a sledgehammer and with a discus, and falling on his head from the top of a forty-foot ladder), used to walk in absolutely straight lines, splashing through puddles instead of walking around them, and he would tear his pants on a barbed-wire fence instead of using a gate a few feet away. That's the kind of behavior Pincus tries to correlate with abnormalities on the neurological examination. "In the Wisconsin Card Sorting Test, the psychologist shows the subject four playing cards—three red ones, one black one—and asks which doesn't fit," Pincus said. "Then he shows the subject, say, the four of

diamonds, the four of clubs, the four of hearts, and the three of diamonds. Somebody with frontal-lobe damage who correctly picked out the black one the first time—say, the four of clubs—is going to pick the four of clubs the second time. But the rules have changed. It's now a three we're after. We're going by numbers now, not color. It's that kind of change that people with frontal-lobe damage can't make. They can't change the rules. They get stuck in a pattern. They keep using rules that are demonstrably wrong. Then there's the word-fluency test. I ask them to name in one minute as many different words as they can think of which begin with the letter 'f.' Normal is fourteen, plus or minus five. Anyone who names fewer than nine is abnormal."

This is not an intelligence test. People with frontal-lobe damage might do just as well as anyone else if they were asked, say, to list the products they might buy in a supermarket. "Under those rules, most people can think of at least sixteen products in a minute and rattle them off," Pincus said. But that's a structured test, involving familiar objects, and it's a test with rules. The thing that people with frontal-lobe damage can't do is cope with situations where there are no rules, where they have to improvise, where they need to make unfamiliar associations. "Very often, they get stuck on one word—they'll say 'four,' 'fourteen,' 'forty-four,'" Pincus said. "They'll use the same word again and again—'farm' and then 'farming.' Or, as one fellow in a prison once said to me, 'fuck,' 'fucker,' 'fucking.' They don't have the ability to come up with something else."

The Effect of Brain Damage

What's at stake, fundamentally, with frontal-lobe damage is the question of inhibition. A normal person is able to ignore the tapping after one or two taps, the same way he can ignore being jostled in a crowded bar. A normal person can screen out and dismiss irrelevant aspects of the environment. But if you can't ignore the tapping, if you can't screen out every environmental annoyance and stimulus, then you probably can't ignore being jostled in a bar, either. It's living life with a hair trigger.

A recent study of two hundred and seventy-nine veterans who suffered penetrating head injuries in Vietnam showed that those with frontal-lobe damage were anywhere from two to six times as violent and aggressive as veterans who had not suffered such injuries. This kind of aggression is what is known as neurological, or organic, rage. Unlike normal anger, it's not calibrated by the magnitude of the original insult. It's explosive and uncontrollable, the anger of someone who no longer has the mental equipment to moderate primal feelings of fear and aggression.

"There is a reactivity to it, in which a modest amount of stimulation results in a severe overreaction," Stuart Yudofsky told me. "Notice that reactivity implies that, for the most part, this behavior is not premeditated. The person is rarely violent and frightening all the time. There are often brief episodes of violence punctuating stretches when the person does not behave violently at all. There is also not any gain associated with organic violence. The person isn't using the violence to manipulate someone else or get something for himself. The act of violence does just the opposite. It is usually something that causes loss for the individual. He feels that it is out of his control and unlike himself. He doesn't blame other people for it. He often says, 'I hate myself for acting this way.' The first person with organic aggression I ever treated was a man who had been inflating a truck tire when the tire literally exploded and the rim was driven into his prefrontal cortex. He became extraordinarily aggressive. It was totally uncharacteristic: he had been a religious person with strong values. But now he would not only be physically violent—he would curse. When he came to our unit, a nurse offered him some orange juice. He was calm at that moment. But then he realized that the orange juice was warm, and in one quick motion he threw it back at her, knocking her glasses off and injuring her cornea. When we asked him why, he said, 'The orange juice was warm.' But he also said, 'I don't know what got into me.' It wasn't premeditated. It was something that accelerated quickly. He went from zero to a hundred in a millisecond." At that point, I asked Yudofsky an obvious ques-

tion. Suppose you had a person from a difficult and disadvantaged background, who had spent much of his life on the football field, getting his head pounded by the helmets of opposing players. Suppose he was involved in a tempestuous on-again, off-again relationship with his ex-wife. Could a vicious attack on her and another man fall into the category of neurological rage? "You're not the first person to ask that question," Yudofsky replied dryly, declining to comment further.

Pincus has found that when he examines murderers neurological problems of this kind come up with a frequency far above what would be expected in the general population. For example, Lewis and Pincus published a study of fifteen death-row inmates randomly referred to them for examination; they were able to verify forty-eight separate incidents of significant head injury. Here are the injuries suffered by just the first three murderers examined:

1. three years: beaten almost to death by father (multiple facial scars)
   early childhood: thrown into sink onto head (palpable scar)
   late adolescence: one episode of loss of consciousness while boxing
2. childhood: beaten in head with two-by-fours by parents
   childhood: fell into pit, unconscious for several hours
   seventeen years: car accident with injury to right eye
   eighteen years: fell from roof apparently because of a blackout
3. six years: glass bottle deliberately dropped onto head from tree (palpable scar on top of cranium)
   eight years: hit by car
   nine years: fell from platform, received head injury
   fourteen years: jumped from moving car, hit head.

The Effect of Child Abuse on the Brain

Dorothy Lewis's task is harder than Jonathan Pincus's. He administers relatively straightforward tests of neurological function. But she is interested in the psychiatric picture, which means getting a murderer to talk about his family, his feelings and behavior, and, perhaps most important, his childhood. It is like a normal therapy session, except that Lewis doesn't have weeks in which to establish intimacy. She may have only a session or two. On one occasion, when she was visiting a notorious serial killer at San Quentin, she got lucky. "By chance, one of the lawyers had sent me some clippings from the newspaper, where I read that when he was caught he had been carrying some Wagner records," she told me. "For some reason, that stuck in my mind. The first time I went to see him, I started to approach him and he pointed at me and said, 'What's happening on June 18th?' And I said, 'That's the first night PBS is broadcasting "Der Ring des Nibelungen."' You know, we'd studied Wagner at Ethical Culture. Granted, it was a lucky guess. But I showed him some respect, and you can imagine the rapport that engendered." Lewis says that even after talking for hours with someone guilty of horrendous crimes she never gets nightmares. . . .

At the heart of Lewis's work with murderers is the search for evidence of childhood abuse. She looks for scars. She combs through old medical records for reports of suspicious injuries. She tries to talk to as many family members and friends as possible. She does all this because, of course, child abuse has devastating psychological consequences for children and the adults they become. But there is the more important reason—the one at the heart of the new theory of violence—which is that finding evidence of prolonged child abuse is a key to understanding criminal behavior because abuse also appears to change the anatomy of the brain.

When a child is born, the parts of his brain that govern basic physiological processes—that keep him breathing and keep his heart beating—are fully intact. But a newborn can't walk, can't crawl, can't speak, can't reason or do much of anything besides sleep and eat, because the higher regions of his brain—the cortex, in particular—aren't developed yet. In the course of child-

hood, neurons in the cortex begin to organize themselves—to differentiate and make connections—and that maturation process is in large part responsive to what happens in the child's environment. Bruce Perry, a psychiatrist at Baylor College of Medicine, has done brain scans of children who have been severely neglected, and has found that their cortical and subcortical areas never developed properly, and that, as a result, those regions were roughly twenty or thirty per cent smaller than normal. This kind of underdevelopment doesn't affect just intelligence; it affects emotional health. "There are parts of the brain that are involved in attachment behavior—the connectedness of one individual to another—and in order for that to be expressed we have to have a certain nature of experience and have that experience at the right time," Perry told me. "If early in life you are not touched and held and given all the somatosensory stimuli that are associated with what we call love, that part of the brain is not organized in the same way."

According to Perry, the section of the brain involved in attachment—which he places just below the cortex, in the limbic region—would look different in someone abused or neglected. The wiring wouldn't be as dense or as complex. "Such a person is literally lacking some brain organization that would allow him to actually make strong connections to other human beings. Remember the orphans in Romania? They're a classic example of children who, by virtue of not being touched and held and having their eyes gazed into, didn't get the somatosensory bath. It doesn't matter how much you love them after age two—they've missed that critical window."

In a well-known paper in the field of child abuse, Mary Main, a psychologist at Berkeley, and Carol George, now at Mills College, studied a group of twenty disadvantaged toddlers, half of whom had been subjected to serious physical abuse and half of whom had not. Main and George were interested in how the toddlers responded to a classmate in distress. What they found was that almost all the nonabused children responded to a crying or otherwise distressed peer with concern or sadness or, alternatively, showed interest and made some attempt to provide comfort. But not one of the abused toddlers showed any concern. At the most, they showed interest. The majority of them either grew distressed and fearful themselves or lashed out with threats, anger, and physical assaults. Here is the study's description of Martin, an abused boy of two and a half, who—emotionally retarded in the way that Perry describes—seemed incapable of normal interaction with another human being:

> Martin . . . tried to take the hand of the crying other child, and when she resisted, he slapped her on the arm with his open hand. He then turned away from her to look at the ground and began vocalizing very strongly. "Cut it out! CUT IT OUT!," each time saying it a little faster and louder. He patted her, but when she became disturbed by his patting, he retreated "hissing at her and baring his teeth." He then began patting her on the back again, his patting became beating, and he continued beating her despite her screams.

Abuse also disrupts the brain's stress-response system, with profound results. When something traumatic happens—a car accident, a fight, a piece of shocking news—the brain responds by releasing several waves of hormones, the last of which is cortisol. The problem is that cortisol can be toxic. If someone is exposed to too much stress over too long a time, one theory is that all that cortisol begins to eat away at the organ of the brain known as the hippocampus, which serves as the brain's archivist: the hippocampus organizes and shapes memories and puts them in context, placing them in space and time and tying together visual memory with sound and smell. J. Douglas Bremner, a psychiatrist at Yale, has measured the damage that cortisol apparently does to the hippocampus by taking M.R.I. scans of the brains of adults who suffered severe sexual or physical abuse as children and comparing them with the brains of healthy adults. An M.R.I. scan is a picture of a cross-section of the brain—as if someone's head had been cut into thin slices like a tomato, and then each slice had been photographed—and in the horizontal section taken by Bremner the normal hippocampus is visible as

two identical golf-ball-size organs, one on the left and one on the right, and each roughly even with the ear. In child-abuse survivors, Bremner found, the golf ball on the left is on average twelve per cent smaller than that of a healthy adult, and the theory is that it was shrunk by cortisol. Lewis says that she has examined murderers with dozens of scars on their backs, and that they have no idea how the scars got there. They can't remember their abuse, and if you look at Bremner's scans that memory loss begins to make sense: the archivist in their brain has been crippled.

Abuse also seems to affect the relationship between the left hemisphere of the brain, which plays a large role in logic and language, and the right hemisphere, which is thought to play a large role in creativity and depression. Martin Teicher, a professor of psychiatry at Harvard and McLean Hospital, recently gave EEGs to a hundred and fifteen children who had been admitted to a psychiatric facility, some of whom had a documented history of abuse. Not only did the rate of abnormal EEGs among the abused turn out to be twice that of the nonabused but all those abnormal brain scans turned out to be a result of problems on the left side of the brain. Something in the brain's stress response, Teicher theorized, was interfering with the balanced development of the brain's hemispheres.

Then Teicher did M.R.I.s of the brains of a subset of the abused children, looking at what is known as the corpus callosum. This is the fibre tract—the information superhighway—that connects the right and the left hemispheres. Sure enough, he found that parts of the corpus callosum of the abused kids were smaller than they were in the nonabused children. Teicher speculated that these abnormalities were a result of something wrong with the sheathing—the fatty substance, known as myelin, that coats the nerve cells of the corpus callosum. In a healthy person, the myelin helps the neuronal signals move quickly and efficiently. In the abused kids, the myelin seemed to have been eaten away, perhaps by the same excess cortisol that is thought to attack the hippocampus.

The Link Between Brain Damage and Emotional Health

Taken together, these changes in brain hardware are more than simple handicaps. They are, in both subtle and fundamental ways, corrosive of self. Richard McNally, a professor of psychology at Harvard, has done memory studies with victims of serious trauma, and he has discovered that people with post-traumatic-stress disorder, or P.T.S.D., show marked impairment in recalling specific autobiographical memories. A healthy trauma survivor, asked to name an instance when he exhibited kindness, says, "Last Friday, I helped a neighbor plow out his driveway." But a trauma survivor with P.T.S.D. can only say something like "I was kind to people when I was in high school." This is what seems to happen when your hippocampus shrinks: you can't find your memories. "The ability to solve problems in the here and now depends on one's ability to access specific autobiographical memories in which one has encountered similar problems in the past," McNally says. "It depends on knowing what worked and what didn't." With that ability impaired, abuse survivors cannot find coherence in their lives. Their sense of identity breaks down.

It is a very short walk from this kind of psychological picture to a diagnosis often associated with child abuse; namely, dissociative identity disorder, or D.I.D. Victims of child abuse are thought sometimes to dissociate, as a way of coping with their pain, of distancing themselves from their environment, of getting away from the danger they faced. It's the kind of disconnection that would make sense if a victim's memories were floating around without context and identification, his left and right hemispheres separated and unequal, and his sense of self fragmented and elusive. It's also a short walk from here to understanding how someone with such neurological problems could become dangerous. Teicher argues that in some of his EEG and M.R.I. analyses of the imbalance between the left and the right hemispheres he is describing the neurological basis for the polarization so often observed in psychiatrically disturbed patients—the mood swings, the sharply contrasting temperaments.

Instead of having two integrated hemispheres, these patients have brains that are, in some sense, divided down the middle. "What you get is a kind of erraticness," says Frank Putnam, who heads the Unit on Developmental Traumatology at the National Institute of Mental Health, in Maryland. "These kinds of people can be very different in one situation compared with another. There is the sense that they don't have a larger moral compass."

Several years ago, Lewis and Pincus worked together on an appeal for David Wilson, a young black man on death row in Louisiana. Wilson had been found guilty of murdering a motorist, Stephen Stinson, who had stopped to help when the car Wilson was in ran out of gas on I-10 outside New Orleans; and the case looked, from all accounts, almost impossible to appeal. Wilson had Stinson's blood on his clothes, in his pocket he had a shotgun shell of the same type and gauge as the one found in the gun at the murder scene, and the prosecution had an eyewitness to the whole shooting. At the trial, Wilson denied that the bloody clothes were his, denied that he had shot Stinson, denied that a tape-recorded statement the prosecution had played for the jury was of his voice, and claimed he had slept through the entire incident. It took the jury thirty-five minutes to convict him of first-degree murder and sixty-five minutes more, in the sentencing phase, to send him to the electric chair.

But when Lewis and Pincus examined him they became convinced that his story was actually much more complicated. In talking to Wilson's immediate family and other relatives, they gathered evidence that he had never been quite normal—that his personality had always seemed fractured and polarized. His mother recalled episodes from a very early age during which he would become "glassy-eyed" and seem to be someone else entirely. "David had, like, two personalities," his mother said. At times, he would wander off and be found, later, miles away, she recalled. He would have violent episodes during which he would attack his siblings' property, and subsequently deny that he had done anything untoward at all. Friends would say that they had seen someone who looked just like Wilson at a bar, but weren't sure that it had been Wilson, because he'd been acting altogether differently. On other occasions, Wilson would find things in his pockets and have no idea how they got there. He sometimes said he was born in 1955 and at other times said 1948.

What he had, in other words, were the classic symptoms of dissociation, and when Lewis and Pincus dug deeper into his history they began to understand why. Wilson's medical records detailed a seemingly endless list of hospitalizations for accidents, falls, periods of unconsciousness, and "sunstroke," dating from the time Wilson was two through his teens—the paper trail of a childhood marked by extraordinary trauma and violence. In his report to Wilson's attorneys, based on his examination of Wilson, Pincus wrote that there had been "many guns" in the home and that Wilson was often shot at as a child. He was also beaten "with a bull whip, 2x4's, a hose, pipes, a tree approximately 4 inches in diameter, wire, a piece of steel and belt buckles . . . on his back, legs, abdomen and face," until "he couldn't walk." Sometimes, when the beatings became especially intense, Wilson would have to "escape from the house and live in the fields for as long as two weeks." A kindly relative would leave food surreptitiously for him. The report goes on:

> As a result of his beatings David was ashamed to go to school lest he be seen with welts. He would "lie down in the cold sand in a hut" near his home to recuperate for several days rather than go to school.

At the hearing, Lewis argued that when Wilson said he had no memory of shooting Stinson he was actually telling the truth. The years of abuse had hurt his ability to retrieve memories.

Lewis also argued that Wilson had a violent side that he was, quite literally, unaware of; that he had the classic personality polarization of the severely abused who develop dissociative identity disorder. Lewis has videotapes of her sessions with Wilson: he is a handsome man with long fine black hair, sharply defined high cheekbones, and large, soft eyes. In the videotapes, he looks gentle. "During the hearing," Lewis recalls, "I was testifying, and I looked down at the defense table and David wasn't there. You know, David is a sweetie. He has a softness and a lovable quality. Instead, seated in his place there was this glowering kind of character, and I interrupted myself. I said, 'Excuse me, Your Honor, I just wanted to call to your attention that that is not David.' Everyone just looked." In the end, the judge vacated Wilson's death sentence.

Lewis talks a great deal about the Wilson case. It is one of the few instances in which she and Pincus succeeded in saving a defendant from the death penalty, and when she talks about what happened she almost always uses one of her favorite words—"poignant," spoken with a special emphasis, with a hesitation just before and just afterward. "In the course of evaluating someone, I always look for scars," Lewis told me. We were sitting in her Bellevue offices, watching the video of her examination of Wilson, and she was remembering the *poignant* moment she first met him. "Since I was working with a male psychologist, I said to him, 'Would you be good enough to go into the bathroom and look at David's back?' So he did that, and then he came back out and said, 'Dorothy! You must come and see this.' David had scars all over his back and chest. Burn marks. Beatings. I've seen a lot. But that was really grotesque."

An Explosive Mix

Abuse, in and of itself, does not necessarily result in violence, any more than neurological impairment or psychosis does. Lewis and Pincus argue, however, that if you mix these conditions together they become dangerous, that they have a kind of pathological synergy, that, like the ingredients of a bomb, they are troublesome individually but explosive in combination.

Several years ago, Lewis and some colleagues did a followup study of ninety-five male juveniles she and Pincus had first worked with in the late nineteen-seventies, in Connecticut. She broke the subjects into several groups: Group 1 consisted of those who did not have psychiatric or neurological vulnerabilities or an abusive childhood; Group 2 consisted of those with vulnerabilities but no abuse at home; Group 3 consisted of those with abuse but no vulnerabilities; yet another group consisted of those with abuse *and* extensive vulnerabilities. Seven years later, as adults, those in Group 1 had been arrested for an average of just over two criminal offenses, none of which were violent, so the result was essentially no jail time. Group 2, the psychiatrically or neurologically impaired kids, had been convicted of an average of almost ten offenses, two of which were violent, the result being just under a year of jail time. Group 3, the abused kids, had 11.9 offenses, 1.9 of them violent, the result being five hundred and sixty-two days in jail. But the group of children who had the most vulnerabilities and abuse were in another league entirely. In the intervening seven years, they had been arrested for, on average, 16.8 crimes, 5.4 of which were violent, the result being a thousand two hundred and fourteen days in prison.

In another study on this topic, a University of Southern California psychologist named Adrian Raine looked at four thousand two hundred and sixty-nine male children born and living in Denmark, and classified them according to two variables. The first was whether there were complications at birth—which correlates, loosely, with neurological impairment. The second was whether the child had been rejected by the mother (whether the child was unplanned, unwanted, and so forth)—which correlates, loosely, with abuse and neglect. Looking back eighteen years later, Raine found that those children who had not been rejected and had had no birth complications had roughly the same chance of becoming criminally violent as those with only one of the risk factors—around three per cent. For the children with both complications and rejection, however, the risk of violence tripled: in fact, the children with both problems accounted for eighteen per cent of all the violent crimes, even though they made up only 4.5 per cent of the group.

Implications for Preventing Crime

There is in these statistics a powerful and practical suggestion for how to prevent crime. In the current ideological climate, liberals argue that fighting crime requires fighting poverty, and conservatives argue that fighting crime requires ever more police and prisons; both of these things may be true, but both are also daunting. The studies suggest that there may be instances in which more modest interventions can bring large dividends. Criminal behavior that is associated with specific neurological problems is behavior that can, potentially, be diagnosed and treated like any other illness. Already, for example, researchers have found drugs that can mimic the cortical function of moderating violent behavior. The work is preliminary but promising. "We are on the cusp of a revolution in treating these conditions," Stuart Yudofsky told me. "We can use anticonvulsants, antidepressants, antihypertensive medications. There are medications out there that are F.D.A.-approved for other conditions which have profound effects on mitigating aggression." At the prevention end, as well, there's a strong argument for establishing aggressive child-abuse-prevention programs. Since 1992, for example, the National Committee to Prevent Child Abuse, a not-for-profit advocacy group based in Chicago, has been successfully promoting a program called Healthy Families America, which, working with hospitals, prenatal clinics, and physicians, identifies mothers in stressful and potentially abusive situations either before they give birth or immediately afterward, and then provides them with weekly home visits, counselling, and support for as long as five years. The main thing holding back nationwide adoption of programs like this is money: Healthy Families America costs up to two thousand dollars per family per year, but if we view it as a crime-prevention measure that's not a large sum.

These ideas, however, force a change in the way we think about criminality. Advances in the understanding of human behavior are necessarily corrosive of the idea of free will. That much is to be expected, and it is why courts have competency hearings, and legal scholars endlessly debate the definition and the use of the insanity defense. But the new research takes us one step further. If the patient of Yudofsky's who lashed out at his nurse because his orange juice was warm had, in the process, accidentally killed her, could we really hold him criminally responsible? Yudofsky says that that scenario is no different from one involving a man who is driving a car, has a heart attack, and kills a pedestrian. "Would you put *him* in jail?" he asks. Or consider Joseph Paul Franklin. By all accounts, he suffered through a brutal childhood on a par with that of David Wilson. What if he has a lesion on one of his frontal lobes, an atrophied hippocampus, a damaged and immature corpus callosum, a maldeveloped left hemisphere, a lack of synaptic complexity in the precortical limbic area, a profound left-right hemisphere split? What if in his remorselessness he was just the grownup version of the little boy Martin, whose ability to understand and relate to others was so retarded that he kept on hitting and hitting, even after the screams began? What if a history of abuse had turned a tendency toward schizophrenia—recall Franklin's colorful delusions—from a manageable impairment into the engine of murderousness? Such a person might still be sane, according to the strict legal definition. But that kind of medical diagnosis suggests, at the very least, that his ability to live by the rules of civilized society, and to understand and act on the distinctions between right and wrong, is quite different from that of someone who had a normal childhood and a normal brain.

What is implied by these questions is a far broader debate over competency and responsibility—an attempt to make medical considerations far more central to the administration of justice, so that we don't bring in doctors only when the accused seems really crazy but, rather, bring in doctors all the time, to add their expertise to the determination of responsibility.

One of the state-of-the-art diagnostic tools in neurology and psychiatry is the PET scan, a computerized X-ray that tracks the movement and rate of the body's metabolism. When you sing, for instance, the neurons in the specific regions that govern singing will start to fire. Blood will flow toward those regions, and if you take a PET scan at that moment the specific areas responsible for singing will light up on the PET computer moni-

tor. Bremner, at Yale, has done PET scans of Vietnam War veterans suffering from post-traumatic-stress disorder. As he scanned the vets, he showed them a set of slides of Vietnam battle scenes accompanied by an appropriate soundtrack of guns and helicopters. Then he did the same thing with vets who were not suffering from P.T.S.D. Bremner printed out the results of the comparison for me, and they are fascinating. The pictures are color-coded. Blue shows the parts of the brain that were being used identically in the two groups of veterans, and most of each picture is blue. A few parts are light blue or green, signifying that the P.T.S.D. vets were using those regions a little less than the healthy vets were. The key color, however, is white. White shows brain areas that the healthy vets were using as they watched the slide show and the unhealthy vets were hardly using at all; in Bremner's computer printout, there is a huge white blob in the front of every non-P.T.S.D. scan.

"That's the orbitofrontal region," Bremner told me. "It's responsible for the extinction of fear." The orbitofrontal region is the part of your brain that evaluates the primal feelings of fear and anxiety which come up from the brain's deeper recesses. It's the part that tells you that you're in a hospital watching a slide show of the Vietnam War, not in Vietnam living through the real thing. The vets with P.T.S.D. weren't using that part of their brain. That's why every time a truck backfires or they see a war picture in a magazine they are forced to relive their wartime experiences: they can't tell the difference.

Should We Focus on the Act or the Actor?

It doesn't take much imagination to see that this technique might someday be used to evaluate criminals—to help decide whether to grant parole, for example, or to find out whether some kind of medical treatment might aid reentry into normal society. We appear to be creating a brand-new criminal paradigm: the research suggests that instead of thinking about and categorizing criminals merely by their acts—murder, rape, armed robbery, and so on—we ought to categorize criminals also according to their disabilities, so that a murderer with profound neurological damage and a history of vicious childhood abuse is thought of differently from a murderer with no brain damage and mild child abuse, who is, in turn, thought of differently from a murderer with no identifiable impairment at all. This is a more flexible view. It can be argued that it is a more sophisticated view. But even those engaged in such research—for example, Pincus—confess to discomfort at its implications, since something is undoubtedly lost in the translation. The moral force of the old standard, after all, lay in its inflexibility. Murder was murder, and the allowances made for aggravated circumstances were kept to a minimum. Is a moral standard still a moral standard when it is freighted with exceptions and exemptions and physiological equivocation?

When Lewis went to see Bundy, in Florida, on the day before his execution, she asked him why he had invited her—out of a great many people lining up outside his door—to see him. He answered, "Because everyone else wants to know what I did. You are the only one who wants to know why I did it." It's impossible to be sure what the supremely manipulative Bundy meant by this: whether he genuinely appreciated Lewis, or whether he simply regarded her as his last conquest. What is clear is that, over the four or five times they met in Bundy's last years, the two reached a curious understanding: he was now part of her scientific enterprise.

"I wasn't writing a book about him," Lewis recalls. "That he knew. The context in which he had first seen me was a scientific study, and this convinced him that I wasn't using him. In the last meeting, as I recall, he said that he wanted any material that I found out about him to be used to understand what causes people to be violent. We even discussed whether he would allow his brain to be studied. It was not an easy thing to talk about with him, let me tell you." At times, Lewis says, Bundy was manic, "high as a kite." On one occasion, he detailed to her just how he had killed a woman, and, on another occasion, he stared at her and stated flatly, "The man sitting across from you did not commit any murders." But she says that at the end she sensed a certain breakthrough. "The day before he was executed, he asked me to turn off the tape recorder. He said he wanted to tell me things that he didn't want recorded, so I didn't record them. It was very confidential." To this day, Lewis has never told anyone what Bundy said. There is something almost admirable about this. But there is also something strange about extending the physician-patient privilege to a killer like Bundy—about turning the murderer so completely into a patient. It is not that the premise is false, that murderers can't also be patients. It's just that once you make that leap—once you turn the criminal into an object of medical scrutiny—the crime itself inevitably becomes pushed aside and normalized. The difference between a crime of evil and a crime of illness is the difference between a sin and a symptom. And symptoms don't intrude in the relationship between the murderer and the rest of us: they don't force us to stop and observe the distinctions between right and wrong, between the speakable and the unspeakable, the way sins do. It was at the end of that final conversation that Bundy reached down and kissed Lewis on the cheek. But that was not all that happened. Lewis then reached up, put her arms around him, and kissed him back.

READING 4

CRIME CAUSATION FROM THE INMATES' STANDPOINT

Robert J. Kelly

Robert J. Kelly based this article on interviews and observations with inmates and correction officers at the Central Punitive Segregation Unit, Rikers Island. Kelly is Broeklundian Professor at Brooklyn College and the Graduate School, City University of New York.

In their own words, many inmates experience themselves as putty in the hands of fate. The language of inmates, the ways in which they choose to describe their lives and predicaments, is always informative. Their talk is typically about the happenstance leading to arrest and incarceration. One inmate, awaiting placement in an upstate prison on a charge of armed robbery in which a victim was shot, spoke about his lack of luck after he had already served numerous prison sentences, many for violent crimes. It was bad luck, he said, for he was blameless. The damned victim happened to wander into the store—that's what led to the shooting; had the man not been there, he would not have been shot.

This inmate was by no means alone in explaining his behavior as a consequence of fortu-

Reprinted from Robert J. Kelly, "Vindictive Vindications: Crime Causation from the Inmates' Standpoint," *The Keepers' Voice*, Spring 1996, by permission of *The Keepers' Voice*, a publication of The International Association of Correctional Officers.

itous circumstances beyond his control. A young man convicted of murder in a "drive-by" shooting when asked what happened and why spoke of "bullets flying all over the place." Apparently, the explanatory system here is that no one could be held accountable because the streets were ablaze with gunfire. The victims were not sought out. That guns were taken to the scene, and intended for use, did not seem particularly relevant.

Some psychotherapists might argue that it is natural to deny or repress violent criminal acts as one's own doing. Within a pseudo-Freudian perspective it makes perfectly good sense to ascribe the lethal outcomes of irrational and impulsive behavior to the victims, to attribute their deaths to forces beyond anyone's control. A frank and sincere acknowledgment of responsibility would result in a collapse of the psyche and possibly deep depression. Hence the evasion of responsibility became a psychologically and emotionally healthy response.

Those who commit less serious crimes exhibit a similar type of rationale in re-visioning their criminal acts. A mercurial, compulsive burglar of churches and temples, who also molested clergy, complained that had ecclesiastical authorities shown more concern for security, he would not be locked up. It was the laxness of security not the valuable gold and silver instruments used in ceremonies that compelled this individual. In short, the churches were to blame. In some ways, the criminal echoes the police who too often appear to lay some blame on the victims for failing to take proper precautions, rather than on the persons who actually carry out criminal acts.

Inmates at the "Bing"

In the New York City Department of Correction, many inmates assigned to the Central Punitive Segregation Unit (CPSU), known as the "Bing," suffer from the same delusional thinking. Those who assault other inmates or correction personnel, or commit serious rule infractions (fighting, carrying weapons), are assigned to the Bing for varying lengths of time depending upon the frequency or seriousness of the offense. Many actually see themselves as blameless, as victims rather that perpetrators.

An inmate who routinely assaulted female correction officers claimed to be under so strong a compulsion to attack women in uniforms that it was for him irresistible—nothing less than an "addiction." In spite of his "afflictions," he considered himself a fundamentally good person because his victims never suffered serious physical damage. He fondled them, made salacious comments and gestured obscenely, but never stabbed, sliced, strangled, or beat female officers.

The isolation and control in the Bing with its 23-hour lockup and high security conditions did not cure but exacerbated his problem. He said he became restless, anxious, depressed, and often enraged. In his opinion, attacking women was an addiction that was magnified by denial and made more intolerable by the indignity of additional constraints and the removal of privileges.

Addiction is generally thought to be an illness characterized by an irresistible urge that is driven by a combination of neurochemical, hereditary and social factors, which compel individuals to behave in a repetitively self-destructive or anti-social manner. Popular wisdom holds that addicts cannot help themselves and, more importantly for this discussion, that such compulsive behavior is a manifestation of illness and thus has, or

should have, no moral content. The man who molested a female officer claimed that he was not responsible for his actions and that it was the duty of the Department of Correction to treat him, not just constrain him.

Criminals and inmates shrewdly shift the locus of responsibility for their acts onto others. For example, some inmates placed in the Bing because of their chronically violent behavior and assaults talk about "losing their heads" or "going off the deep end." Apparently they consider themselves suffering from a pathology that causes explosive anger and uncontrollable involuntary rage, which it is the medical professions' duty to deal with. These putative illnesses, they believe, absolve them from any accountability for their misconduct. The self-diagnosis essentially enables the inmate to define himself or herself as a victim rather than a perpetrator. The criminals, by informing counseling personnel, correction officers and interviewers—by telling the authorities what they might do, if they do engage in crime again—feel both relieved and aggrieved that the system did nothing when they pleaded for help. If, on the other hand, inmates are asked their views about preventive detention (as a pre-emptory strategy to forestall future violent crime until such time after confinement and treatment as they feel confident in controlling their tempers), they usually became outraged, and indignant, and begin talking about their legal rights, the principle of the presumption of innocence and habeas corpus proceedings.

Bing inmates often talked about "getting their heads together," when explaining their criminal histories. Whether they know it or not, their cognitive theories entail a conceptual distinction between the actor, the "social me,"—to use William James' form—and the "real me," that deeper, spiritual entity some might call the soul or that collection of states of consciousness, mental faculties and emotional dispositions that constitute a person's psyche. Within the jail population, the social-me personality actually wields razors, carries guns, steals, robs and assaults other persons. That other psychic territory—the non-material, non-social self—is not at all reflected in a social deviant behavior; what one is in this Jekyll and Hyde imagery is determined by what one does; there is an unassailable core of virtue that thrives beneath the physical and social realities that enables the individual to retain self-respect even if their overt actions lack any moral significance. The rationale for splitting oneself is not that far fetched: finding themselves in a world governed by a code of behavior, a set of tough regulations that reward aggression (even among those who deplore it) and that is full of permissions and vetoes that would shock straight society but is unfortunately viable in the world of confinement, the inmate comes to the view that prison life is essentially dominated by the powerful and violent who invade private space, appropriate goods and services with impunity and scant regard for principles and moral imperatives that they otherwise proclaim for their secret, deeper selves.

That said, the idea of "getting one's head together" has social and psychological utilities that facilitate the inmates' negotiation of the official side of the prison world. Since the true, virtuous self is submerged in the turbulence of the penitentiary environment, until adjustments are made and conditions improved, constructive suggestions obliging inmates to comply with rules and regulations may be ignored.

The Inmates' Game of "Getting Over"

At the center of this refusal to assume responsibility is a deceitfulness and disenchantment—what Jean Paul Sartre famously called mauvaise foi ("bad faith"). To be an inmate means a sense of defeat and often bewildering uncertainty. Perhaps inmates feel compelled, almost humiliatingly, to keep to a testimonial level in their contacts, discussions, explanations, justifications, pleadings, demands and confessions with other inmates, correctional personnel, lawyers, judges and even families. However inmates attempt to blame others—the correction officer, the crowded facilities, the lawyers—and whatever appearance of sincerity they manage to convey, some, at least, know that their complaints and explanations are untrue. Much of what they say is part of the complex interactional game known as "Getting Over."

Drug addicts, for instance, explain their actions differently depending upon their audience. With physicians, drug dispensary workers, probation officers—anyone who might be useful in arranging or maintaining a prescription or social support—addicts emphasize their overpowering craving for the drug, the profound impact it has on their lives, and the intolerable effects of drug withdrawal. Among other drug users, however, addicts discuss "copping and scoring" (obtaining illegal street supplies); and about which dealer has the best quality and best prices.

This hustle seems similar with the "cons" of prison and jail inmates. It is scarcely a fresh observation that prisons and jails are "schools of crime." A place where some apprentices learn new criminal and linguistic skills. Good "students" develop into amateur social scientists and learn how to manipulate physicians, psychiatrists, attorneys and social workers with stories about their squalid pasts; dysfunctional families; abusive, alcoholic parents; and tough, unforgiving slum neighborhoods. These "raps" (discussions) are meant to explain the genesis of an inmate's criminal career.

Inmates fail to see how sociological explanations that may apply to them, might also apply to police and correctional officers who commit violent acts. Inmates rarely ascribe police and correctional officer misconduct to an early childhood trauma or an abusive environment. Unlike inmates, officers do not need sympathy and understanding, counseling and therapy to "get their heads together." "Those motherfucker officers should know better." Implicit in the inmate's hostility is the assumption that unlike themselves—the offspring of poverty and discrimination, circumstances beyond their control—officers act out of free will that is simply and purely malevolent. Skillful impression management of the self is an art inmates cleverly contrive to suit their own needs.

The Presentation of Self in Jail and Prison

Erving Goffman's notable contributions to the understanding of self identity formation can be usefully applied here.[1] Using theatrical performance as a metaphor, Goffman sees individuals presenting themselves and their activities to others as a means to guide and control the impressions formed of them, in much the same way that an actor portrays a character to an audience. These characterizations are played out on a prison or jail stage.

Goffman calls this stage a "total institution"—a confining place of residence and work where a large number of individuals who are cut off from society for an appreciable period of time lead an enclosed, formally administered way of life. In a coercive institution such as a correctional facility everything that goes on, including bargaining for privileges, must be legitimated by assimilating it or translating it to fit the institutional frame of reference. Staff actions must be defined and presented to the inmates as expressions of treatment and control. It is the institutional structure itself, according to Goffman, that produces two unmistakable categories of persons that give depth and color to inmate/officer arrangements; and insofar as the disparities between their social qualities and moral character are successfully staged and verified through the roles each group plays, differences in perceptions of self and others are heightened. This stratification of staff and inmates also regiments and distributes power unevenly such that the inmate is obliged to invent exculpatory narratives of self.

Simultaneously, as if to withstand the psychological stress and deprivational effects which is much like a dead sea of predictable, monotonous routine, the inmate sculpts some "resting points" much like the non-criminal in civil society who when pushed to the wall usually has the opportunity to crawl into some shielded place where commercialized paleo-fantasies—movies, TV, alcohol, vacations,—can be indulged. In correctional facilities imaginative substitutes must be found or created because these conventional release mechanisms, common in the "home world," are in short supply. It is not that the jail or prison seeks a cultural victory over the inmate by means of its mortification processes that denude inmates of their "identity kits," but rather that the prison

and jail are of necessity social hybrids, part residential community, part formal custodial organization; and given their bastardized structure and mission they generate and sustain a tension between the home world of the inmates' community and neighborhood and the institutional world of bureaucratic protocols whose rationalized regimens, procedures, strictures, confinements and legalized prohibitions provide strategic leverage in the management of incarcerated populations. All of this amounts to the palpable meaning of punishment inflicted as it unfolds in fact and in the minds of inmates.

The inmates' presentations of themselves are enriched by the medley of theories circulating among staff including an open acknowledgment of wrong doing that was, perhaps, a momentary lapse, the result of a faulty character; or crime as the outcome of self that concurs with staff philosophies as to what constitutes rehabilitation and personal change. Although rehabilitation is often openly ridiculed as a failed policy, many correctional professionals, criminologists—especially psychiatrists and social workers—secretly nurse the hope that incarceration in itself may change minds and hearts and produce a willingness among inmates to embrace paradigms of personal restoration and psychological re-conditioning.

As a way of securing some surcease from the degradation of confinement, an inmate can agree that he did wrong but that there are important mitigating circumstances (a victim of circumstances, racism, poverty), or that their responsibility must be qualified because of reduced competencies induced by drugs, alcohol, ignorance or even youthfulness.

Professional Redemptions

Personally selecting an explanation or "treatment" regimen for one's criminal behavior is not difficult: there now exists an enlarged constituency of helpers, therapists, attorneys and social workers whose incomes and careers depend on the supposed incapacities of inmates to behave reasonably or fend for themselves economically on the outside. Without the presumed powerlessness of career criminals to cope with their own deviant inclinations, an entire infrastructure of intellectual entrepreneurs, therapists and moral crusaders would be without work. They have a steep investment in the putative psychopathologies that hound criminals. Indeed, their therapeutic ethos of the criminal/inmate or patient/client as essentially the passive victim of illness in some ways legitimizes the behaviors from which they hope to rescue the inmate. Thus, there are tangible advantages for offenders in appearing as helpless victims of social, cultural and psychological forces over which they have little influence.

Added to this therapeutic atmosphere is the widespread dissemination of psychotherapeutic jargon, concepts and sociological descriptions that give currency to these ideas. The major perspectives of sociological determinism are gaining public acceptance. Statistical associations between criminal behavior and poverty, for example, are construed indiscriminately as proving causation between the two. Congress and public officials, those who could have these things lucidly explained to them, conclude wrongly that if criminal behavior is more common among the poor, then it must be poverty that causes crime.

This view may be eagerly embraced by inmates who sense that it provides viable excuses for their conduct, and by citizens who are guilt-ridden by so much imprisonment. However, these perspectives contain profound dehumanizing consequences. If poverty were the cause of crime, then those who take up guns and those who steal or deal drugs as a career do not decide to do so any more than a bacteria reacts in predictable ways to chemical manipulations. These popular and fashionable explanations—from social conditions direct to behavior, without passing through the filtering agency of the individual's mind—have just enough plausibility to suggest that crime is not a moral problem after all. Just as importantly, those who commit crimes have an excuse which is useful and convenient in dealing with law enforcement authorities. Encouraged by professionals, these explanations, if repeated enough, allow inmates to deny (at least part of the time) their guilt and indignantly insist upon sentence reductions, release, or alternative placements. Ironically, the structure of care and help afforded inmates in coming to terms with their problems can be easily sabotaged when the tables are turned. The inmate whose well-oiled production of a pliable self seeking help may assimilate explanations that provide partial exculpation and act on these opportunistically defeating the very purposes which professional ancillary help agencies in correctional services seek to achieve. "I need help" is transmuted into, "I'm a victim too, why am I being punished for accidents of birth and social injustices!"

The Malleability of Character

It is well to remember the observations of Goffman, whose views on the self illuminate the behavior of those confined in prisons and jails. His key insights help us to understand the malleability of character and its capacities for deceit, dissembling and self-delusion. If we accept a psychobiology of personality which equates a social performance as an expression of the attributes of character housed in the body of the processor, then social behavior will appear to emanate intrinsically from its performer. Actions that are for the most part consistent with social expectations are deemed creditable; they lead an audience (in this case, corrections personnel, mental health professionals and social scientists) to impute a self to a performed character rather than interpreting that self as a manufactured projection, since a performed character is not a classifiable organic thing that can be diagnosed but a dramatic effect arising out of the context in which it is presented. The means for producing and sustaining a self are not deeply rooted in the person but reside in the opportunities to shape behavior that social establishments provide.

And what do these claims amount to for the corrections professional? They suggest much about the complex structure of social encounters and the protean nature of the self. They say something about the bewildering conditions both inmates and correctional personnel confront on a daily basis in prisons and jails; how the coherence of institutional priorities and inputs that make up the inmates experience can be jeopardized by the baffling multitude of professional inputs, however well-intended, that can exacerbate tensions and precipitate disruptions. One can only wonder at the thief who glows with self-satisfaction and cal-culated, provisional ethicality: "I steal only Mercedes . . . hey, if they can afford one, they can stand the loss. I leave the poor alone." The threat is that such a mood may be sincere.

REFERENCES

1. Erving Goffman. (1959) *The Presentation of Self in Everyday Life.* NY: Doubleday Anchor Books; (1971) *Relations in Public: Microstudies of the Public Order.* NY: BasicBooks; and (1961) *Asylums: Essays on the Social Situation of Mental Patients and Other Inmates.* NY: Doubleday Anchor Books.

DISCUSSION QUESTIONS

1. Gladwell suggests that some violent criminals may be victims of their own neurological dysfunctions. Should, he asks, such "victims" be responded to as less culpable for their actions? Respond to that question, but also respond to the idea that some violent criminals may in fact be victims of societal dysfunctions (e.g., employment discrimination, institutional racism, unequal enforcement of laws). Should these "victims" also be considered less culpable for their actions?

2. This chapter's introduction suggested that a complete understanding of criminal behavior may benefit from research in biology as well as in sociology and psychology. Explain why you agree or disagree with this assessment.

3. In this chapter's introduction, you were asked to consider how any explanation (e.g., biological, psychological, sociological) for crime inevitably provides criminals with an excuse for their criminality. How can society reach a compromise between a need to know why people commit crime while also being able to convince criminals to take responsibility for their actions? Or, if we come to believe that criminals are not, in fact, personally responsible for their actions (that is, behavior is determined by forces beyond the individual's control), how should we modify our criminal justice system?

WEBSITES

www.webserve.net/iandi/org/cave/welcome.html

Citizens Against Violent crimE (CAVE) is a grassroots organization designed to mobilize citizens into action against the problems of violent crime. At their home page, you will find information geared specifically for victims and family members of victims.

www.bsos.umd.edu/asc

Research into the causes of crime is of particular interest to criminologists. At this home page for the American Society of Criminology you will find an excellent listing of criminal justice websites that you can use to track down additional information about explanations for crime.

sun.soci.niu.edu/~ascmentr/mentor.html

As a service to its student members (call 614-292-9207 for membership information), the American Society of Criminology provides a list of faculty and researchers from around the world who have agreed to serve as informal mentors by answering e-mail inquiries. Check out the mentor list and see if there is someone who is offering assistance on a particular crime topic (e.g., violent crime) of interest to you.

CHAPTER 3: OTHER LEGAL SYSTEMS

Scholars typically identify four major contemporary legal traditions: common, civil, socialist, and Islamic. Since a goal of this book is to help people better understand the American criminal justice system, it seems appropriate that the selected readings be geared toward the common legal tradition, in which the American system developed. However, scholars of comparative studies believe people can come to a better understanding of their own system by contrasting it with another. That perspective has influenced the choice of several readings throughout this book. To discover similarities and differences in the way countries respond to law violators, one must first have a basic understanding of other systems. This chapter begins that process by presenting overviews of two legal traditions—the civil and the Islamic.

The common legal tradition stemmed especially from efforts of England's Henry II (1154–1189) and spread with colonization to English-speaking countries like the United States, Australia, Canada (outside Quebec), and British colonies in Africa and Asia. The most notable alternative to the common legal tradition—at least from an American point of view—is the civil legal tradition, which stemmed from Roman law and spread throughout Europe and into those areas of Africa and Latin America that were colonies of continental European countries. These two great legal traditions are sometimes distinguished by a reliance on written law, or codes (the civil tradition), versus a reliance on custom (the common tradition). In the selection by John Merryman we find that such a distinction can be misleading. Merryman explains that although jurisdictions under common law might write down their laws (and perhaps call them "codes"), these are not codes in the civil law sense because they are not replacing existing law. That is, when laws are written down in U.S. jurisdictions it is to perfect and supplement existing law. When laws are written down in Italy, Germany, or other civil law countries, the existing law is being replaced. To help show the impact of this view of law on how the law is applied, Merryman goes on to describe the role of judges under civil law. As you read this section, notice that civil law judges are expected simply to apply the law as found in the relevant code, ignoring the decisions of other judges in similar cases. This lack of attention to judicial precedent is a rejection of stare decisis that Americans might find disconcerting.

Many Americans' knowledge of Islamic law does not extend past the cutting off of a thief's hand. The reading by Wiechman, Kendall, and Azarian shows that this legal tradition is much more complex than might first appear. Of the four contemporary legal traditions, Islamic law is the only one that is solely religious in nature. Muslims ("those who submit to Allah") believe that God set down the rules and regulations for all behavior. The Sharia ("the path to follow") presents Allah's rules in the Quran (Islam's holy book) and the Sunna (the statements and deeds of the prophet Muhammad). As you read this selection consider how media reports of Muslim extremists may give non-Muslims a misunderstanding of Islam and Islamic law.

READING 5

THE CIVIL LEGAL TRADITION

John Henry Merryman

John Henry Merryman compares two great legal traditions—the civil legal tradition and the common legal tradition. As a specific example of their differences, the role of judges in each system is examined. Merryman is emeritus professor of law at Stanford University.

One often hears it said, sometimes by people who should know better, that civil law systems are codified statutory systems, whereas the common law is uncodified and is based in large part on judicial decisions. The purpose of this article is to indicate the extent to which this observation oversimplifies and misrepresents, and at the same time the extent to which it expresses, an important set of basic differences between the two legal traditions.

The distinction between legislative and judicial production of law can be misleading. There is probably at least as much legislation in force in a typical American state as there is in a typical European or Latin American nation. As in a civil law nation, legislation validly enacted in the United States is the law, which the judges are expected to interpret and apply in the spirit in which it was enacted. The authority of legislation is superior to that of judicial decisions; statutes supersede contrary judicial decisions (constitutional questions aside), but not vice versa. The amount of legisla-

tion and the degree of authority of legislation are not useful criteria for distinguishing civil law systems from common law systems.

Nor is the existence of something called a code a distinguishing criterion. California has more codes than any civil law nation, but California is not a civil law jurisdiction. Codes do exist in most civil law systems, but bodies of systematic legislation covering broad areas of the law and indistinguishable in appearance from European or Latin American codes also exist in a number of common law nations. Conversely, a civil law system need not have codes. Hungary and Greece were civil law countries even before they enacted their civil codes: Hungarian civil law was uncodified until Hungary became a socialist state, and Greece enacted its first civil code after World War II. South Africa, whose legal system is based on Roman-Dutch law, is still uncodified, and citations of Justinian's *Digest* in South African judicial opinions are still encountered. The code form is thus not a distinctive identifying mark of a civil law system.

If, however, one thinks of codification not as a form but as the expression of an ideology, and if one tries to understand that ideology and why it achieves expression in code form, then one can see how it makes sense to talk about codes in comparative law. It is true that California has a number of what are called codes, as do some other states in the United States, and that the Uniform Commercial Code has been adopted in most

Adapted from *The Civil Law Tradition*, 2nd ed., by John Henry Merryman, with the permission of the publishers, Stanford University Press. Copyright ©1969, 1985 by the Board of Trustees of the Leland Stanford Junior University.

American jurisdictions. However, although these look like the codes in civil law countries, the underlying ideology—the conception of what a code is and of the functions it should perform in the legal process—is not the same. There is an entirely different ideology of codification at work in the civil law world.

It will be recalled that Justinian [Eastern Roman emperor, 527–575], when he promulgated the *Corpus Juris Civilis,* sought to abolish all prior law. Certain elements of the prior legal order were, however, included in the *Corpus Juris Civilis* itself, and were consequently preserved when he promulgated it. Similarly, the French, when they codified their law, repealed all prior law in the areas covered by the codes. Any principles of prior law that were incorporated in the codes received their validity not from their previous existence, but from their incorporation and reenactment in codified form. Justinian and the French codifiers sought to destroy prior law for different but analogous reasons: Justinian sought to reestablish the purer law of an earlier time, the French to establish an entirely new legal order. In both cases, the aims were essentially utopian. Let us look more closely at the utopia of the French codification.

The French Code

The ideology of the French codification, though more temperate than that of the immediate post-revolutionary period, accurately reflects the ideology of the French Revolution. For example, one reason for the attempt to repeal all prior law, and thus limit the effect of law to new legislation, was statism—the glorification of the nation-state. A law that had its origins in an earlier time, before the creation of the state, violated this statist ideal. So did a law that had its origin outside the state—in a European common law, for instance. The nationalism of the time was also an important factor. Much of the prerevolutionary law in France was European rather than French in origin (the *jus commune*), and was consequently offensive to the rising spirit of French nationalism. At the same time, much that was French (the *coutumes* of the northern regions in particular)

now appeared as the logical object of preservation and glorification. The drive toward a centralized state made it important to bring some unity out of the diversity of legal systems and materials in the French regions. The secular natural law ideal of one law applicable to all Frenchmen pointed the same way.

The rampant rationalism of the time also had an important effect on French codification. Only an exaggerated rationalism can explain the belief that history could be abolished by a repealing statute. Such an attitude is implicit also in the hypothesis that an entirely new legal system, incorporating only certain desirable aspects of the generally undesirable prior legal system, could be created and substituted for the old system. The assumption was that by reasoning from basic premises established by the thinkers of the secular natural law school, one could derive a legal system that would meet the needs of the new society and the new government. The legal scholars of the time were, of course, trained in an earlier period, and they found their working legal conceptions, institutions, and processes in the old law. Those who participated in drafting the French codes consequently incorporated a good deal of the prior law and legal learning into them. In this way some continuity with the prior legal culture was retained. This tempered the legal consequences of the French Revolution, but it did not entirely avoid them. For several decades after the enactment of the Code Napoléon (the French Civil Code of 1804), the fiction was stoutly maintained by a large group of French jurists that history was irrelevant to interpretation and application of the code. This point is illustrated by the frequently quoted statement of a French lawyer of the period: "I know nothing of the civil law; I know only the Code Napoléon."

As in many utopias, one of the objectives of the Revolution was to make lawyers unnecessary. There was a desire for a legal system that was simple, nontechnical, and straightforward—one in which the professionalism and the tendency toward technicality and complication commonly blamed on lawyers could be avoided. One way to do this was to state the law clearly and in a straightforward fashion, so that the ordinary citizen could read the law and understand what his rights and obligations were, without having to consult lawyers and go to court. Thus the French Civil Code of 1804 was envisioned as a kind of popular book that could be put on the shelf next to the family Bible. It would be a handbook for the citizen, clearly organized and stated in straightforward language, that would allow citizens to determine their legal rights and obligations by themselves.

Fear of a "gouvernement des juges" hovered over French post-revolutionary reforms and colored the codification process. The emphasis on complete separation of powers, with all lawmaking power lodged in a representative legislature, was a way of insuring that the judiciary would be denied lawmaking power. Experience with the prerevolutionary courts had made the French wary of judicial lawmaking disguised as interpretation of laws. Therefore some writers argued that judges should be denied even the power to interpret legislation. . . . At the same time, however, the judge had to decide every case that came before him. The premises of secular natural law required that justice be available to all Frenchmen; there could be no area for judicial selection or discretion in the exercise of jurisdiction.

But if the legislature alone could make laws and the judiciary could only apply them (or, at a later time, interpret and apply them), such legislation had to be complete, coherent, and clear. If a judge were required to decide a case for which there was no legislative provision, he would in effect make law and thus violate the principle of separation of powers. Hence it was necessary that the legislature draft a code without gaps. Similarly, if there were conflicting provisions in the code, the judge would make law by choosing one rather than another as more applicable to the situation. Hence there could be no conflicting provisions. Finally, if a judge were allowed to decide what meaning to give to an ambiguous provision or an obscure statement, he would again be making law. Hence the code had to be clear.

If insistence on a total separation of legislative from judicial power dictated that the codes be complete, coherent, and clear, the prevailing spirit of optimistic rationalism persuaded those in its spell that it was possible to draft systematic legislation that would have those characteristics to such a degree that the function of the judge would be limited to selecting the applicable provision of the code and giving it its obvious significance in the context of the case. Actually, the Code Napoléon is not the most extreme example of this type of codification. That dubious honor falls to the Prussian Landrecht of 1794, enacted under Frederick the Great and containing some seventeen thousand detailed provisions setting out precise rules to govern specific "fact situations." The French civil code was drafted by experienced and intelligent jurists who were familiar with the rather spectacular failure of the Prussian attempt to spell it all out. Indeed, if we read the comments of Jean-Etienne-Marie Portalis, one of the most influential of the compilers of the code, we find a constant realistic concern to avoid the extremes of rationalist ideology. Portalis shows us that the code builds on much prerevolutionary law and legal scholarship; and he remarks that the provisions of the code are best thought of as principles or maxims, "féconds en consequences," to be developed and applied by judges and other jurists.

This kind of professional realism was, however, easily and quickly submerged by the rhetoric of the Revolution and by the excesses of the prevailing rationalism. The code became a victim of the revolutionary ideology and was uniformly treated as though it were a conscious expression of that ideology, both in France and in the many nations in other parts of the world that were heavily influenced by the French Revolution. . . .

The German Code

In contrast to the essentially revolutionary, rationalistic, and nontechnical character of the Code Napoléon, the German Civil Code of 1896 (effective in 1900) was historically oriented, scientific, and professional. A large share of the credit (or blame) for the differences between the German and the French civil codes is owed to Friedrich Karl von Savigny, one of the most famous names in the history of the civil law tradition.

The idea of codification aroused widespread interest in Germany and other parts of Europe and in Latin America during the first part of the nineteenth century. The French code was widely admired and copied, and in the course of time it was proposed that Germany follow France's lead. However, Savigny and his followers—influenced by Kant, Hegel, and German Romanticism—opposed this effort, persuasively arguing a thesis that became very influential in Germany. Proponents of what came to be known as the "historical school," these scholars maintained that it would be wrong for Germany to attempt to devise a civil code by reasoning from principles of secular natural law. In their view, the law of a people was a historically determined organic product of that people's development, an expression of the *Volksgeist.* Consequently, a thorough study of the existing German law and of its historical development was a necessary prelude to proper codification. Since the Roman civil law as interpreted by the medieval Italian scholars had been formally received in Germany some centuries before, a thorough historical study of German law had to include Roman law and old Germanic law as well as more recent elements of the contemporary German legal system. Under the influence of Savigny and the historical school, many German scholars turned their energies to the intensive study of legal history.

Savigny's idea was that by thoroughly studying the German legal system in its historical context legal scholars would be able to draw from it a set of historically verified and essential principles. These features of the law could then be individually studied, studied in relation to other such principles, and eventually systematically restated. The result would be a reconstruction of the German legal system according to its inherent principles and features. This, in turn, would provide the necessary basis for the codification of German law.

The components of the German legal system, in their historical context, came to be thought of by certain successors of Savigny as something like natural data. Just as natural data in biology, chemistry, or physics could be studied in order to determine the more general principles of which they were specific manifestations, so the data of German law could be studied in order to identify and extract from them chose inherent principles of the German legal order of which they were specific expressions. Hence the proposed reconstruction of the German legal system was to be a *scientific* reconstruction. . . . Finally, the Germans were convinced that it was neither desirable nor possible to rid the world of lawyers. The idea that the law should be clearly and simply stated so that it could be correctly understood and applied by the popular reader was expressly rejected. The German view was that lawyers would be needed, that they would engage in interpreting and applying the law, and that the code they prepared should be responsive to the needs of those trained in the law.

Consequently, the German Civil Code of 1896 is the opposite of revolutionary. It was not intended to abolish prior law and substitute a new legal system; on the contrary, the idea was to codify those principles of German law that would emerge from careful historical study of the German legal system. Instead of trying to discover true principles of law from assumptions about man's nature, as the French did under the influence of secular natural law, the Germans sought to find fundamental principles of German law by scientific study of data of German law: the existing German legal system in historical context. Rather than a textbook for the layman, the German civil code was thought of as a tool to be used primarily by professionals of the law.

Does this mean that the German civil code and the French civil code are totally dissimilar? It does not. There are differences, and they are important, but some overriding similarities remain. The Germans, like the French, have incorporated a sharp separation of powers into their system of law and government. It is the function of the legislator to make law, and the judge must be prevented from doing so. While displaying a more sophisticated awareness of the difficulty of making a code complete, coherent, and clear, the Germans nevertheless sought to do exactly that, and for the same basic reasons that motivated the French. The German code also served a unifying function, providing a single body of law for the recently unified nation. And like the French code, it thus supported the emergence of the monolithic nation-state.

How Codes in Common Law Are Different

An entirely different set of ideals and assumptions is associated with the California Civil Code, or with the Uniform Commercial Code as adopted in any American jurisdiction. Even though such codes may look very much like a French or a German code, they are not based on the same ideology, and they do not express anything like the same cultural reality. Where such codes exist, they make no pretense of completeness. The judge is not compelled to find a basis for deciding a given case within the code. Usually, moreover, such codes are not rejections of the past; they do not purport to abolish all prior law in their field, but rather to perfect it and, except where it conflicts with their specific present purposes, to supplement it. Where some provision of a code or other statute appears to be in possible conflict with a deeply rooted rule of the common law, the tendency will be to interpret the code provision in such a way as to evade the conflict. "Statutes in derogation of the common law," according to a famous judicial quotation, "are strictly construed."

Thus the conservative tendencies of the common law tradition stand in marked contrast to the ideology of revolution from which the spirit of civil law codification emerged. It is this ideology, rather than the form of codification, that helps to bind civil law nations together. . . .

[To see the practical application of that ideology, we can look at how the civil law views the role of judges.]

Civil Law Judges

We in the common law world know what a judge is. He is a culture hero, even something of a father figure. Many of the great names of the common law are those of judges: Coke, Mansfield, Marshall, Story, Holmes, Brandeis, Cardozo. We know that our legal tradition was originally created and has grown and developed in the hands of judges, reasoning closely from case to case and building a body of law that binds subsequent judges, through the doctrine of *stare decisis*, to decide similar cases similarly. We know that there is an abundance of legislation in force, and we recognize that there is a legislative function. But to us the common law means the law created and molded by the judges, and we still think (often quite inaccurately) of legislation as serving a kind of supplementary function. We are accustomed, in the common law world, to judicial review of administrative action, and in the United States the power of judges to hold legislation invalid if unconstitutional is accepted without serious question. We know that our judges exercise very broad interpretative powers, even where the applicable statute or administrative action is found to be legally valid. We do not like to use such dramatic phrases as "judicial supremacy," but when pushed to it we admit that this is a fair description of the common law system, particularly in the United States.

We also know where our judges come from. We know that they attend law school and then have successful careers either in private practice or in government, frequently as district attorneys. They are appointed or elected to judicial positions on the basis of a variety of factors, including success in practice, their reputation among their fellow lawyers, and political influence. Appointment or election to the bench comes as a kind of crowning achievement relatively late in life. It is a form of recognition that brings respect and prestige. The judge is well paid, and if he is among the higher judicial echelons, he will have secretaries and research assistants. If he sits on the highest court of a state or is high in the federal judiciary, his name may be a household word. His opinions will be discussed in the newspapers and dissected and criticized in the legal periodicals. He is a very important person.

This is what common lawyers mean when they talk about judges. But in the civil law world, a judge is something entirely different. He is a civil servant, a functionary. Although there are important variations, the general pattern is as follows. A judicial career is one of several possibilities open to a student graduating from a university law school. Shortly after graduation, if he wishes to follow a judicial career, he will take a state examination for aspirants to the judiciary and, if successful, will be appointed as a junior judge. (In France and a few other nations, he must first attend a special school for judges.) Before very long, he will actually be sitting as a judge somewhere low in the hierarchy of courts. In time, he will rise in the judiciary at a rate dependent on some combination of demonstrated ability and seniority. He will receive salary increases according to preestablished schedules and will belong to an organization of judges that has improvement of judicial salaries, working conditions, and tenure as a principal objective.

Lateral entry into the judiciary is rare. Although provision is made in some civil law jurisdictions for the appointment of distinguished practicing attorneys or professors to high courts (particularly to the special constitutional courts established since World War II), the great majority of judicial offices, even at the highest level, are filled from within the ranks of the professional judiciary. Judges of the high courts receive, and deserve, public respect, but it is the kind of public respect earned and received by persons in high places elsewhere in the civil service.

One of the principal reasons for the quite different status of the civil law judge is the existence of a different judicial tradition in the civil law, beginning in Roman times. The judge (*iudex*) of Rome was not a prominent man of the law. Prior to the Imperial period he was, in effect, a layman discharging an arbitral function by presiding over the settlement of disputes according to formulae supplied by another official, the *praetor*. The *iudex* was not expert in the law and had very limited power. For legal advice he turned to the jurisconsult. Later, during the Imperial period, the adjudication of disputes fell more and more into the hands of public officials who were also learned in the law, but by that time their principal function

was clearly understood to be that of applying the emperor's will. The judge had no inherent lawmaking power. He was less limited in medieval and pre-revolutionary times, when it was not unusual for continental judges to act much like their English counterparts. That, indeed, was the problem: they were interpreting creatively, building a common law that was a rival to the law of the central government in Paris and even developing their own doctrine of *stare decisis*.

With the revolution, and its consecration of the dogma of strict separation of powers, the judicial function was emphatically restricted. The revolutionary insistence that law be made only by a representative legislature meant that law could not be made, either directly or indirectly, by judges. One expression of this attitude was the requirement that the judge use only "the law" in deciding a case, and this meant . . . that he could not base his decision on prior judicial decisions. The doctrine of *stare decisis* was rejected. An extreme expression of the dogma of strict separation of the legislative and judicial powers was the notion that judges should not interpret incomplete, conflicting, or unclear legislation. They should always refer such questions to the legislature for authoritative interpretation. It was expected that there would not be very many such situations, and that after a fairly brief period almost all the problems would be corrected and further resort to the legislature for interpretation would be unnecessary. . . .

The Judge as Clerk

The picture of the judicial process that emerges is one of fairly routine activity. The judge becomes a kind of expert clerk. He is presented with a fact situation to which a ready legislative response will be readily found in all except the extraordinary case. His function is merely to find the right legislative provision, couple it with the fact situation, and bless the solution that is more or less automatically produced from the union. The whole process of judicial decision is made to fit into the formal syllogism of scholastic logic. The major premise is in the statute, the facts of the case furnish the minor premise, and the conclusion inevitably follows. In the uncommon case in which some more sophisticated intellectual work is demanded of the judge, he is expected to follow carefully drawn directions about the limits of interpretation.

The net image is of the judge as an operator of a machine designed and built by legislators. His function is a mechanical one. The great names of the civil law are not those of judges (who knows the name of a civil law judge?) but those of legislators (Justinian, Napoléon) and scholars (Gaius, Irnerius, Bartolus, Mancini, Domat, Pothier, Savigny, and a host of other nineteenth- and twentieth-century European and Latin American scholars). The civil law judge is not a culture hero or a father figure, as he often is with us. His image is that of a civil servant who performs important but essentially uncreative functions.

It is a logical, if not a necessary, consequence of the quite different status of the civil law judge that he is not widely known, even among lawyers. His judicial opinions are not read in order to study his individual ways of thinking and his apparent preconceptions and biases. Although there are exceptions, the tendency is for the decisions of higher courts in civil law jurisdictions to be strongly collegial in nature. They are announced as the decision of the court, without enumeration of votes pro and con among the judges. In most jurisdictions separate concurring opinions and dissenting opinions are not written or published, nor are dissenting votes noted. The tendency is to think of the court as a faceless unit.

The result is that although there is a superficial similarity of function between the civil law judge and the common law judge, there are substantial disparities in their accepted roles. In part the contemporary civil law judge inherits a status and serves a set of functions determined by a tradition going back to the *iudex* of Roman times. This tradition, in which the judge has never been conceived of as playing a very creative part, was reinforced by the anti-judicial ideology of the European revolution and the logical consequences of a rationalistic doctrine of strict separation of powers. The civil law judge thus plays a substantially more modest role than the judge in the common law tradition, and the system of selection and tenure of civil law judges is consistent with this quite different status of the judicial profession.

The establishment of rigid constitutions and the institution of judicial review of the constitutionality of legislation in some civil law jurisdictions has to some extent modified the traditional image of the civil law judge. In some jurisdictions (e.g. Austria, Italy, Germany, and Spain), special constitutional courts have been established. These special courts, which are not part of the ordinary judicial system and are not manned by members of the ordinary judiciary, were established in response to the civil law tradition that judges (i.e. *ordinary* judges—the modern successors of the Roman *iudex* and the civil judges of the *jus commune*) cannot be given such power. With the establishment of these special courts manned by specially selected judges, tradition is, at least in form, observed. Indeed, a few purists within the civil law tradition suggest that it is wrong to call such constitutional courts "courts" and their members "judges." Because judges cannot make law, the reasoning goes, and because the power to hold statutes illegal is a form of lawmaking, these officials obviously cannot be judges and these institutions cannot be courts. But even where, as in some nations in Latin America, the power of judicial review resides in the highest ordinary courts, the traditional civil law image of the judge retains most of its power. Judicial service is a bureaucratic career; the judge is a functionary, a civil servant; the judicial function is narrow, mechanical, and uncreative.

THE ISLAMIC LEGAL TRADITION

Dennis J. Wiechman, Jerry D. Kendall, and Mohammad K. Azarian

The legal tradition of Islamic law is based on the teachings of the prophet Muhammad. Three professors at the University of Evansville in Indiana discuss aspects of Islamic law that are difficult for Westerners to grasp and identify misconceptions about Islamic legal practices. Dennis Wiechman is professor of criminal justice with an emphasis on comparative justice. Jerry Kendall is a professor of geography and specializes in Middle Eastern issues. Mohammad Azarian is a professor of mathematics.

The general public and many academics have several preconceived notions about Islamic Law. One such notion is that Islamic judges are bound by ancient and outdated rules of fixed punishments for all crimes. This article explores that idea and looks at other myths in an attempt to present Islamic Law from a nonbiased view of Sharia Law.

Some contemporary scholars fail to recognize Islamic Law as an equal to English Common Law, European Civil Law and Socialist Law. A few academics have even attempted to place Islamic Law into the Civil Law tradition. Other writers have simply added a footnote to their works on comparative justice on the religious law categories of Islamic Law, Hindu Law, which is

Reprinted from Dennis J. Wiechman, Jerry D. Kendall, and Mohammad K. Azarian, "Islamic Law: Myths and Realities," *CJ International*, vol. 12, no. 3, May/June 1996, with permission of the Office of International Criminal Justice, University of Illinois at Chicago.

still used in some parts of India, and the Law of Moses from the Old Testament, which still guides the current thought of the Israeli Knesset (Parliament) today. This survey will attempt to alter some of these inaccurate perceptions and treatments in both the contemporary literature and academic writings.

Mohammed Salam Madkoar explains the theoretical assumptions of Islamic Law:

In order to protect the five important indispensables in Islam (religion, life, intellect, offspring and property), Islamic Law has provided a worldly punishment in addition to that in the hereafter. Islam has, in fact, adopted two courses for the preservation of these five indispensables: the first is through cultivating religious consciousness in the human soul and the awakening of human awareness through moral education; the second is by inflicting deterrent punishment, which is the basis of the Islamic criminal system. Therefore "Hudoud," Retaliation (Kisas) and Discretionary (Tazir) punishments have been prescribed according to the type of the crime committed.

Islamic Law and Jurisprudence is not always understood by the Western press. Although it is the responsibility of the mass media to bring to the world's attention violations of human rights and acts of terror, many believe that media stereotyping of all Muslims is a major problem. The bombing of the World Trade Center in New York City is a prime example. The media often used the term "Islamic Fundamentalists" when referring to the accused in the case. It also referred to the Egyptian connections in that case as "Islamic Fundamentalists." The media has used the label of "Islamic Fundamentalist" to imply all kinds of possible negative connotations: terrorists, kidnappers and hostage takers. Since the media does not use the term "Fundamentalist Christian" each time a Christian does something wrong, the use of such labels is wrong for any group, Christians, Muslims, or Orthodox Jews.

A Muslim who is trying to live his religion is indeed a true believer in God. This person tries to live all of the tenets of his religion in a fundamental way. Thus, a true Muslim is a fundamentalist in the practice of that religion, but a true Muslim is not radical, because the Quran teaches tolerance and moderation in all things. When the popular media generalizes from the fundamentalist believer to the "radical fundamentalist" label they do a disservice to all Muslims and others.

No Separation of Church and State

To understand Islamic Law one must first understand the assumptions of Islam and the basic tenets of the religion. The meaning of the word Islam is "submission or surrender to Allah's (God's) will." Therefore, Muslims must first and foremost obey and submit to Allah's will. Mohammed the Prophet was called by God to translate verses from the Angel Gabriel to form the most important book in Islam, the Quran, Muslims believe.

There are over 1.2 billion Muslims today worldwide, over 20% of the world's population. "By the year 2000, one out of every four persons on the planet will be a Muslim," Rittat Hassan estimated in 1990. There are 35 nations with populations over 50% Muslim, and there are another 21 nations that have significant Muslim populations. There are 19 nations which have declared Islam in their respective constitutions. The Muslim religion is a global one and is rapidly expanding. The sheer number of Muslims living today makes the idea of putting Islamic Law into a footnote in contemporary writings inappropriate.

The most difficult part of Islamic Law for most Westerners to grasp is that there is no separation of church and state. The religion of Islam and the government are one. Islamic Law is controlled, ruled and regulated by the Islamic religion. The theocracy controls all public and private matters. Government, law and religion are one. There are varying degrees of this concept in many nations, but all law, government and civil authority rests upon it and it is a part of Islamic religion. There are civil laws in Muslim nations for Muslim and non-Muslim people. Sharia is only applicable to Muslims. Most Americans and others schooled in Common Law have great difficulty with that concept. The U.S. Constitution (Bill of Rights) prohibits the government from "establishing a religion." The U.S. Supreme Court has concluded in numerous cases that the U.S. Government can't favor one religion over another. That concept is implicit for most U.S. legal scholars and many U.S. academicians believe that any mixture of "church and state" is inherently evil and filled with many problems. They reject all notions of a mixture of religion and government.

To start with such preconceived notions limits the knowledge base and information available to try and solve many social and criminal problems. To use an analogy from Christianity may be helpful. To ignore what all Christian religions except your own say about God would limit your knowledge base and you would not be informed or have the ability to appreciate your own religion. The same is true for Islamic Law and Islamic religion. You must open your mind to further expand your knowledge base. Islamic Law has many ideas, concepts, and information that can solve contemporary crime problems in many areas of the world. To do this you must first put on hold the preconceived notion of "separation of church and state."

The Islamic Judge (Qudi)

Another myth concerning Islamic Law is that there are no judges. Historically the Islamic Judge (Qudi) was a legal secretary appointed by the provincial governors. Each Islamic nation may differ slightly in how the judges are selected. Some nations will use a formal process of legal education and internship in a lower court. For example, in Saudi Arabia there are two levels of courts. The formal Sharia Courts, which were established in 1928, hear traditional cases. The Saudi government established a ministry of justice in 1970, and they added administrative tribunals for traffic laws, business and commerce. "All judges are accountable to God in their decisions and practices" (Lippman, p. 66–68).

One common myth associated with Islamic Law is that judges must always impose a fixed and predetermined punishment for each crime. Western writers often point to the inflexible nature of Islamic Law. Judges under Islamic Law are bound to administer several punishments for a few very serious crimes found in the Quran, but they possess much greater freedom in punishment for less serious (non-Had) crimes. Common Law is filled with precedents, rules, and limitations which inhibit creative justice. Judges under Islamic Law are free to create new options and ideas to solve new problems associated with crime.

Elements of Sharia Law

Islamic Law is known as Sharia Law, and Sharia means the path to follow God's Law. Sharia Law is holistic or eclectic in its approach to guide the individual in most daily matters. Sharia Law controls, rules and regulates all public and private behavior. It has regulations for personal hygiene, diet, sexual conduct, and elements of child rearing. It also prescribes specific rules for prayers, fasting, giving to the poor, and many other religious matters. Civil Law and Common Law primarily focus on public behavior, but both do regulate some private matters.

Sharia Law can also be used in larger situations than guiding an individual's behavior. It can be used as a guide for how an individual acts in society and how one group interacts with another. The Sharia Law can be used to settle border disputes between nations or within nations. It can also be used to settle international disputes, conflicts and wars. This Law does not exclude any knowledge from other sources and is viewed by the Muslim world as a vehicle to solve all problems civil, criminal and international.

Sharia Law has several sources from which to draw its guiding principles. It does not rely upon one source for its broad knowledge base. The first and primary element of Sharia Law is the Quran. It is the final arbitrator and there is no other appeal. The second element of Sharia Law is known as the Sunna, the teachings of the Prophet Mohammed not explicitly found in the Quran. The Sunna are a composite of the teachings of the Prophet and his works. The Sunna contain stories and anecdotes, called Hadith, to illustrate a concept. The Quran may not have all the information about behavior and human interaction in detail; the Sunna gives more detailed information than the Quran.

The third element of Sharia Law is known as the Ijma. The Muslim religion uses the term Ulama as a label for its religious scholars. These Ulamas are consulted on many matters both personal and political. When the Ulamas reach a consensus on an issue, it is interpreted as a Ijma. The concepts and ideas found in the Ijma are not found explicitly in the Quran or the teachings of the Prophet (Sunna). Islamic judges are able to examine the Ijma for many possible solutions which can be applied in a modern technical society. They are free to create new and innovative methods to solve crime and social problems based upon the concepts found in the Ijma. These judges have great discretion in applying the concepts to a specific problem.

The Qiyas are a fourth element of Sharia Law. The Qiyas are not explicitly found in the Quran, Sunna, or given in the Ijma. The Qiyas are new cases or case law which may have already been decided by a higher judge. The Sharia judge can use the legal precedent to decide new case law and its application to a specific problem. The judge can use a broad legal construct to resolve a very specific issue. For example, a computer crime or theft of computer time is not found in the Quran or Sunna. The act of theft as a generic term is prohibited so the judge must rely on logic and reason to create new case law or Qiyas.

The fifth element of Sharia Law is very broad and "all encompassing." This secondary body of knowledge may be ideas contained in the other written works. The New Testament is an example of this area of information, and legal discourses based upon Civil Law or Common Law may be another example. All information can be examined for logic and reason to see if it applies to the current case. It also may be a local custom or norm that a judge may find helpful in applying to the issue before him. The judge may also weigh the impact of his decision upon how it will affect a person's standing in the community.

Crimes in Islam

Crimes under Islamic Law can be broken down into three major categories. Each will be discussed in greater detail with some common Law analogies. The three major crime categories in Islamic Law are:

1. Had Crimes (most serious).
2. Tazir Crimes (least serious).
3. Qesas Crimes (revenge crimes restitution).

Had crimes are the most serious under Islamic Law, and Tazir crimes are the least serious. Some Western writers use the felony analogy for Had crimes and misdemeanor label for Tazir crimes. The analogy is partially accurate, but not entirely true. Common Law has no comparable form of Qesas crimes.

Fairchild, in her excellent book on comparative justice, makes the following observation of Islamic Law and punishment (Fairchild, p. 41).

> Punishments are prescribed in the Quran and are often harsh with the emphasis on corporal and capital punishment. Theft is punished by imprisonment or amputation of hands or feet, depending on the number of times it is committed . . .

Had Crimes

Had crimes are those which are punishable by a pre-established punishment found in the Quran. These most serious of all crimes are found by an exact reference in the Quran to a specific act and a specific punishment for that act. There is no plea bargaining or reducing the punishment for a Had crime. Had crimes have no minimum or maximum punishments attached to them. The punishment system is comparable to the determinate sentence imposed by some judges in the United States. If you commit a crime, you know what your punishment will be. There is no flexibility in the U.S. determinate model or in the punishment for Had crimes of Islamic Law.

No judge can change or reduce the punishment for these serious crimes. The Had crimes are:

1. Murder;
2. Apostasy from Islam (making war upon Allah and his messengers);
3. Theft;
4. Adultery;
5. Defamation (false accusation of adultery or fornication);
6. Robbery;
7. Alcohol-drinking.

The first four Had crimes have a specific punishment in the Quran. The last three crimes are mentioned but no specific punishment is found (Schmalleger, p. 603).

Some more liberal Islamic judges do not consider apostasy from Islam or wine drinking as Had crimes. The more liberal Islamic nations treat these crimes as Tazir or a lesser crime.

Had crimes have fixed punishments because they are set by God and are found in the Quran. Had crimes are crimes against God's law and Tazir crimes are crimes against society. There are some safeguards for Had crimes that many in the media fail to mention. Some in the media only mention that if you steal, your hand is cut off. The Islamic judge must look at a higher level of proof and reasons why the person committed the crime. A judge can only impose the Had punishment when a person confesses to the crime or there are enough witnesses to the crime. The usual number of witnesses is two, but in the case of adultery four witnesses are required. The media often leaves the public with the impression that all are punished with flimsy evidence or limited proof. Islamic Law has a very high level of proof for the most serious crimes and punishments. When there is doubt about the guilt of a Had crime, the judge must treat the crime as a lesser Tazir crime. If there is no confession to a crime or not enough witnesses to the crime, Islamic Law requires the Had crime to be punished as a Tazir crime.

Tazir Crimes

Modern Islamic Society has changed greatly from the time of the Prophet. Contemporary Sharia Law is now in written form and is statutory in nature. Islamic concepts of justice argue that a person should know what the crime is and its possible punishment. For example, Egypt has a parliamentary process which has a formal penal code written and based upon the principles of Islamic Law, but Saudi Arabia allows the judge to set the Tazir crimes and punishments. Modern Islamic Law recognizes many differences between these two nations. It also allows for much greater flexibility in how it punishes an offender. The major myth of many people is that judges in Islamic nations have fixed punishments for all crimes. In reality the judges have much greater flexibility than judges under Common Law.

Tazir crimes are less serious than the Had crimes found in the Quran. Some Common Law writers use the analogy of misdemeanors, which is the lesser of the two categories (felony and misdemeanor) of Common Law crimes. Tazir crimes can and do have comparable "minor felony equivalents." These "minor felonies" are not found in the Quran so the Islamic judges are free to punish the offender in almost any fashion. Mohammed Salam Madkoar, who was the head of Islamic Law at the University of Cairo, makes the following observation:

> Tazir punishments vary according to the circumstances. They change from time to time and from place to place. They vary according to the gravity of the crime and the extent of the criminal disposition of the criminal himself.

Tazir crimes are acts which are punished because the offender disobeys God's law and word. Tazir crimes can be punished if they harm the societal interest. Sharia Law places an emphasis on the societal or public interest. The assumption of the punishment is that a greater "evil" will be prevented in the future if you punish this offender now.

Historically Tazir crimes were not written down or codified. This gave each ruler great flexibility in what punishments the judge was able to dispense. The judge under Islamic Law is not bound by precedents, rules, or prior decisions as in Common Law. Judges are totally free to choose from any number of punishments that they think will help an individual offender. The only guiding principle for judges under Sharia Law is that they must answer to Allah and to the greater community of Muslims. Some of the more common punishments for Tazir crimes are counseling, fines, public or private censure, family and clan pressure and support, seizure of property, confinement in the home or place of detention, and flogging.

In some Islamic nations, Tazir crimes are set by legislative parliament. Each nation is free to establish its own criminal code and there is a great disparity in punishment of some of these crimes. Some of the more common Tazir crimes are: bribery, selling tainted or defective products, treason, usury, and selling obscene pictures. The consumption of alcohol in Egypt is punished much differently than in Iran or Saudi Arabia because they have far different civil laws. Islamic Law has much greater flexibility than the Western media portrays. Each judge is free to punish based upon local norms, customs, and informal rules. Each judge is free to fix the punishment that will deter others from crime and will help to rehabilitate an offender.

Qesas Crimes and Diya

Islamic Law has an additional category of crimes that Common Law nations do not have. A Qesas crime is one of retaliation. If you commit a Qesas crime, the victim has a right to seek retribution and retaliation. The exact punishment for each Qesas crime is set forth in the Quran. If you are killed, then your family has a right to seek Qesas punishment from the murderer. Punishment can come in several forms and also may include "Diya." Diya is paid to the victim's family as part of punishment. Diya is an ancient form of restitution for the victim or his family. The family also may seek to have a public execution of the offender or the family may seek to pardon the offender. Traditional Qesas crimes include:

1. Murder (premeditated and non-premeditated).

2. Premeditated offenses against human life, short of murder.
3. Murder by error.
4. Offenses by error against humanity, short of murder.

Some reporters in the mass media have criticized the thought of "blood money" as barbaric. They labeled the practice as undemocratic and inhumane. Qesas crimes are based upon the criminological assumption of retribution. The concept of retribution was found in the first statutory "Code of Hammurabi" and in the Law of Moses in the form of "an eye for an eye." Muslims add to that saying "but it is better to forgive." Contemporary Common Law today still is filled with the assumptions of retribution. The United States federal code contains "mandatory minimum" sentences for drug dealing, and many states have fixed punishment for drugs and violence and using weapons. The United States justice system has adopted a retribution model which sets fixed punishments for each crime. The idea of retribution is fixed in the U.S. system of justice. Qesas crime is simple retribution: if one commits a crime he knows what the punishment will be.

Diya has its roots in Islamic Law and dates to the time of the Prophet Mohammed when there were many local families, tribes and clans. They were nomadic and traveled extensively. The Prophet was able to convince several tribes to take a monetary payment for damage to the clan or tribe. This practice grew and now is an acceptable solution to some Qesas crimes.

Today, the Diya is paid by the offender to the victim if he is alive. If the victim is dead, the money is paid to the victim's family or to the victim's tribe or clan. The assumption is that victims will be compensated for their loss. Under Common Law, the victim or family must sue the offender in a civil tort action for damages. Qesas law combines the process of criminal and civil hearings into one, just as the "civil law" is applied in many nations of the world. Qesas crimes are compensated as restitution under Common Law and Civil Law.

The Qesas crimes require compensation for each crime committed. Each nation sets the dam-

age before the offense and the judge then fixes the proper Diya. If an offender is too poor to pay the Diya, the family of the offender is called upon first to make good the Diya for their kin. If the family is unable to pay, the community, clan or tribe may be required to pay. This concept is not found in Common Law or the Civil Law of most nations. It acts as a great incentive for family and community to teach responsible behavior. What happens to the debt if the offender dies and has not paid it? Historically, it was passed on to the offender's heirs; today, most nations terminate the debt if the offender left no inheritance.

One question that is often raised is "What happens if a victim takes the Diya without government approval?" The victim or family has committed a Tazir crime by accepting money which was not mandated by a judge: taking Diya must be carried out through proper governmental and judicial authority.

Another concept of Qesas crimes is the area of punishment. Each victim has the right to ask for retaliation and, historically, the person's family would carry out that punishment. Modern Islamic Law now requires the government to carry out the Qesas punishment. Historically, some grieving family member may have tortured the offender in the process of punishment. Now the government is the independent party that administers the punishment, because torture and extended pain is contrary to Islamic teachings and Sharia Law.

Conclusions

Contemporary treatment of Islamic Law and "Radical Muslims" is filled with stereotypical characterizations. Some in the Western media have used the "New York City bombings" as a way to increase hate and prejudice. They have taken the views of a few radicals and projected them onto all Muslims. This action has done a great disservice to the Muslim world. Some academic writings also have been distorted and not always completely accurate and some researchers have concluded that Islamic Law requires a fixed punishment for all crimes. These writers also have concluded that Islamic judges lack discretion in their sentences of defendants in the Sharia

Court System. There are four Had crimes that do have fixed punishments set forth in the Quran, but not all the Had crimes are bound by mandatory punishment.

Islamic Law is very different from English Common Law or the European Civil Law traditions. Muslims are bound to the teachings of the Prophet Mohammed whose translation of Allah or God's will is found in the Quran. Muslims are held accountable to the Sharia Law, but non-Muslims are not bound by the same standard (apostasy from Allah). Muslims and non-Muslims are both required to live by laws enacted by the various forms of government such as tax laws, traffic laws, white collar crimes of business, and theft. These and many other crimes similar to Common Law crimes are tried in modern "Mazalim Courts." The Mazalim Courts can also hear Civil Law, family law and all other cases. Islamic Law does have separate courts for Muslims for "religious crimes" and contemporary non-religious courts for other criminal and civil matters.

SELECTED BIBLIOGRAPHY

Al-Alfi, Ahmad Abd al-aziz. "Punishment in Islamic Criminal Law," found in Bassiouni, M. Cherif. *The Islamic Criminal Justice System.* New York: Oceana Publications, Inc., 1982, pp. 227–236.

Al-Thakeb, Fahed and Scott, Joseph E. "Islamic Law: An Examination of Its Revitalization." *British Journal of Criminology.* Vol. 21, No. 1 (Jan. 1981), pp. 58–69.

Ali, B. "Islamic Law and Crime: The Case of Saudi Arabia." *International Journal of Comparative and Applied Criminal Justice.* Vol. 9, No. 2 (Winter, 1985), pp. 45–57.

Badr, Gamal Mouri. "Islamic Law: Its Relation to Other Legal Systems." *American Journal of Comparative Law.* Vol. 26 (1978), pp. 187–198.

Bassiouni, M. Cherif. Editor. *The Islamic Criminal Justice System.* New York: Oceana Publications, Inc., 1982.

Doi, Abdur Rahman I. *Shariah: The Islamic Law.* London: Ta-Ha Publishers, 1984.

Doi, Abdur Rahman I. *Shariah in the 1500 Century of Hijra Problems and Prospects.* London: Ta-Ha Publishers, 1981.

El-Awa, Mohamed S. *Punishment in Islamic Law: A Comparative Study.* Indianapolis: American Trust Publishers, 1982.

Ezeldin, Ahmed Galal. "Judicial Control of Policing in Egypt." *CJ International.* Vol. 7, No. 4 (July–August, 1991), pp. 3, 4.

Fairchild, Erika S. *Comparative Criminal Justice Systems.* Belmont, CA: Wadsworth Publishing Co., 1993.

Fitzgerald, S.V. "The Alleged Debt of Islamic Law to Roman Law." *The Law Quarterly.* Vol. 67 (Jan. 1951), pp. 81–102.

Ghanem, Isam. *Outlines of Islamic Jurisprudence.* Riyadh, Saudi Arabia: Saudi Publishing and Clearing House, 1983.

Griffiths, Curt Taylor. "The Criminal Justice System of Egypt." *International Criminal Justice Systems II.* Omaha, Nebraska: Academy of Criminal Justice Sciences, 1986, pp. 13–26.

Hassan, Rittat. "Muslims in America: A Living Presence." *Horizons.* (November/December, 1990), pp. 10–11.

Heer, Nicholas. Editor. *Islamic Law and Jurisprudence.* Seattle, WA: University of Washington Press, 1990.

Khadduri, Majid and Herbert J. Liebesny, eds. *Origin and Development of Islamic Law.* Volume 1 of *Law in the Middle East.* Ed. Majid Khadduri and Herbert J. Liebesny. New York: AMS Press, 1984.

Laliwala, Jafer Ismail. *The Islamic Jurisprudence.* India: The India Institute of Islamic Studies.

Lamb, David. *The Arabs: Journeys Beyond the Mirage.* New York: Vintage Books, 1987.

Lippman, Matthew and McConnville, Sean and Yerushalmi, Mordechai. *Islamic Criminal Law and Procedure and Introduction.* New York: Praeger, 1988.

Madkoar, Mohammad Salam. "Defining Crime According to Islamic Legislation." *The Effect of Islamic Legislation on Crime Prevention in Saudi Arabia.* Riyadh, Saudi Arabia: Minister of Interior, Kingdom of Saudi Arabia, 1976, pp. 89–146.

Masud, Muhammad Khalid. *Islamic Legal Philosophy.* Pakistan: Islamic Research Institute, Reprint 1984.

Mernissi, Fatima. *The Veil and the Male Elite.* New York: Addison-Wesley Publishing Company, Inc., 1987.

Moore, Richter H. "The Criminal Justice System of Saudi Arabia." *International Criminal Justice Systems II.* Omaha, Nebraska: Academy of Criminal Justice Sciences, 1986, pp. 139–198.

Moore, Richter H. "Islamic Legal Systems: A Comparison—Saudi Arabia, Bahrain and Pakistan." *Comparative Criminal Justice.* Chicago, IL: Office of International Criminal Justice, 1989, pp. 243–250.

Qadri, Anwar Ahmad. *A Sunni Shafi'i Law Code.* Sh. Muhammad Ashraf. (Available at Mahmud's Bazaar, P.O. Box 505, Conley, GA 30027)

"Rising Fundamentalist Movement Takes Center Stage." *CJ International.* Vol. 8, No. 2 (March–April, 1992), pp. 1–6.

Schmalleger, Frank. *Criminal Justice Today.* 2nd ed. Englewood Cliffs, NJ: Prentice Hall, 1993.

Trojan, Carol. "Egypt: Evolution of a Modern Police State." *Comparative Criminal Justice.* Chicago, IL: Office of International Criminal Justice, University of Illinois at Chicago, 1989, pp. 235–242.

United Nations Social Defense Research Institute. *The Effect of Islamic Legislation on Crime Prevention in Saudi Arabia.* Proceedings of the Symposium held in Riyadh. 16–21 Sharia 1396 A.H. (9–13 October, 1976) Riyadh, Saudi Arabia, Ministry of Interior, Kingdom of Saudi Arabia, 1980.

Ward, Dick. "Fanatic Fundamentalism Brings Renewed Strife and Concern in Region." *CJ International.* Vol. 9, No. 2 (March–April, 1993), p. 14.

Weiss, Bernard. "Interpretation in Islamic Law: The Theory of Ijtihad." *American Journal of Comparative Law.* Vol. 26 (1978), pp. 199–212.

DISCUSSION QUESTIONS

1. U.S. Supreme Court justices and judges at state and other federal levels are sometimes criticized for "making law" instead of simply applying it. For example, if Congress were to pass a law prohibiting the burning of the American flag, that law would not be authoritative until the courts had ruled on its constitutionality. In a civil law country, presumably, when legislators pass a law against burning the country's flag, the courts would be obliged simply to enforce the law. What advantages and disadvantages do you see in each approach?

2. The Sharia guides Muslims in all aspects of life: In school, at work, in sports, or at worship in the mosque, the Sharia governs their behavior and interactions. In the United States, by contrast, different rules or laws apply in different situations. The code of criminal law (which may differ from state to state) governs some situations, while school regulations, business ethics, a coach's orders, and religious guidelines restrict other types of behavior and interactions. Would America have a lower crime rate if a single set of rules governed all aspects of daily life? If reduction in crime was a certainty, would possibly drastic changes in lifestyle be justified? Explain your answers.

WEBSITES

lcweb2.loc.gov/glin/worldlaw.html

At this site you will find the Guide to Law Online, prepared by the U.S. Law Library of Congress. This guide to worldwide sources of information on government and law is an excellent place to begin a search on other legal systems.

endjinn.soas.ac.uk/Centres/Islamiclaw/Home.html

The Center of Islamic and Middle Eastern Law has information on Islamic law and other systems of law in the Islamic and Middle Eastern world, as well as links to other Internet materials on Islamic law.

PART II

LAW ENFORCEMENT

CONTENTS

CHAPTER 4: POLICE HISTORY

The two readings for this chapter contrast historical and contemporary aspects of American law enforcement. Laura Hauth's history of the New York police provides important information on the social forces that shaped America's first modern police department. She also gives us some interesting factoids on topics like the origin of "cop." As you read this selection, notice some similarities and contrasts with contemporary policing. For example, Hauth tells us that the printed rules and regulations issued to the police in 1845 set crime prevention as the primary duty of the police officer, a key feature of modern policing. The forerunners to the modern era were typically reactive; that is, they responded to a committed crime rather than trying to keep crime from occurring in the first place.

Like many occupations, police work was initially a male-only job. London's Metropolitan Police of 1829 was a force of one thousand men. In New York, two hundred men, quickly growing to eight hundred, formed that city's police. In her review of women in American policing, Dorothy Moses Schulz describes the evolution of women in law enforcement, beginning in the eighteenth century when women worked as jail and prison matrons. The modern era of women in law enforcement is said to have begun in 1910, when the Los Angeles Police Department made Alice Stebbins Wells the first policewoman in the United States. The social forces that influenced, and continue to influence, women in law enforcement are interesting and important. Schulz's conclusion that police work in the future might include a female perspective and leadership that could change the very nature of policing is a forecast that gives rise to many intriguing questions.

READING 7
THE HISTORY OF NEW YORK'S FINEST

Laura A. Hauth

Laura A. Hauth, a police officer with the New York City Police Department, traces the almost four-century history of policing in New York.

The Humble Beginnings

The Dutch Era (1625–1664) When the Dutch colonists first arrived on Manhattan Island, they found themselves faced with a harsh and often hostile frontier. Armed with hope and determination, these hardy settlers struggled daily with fear, hunger, sickness and poverty. They realized they had to establish a system of law and order, or their community would perish.

Relying on their European experience, they formed a council to make and interpret the law. The council then appointed a *schout-fiscal*— Dutch for legal officer—to see that its edicts were obeyed. It was the *schout-fiscal*'s job to punish each law-breaker in a manner befitting the crime. He served as both sheriff and prosecutor throughout New Netherland, an area covering what is now lower New York State and eastern New Jersey.

In 1651 the first professional police department was created in New Amsterdam—the *Rattlewatch*. It was a voluntary patrol composed of citizens appointed by the council. In addition to muskets, its members were equipped with the hand-rattles that gave their fledgling police force its name. They

Reprinted from Laura A. Hauth, "The History of New York's Finest," *Spring 3100*, Memorabilia column, March/April 1989, by permission of *Spring 3100*.

strolled the streets to discourage crime and search for law-breakers. In times of emergency, they noisily spun their rattles to summon assistance from fellow *Rattlewatch* members. They also served as town criers, announcing the hours from 9 P.M. to daybreak at all street corners.

In late 1658, the eight members of the *Rattlewatch* began drawing pay, making them our first municipally funded police organization.

Under British Rule (1664–1783) In 1664, the British seized New Amsterdam and its outskirts and renamed the territory New York. Although immediate steps were taken to make the region's 1,500 settlers conform to the English system, peace-keeping activities underwent few changes.

Instead of a *schout-fiscal*, there was an English constable. His job was to keep the peace, suppress excessive drinking, gambling and prostitution, and prevent disturbances when church services were in progress.

During the late 1600s, with the first of the French and Indian wars underway, the military assumed responsibility for maintaining law and order in the city. Officials appointed a *bellman* to do the job. His title came from the bell he rang while making his rounds and calling out the hours. In addition to the bell, he was issued a gun, uniform, badge, shoes and stockings, becoming the city's first uniformed policeman.

The start of the 18th century brought radical changes to the city's system of public protection. The post of *bellman* was abolished and the English introduced the constable's watch to protect New York's 6,000 residents. What is now lower to mid-Manhattan was divided into six sectors, with a *high constable* and 12 *sub-constables* sworn to "take care, and keep and preserve the peace" throughout the area. In 1731 a *watch-house*—or jail—was built at the corner of Wall and Broad Streets. Punishment for "ruffians and evil-doers" was carried out in the *"cage," stocks, whipping post* or *ducking stool* in front of City Hall.

The Revolutionary War (1776–1783) The city was occupied by the British during most of the Revolution—from September 1776 to November 1783. The redcoats seized control of the provincial and municipal governments and a military governor was made responsible for providing police protection for the citizenry.

New Yorkers, however, were dissatisfied with the level of protection provided by the British army, and in January 1777 they decided to do something about it. History repeated itself as they banded together to form a civilian watch. With the city larger in size and population, and its problems greater than in the days of Dutch rule, instead of a small *Rattlewatch* they had a force of 80 men patrolling the streets during the evening hours.

In May 1778, the British military commandant appointed three citizens to form a quasi-civil police department to administer and direct the night watch.

Period of Independence (1783–1830) By the time the Revolutionary War ended, the city's population had grown to 60,000—and police protection had become a major problem. But little was done to deal with it. Crime continued to increase through the late 1820s. Although more watchmen were hired, they were widely regarded as incompetent and the protection they provided was considered inadequate.

For years the situation remained this way. Nothing was done until contempt for the city's weak police force finally gave way to fear—fear that the city's social disintegration was imminent. And with that fear came the realization that something had to be done about providing New York with a strong, effective police department.

New York's Finest Finally Finds Its Way

During the mid-1800s, New York became home to thousands of destitute and desperate immigrants from Ireland and Germany. Many could barely afford housing in the rat-infested, unlit, unheated and horribly overcrowded tenements and wooden shanties on the city's outskirts.

Salaries at the time scarcely provided working people with enough to cover their living expenses. Men and women—and children as young as ten—earned less than 30 cents a day for laboring 12 to 15 hours in unhealthy and hazardous factories.

City streets were unpaved, lacked proper drainage, and were cluttered with uncollected trash. When it rained, they became quagmires of mud and filth.

Many people fell sick from contaminated water, and overcrowded living conditions caused disease to spread rapidly and uncontrollably.

Crime was rampant on the unlit streets, especially when moonless nights left large parts of the city in total darkness. It was common for thieves to roam the streets burglarizing buildings and attacking people as they hurried home.

Living conditions such as these caused anger and despair, making New York fertile ground for a tremendous growth in crime, vice and disorder.

Frightened and enraged by this criminal onslaught, New Yorkers looked at police departments far and near in hopes of finding a strong, effective model to copy. They settled on the Metropolitan Police of London.

The London Police Model (1830–1845) In 1828, Sir Robert Peel of England had introduced a bill establishing a paid professional police force—one that wore uniforms, was well-drilled and devoted itself full-time to protecting the peace. Nicknamed "bobbies" and "peelers," this police force had been created because of a marked increase in criminal activity in England. With a similar upsurge in crime in their own city, New Yorkers decided to try a similar solution.

The Municipal Police (1845–1857) The city's old system of policing—the 80-member Night-watch that patrolled the streets during evening hours—was finally legislated out of existence in 1844 and replaced with a new system—the Day and Night Police.

The State Legislature approved the creation of the new force and authorized the hiring of up to 800 men. But the City Council, rather than adopting the concept, decided it could get by with a municipal police force of only 200 men. This small force, of course, quickly proved inadequate. In 1845, the original act of the State Legislature was adopted and a uniformed Municipal Police Force of 800 men was established.

The First Shield (May 23, 1845) Many policemen strongly objected to wearing a specially designed uniform, preferring to dress in their own clothes. They viewed the uniform as a British innovation and an infringement on their rights as free-born American citizens. Many citizens shared this contempt and publicly condemned a uniformed force as nothing more than a "standing army" or "liveried lackeys."

A compromise was finally reached under which police officers wore an eight-point, star-shaped copper badge over the left breast of their coats in lieu of a complete uniform. The policemen became known as "star police" and later on as "coppers" and "cops."

The First Patrol Guide (July 16, 1845) The first set of printed rules and regulations was issued to the force in 1845. These "Regulations for the Day and Night Police of the City of New York with Instructions as to the Legal Powers and Duties of Policemen" dealt with the statutory and administrative aspects of the job.

Policemen were instructed that "the prevention of crime being the most important object in your view, your exertions must be constantly used to accomplish that end," and "the absence of crime will be considered the best proof of the efficiency of the police."

The First Official Uniform (1853) Full uniforms were finally adopted in 1853. The first uniform consisted of a leather helmet and a blue, single-breasted cloth frock coat buttoned to the neck with the letters M.P. (Municipal Police) on a standing collar. Gray trousers, with a half-inch black stripe running down the side of each leg,

completed the outfit.

Each officer was equipped with a baton that was 22 inches long and three-quarters of an inch thick. The department "Rules and Regulations" required that the club be used only "in urgent self defense." The Municipal Police were not authorized to carry sidearms for patrol duty.

Formal Training Formal training came into existence in 1853. Police captains instructed officers in the "school of soldier" and drill instructors were appointed to train and discipline officers in riot and crowd control.

Communications During the early 1850s, the New York Police constructed a simple telegraph network between their chief's office and the various precincts. The primary purpose of this communications system was to speed the dispatch of extra officers to fire and riot scenes. However, most of the messages dealt with lost children and stray horses.

New York's Finest Triumph

Concerned about the city's mushrooming crime rate, officials decided that sweeping and radical changes had to be made in police protection. A state-controlled Metropolitan Police District was established to step in and slowly phase out the Municipal Police Department.

Members of the municipal force were reluctant to relinquish their jobs and continued to patrol the city's streets, often clashing with the metropolitan police over turf. While the courts attempted to resolve the problem, the two blue-coated forces competed with one another in arresting the ringleaders of the Bowery Boys and the Plug Uglies, gangs of hardened street toughs that terrorized the city.

Eventually an agreement was reached and many municipal officers joined the ranks of the Metropolitan Police.

Under the Metropolitan Police Act, the "Mets" were governed by three police commissioners and consisted of a general superintendent, two deputy superintendents, five surgeons, and assorted inspectors, captains, sergeants and patrolmen. All were outfitted in similar uniforms—the chief difference being the frock coat. Those worn by superior officers were double-breasted; all others were single-breasted.

Under Frederick Tallmadge, the first general superintendent, the Metropolitan Police District was divided into precincts, which in turn were subdivided into patrol beats. The precincts, some having more than one stationhouse, were each staffed with one inspector, one captain, four sergeants, and patrolmen and officers assigned to details.

Among the improvements introduced in the 1850s was the "Rogues Portrait Gallery"—a collection of photos of hundreds of known criminals. Also established was a harbor police force of 25 men and a more sophisticated telegraphic link among precincts.

Civil War Draft Riots In 1863, the Mets were confronted with their new first major crisis—the Civil War draft riots. With tempers flaring in response to President Lincoln's proclamation that 300,000 men would be inducted into the Union Army, rioters wreaked mayhem on the streets of New York. The violence and destruction went on for four days before the frenzied protest was quelled. Many lives were lost and injuries suffered, and several stationhouses were burned to the ground after officers abandoned them as they fled for their lives.

As the Civil War wound down, crimes of violence in the city increased. In 1864 a "police insurance fund" was established to guarantee financial security to the families of policemen killed or disabled in the line of duty.

In 1868, with the Mets' ranks largely comprised of aged veterans from the old Municipal Police Department, the commissioners successfully lobbied for half-pay retirement pensions for its loyal public servants.

The Municipal Police Department Is Restored In 1870 the State Legislature passed an act known as the "Tweed Charter" that returned police powers to the Municipal Police. The Mets merged with the restored Municipal Police, which was governed by four commissioners appointed by the mayor.

A "Flag of Honor" was presented to the Department in 1872 by the people of the city in recognition of the outstanding performance by the police during times of public disturbance, particularly the draft riots. The flag, reserved for display at annual parades and funerals of officers killed in the line of duty, was inscribed on one side with the Department motto—"Faithful unto Death"—and with the city seal on the other.

In 1873 the Department was reorganized. The number of commissioners was upped to five and the force now comprised a superintendent, three inspectors, captains, sergeants, patrolmen, civilian clerks and doormen [civilians licensed by the police to act as security guards for residential buildings].

Hiring standards were tightened and police candidates were required to be U.S. citizens, residents of the state for at least a year, and free of any criminal convictions. In addition, a Board of Surgeons was established to examine candidates and supervise the medical and surgical services of the Department.

Also changed was the procedural manual, which was not only revised and updated, but introduced a new title for the police force—the "Department of Police for the City of New York."

From 1872 to 1881, in a bid to improve sanitary conditions in the city, the Department was put in charge of hiring, overseeing and providing equipment to a street-cleaning task force.

In 1874, Mayor William Havemeyer tagged the Department with its popular nickname—"the Finest."

The improvements kept coming. Telephone links between all police facilities replaced the sporadically placed, outdated telegraph system in 1880. A year later a central office for the Bureau of Detectives was established at Police Headquarters, located at 300 Mulberry Street.

In 1888, the Department got its first women when four women joined the force and were assigned as precinct matrons. It wasn't until a year later, however, that they were officially considered uniformed members of the service.

By 1894, with the restructuring of the Police Department in full swing, the State Senate appointed a committee to investigate alleged abuses of authority by police. The office of superintendent was abolished and replaced with a chief of police who had the power to assign and transfer and to suspend policemen for up to 10 days prior to trial by the police commissioners.

Teddy Roosevelt: The Innovator In 1895, Theodore Roosevelt was appointed to a newly installed board of police commissioners. He immediately set about strengthening qualifications for appointment to ensure that physical and mental ability would be given more weights than political influence.

Advocating progressive recruitment, he hired the first female civilian secretary and campaigned to have Jewish officers join the ranks of the primarily Irish Catholic police force.

Roosevelt helped pave the way for the modernization of the Department. During his tenure as a commissioner, telephone call boxes were installed on city sidewalks, permitting officers to communicate with their stationhouses. Stationhouses were renovated and more matrons were assigned to them. A patrol wagon service was introduced to help patrolmen get to their posts and to emergencies more quickly.

To relieve overcrowding and improve hygiene, sleeping quarters for transients were abolished at stationhouses and replaced with separate lodging houses. The .32-calibre revolver became the standard on-duty sidearm, and a bicycle squad was established and quickly expanded to 100 officers.

Department morale greatly increased as a result of Roosevelt's innovations. It was boosted even further when he instituted a recognition system for meritorious police service before he resigned in 1897 to become Secretary of the Navy.

In 1898, the State Legislature ordered that 24 local governments—cities, towns, and villages—consolidate into a single entity: New York City. As a result the Police Department of the Greater City of New York assimilated 18 smaller police agencies from various parts of Queens, Kings, Richmond, Bronx and New York counties. The greatly expanded force was renamed the "New York Police Department."

A year later plainclothes officers were used for the first time. They traveled in cars, protecting streetcars from attack by strikers.

The city's governmental expansion made the problems of policing more complex in the early years of the 20th century.

In 1901, to curb confusion and dissent within the Department's administration, the State Legislature adopted a bill giving a single commissioner of police full responsibility for overseeing the agency. Colonel Michael Murphy was the first to hold the position, and he appointed William Devery as first deputy police commissioner.

Working seven days a week, the policemen of the early 1900s got to know residents, merchants, and ruffians on their eight-block foot-posts. The round-the-clock chart included tours of 7 A.M. to 3 P.M.; 3 P.M. to 11 P.M.; and 11 P.M. to 7 A.M. Officers rarely got a day off—and when they did, it was usually after 45 to 50 days of work.

Modern-Day Police Department at the Turn of the Century

The city and its Police Department now faced an era of modernization and growth spurred on by community needs and the "needs of the time."

Many exciting innovations were ushered in with the first decade. The first automobile could be seen puttering about, bridges and tunnels connected the city to neighboring areas, railway construction began, mechanical traffic control devices were installed, a more scientific technique replaced the antiquated criminal identification system and the Department continued to organize specialized units.

In the autumn of 1904 the Mounted Division, recognized for its mobility and range of vision, was used to calm labor unrest, control crowds and regulate traffic. A year later the Motorcycle Bureau was formed to help handle traffic duties.

By 1909 folks were regularly moseying into and about the city in "horseless carriages" via the newly opened Brooklyn, Williamsburg, Queensboro and Manhattan bridges. Police Headquarters had been relocated to Centre Street and a Bureau of Criminal Identification was established to maintain criminal records.

An effective new method of fingerprint identification was used for the first time by the "Safe and Loft Squad" in 1911 to positively identify a burglar through fingerprints left behind on a windowsill. Later renamed the Safe, Loft and Truck Squad, this unit protected businessmen from skilled thieves who made a habit of going after and making off with valuables stored in safes, lofts and trucks.

As the city's population grew, so did its crime problem. In 1914, recognizing that "the youth of today could turn into the criminal of tomorrow," Captain John Sweeney founded the Police Athletic League (PAL) on Manhattan's Lower East Side. Initially called the Junior Police Corps, its mission was to keep youngsters out of trouble by channelling their energies into recreational and athletic activities.

Entering Difficult Times: The 1920s In 1917 America entered World War I. That same year, the Department put its first radio-equipped patrol car on the road and established a Missing Persons Bureau.

The war ended in November 1918 and was quickly followed by the "Roaring 20s." Police faced huge problems trying to enforce the constitutional ban on alcohol. Gangster-controlled speakeasies reaped profits through the illegal sale of liquor. "Prohibition" and economic hard times caused criminal behavior to flourish.

In 1924 a course of comprehensive training for all members of the Department was introduced at the "Police College" on Broome Street in Manhattan. New officers spent an arduous three months studying police doctrine. Know-how and in-service courses were given on all levels to keep Department members abreast of the latest developments in police work.

In 1929 the Aviation Unit was born and more radio-equipped patrol cars were put on the road.

In October 1929 the stock market crashed, with panic on Wall Street spreading and soon engulfing most of the world. The Great Depression devastated the economy, creating widespread poverty and desperation.

Police officers proved their commitment to public service by making hearty attempts to secure food, fuel, clothing and jobs for the needy and by generously donating to a relief fund.

The District Attorney's Office Squad was set up as an undercover unit operating out of the Manhattan Criminal Courts Building. Its job was to fight organized crime and racketeers who were attempting to capitalize on the city's plight.

Coping with Traffic and Teenagers: The 1930s By 1930 Manhattan's neatly organized streets and avenues had become the setting for a growing number of traffic accidents and deaths. Juvenile delinquency had also become a problem. The Department met both of these challenges with long-term solutions.

In response to the traffic problem, it implemented a three-pronged program of regulation, enforcement and safety education.

The juvenile delinquency problem was met through the development of a unit called the Crime Prevention Bureau. Consistent with PAL's philosophy, the bureau offered counseling as well as educational and recreational activities to the city's youth in hopes that they would keep them from turning to crime.

In 1939 the Department played an exciting role policing a big event—the New York World's Fair in Flushing Meadows, Queens.

Shell Shocked and "Blue": The 1940s and 1950s In 1941, America entered World War II.

Months before the costly lesson of Pearl Harbor, a civil defense strategy had been formulated to ensure the safety of New York City's citizens in event of enemy attack.

Working with other federal, state and city agencies, the NYPD was entrusted with reuniting separated families and providing relief.

In addition to their police duties, officers also enforced the nation's rationing of such staples as canned food, fuel, rubber products and women's nylons.

In 1945 the war ended. With the city's population continuing to grow by leaps and bounds, the Department concentrated on expansion. By 1957 its strength had reached 23,590.

The 1960s: A Time of Civil Unrest With the 1960s came great advances in income, education and housing, but not in civil rights. The mood of contentment and confidence that had characterized the 1950s was shattered not only by a skyrocketing crime wave but by civil disorder, alarming rises in welfare cases, drug abuse and youth unemployment.

Youth crime again became rampant. The city was entering a time of "urban crisis." Community cohesion began to disintegrate and inner-city crime rates rose alarmingly.

The police officer's capacity to understand the law, to deal with explosive situations and to cope with social and economic problems was continually tested during this decade.

In 1964 Harlem erupted in civil disorder, leaving many seriously injured, one dead and hundreds arrested. In 1968 citywide disorder followed the assassination of Martin Luther King, Jr.

Striving to Meet the Needs of the Time: The 1970s After the violent conclusion of the 60s there was a need to rebuild police-community relations. The Department recognized that increased foot patrols would best accomplish this goal. A foot officer could be a source of information, a counselor to the public and the eyes and ears of the Department.

In 1972 an equal opportunity policy was implemented. It directed that women be hired and assigned to perform the same duties as male officers. Women were given equal promotional opportunities and the right to undertake the same law enforcement roles as men.

As the 20th century moved along, so did the wheels of progress for the NYPD. Today, it stands as an example to the world of what modern policing is all about.

READING 8

A SOCIAL HISTORY OF WOMEN IN U.S. POLICING

Dorothy Moses Schulz

Dorothy Moses Schulz summarizes the rich history of the evolution of women police in the United States. Schulz is an assistant professor of police science and criminal justice administration at John Jay College of Criminal Justice (CUNY) and was previously a captain in the MetroNorth Commuter Railroad Police Department.

U.S. policewomen officially came into existence in 1910, but their roots are in the early decades of the nineteenth century—the jail and prison matron era. This era began in the 1820s, when volunteer Quaker women, following the example set by British Quakers, entered locked institutions to provide religious and secular training for women inmates. These volunteers, soon pined by other upper-middle-class women, wanted to reform the morals of the inmates and train them for respectable jobs, primarily as domestics in Christian homes. As the reformers became aware of the poor conditions under which these "fallen women" served their prison terms, they attributed a large portion of the neglect to the fact that the inmates were supervised by men. Foremost among their concerns was the sexual vulnerability of the inmates, who were frequently

Reprinted from Dorothy Moses Schulz, "Invisible No More: A Social History of Women in U.S. Policing," in *The Criminal Justice System and Women: Offenders, Victims, and Workers*, 2nd ed., compiled and edited by Barbara Raffel Price and Natalie J. Sokoloff, by permission of The McGraw-Hill Companies. Copyright ©1995 by McGraw-Hill, Inc.

impregnated while in prison by either male inmates or male keepers.

Efforts by the volunteers to create better living conditions and a moral environment for the women they termed their "less fortunate sisters" evolved into a new profession for women—prison matron. These matrons were part of a general benevolent movement of the time, which brought religious, middle-class women into contact with poor women through charitable efforts and sought to create a sense of female solidarity across class lines. Clarice Feinman, who has traced the history of women in corrections, observed that these women reformers believed that women criminals could be saved only if they were removed from the corrupting influences of cities and men.[1] Prisons were therefore set in the countryside and staffed with women only. At the same time that these women reformers were attempting to improve conditions for women inmates, they were also creating a new profession for those who would follow them as paid matrons in these prisons. For almost 50 years, from the 1820s to the 1870s, this remained the only position in corrections open to women. Despite what appears to have been a revolution in women's roles, a second look negates this view, for by reinforcing women's traditional role as the caregiver to other women, these early matrons stayed within the then acceptable sexual boundaries even while ensuring new careers for themselves.[2]

At the end of the Civil War another generation

of women expanded this philosophy of "women's sphere," taking it far beyond jail and prison walls into other public sector areas. Women's sphere, the "special responsibility to alleviate harsh conditions," developed from women's traditional, maternal role but allowed activist women to develop a concept of municipal housekeeping that eventually encompassed virtually all activities that placed government or voluntary agencies in contact with women or children. Since women at this time were believed to be morally superior to men, these women argued that it was only proper that they be responsible for the protection of other women in need of moral guidance.[3]

Phase One: Police Matrons

The care of those in police custody became an area of special concern. At a time when components of what today constitutes the criminal justice system were less distinct, the handling of sentenced inmates and those awaiting court appearances was ill-defined. Additionally, police stations frequently functioned as homeless shelters, and many of those who sought refuge were women and their children. The women were almost always poor and frequently intoxicated, two conditions that made them vulnerable to advances by the men responsible for their care.

Using as their model the prison matrons, these post–Civil War women activists demanded and won an expanded role for women caring for women and children in police custody. That their tactics and arguments were similar to those of the women who came before them was to be expected. Their social characteristics were virtually identical with those of the women in whose path they followed. They, too, were primarily socially prominent or politically well-connected upper-middle-class women of native-born families. Many had been abolitionists prior to the Civil War, and now they turned their attention to religious, temperance, and benevolent associations. By the 1880s these women succeeded in creating another new profession for women—police matron.

Police matrons brought custodial care into police stations throughout the nation. They represented another phase of women's involvement in

the criminal justice system—their first entry into the police portion of the system. Within a short period of time, police matrons began to perform more than strictly custodial roles. They interviewed accused women and made sentencing recommendations, duties today assigned to probation officers. By the early years of the twentieth century they had ushered in the policewoman era, the second phase of women in policing.

Phase Two: Policewomen

This period is often defined as having begun in 1910, when Alice Stebbins Wells became the first woman in the United States to be called a policewoman. In reality it overlapped the matron movement and was not a new phenomenon but a continuation of women's professionalization within the police environment. Although the women who lobbied for police matrons and policewomen had little work experience outside their own homes and lacked the right to vote, in the period from 1880 to 1910 they created two new professions in the public sector for women. Because in some cities it took "as many" as three years for them to achieve their aims, they frequently voiced frustration.

Within this context, both the matrons' and the policewomen's movements provide insights into how women from a variety of organizations were able to join together and win the support of like-minded men to achieve goals and employment opportunities for women in fields that had previously been closed to them. These movements also indicate how firmly intertwined policewomen were with social purity and early female reform traditions. Social purity (a term generally relating to sexual morality, eradication of prostitution, and control of venereal diseases) was a major national concern for much of the nineteenth and early twentieth centuries. It led to the creation of numerous organizations whose primary purpose was to control vice and sexual activity outside of marriage by women and young people. Many leaders of these social purity organizations were vocal advocates for and allies of policewomen.

Wells, just as the few women who came before

her and the many who came after her (sometimes women who had been matrons), conceived her police role in order to fulfill her vision of women helping other women. These women police embodied the concept of the policewoman-as-social worker. During this period, when social work was developing as a profession, it attracted to its ranks a class of women who, under the guise of helping others, actually were as much social controllers as social workers.

The prevention and protection theories these policewomen espoused gave them the opportunity to intervene in the lives of the women and children they claimed to be saving from a life of crime and delinquency. Although this philosophy of moral and social control gave way in the post-Depression era to a more middle-class, female careerist outlook, it was not until the modern, women-on-patrol period (which began somewhat tentatively in 1968 and wholeheartedly in 1972) that the path set by early policewomen was seriously altered. Thus, the history of the policewomen's movement is also a history of intervention by upper-middle-class women into the lives of poor women and children.

Policewomen as Social Workers

These upper-middle-class, educated policewomen used social work, not law enforcement, as their frame of reference. Their allies and peers were female (and male) social workers, feminists, temperance leaders, and members of women's civic clubs, not male police officers or chiefs. The women formed two professional organizations that fostered high entry standards and ongoing training far in excess of male requirements or interest in these areas. The International Association of Policewomen (IAP), which existed from 1915 to 1932, was modeled after and affiliated with the National Conference of Charities and Correction (NCCC—later the National Conference of Social Work [NCSW]). IAP leaders scheduled annual and regional meetings in conjunction with social workers' meetings. The International Association of Women Police (IAWP), formed in 1956 as a reincarnation of the IAP, was not as closely aligned with the social work establishment but

continued to have a strong social service and women's sphere orientation well after policewomen had expanded their roles within policing.

Rooted in a value system that stressed the moral superiority of women over men and the differences between men and women, early policewomen were eager to act as municipal mothers to those whose lifestyles they believed needed discipline. Some were actually called "city mothers." In attempting to serve their female and juvenile clients in a professional, nonthreatening atmosphere, they tried to separate themselves physically from policemen and elements of the police world they viewed as hampering their mission. They stressed the need for offices away from police stations, which they viewed as inhospitable to their efforts to prevent crime and delinquency among women and juveniles. Although they felt they needed the legal authority the title "police" represented, policewomen did not view themselves as female versions of policemen, a concept they disparagingly termed "little men." Nor did they view policemen—usually of a lower class and education level than theirs—as their equals, although they did stress the need for cooperation with male personnel.

Their view of themselves was, therefore, based on both gender and class, and they consciously sought a peripheral, rather than an integrated, role in policing. The concept of equality of assignment with their male colleagues did not enter their world. It was inconceivable to them, just as it was to policemen. They also eschewed the most obvious trappings of policing. They were vehemently opposed to uniforms, and most chose not to carry firearms even if permitted to do so. The women's willingness to accept assignments men did not want made their presence less threatening to policemen and senior officers, but support from within the police environment was usually unenthusiastic, reluctant, and grudging.

The few African-American policewomen were even further segregated—very much a minority within a minority. Hired to work specifically with African-American women and juveniles, they shared many of the characteristics of their white sisters. They, too, were usually better educated than the average African-American man or woman, and they were often teachers, social workers, or ministers' wives with status in their communities.

The specialized roles filled by early white and African-American policewomen were not forced on them by the male police establishment but were the roles they sought. Understanding women's traditional place in policing puts recent studies into a historical perspective, because it shows that women's acceptance by male peers has always been marginal. From the first day women entered police stations, their presence was imposed on male police executives by outside forces. It was a rare municipal government official or police chief who sought to hire policewomen. Demands for women in the police environment almost always came from outsiders.

Policing to Impose Morality

If early policewomen, who numbered about 125 employed in about 30 cities in the years from 1910 to 1917, sought neither the trappings of police nor interaction with male officers, the obvious question is, Why did they want to be police rather than purely social workers operating out of municipal or voluntary agencies? The answer lies in the class and ethnic distinctions in the United States that were partially responsible for the movement. Although these policewomen saw themselves as benevolent helpers, their assistance was not always perceived as such. Their views on prostitution, sexual morality, dance halls, penny arcades, curfews for minors, and temperance were rarely shared by those to whom they offered their "preventive help." While policewomen were overwhelmingly college-educated, native-born, upper-middle-class women, those on whom they sought to bestow their benevolence were usually uneducated, poor, and immigrant. Despite the rhetoric of the policewomen, what they viewed as benevolence was viewed by their clients as coercive social control and placed them squarely within the group Anthony Platt has called "the child savers."

Platt coined the term "child savers" to describe a group of juvenile justice system reformers who viewed themselves as "disinterested" and who "regarded their cause as a matter of conscience and morality, serving no particular class or political interests." Just as the policewomen did, these reformers saw themselves as "altruists and humanitarians dedicated to rescuing those . . . less fortunately placed in the social order." But, as Platt has observed, they went beyond this—by highlighting certain behaviors, they "invented new categories of youthful misbehavior which had been hitherto unappreciated" and not viewed as criminal or requiring correction.[4] Just as the child savers diminished the civil liberties and privacy of youths by calling for civic supervision of their activities, so, too, did policewomen bring under municipal control behavior by women and children that had previously not been viewed as requiring the attention or intervention of the police.

Because of their class distance from those they sought to save, child savers and policewomen had different definitions of morality and delinquency than those on whom they imposed their standards of behavior. Their presence in poor, immigrant neighborhoods was often unwelcome and unappreciated, as they tried to force their values on others in a maternal, yet coercive manner.

Reinforcing their class and nativist orientation, policewomen turned for support during World War I to the social purity and social hygiene agencies created to combat prostitution and liquor law violations in and around cities with military installations. Efforts by these agencies—whether voluntary or governmental—resulted in severe limitations on women's mobility and in the majority of instances placed legal and moral blame on women, rather than on the military men who sought their companionship.

Moral reform sentiments continued in the post–World War I period, providing additional allies for the growing numbers of policewomen, particularly among the Progressives, a label given by historians to various well-educated and often well-to-do individuals who joined together during the late nineteenth and early twentieth centuries to advance social and political reform. By the end of the war, the number of policewomen had doubled to about 300 working in more than 200 cities.[5]

Despite increased numbers of policewomen, there were no demands for greater integration into the police environment. In fact, the postwar era, a time when workplace gender segregation was the norm, brought about greater segregation. Women actively sought women's bureaus, some of which operated virtually as independent agencies. They processed all matters pertaining to women and children, sometimes including pre- and postsentencing incarceration for morality offenses. Demands for women's bureaus were a continuation of the ideology of women's sphere, but a new element entered the debate.

When these highly educated and motivated policewomen compared their careers with those of women in correctional facilities, settlement houses, and similar institutions, it was obvious that they lagged behind in achieving policy-making roles. These other women held managerial titles and supervised other women. Yet policewomen, despite their self-segregation within police departments, were not sufficiently independent to warrant their own rank structure. Intertwined with the advocacy of women's bureaus was their recognition that only greater segregation could justify an independent rank structure similar to that in specialized bureaus elsewhere in the police department. Not coincidentally, policewomen and their supporters not only demanded women's bureaus—they demanded that women be in charge of them. Thus, women's bureaus met the two major goals of post–World War I policewomen. They more fully defined women's specialized roles, and they created a mechanism for women to rise through the ranks, if not to the very top, then at least to the middle of the police hierarchy.

Many of the gains—both numerical and bureaucratic—made by policewomen during and after World War I were eradicated by the Depression. Although by 1929 there were close to 600 policewomen serving in 150 to 175 cities,[6] between 1929 and 1931 the number of departments employing policewomen decreased. Additionally, the 1930s spotlighted for the first time the image of the policeman as crimefighter, an image dia-metrically opposed to how social-work-oriented policewomen saw themselves. By 1940 there were no more than 500 policewomen, the vast majority working in the largest cities.

World War II renewed the nation's concerns with morality and delinquency, and policewomen were able to regain their World War I momentum and allies. Although World War II did not create new roles for policewomen, the women hired were not temporary replacements for men fighting the war but permanent additions to their police departments. Unlike the women personified by Rosie the Riveter, a woman hired to fill a man's industrial job during World War II, policewomen were hired for traditional policewomen's jobs, not to replace policemen who had gone to war. Because policewomen's gender-specific roles in law enforcement were not altered by the war, neither was their employment dependent on the continued absence of men. Therefore, policewomen were not faced with layoffs when the soldiers returned. While Rosie the Riveter is an enduring image from the war years, she represents a highly specialized form of women's entry into previously male occupations and had no parallel in policewomen's history.

Concerns with morality and juvenile delinquency intensified in the postwar years, allowing women to increase their wartime gains. Women's assignments also began to diversify. Policewomen often were teamed with male officers on undercover assignments and more frequently investigated other than morality-based crimes. They were issued uniforms (which were usually based on female military garb and which they rarely wore) and were trained in the use of and expected to carry their firearms. The 1950 U.S. Census reported more than 2,500 publicly employed policewomen, slightly more than 1 percent of all police and detectives and a considerable increase since 1940, when 1,775 women were counted in public and private agencies combined.

Policing as a Career

The post–World War II period and the decade of the 1950s are vital to policewomen's history not only because women's assignments and responsibilities expanded but also because a different type of woman was brought into policing. Often military veterans and no longer aligned with the social work establishment, the women entering police departments in this period were middle-class careerists, not upper-middle-class feminists and child savers. Although still better educated and higher in class orientation than their male peers, these women were less different from policemen than their predecessors had been. Their goal of upward mobility through civil service and through attainment of rank resembled the goals of policemen and underlined their differences from the first generation of policewomen. This began a trend that was accentuated in the late 1970s, when the requirements for women to become police officers were lowered to the same requirements as for men, rather than qualifications for both men and women being raised to the level they had been for policewomen.

The 1950s are normally viewed as a quiet time in the expansion of women's roles, but these "second generation" policewomen made professional gains. Factors inside and outside police departments led many of the women hired during and after the war to become dissatisfied with the philosophy of women's sphere.

Externally, societal changes pertaining to women's self-image convinced them that occupational segregation was hampering their chances for lateral or upward mobility. Since these women had entered policing to take advantage of its career opportunities rather than to impose their morality on others, their concerns were as much for their own professional development as for societal benefit. In 1956 they reestablished the International Association of Policewomen, changing its name to the International Association of Women Police (IAWP), and began to develop a group consciousness distinct from that of social workers.

Internally, larger numbers and a greater range of assignments, combined with differences in their educational and class orientation, brought policewomen into closer contact with policemen. They saw that even men who were not in traditional uniform patrol had greater career range. Men were el-

igible for transfer to any bureau. More important, they were eligible for civil service promotion that could increase their status and their incomes. By the 1960s, these women demanded and won similar promotional opportunities.

In 1961, two New York City policewomen sued the New York City Police Department after they were barred from taking a promotion test for sergeant. The case took more than two years to be decided, but they won. Three years later, they were promoted to sergeant; in 1967 both were promoted again, becoming the department's first female lieutenants.[7]

In the years during and soon after this and similar lawsuits, employment law changed considerably as a result of major forces in society, particularly the civil rights and women's movements. This provided new impetus for women and minorities to seek expanded roles in policing. Once again, internal and external factors came to alter the perceptions of policewomen. In 1963 Congress passed the Equal Pay Act, prohibiting unequal pay for equal work. Although the 1964 Omnibus Civil Rights Law's Title VII, prohibiting discrimination based on sex, race, color, religion, or national origin, pertained only to private employers, not government agencies, it began a string of laws and cases limiting employers' control over employment selection.

In 1969 President Richard Nixon issued Executive Order 11478, which declared that the federal government could not use sex as a qualification for hiring, forcing a number of federal law enforcement agencies to begin hiring women agents. In 1971, the Supreme Court ruled in *Griggs v. Duke Power Company* that preemployment tests had to be job-related, and in 1972 Congress passed the Revenue Sharing Act, which prohibited discriminatory use of revenue-sharing funds. Also in 1972, Congress, through the Equal Employment Opportunity Act, extended the provisions of the Civil Rights Act to government employment—including police departments.

The Law Enforcement Assistance Administration (LEAA), a Justice Department agency created under the Omnibus Crime Control and Safe Streets Act of 1968, also pushed police departments to accept equal employment. Forty percent of the funds for the improvement of law enforcement dispensed by LEAA went to local governments, and the Crime Control Act of 1973, which amended the 1968 act, specified that LEAA grantees were prohibited from discriminating in employment practices. This meant that departments that discriminated against women risked losing the federal grants that many were using to upgrade training, equipment, and facilities. In reality, no department met this fate. Yet because LEAA funds were important to job expansion in policing, combined with the new guidelines of the federal government, more positions became available to women and minorities than ever before.

With new promotional rights and newly acquired court and legislative support, more aggressive and less social-service-oriented policewomen in the 1960s moved into areas of the police department that their foremothers would never have dreamed of entering. Although their demands for greater equality were spurred at least in part by the women's movement, this was the first time in their history that women police officers were not assisted by other professional women; instead, they were aided by new allies—federal legislation and the courts.

Yet in 1960, IAWP President Lois Lundell Higgins, reviewing the golden anniversary of women in the police service, confidently echoed earlier policewomen in the belief that if they were here to stay, it was only because they did not try to compete with men in "work that has been and always will be predominantly a man's job." Women would continue to succeed, she predicted, because "they have brought to their work talents that are peculiarly feminine—usually a highly developed interest in human relationships—and have accentuated, rather than subordinated, their femininity."[8]

Women Police Officers on Patrol

Speakers at annual IAWP meetings until the 1970s were more likely to be social work professionals or women's bureau directors than policewomen on patrol or in other nontraditional as-

signments. But since the 1980s IAWP meetings have acquired the trappings of law enforcement, including firearms competitions and awards that frequently honor bravery under gunfire. While the IAP could exist from 1915 to 1932 with few leadership changes and still reflect the views of its members, by the time the IAWP was formed, change was coming too rapidly for the association to keep pace, forcing it to follow, rather than lead, its members. Many leaders remained at least partially committed to the older, social work ideal; they no longer represented the younger, more law-enforcement-oriented women. Also, since many leaders were in appointed ranks in their police departments, they could not risk taking positions that contradicted the wishes of their chiefs. Ironically, their vulnerable positions were often the result of the very policies they espoused.

Less than ten years after Higgins made her prediction, Indianapolis in 1968 assigned Betty Blankenship and Elizabeth Coffal to patrol. They became the first policewomen to wear uniforms, strap gun belts to their waists, drive a marked patrol car, and answer general-purpose police calls for service on an equal basis with policemen. Although they eventually returned to traditional policewomen's duties, they were the forerunners of a break with the past. Thus began the demise of the mothering concept. The women who followed them were no longer policewomen in the traditional sense of women social workers in the police environment. They were police officers, women with a law enforcement concept similar to that of their male peers. As crimefighters, they now enforced the law, maintained order, and provided for the public's safety, just as men did.

In the six decades (1910 to 1968) from Alice Stebbins Wells to Betty Blankenship and Elizabeth Coffal, a revolution had occurred. Demands by policewomen no longer reflected their historical feminist, upper-middle-class, educated roots. Modern women, hired under the same rules as men, rejected the constraints of women's sphere and sought equality with male peers. Recent discussion over whether uniform patrol is as much service as crimefighting may have aided these women in breaking down male police resistance to placing them on patrol, but their primary focus is not the components of patrol but the opportunity it presents for equal treatment from and within the police hierarchy, including assignment and promotional equality.

Moving Toward Equality

For the first time, the majority of women now enter criminal justice professions for the same reasons as men. In this regard, they are similar to other women who have in the past 20 years entered male fields on an equal basis with male colleagues. They do not seek to change their chosen professions; rather, they wish to benefit from the financial or status rewards these fields offer. Today's women became police officers for the tangible rewards of pay, promotions, and pensions. Their attitudes and goals are similar to those of the men with whom they train and ride in patrol cars, and against whom they compete for assignment and promotion. Although not aligned with traditional women's advocacy groups, today's women police officers are part of a broader social movement which they unwittingly may have helped to create but from which they, too, profited.

Equality, though, has brought new issues for study. As of 1993, only four women have been appointed police chiefs in major cities. Elizabeth Watson, an 18-year veteran of the Houston Police Department, was appointed chief in February 1990. Although a new mayor chose not to retain her two years later and she was forced to return to the rank of assistant chief, by the end of 1992 she was heading to Austin, Texas, as chief. Other women serving as large-city chiefs in early 1993 included Elaine S. Hedtke in Tucson, Arizona; Leslie Martinez in Portsmouth, Virginia; and Mary F. Rabadeau in Elizabeth, New Jersey.[9]

The proportionately small number of women moving up the ranks is of concern to many women officers, as well as to researchers studying their career patterns and paths. Achieving rank in paramilitary organizations that depend overwhelmingly on periodic civil service testing as the means of upward mobility is a slow progression. The process for women has been further slowed, according to some researchers, indicating that women are not availing themselves of promotional opportunities because of personal reasons and also because systemic discrimination against them still exists. The personal reasons women list include not wanting to give up positions with daylight hours owing to family and child-care requirements. Systemic reasons include lack of assignment to high-profile units, seniority beyond the minimal eligibility requirements (often keyed to veteran status), negative (possibly biased) supervisory evaluations, and general attitudes of male coworkers that psychologically discourage ambition.[10]

These systemic reasons belie the legal equality women have achieved and highlight issues pertaining to the subtle and not so subtle discrimination women face as they compete with men on terms defined by and for men.

Recently, these barriers to real equality have spawned new debates. No longer concerned with whether women provide police service in the same way men do, or whether women will somehow change (i.e., soften and humanize) U.S. policing, a growing number of feminist criminologists have argued that women should not have to become "little men" to succeed in policing. As feminists rethink the meaning of equality and pose new theories of its effect on women in the workplace, their views could lessen the demands on women police officers to conform to male definitions of a "good cop," but such views could also provide ammunition for opponents of equality who continue to believe that women's place in policing should be determined by gender—by women's sphere.

Previous feminists writing about women's roles in the criminal justice system (particularly Dorothy Bracey, Clarice Feinman, and Barbara Raffel Price) criticized any vestiges of women's sphere. They advocated gender-neutral policing as the only way women could achieve equality, as well as supervisory and policy-making positions, within the police world.[11] While not in agreement with all the prevailing definitions of success in the police environment, these observers believed that women would be unable to advance professionally by stressing only their differences from, rather than their similarities to, the men who make up the overwhelming majority of police. In this belief they reflected the views of many women officers, who came to believe that "equal" meant "the same as" rather than "different but just as good as."

Those staking out the new feminist criminology disagree; they do not view gender neutrality positively. Kathleen Daly and Meda Chesney-Lind, discussing postfeminist consciousness, believe that feminists who "sought to achieve equality with men in the public sphere . . . omitted more subtle questions of equality and difference now being raised." Although they are referring to offenders when they observe that "feminist legal scholars are more skeptical of a legal equality model because the very structure of law continues to assume that men's lives are the norm," they could just as easily be discussing women's experiences in the police environment.[12]

Addressing policing directly, Nanci Koser Wilson believes that "not only should there be female police; but there should also be room for women's perspective on what policing should be. Not only should there be female detectives; but women's style of detective work . . . should receive attention." She echoes an earlier view when she states that "women were not introduced to policing . . . to mimic policemen or become stilted versions of men."[13]

If this postfeminist view begins to predominate, we may see the day when Lois Lundell Higgins's 1960 prediction that women will succeed by accentuating, rather than subordinating, their femininity will again prove correct!

NOTES

1. Clarice Feinman, *Women in the Criminal Justice System* (New York: Praeger Publishers, 1980), 27.

2. Ibid., 108–109.

3. Lori D. Ginzberg, *Women and the World of Benevolence: Morality, Politics, and Class in the Nineteenth-Century United States* (New Haven: Yale University Press, 1990), 17, 37; Ann Firor Scott (ed.), *The American Woman: Who Was She?* (Englewood Cliffs, N.J.: Prentice-Hall, 1971), 88. For a detailed look at how women used the concept of women's sphere to enter policing and eventually expand their roles, see Dorothy M. Schulz, *From Social Worker to Crimefighter: A History of Women in United States Policing* (Ann Arbor, Mich.: University Microfilms International, 1992).

4. Anthony M. Platt, *The Child Savers: The Invention of Delinquency* (Chicago: University of Chicago Press, 1969), 3–4.

5. *The Woman Citizen,* May 3, 1919, 1055; Peter Horne, *Women in Law Enforcement,* 2d ed. (Springfield, Ill.: Charles C. Thomas, 1980), 29.

6. Edith Rockwood and Augusta J. Street, *Social Protective Work of Public Agencies: With Special Emphasis on the Policewoman* (Washington, D.C.: Committee on Social Hygiene—National League of Women Voters, 1932), 10.

7. *Shpritzer v. Lang*, 32 Misc. 2d 693, 1961, modified and affirmed, 234 NYS 2d 1962; Felicia Shpritzer, interview with author, Nov. 21, 1991.

8. Lois Lundell Higgins, "Golden Anniversary of Women in Police Service," *Law and Order*, August 1960, 4.

9. Barbara Hustedt Crook, "Cosmo Talks to Elizabeth Watson: Houston's Pioneering Police Chief," *Cosmopolitan*, October 1990, 116+. On Feb. 17, 1992, Mayor Bob Lanier replaced Chief Watson with a male former member of the Houston PD. Lanier stated that despite "generally a positive impression" of Watson, he preferred to begin a new administration with a new police chief. See Roberto Suro, "Houston Mayor Removes Female Police Chief," *New York Times*, Feb. 18, 1992, A20:1–6. See also "A Few More Glass Ceilings Are Shattered," *Law Enforcement News*, Jan. 15/31, 1993, 18:1–3.

10. Comments typical of the concern over promotional patterns are from Susan Ehrlich Martin, *Women on the Move? A Report on the Status of Women in Policing* (Washington, D.C.: Police Foundation, 1989), 1, 3–4, and Cynthia G. Sulton and Roi D. Townsey, *A Progress Report on Women in Policing* (Washington, D.C.: Police Foundation, 1981), 4–5.

11. See Feinman, *Women in the Criminal Justice System*, 121 pp.; Barbara Raffel Price and Swan Gavin, "A Century of Women Policing," in Donald O. Schultz (ed.), *Modern Police Administration* (Houston: Gulf Publishing Co., 1979), 109–122; Dorothy Bracey, "Women in Criminal Justice: The Decade after the Equal Employment Opportunity Legislation," in William A. Jones, Jr. (ed.), *Criminal Justice Administration: Linking Practice and Research* (New York: Marcel Dekker, 1983), 57–78; and Edith Linn and Barbara Raffel Price, "The Evolving Role of Women in American Policing," in *The Ambivalent Force: Perspectives on the Police,* 3d ed. Abraham S. Blumberg and Elaine Niederhoffer (eds.), (New York: Holt, Rinehart and Winston, 1985), 69–80.

12. Kathleen Daly and Meda Chesney-Lind, "Feminism and Criminology," *Justice Quarterly* 5, no. 4 (December 1988): 509, 524.

13. Nanci Koser Wilson, "Feminist Pedagogy in Criminology," *Journal of Criminal Justice Education* 2, no. 1 (Spring 1991): 91.

DISCUSSION QUESTIONS

1. Laura Hauth's article on the history of the NYPD notes that crime prevention was the primary duty of the police officer in 1845 and police efficiency was determined by the relative absence of crime. Do we hold similar expectations for today's police? How should police efficiency be judged, if not in relation to the community's crime rate?

2. Dorothy Moses Schulz suggests that police work in the future will be influenced by what one writer calls a "woman's perspective." Will the growing number of women at all levels of law enforcement change the nature of policing? Describe some of those possible changes.

WEBSITES

www.officer.com

From the Police Officer's Internet Directory at this site you can link to web pages of police departments throughout the world.

www.ci.nyc.ny.us/html/nypd/finest.html

The home page of the New York Police Department provides an interesting contrast to the historical perspective in the reading for this chapter.

www.open.gov.uk/police/mps/home.htm

The home page of the first modern police department includes links to historical information about the Metropolitan Police Service and to pages providing the latest information about the department.

www.anet-dfw.com/~iawpol

This home page of the International Association of Women Police offers information about the organization and its publications.

www.ncjrs.org/unojust/policing/int627.htm

This hypertext article by Jennifer Brown provides information about how European countries are integrating women into policing.

CHAPTER 5: POLICE MANAGEMENT

B etween 1993 and 1995, New York City had double-digit decreases in major crime. Murder and non-negligent manslaughter, for example, were down 39.5 percent, robbery declined by 31.1 percent, and auto theft dropped by 35.4 percent. As Sarah Glazer explains in her article on declining crime rates, some people attribute the reduction in crime to police tactics while others point to an improving economy and changing demographics, with fewer people in the younger, and more crime-prone, age brackets. Glazer's article, which emphasizes the police tactics argument, uses examples from several cities to provide an overview of community policing issues.

In the perpetual confrontation between "cops and robbers" there is constant maneuvering on both sides for advantage. To get clear descriptions of offenders at places where robberies might occur, the cops place video cameras; the robbers respond by wearing disguises. To gain an edge in firepower and lethality, the "bad guys" take quick advantage of advances in automatic weapons and armor-piercing bullets; the cops respond by upgrading their own weapons and by wearing even newer versions of body armor. In his article on high-tech crooks, Dennis McCauley suggests that the "game" of cops and robbers is taking a technological turn that requires both sides to become increasingly familiar with computers, fiber optics, and cellular technology. Street crime will remain an important, and probably primary, concern for law enforcement well into the twenty-first century. But McCauley presents an interesting argument on the need for contemporary officers to think in terms of patrolling cyberspace as well as the city streets.

DOES BETTER POLICING REDUCE CRIME?

Sarah Glazer

Crime has been decreasing in the United States since 1991. In New York, Fort Worth, and other cities, police are cracking down on quality-of-life offenses like public drinking and aggressive panhandling and claiming credit for the big drops in violent crime that follow. But New York, traditionally a high-crime city, is responsible for a big chunk of the nationwide decline. Skeptics credit the declining statistics to the improving economy, the fading of the crack wars, and the maturing of the baby boomers, rather than new policing tactics. The only way to drive down crime in the long run, these experts argue, is to mend the nation's social fabric, especially racial and class disparities in education and employment. Sarah Glazer is a freelance writer in New York who specializes in social policy issues.

Real estate agent Laurie Bloomfield used to leave her Upper West Side brownstone in the morning and find the sidewalk shimmering with glass from smashed car windows. Not anymore. In fact,`it has been two years since her own car was broken into.

Like many New Yorkers, Bloomfield has her own theories for why things improved. "It was the crack addicts," she says. "They were looking for radios." She often found empty crack cocaine vials amid the glass shards.

Today, however, fewer drug addicts seem to be hitting the neighborhood, a favorite with upscale professionals. Bloomfield sees more police patrolling—on bicycles in the summer. And just a few blocks away, prosecutors crushed several drug-selling gangs whose turf wars led to shooting in the streets.

Crime statistics bear out Bloomfield's perceptions. In the 24th Precinct, which encompasses Bloomfield's neighborhood as well as the run-down area known as Manhattan Valley, overall crime has dropped 50 percent since 1993, according to the New York City Police Department. There were just seven murders last year, compared with 23 in 1993.

In previous years, most of the victims were members of gangs with names like Red Top and Yellow Top, named for the color of the cap on the vials of crack they peddled. The shooting also claimed some innocent victims: 14-year-old Lamont Williams, killed while sitting on a park bench, and 9-year-old John Paul Valentine, wounded by crossfire on the way to school.[1]

Nationwide, crime began dropping in 1992. But nowhere has the drop been as dramatic as in New York City. Serious crimes as measured by the Federal Bureau of Investigation dropped 3 percent across the country in the first six months of 1996, compared with 1995. In New York City, the drop was 10.5 percent, according to the FBI.

New York's double-digit drops since Republican Mayor Rudolph W. Giuliani instituted a

Reprinted from Sarah Glazer, "Declining Crime Rates," *CQ Researcher*, April 4, 1997, courtesy of the *CQ Researcher*.

campaign against "quality-of-life" crimes have dwarfed national declines. Between 1993 and 1996 in New York City, murder dropped 49 percent and auto theft 47 percent, according to the NYPD.[2]

Explaining the Declining Crime Rates

Like Bloomfield, the experts also have their theories to explain the decreases. Some criminologists believe the nation's downward trend is largely driven by what's happening in New York City. Several other big cities—Los Angeles and Dallas among them—are also experiencing drops in crime, but none has been as fast or as large as New York's. The Big Apple accounted for nearly three-quarters of the nation's decrease in serious crimes in 1996.

New York City's police department has been quick to claim credit for the drops. "One of the reasons we've been able to decrease crime is a complete focus on minor crimes—quality-of-life crimes that drive people crazy," says department spokesman Lenny Alcivar. "Aggressive panhandling, people acting as doormen at the automatic teller machine (ATM), squeegee men at the intersection, graffiti, public urination—all these problems New Yorkers have been told they have to put up with are out the window."

The quality-of-life campaign launched by Giuliani and former Police Chief William Bratton embraced the "broken windows" theory put forward by criminologists James Q. Wilson and George L. Kelling in a 1982 *Atlantic Monthly* article. They argued that broken windows in a neighborhood convey the message that nobody is in charge. The sense of disorder becomes an invitation to delinquents to break more windows, causes citizens to abandon the streets and eventually leads to more serious crimes.

Until recently, it was common in New York to see unkempt men with styrofoam cups standing guard at night over isolated ATM lobbies. Some New Yorkers shrugged and went inside. But others, fearful of getting ripped off, were reluctant to enter. Now New York outlaws aggressive panhandling near ATM machines.

National Crime Rate Began Falling in 1992

The FBI's index of seven serious crimes more than doubled from 1960 to 1970, when today's middle-aged baby boomers were in their young, crime-prone years (graph). The index's rise slowed after the 1970s, and by 1992 the rate had begun dropping. From 1960 to 1995, rates for burglary and murder rose relatively slowly, while rape, robbery and assault at least quadrupled (table).

Number of offenses
(per 100,000 inhabitants)

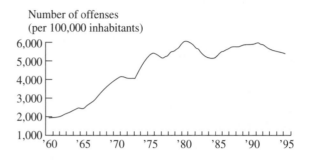

U.S. Crime Index, 1960–1995

	Murder	Forcible rape	Robbery	Aggrav. assault	Burglary	Larceny theft	Motor vehicle theft
1960	5.1	9.6	60.1	86.1	508.6	1,034.7	183.0
1962	4.6	9.4	59.7	88.6	535.2	1,124.8	197.4
1964	4.9	11.2	68.2	106.2	634.7	1,315.5	247.4
1966	5.6	13.2	80.8	120.3	721.0	1,442.9	286.9
1968	6.9	15.9	131.8	143.6	932.3	1,746.6	393.0
1970	7.9	18.7	172.1	164.8	1,084.9	2,079.3	456.8
1972	9.0	22.5	180.7	188.6	1,140.8	1,993.6	426.1
1974	9.8	26.2	209.3	215.8	1,437.7	2,489.5	462.2
1976	8.8	26.6	199.3	233.2	1,448.2	2,921.3	450.0
1978	9.0	31.0	195.8	262.1	1,434.6	2,747.4	460.5
1980	10.2	36.8	251.1	298.5	1,684.1	3,167.0	502.2
1982	9.1	34.0	238.9	289.2	1,466.8	3,084.8	458.8
1984	7.9	35.7	205.4	290.2	1,263.7	2,791.3	437.1
1986	8.6	37.9	225.1	346.1	1,344.6	3,010.3	507.8
1988	8.4	37.6	220.9	370.2	1,309.2	3,134.9	582.9
1990	9.4	41.2	257.0	424.1	1,235.9	3,194.8	657.8
1991	9.8	42.3	272.7	433.3	1,252.0	3,228.8	659.0
1992	9.3	42.8	263.6	441.8	1,168.2	3,103.0	631.5
1994	9.0	39.3	237.7	427.6	1,042.0	3,026.7	591.3
1995	8.2	37.1	220.9	416.3	987.6	3,044.9	560.5

Source: Federal Bureau of Investigation

"The notion is if you affect signs of crime and disorder, people feel more comfortable about using public spaces, and the opportunity for crime is less," says Deputy Police Commissioner Michael Farrell. The other dividend, he says, is a reduction in serious crimes. Stopping someone for a minor offense like aggressive panhandling or public drinking allows police to check outstanding warrants for other crimes, to frisk the individual and confiscate illegal guns.[3]

"We've had a reduction in the number of shootings and even in the number of gun arrests, although overall arrests have increased," Farrell says. "The fact that there are fewer gun charges means [suspects] are not carrying them. In the past, murders would be the result of spontaneous disputes. Shooting is way down."

Social Roots Versus Broken Windows

The declines have caught some experts by surprise. Andrew Karmen, a sociologist at John Jay College of Criminal Justice at the City University of New York, sees an "ideological war" surrounding the decreases: "One side is saying you can't bring crime to its lowest levels without attacking the social roots of crime: limited educational opportunities, poverty. The other side is saying you can suppress crime with tough police tactics, and you don't have to tackle poverty, discrimination and the schools."

Karmen says he's squarely on the side of the social-roots school. But he concedes that his skeptical investigation of New York's declining murder rate indicates the police "deserve some of the credit." He's found that gun-related murders began declining sharply in 1994 after Giuliani's approach had a year to work. He also found that a drop in killings in outdoor locations visible to officers on patrol accounts for most of the decline in murders.[4] The police department credits its strategy of saturating specific high-crime neighborhoods with police officers as another reason for sharp crime drops in neighborhoods like drug-infested Washington Heights, north of Harlem.

Assistant Manhattan District Attorney Walter M. Arsenault, who specializes in gang cases, has noticed fewer shootouts on the street and more murders in stairwells or elevators. "Mostly it's because police do patdown frisks, and people are not carrying their weapons out," he says. "We've had dozens of people say they're keeping their guns in their hubcaps or the sunroof of their cars. So they don't have the opportunity to reach in and start blasting. By the time they go get the gun, their heads may have cooled."

Kelling, who teaches at Rutgers University, believes New York–style approaches are helping to decrease crime in some other cities, though he says few cities have seen New York's drops in virtually all crimes and all precincts. In downtown Dallas, he says "order maintenance" along the lines he recommends has reduced serious crime 60 percent in a little over a year. But he adds, "Very few chiefs have been willing to push across the board like Bratton did."

One confirmed skeptic, criminology and sociology Professor Richard Moran of Mount Holyoke College, contends that a new factory does more to reduce crime in a bad neighborhood than anything police do. He believes New York's crime drops, like other cities', should be attributed to three broad social trends: an improving economy that sent thousands of idle, young men back to work; the winding down of the crack wars among gangs; and the increased incarceration of young criminals—at a rate that has almost doubled over the last 10 years.

"When you talk about new policing tactics [Giuliani and Bratton] have no scientific, solid evidence that what they did made a difference," Moran says. "They did a rain dance and it rained." He adds, "We have over 30 years of research that shows police tactics don't make any difference in the rates of crime."

Unfortunately, counters Kelling, "a lot of police adopted the Moran position as well: crime is caused by poverty, social injustice, racism. Ergo, police can't do anything about crime."

Now, however, the downward trend in crime has given police departments across the country new confidence that they can affect crime. As a vigorous debate continues over whether police action or social trends are more important in driving crime down, these are key questions being asked.

Fighting Crime by Busting "Squeegee" Men

In the late 1980s, "lawlessness reigned" in the subways of New York, according to Kelling.[5] In his 1996 book *Fixing Broken Windows,* he describes aggressive panhandlers demanding money from passengers, indigents sprawled full length on the seats and young people jumping the turnstiles without paying. During rush hour, intimidating youths stood at subway gates extorting money from confused passengers and creating general chaos. Petty crimes, robbery and felonies started a steep increase in 1987.

In April 1990, Bratton was recruited to lead the Transit Police Department. He started cracking down on fare beating, disorder and robbery. One development of arresting fare beaters was unexpected, writes Kelling, who was a consultant to the New York City Transit Authority during this period. One arrestee out of seven either had an outstanding warrant for a felony charge or was carrying an illegal weapon. Would-be robbers, it appeared, had been interrupted on the way to victimizing subway passengers. The increasing arrests of fare beaters brought crime down and, Kelling adds, police morale soared. (Felonies in the subway system are down by 80 percent since 1990.)[6]

The subway experience provided the "blueprint for restoring order on the streets of New York," Kelling writes, when Bratton was appointed police commissioner in early 1994 by the newly elected Giuliani.[7] Police began handing out summonses for minor offenses like urination and public drinking, which they had once routinely ignored, and made follow-up arrests for offenders who didn't show up in court.

The breakthrough in attacking quality-of-life crimes on city streets actually occurred under Bratton's predecessor as police commissioner, Raymond Kelly, according to Kelling. In 1993, in a highly publicized initiative, Kelly focused on the problem of the "squeegee" men.

Groups of these window-washers had taken to congregating at the entrances to tunnels and bridges where traffic was backed up. As Kelling recalls, some worked hard at washing windshields to earn money or retreated politely when drivers declined their services. But others had a more menacing style, spitting on the windshields of drivers who turned them down or draping themselves over the hoods of cars to prevent them from moving, even after traffic lights changed.

Obstructing traffic, the squeegeemen's main offense under the law, was a minor infraction punishable only by a fine or community service. Officers could not make arrests, they could only give out "Desk Appearance Tickets."

"Youths would sneer at [the officers] and say 'I've got plenty of these,'" Kelling recalls. Offenders generally failed to appear or pay their fines. They could be arrested for failure to appear, but warrants for non-appearance would generally disappear into a "black hole"—the warrant room of the police department—and were never served. Working with the Manhattan district attorney, the Transit Authority arranged to have warrants for non-appearance served by the officer who had written the squeegee ticket in the first place. Finally, officers could say to the squeegeemen, "You're going to jail tonight for not appearing." Within a few weeks, the squeegeeing epidemic died out.

According to Kelling, about half of the squeegeemen arrested had previous arrests for serious felonies like robbery, assault or carrying a gun, and almost half had arrests for drug-related offenses.

Kelling argues that stopping people for minor crimes actually prevents them from escalating to more serious crimes. "Once the word got out about squeegeeing, we didn't have to prosecute," he says. "This is to warn people, to alert people to set boundaries earlier. . . . We don't wait till they're committing violent crimes to intervene."

He also sees the order-maintenance strategy as sending a warning to young criminal "wannabees" who are getting the "wrong message" about how much society will look the other way. Creating more orderly neighborhoods, he argues, makes it possible for basic social institutions like families and schools to operate normally, thus attacking root causes of criminality.

"We've created an environment in which the streets are out of control," Kelling asserts. "Youths are in charge of the streets. There are kids carrying guns and joining gangs because they're afraid. This [get-tough strategy] is saying, 'Adults will control the streets.'"

Other Explanations for Declining Crime

Other criminologists are unconvinced. Mount Holyoke's Moran says it's mere coincidence that crime dropped as Giuliani mounted his quality-of-life campaign. Indeed, crime in some categories had started to turn down as early as 1989, four years before Giuliani took office.

The lively economy, increasing use of imprisonment and shriveling crack market have produced similar decreases in cities without the hoopla of New York City's creative policing, Moran argues.

He points out that East St. Louis, Ill., one of the nation's poorest cities, experienced an even sharper drop in murders than New York City—60 percent between 1991 and 1996. (New York City murders dropped 55 percent.) Yet East St. Louis introduced no new policing strategies during this period, according to Moran. Because of a budget crisis, the department often lacked enough gas to run all its police cars or keep its two-way radios in repair, he says.

Los Angeles, long the target of criticism for its slowness to shift from patrol-car-based military-style policing to community policing, also experienced a decrease in serious crimes last year—9 percent in the first six months of 1996 compared with the first six months of 1995, according to the FBI.[8]

"The most fuddy-duddy, old-fashioned police departments in the country are now able to claim that whatever they are doing is making crime drop," says Michael Tonry, a professor of law and public policy at the University of Minnesota, who strongly advocates attacking the social roots of crime in his 1995 book *Malign Neglect*.[9] "If you want to change crime rates, you have to get at underlying social and economic realities."

New York Police Department officials counter that East St. Louis is a poor comparison statistically. Because the number of murders involved is relatively small—it dropped from 67 in 1991 to 27 in 1996, Moran says—there could easily be questions about the margin of error, they say. (By comparison, New York City had more than 2,000 murders in 1991.)

Moreover, although New York's crime started to decline in 1991, it accelerated dramatically after Giuliani took over in 1993, moving into double-digit declines in every category and in every precinct, notes Deputy Commissioner Farrell. Most social trends, such as increased imprisonment, would have taken effect more gradually, he argues.

Other criminologists point to the maturing of drug markets over the last 10 years, arguing that a few remaining large players now dominate the market in big cities and do not have to resort to violence over turf.

But Farrell is not convinced by that explanation either. "We're unaware of any summit meeting where all these groups got together and said, 'We will stop fighting among ourselves' and carved up the territory," he says.

Maybe It's a Combination

In a recent op-ed column, New York University School of Law criminologist Jerome H. Skolnick asserted that "no social scientist, liberal or conservative, really knows the answer" to why crime is declining. He went on to suggest it could be a combination of New York–style quality-of-life policing and long-term social trends.[10]

"The argument that it's a matter of root causes and has nothing to do with policing is as silly as saying it's a matter of sanctions and has nothing to do with families and school and community," agrees Lawrence Sherman, chairman of the criminology department at the University of Maryland-College Park. "We've got to work on both."

Sherman argues that New York's most effective tactic has been getting guns off the street through its crackdown on minor violations. At the same time, he points to studies calculating that most of the nation's gun homicides are concentrated in areas where a majority of the residents live in single-parent households below the poverty line.

"I think it suggests, like AIDS prevention, [that we should] put most of the resources where the problem is concentrated," Sherman says, speaking both of increased police and social programs. "We have proven programs of early-infancy home visitation, preschool Head Start with parental involvement. If we were to concentrate these expensive but effective programs in neighborhoods with high concentrations of poverty and gun violence—both the criminal justice side and social service side working together—we'll get both a short- and long-term payoff in terms of lower levels of gun violence in America."

Where Have All the Homeless Gone?

Investment banker Andrew M. Silberstein, 29, expresses pleasure mixed with moral pangs over New York's recent improvements. "It's a different city. I feel safe walking the streets now," he says. "But I can't help wondering: What have they done with all the homeless people?"

According to Norman Siegel, executive director of the New York Civil Liberties Union (ACLU), the homeless have simply moved to less visible parts of the city where police are less likely to hassle them. A recent *New York Times* account described homeless people who now sleep at the New Jersey end of the Lincoln Tunnel. Squeegee cleaners and panhandlers, who have dwindled markedly in Manhattan, now approach commuters in Newark.[11]

New York's police have "won the war on squeegeeing and panhandling, but I'm not sure they've won much," Siegel says. "They haven't addressed the underlying issue of why we have people living out on the streets."

During the police department's war on squeegeemen, Siegel says he suggested that Bratton gather the men in a midtown hotel room and offer them jobs in lieu of tickets. But Kelling says viewing these men as "homeless" was a misnomer. During a 60-day experiment, the city discovered that approximately three-quarters of the men resided at legitimate addresses, and half had criminal records. Because of their criminal back-grounds, he argues, squeegeers "were not merely a troubled population, they were capable of considerable mayhem."[12]

"To say we can't enforce the law because we don't have a solution to poverty is ridiculous," argues Deputy Commissioner Farrell. "Squeegeemen are stopping and interfering with traffic. It may be helpful to get them into the mainstream of society and get them employment and so on, but that's not what we're set up to do." He adds, "We're not clear on how to eliminate poverty. Frankly, it's not particularly productive for a police agency to pretend that it's able to solve these problems."

Civilian complaints of police abuse have risen about 50 percent since the start of Giuliani's administration, Siegel notes, and he says he personally gets calls about police hassling minorities and young people. Farrell counters that the increase in complaints has been minimal viewed in the context of the increasing number of arrests and summonses by New York City's enlarged police force, which grew from about 25,000 to 38,000 officers between 1990 and 1996.

But the new attack on minor offenses has created tension between the police and minority communities, Siegel contends. Officers targeted drivers in predominantly black Harlem in summer 1995, Siegel says, pulling over drivers for changing lanes without signaling as a pretext for stop-and-frisks. "I didn't know we had lanes in Manhattan," Siegel comments dryly in a reference to New York's predominantly two-lane streets.

Yet Siegel concedes that Giuliani's crime-fighting efforts have been enormously popular. In TV appearances, Siegel has offered to represent citizens who want to mount a constitutional challenge to the increased police searches, but he says no one has stepped forward claiming their rights were violated.

Has Crime Peaked?

A majority of Americans don't believe that crime is going down, but most criminologists say the trend is real. If anything, crime statistics have been getting more accurate in recent years.

The question that divides experts is whether the

downward trend can be sustained or whether new crime spikes hover in the future. Many criminologists attribute the current lull in crime to the small proportion of young men now in their crime-prone years—currently at its lowest point since 1980. Traditionally, the peak age for committing violent crime is 17. Today's baby boomers, born between 1947 and 1964, were 16–33 in 1980, when crime hit a peak. Now they are 33–50, the years when the focus is on raising families not sowing wild oats.

James Alan Fox, a professor at Northeastern University's College of Criminal Justice in Boston, sees a new threat on the horizon as baby boomers' children—an "echo boom"—reach the prime years for criminality over the next 10 years. He has warned against a future juvenile crime wave so bad that "we will look back at the '90s and call them the good old days."[13]

Even as crime rates among adults have been dropping, violent crime rates among youths have been increasing exponentially, and younger teens have become more involved in gun violence. Since 1985, the rate of homicides committed by adults 25 and older declined 25 percent as the baby boomers matured. At the same time, the homicide rate among 18- to 24-year-olds increased 61 percent. Among younger teens 14 to 17, the rate of homicide more than doubled.[14]

Ironically, Fox had predicted in 1978 that crime would drop in the late 1980s as the traditionally crime-prone group of boomers aged and the number of teens declined.[15] Instead crime rose to a new peak. What he hadn't counted on, he now says, was an unprecedented rate of violence among teens—and increasingly younger teens—even though they were dwindling as a proportion of the population.

"What happened in 1986 is teens started picking up guns and shooting one another in record numbers," Fox says. "While historically 15- to 16-year-olds rarely committed homicides, that has all changed. A lot of that has to do with the crack market. It included a larger number of teens in the drug-selling business, and they had to protect themselves with guns."

Arrest rates show that 14- to 17-year-olds have now surpassed 18- to 24-year-olds in violent crimes like murder, rape and robbery. Even if the per-capita rate of teen homicide remains the same, the number of 14- to 17-year-olds who commit murder will increase from 4,000 now to nearly 5,000 annually in 2005 because of population growth alone, Fox predicts.[16]

In 1996, the Justice Department announced that the violent-crime rate among juveniles 10–17 had turned down slightly for the first time in seven years. The announcement raised questions about Fox's dire predictions. The decline was 4 percent from 1994–95.[17]

Fox dismisses the downturn with the comment, "We're having a warm day in December, and people think spring is here." He points to worsening social indicators—millions of children living in poverty and a growing percentage of teens without parental supervision during after-school hours, when most juvenile crime is committed.

"If anything, I believe juvenile crime has plateaued," he says. "Even if we stay at the same rate [of crime] we have now, the future expansion of the teenage population would mean more crime. What I can say for sure is we'll have more kids at risk. Whether these kids commit more muggings and murders partly depends on us—whether we invest in the next generation of teenagers."

Alfred Blumstein, a professor of urban systems at Carnegie Mellon University, is skeptical of Fox's predictions. He calculates the population of young men at crime-prone ages will be increasing at a rate of only about 1 percent a year. "Certainly a demographic story of 1 percent a year shouldn't give us a blood bath," he says, especially if policing and social conditions improve.

Fox concedes that teen growth over the next 10 years does not look that dramatic compared with the baby boomer bulge. But he sees the danger concentrated in the growing numbers of at-risk black children. White baby boomers have had fewer children or had them later than demographers predicted, so growth in the white teen population is going to be modest. "But growth in the black teen population will be much sharper," he says. "Black teens have 10 times the rate of violence of white teens. If you have a disproportionate growth among black teens, you will have a disproportionate impact on the crime problem."

According to the U.S. Census, 46 percent of black teenagers live below the federal poverty level. Criminologists like Fox expect that number to increase. Studies show a strong correlation between living in poverty and entering a life of crime.[18]

The Super-Predators

John J. DiIulio Jr., a professor of politics and public affairs at Princeton University, joins Fox in predicting a ticking demographic time bomb among young, mostly male criminals he dubs "super-predators."

In a recent interview, he describes them as a "small fraction of kids who are simply surrounded by deviant, delinquent, criminal adults in fatherless, godless and jobless settings. . . . They are remorseless, radically present-oriented and radically self-regarding." An important predictor for the future, he says, is the rising rate of child abuse and neglect, which increases the chances of delinquency by 40 percent. While the super-predators may be a small percentage of delinquents, he says, the "most radically impulsive and violent kids tend to be the ones who are leading the more than 200,000 kids who are organized into gangs in this country today."[19]

But the University of Minnesota's Tonry says he has been skeptical of the predictions of a youth crime wave from the beginning. "In the long term, this country has been becoming a more socially and culturally conservative country with greater concerns about personal responsibility for 20 years," he asserts, "and it's been showing up in [decreasing] crime."

While it's true, for example, that the proportion of children born out of wedlock to teens has been rising, Tonry notes, the fertility rate of teens has been declining, yielding a smaller overall number of such children. Having an unmarried, teenage mother is another social factor that has been correlated with criminality.

Other experts agree with Tonry that "demogra-phy isn't destiny." One factor that could make a difference for the better in the future is the declining popularity of crack among 18- to 21-year-olds, Karmen notes. Heroin may be replacing crack among some young users, but street experts suggest heroin users are slower to commit crimes and less violent under the sedating influence of heroin than crack addicts.

Another major factor is the extent of gun carrying among juveniles. Boston and several other cities have been working to reduce the glamour of owning a gun by cracking down on concealed weapons and traffickers. In Charleston, police have offered a bounty of $100 for any report of an illegal gun, which tends to discourage youngsters from brandishing guns in public, Blumstein notes.

"The hula hoop went out, and maybe gun carrying is going to go out," the University of Maryland's Sherman suggests. "If that happens, we're not going to see a blood bath."

"Changes in values among young people" could be explaining the downturn in crime we're starting to see, Karmen says, as AIDS and inner-city funerals bring home the price of drug use and gang involvement. "Young people are learning that life in the fast lane of drugs and gangs is counterproductive." Perhaps, says Karmen, "They've learned from older brothers and sisters and decided not to take that road."

NOTES

1. David Kocieniewski, "Nasty Boys," *Newsday,* June 23, 1994, p. A04, and Lizette Alvarez, "Police Patrols to Increase where Child was Shot," *The New York Times,* Jan. 25, 1996, p. B4. See "Youth Gangs," *The CQ Researcher,* Oct. 11, 1991, pp. 753–776.

2. Clifford Krauss, "Reported Crimes Continue to Show Decline," *The New York Times,* Oct. 2, 1996, p. B3; Office of the Mayor, press release, Dec. 31, 1996. The reductions cited in murder, robbery and auto theft in New York are based on New York City statistics for 1996. Michael Cooper, "Crime Reports Drop Sharply in New York," *The New York Times,* April 1, 1997, p. B1.

3. See "Gun Control," *The CQ Researcher,* June 10, 1994, pp. 505–528.

4. Andrew Karmen, "Why is New York City's Murder Rate Dropping so Sharply?" unpublished paper, October 1996, p. 1.

5. George L. Kelling and Catherine M. Coles, *Fixing Broken Windows* (1996), p. 117.

6. George Kelling, "Restore Order and You Reduce Crime," *The Washington Post,* Feb. 9, 1997, p. C3.

7. Kelling and Coles, *op. cit.,* p. 137.

8. See "Community Policing," *The CQ Researcher,* Feb. 5, 1993, pp. 97–120.

9. Michael Tonry, *Malign Neglect* (1995).

10. Jerome H. Skolnick, "Making Sense of the Crime Decline," *Newsday,* Feb. 2, 1997.

11. Evelyn Nieves, "Chased Out of New York Into a Hole," *The New York Times,* March 13, 1997, p. B1.

12. *Ibid.,* p. 143.

13. Quoted in Rebecca Carr, "Crime," *Congressional Quarterly Weekly Report,* Oct. 5, 1996, p. 2810.

14. James Alan Fox, *Trends in Juvenile Violence: A Report to the United States Attorney General on Current and Future Rates of Juvenile Offending,* March 1996. Prepared for the Bureau of Justice Statistics, U.S. Department of Justice, pp. 1–2.

15. James Alan Fox, *Forecasting Crime Data* (1978).

16. Fox, *Trends in Juvenile Violence, op. cit.,* pp. 1–3.

17. Roberto Suro, "Violent Crime Drops Among Young Teens," *The Washington Post,* Dec. 13, 1996, p. A1.

18. Carr, *op. cit.*

19. Quoted in Michael Cromartie, "Kids Who Kill," *Books and Culture,* January/February 1997, p. 10. The magazine reviews books and ideas from an evangelical Christian point of view.

READING 10
HIGH-TECH CROOKS

Dennis McCauley

Across the country, a new class of high-tech criminals is emerging. Dennis McCauley, a veteran police supervisor and a member of the High-Technology Crime Investigation Association, explores the efforts of law enforcement as it adapts to the demands of the digital age.

Ken Rosenblatt is a deputy district attorney in Santa Clara County, Calif., in the heart of Silicon Valley. He spent four years in charge of his office's High-Technology Unit and is the author of "High-Technology Crime: Investigating Cases Involving Computers," a well-regarded reference work on the topic. Rosenblatt sees the outright theft of high-tech gadgets as a major issue for all levels of law enforcement.

"The biggest concern for the front-line officer is component theft, either by burglary or robbery," said Rosenblatt. This includes memory chips, microprocessor chips, disk drives and computer systems.

"It's a crime that's costing billions in losses throughout the world," he pointed out. "Almost every jurisdiction in the United States has some sort of high-technology business, whether it's the store selling high-tech items or the factory creating them. Officers have to recognize components and know when to suspect they're stolen if they find them during a routine traffic stop. In terms of

Reprinted from Dennis McCauley, "Hi-Tech Crooks," *Police*, vol. 20, December 12, 1996, by permission of *Police* magazine, Bobit Publishing, Torrance, California.

community policing, they also have to be aware of how to prepare their local high-tech businesses to withstand both employee pilferage and robbery."

High-tech bandits can be dangerous, Rosenblatt cautions.

"People come in with guns, take over businesses and clean them out of their high-technology inventory. That started in California and now is a worldwide phenomenon," said Rosenblatt.

Although variable according to demand, Random Access Memory (RAM) and Pentium microprocessor chips were both popular targets at press time.

"The reason they're so hot," Rosenblatt explained, "is that they're very small. You could easily steal $100,000 worth of chips in a pizza box. They are virtually untraceable, and they're easy to sell because there is a large gray market for components."

Rosenblatt advised officers to make an effort to acquaint themselves with the types of companies located on their beats.

"If there are high-technology businesses, think of them as targets, just as you would think of liquor stores as targets. Be very aware of suspicious vehicles casing companies," warned Rosenblatt. "There is a lot of intelligence that goes on before a robbery is committed. These thieves are tactically organized. They are often ex-military. They don't smash and grab. They run military-style operations. Any officer who thinks one of those is going on should get backup and treat it with extreme caution."

High-tech robberies don't just take place at businesses. With security-conscious companies conducting target-hardening at production facilities and offices, thieves are gravitating to the more vulnerable transit points. Truck hijackings and airport thefts are becoming increasingly common methods of illegally obtaining high-tech components.

Suffer the Children

One of the more repulsive crimes of the computer age is the proliferation of child pornography on the Internet. Low-cost technology has proved a boon to those who sexually victimize children. Readily available scanning equipment converts photos into computer graphics, while electronic mail transmits digital images anywhere in the world. Data encryption and anonymous e-mail services make enforcement more difficult.

Law enforcement, however, is fighting back with dedicated investigators like New Jersey State Trooper Mike Geraghty leading the charge. A true cybercop, the 10-year veteran has worked the computer beat since 1992. Currently, he is one of two full-time computer crime investigators working out of the NJSP's Criminal Investigation Section in West Trenton.

Geraghty, who had an off-duty interest in computers, was inspired to tackle computer crime after reading "The Cuckoo's Egg." The 1989 book detailed computer scientist Cliff Stoll's difficulties in getting the criminal justice system to respond to an East German hacker who was breaking into classified systems in the United States. The book led Geraghty to suggest that his agency needed the capability to respond to computer crime. Today, he is deeply immersed in this new aspect of his job.

Most of his investigations involve child pornography transmitted via the Internet and commercial online services. Because of the global nature of cyberspace, Geraghty's work often extends far beyond state lines. He's even traveled to foreign countries to testify about multijurisdictional child pornography investigations he's participated in.

Like Geraghty, Kevin Manson is deeply concerned about the sexual exploitation of kids on the Internet. Manson is a long-time instructor in computer crime investigations who operates cybercop@org, a nonprofit group devoted to interagency cooperation and information sharing about computer crime issues. Manson, whose organization can be accessed via the World Wide Web at http://www.well.com/user/kfarrand/index.htm, has testified before Congress on ways to protect children who use the Internet. He believes the frequent media reports of underage sexual abuse in cyberspace are not the result of sensationalism by the media. He believes it's really happening. "It is very high profile and rightly so," Manson said. "The Internet empowers the individuals that have been doing child pornography. It used to be that they could do it in their own neighborhood. Now they can literally reach across the country or across the globe and recruit children. It gives them much more power than they used to have. Regardless of the numbers, they now have a greater opportunity to commit their crime than they had in the past."

Fortunately for law enforcement, however, many of the areas that are accessible to online perverts can be monitored by police as well. These include public chat rooms where pedophiles have been known to recruit young victims.

Scams on the Net

In many ways, the Internet is a microcosm of society, full of good and bad inhabitants—right down to the presence of scam artists who prey on unsuspecting victims. Jeff Janacek, an investigator with the Minnesota Attorney General's Office, has taken the initiative in battling online fraud.

A few years ago Janacek logged onto America Online (AOL). With over 5 million subscribers, AOL is the largest commercial online service in the world. Browsing through the classified ads in the business opportunities section, Janacek was troubled by what he found.

"There was just an incredible amount of fraud," Janacek said. "I approached my supervisors and suggested we do some cases on it. This was straight-up fraud, with people advertising things they couldn't deliver. Even some of the things they were offering were illegal."

By way of example, Janacek cited a scam that sold information on how to mail first-class letters for two cents each. Janacek also hunted down sports gambling and health care fraud cases. A true modern cybercop, information on each of Janacek's fraud cases can be viewed on the World Wide Web at http://www.state.mn.us/ebranch/ag.

The growth of the Internet in recent years has been so explosive that Janacek sometimes found working with management of the online services difficult. The companies were willing to help but seemed snowed under by the volume, even when subpoenas were issued. Another concern is the position adopted by the services regarding questionable ads. Management generally refused to screen the offerings, fearing that if they did so, they could be held liable for any bogus offerings that slipped through. This laissez-faire approach continues to provide a window of opportunity for scam artists, making online commerce strictly a buyer-beware proposition.

Can You Hack It?

For many, the phrase computer crime conjures up images of clever teenagers like Matthew Broderick's character in the movie "War Games." The reality is quite different. Although hackers generally receive less publicity than in years past, most experts believe that computer intruders are as active as ever.

"One of the reasons that you don't hear about it," commented Janacek, "is that nobody publicizes what happens when the hackers penetrate a system. This is happening on a fairly routine basis to a lot of companies—it's just that they never tell anyone. They don't even take them to court criminally, in most cases, because they don't want the publicity. They don't want to look like fools."

Mike Geraghty agrees that the hackers are still around and scoffs at the popular notion that they are intellectually gifted.

"There are very few hackers who are technically brilliant," the New Jersey trooper said. "There are a lot of copycats out there and a lot of wannabes. Instead of just intellectual curiosity,

they're hacking maliciously and stealing credit card numbers."

Time is of the essence when hackers strike, Ken Rosenblatt pointed out. Having an organizational game plan ready ahead of time is critical.

"The police should be organized internally so there's one person responsible for dealing with computer intrusion problems," Rosenblatt recommended.

"Even the smallest police department can have a designated officer whose function is to call someone regionally. Anyone who receives a report of computer intrusion should bump it upstairs to a detective immediately. Speed is critical. If you're going to catch someone breaking into a computer, you're going to need to get multiple court orders to trace the intrusion, and you need them quickly."

Drop That Keyboard

Okay, so you've made the arrest, and now you're faced with an unfamiliar piece of evidence—a computer. If it was a smoking 9 mm or a bag of rock cocaine, you'd know how to handle it, but now you're scratching your head.

It's probably time to call for an expert. In virtually every case that may involve the seizure of a computer, officers who lack specific expertise should turn to those trained to the task, such as Geraghty.

"Just like any crime scene, don't touch any evidence," Geraghty warned. "One keystroke, and it all can be gone. If you do a good job recovering computer evidence, one case can lead you to 10, 20 or 100 other cases, especially with kiddie porn since there are usually links to who they're receiving it from or sending it to. It just snowballs from there."

"Computer evidence is something that frontline officers are confronting every day," Kevin Manson added. "Often they're not equipped to deal with it. That's a serious problem. If you handle a computer without knowing what you're doing, some very bad things can happen. First, you can damage the computer and lose your evidence. Second, you can get sued. Third, there are some obscure but important federal privacy laws that may interfere with your ability to look in that computer at all."

"Officers need to get training," Manson emphasized. "It is not enough for officers to be avid computer users. The skills required are different. It's much more like being an evidence technician."

Manson advises officers who need help with a computer investigation to contact the largest jurisdiction in their area or the regional chapter of the High Technology Crime Investigation Association (HTCIA). Larger agencies generally either have a dedicated computer crime unit or access to one. With more than 800 members nationwide, the HTCIA can be an invaluable resource in high-tech cases.

Manson, who also recommends the computer crime investigation course offerings at the Federal Law Enforcement Training Center (FLETC) in Glynco, Ga., believes that law enforcement can use the Internet as a training tool as well.

"One of the great difficulties right now is that a lot of agencies are short on travel money and training money. As law enforcement officers become more familiar with communicating online, that's going to become a very valuable place for them to learn. I would encourage those officers that do not have an Internet account to get one. I can't emphasize that enough. There are a lot of good opportunities out there for us to communicate."

It's for You

The cellular phone is fast becoming one of the most popular tools in the law enforcement arsenal. Unfortunately, it's also favored by a cross section of criminals who account for the rapid rise in cellular fraud in the last five years.

Dennis Walters, director of Risk Management for Comcast Cellular Communications in Wayne, Pa., spent 21 years in local and federal law enforcement before entering the private sector. These days he puts his experience to work battling the many faces of cellular phone fraud.

"The most significant issue right now is the ability to clone someone else's phone," Walters said, explaining that every cellular phone emits a unique mobile identification number (MIN) and an electronic serial number (ESN).

"It's possible to capture the ESN/MIN information out of the airwaves," he continued. "Then, using black-market devices, criminals counterfeit that information into another phone so that someone is able to use the cloned version. The legitimate customer ends up getting the bill, typically for a significant amount of air time until the cloned phone is detected."

Crooks use scanning devices called ESN readers to monitor the airwaves and capture MIN and ESN combinations, which can then be programmed into another phone. Cloners typically position themselves near high-density locations such as highways or airport terminals where there's likely to be plenty of cellular phone chatter. Although it varies by jurisdiction, many states have made having an ESN reader for unlawful purposes a crime in itself.

The boom in cloning has had an unfortunate ripple effect, generating supporting crimes.

"Theft is becoming a huge issue," said Walters. "Cloners need access to other phones to program. The theft of cellular phones has become a cottage industry. Some people do nothing but steal phones and sell them to the cloning operations. Other individuals do nothing but harvest numbers out of the air and sell them to cloners."

Who are the end users of cloned phones? The answer might surprise you.

"It started out being principally drug dealers," said Walters. "But today, it's become attractive to all sections of the community—people who are doing business with their cellular phones and want to avoid the cost, college students, over-the-road truck drivers—virtually all sectors of the community are buying cloned phones now."

Amazingly, cloning has become so prevalent that the prices have come down and the bad guys are giving warranties, Walters explained.

"The average price to have a phone cloned is anywhere from $60–100 per month. Typically, the cloner guarantees 30 days of service. If the carrier or the customer detects that phone and it's shut down before the 30 days are up, you bring it back and they reprogram another number for free."

There are obvious clues to cloned phones that street officers can look for.

"One is the phone itself," Walters explained. "Does the suspect know the phone number?"

Walters also advises officers to look at the phone when it's activated, since some phones are programmed to distant carriers if their local carriers require PIN numbers.

"If it's in roaming mode and the person is local, that's an immediate clue to an officer that there's reason to follow up on the questioning. There's no likely reason to have a phone that's programmed to an out-of-market number."

Cloners often unwittingly assist law enforcement by leaving trademarks on cloned phones—usually a sticker inside the battery case with their symbol and the date the phone was reprogrammed. This helps them keep their warranties straight and helps officers identify illegal phones.

Walters cautions officers who seize cellular phones that they are considered computers under the law for purposes of accessing data stored within. Either the consent of the suspect or a search warrant is required to extract this information.

In general, cooperation between cellular phone carriers and law enforcement is at an all-time high. The companies are losing substantial revenue to fraud and are eager to build working relationships with police agencies. Often they're willing to provide training since they realize many officers have only a vague notion of cellular fraud and how it occurs.

Keeping Current

As we approach the millennium, one thing's for certain: Crooks and their gadgets are getting increasingly more sophisticated. As protectors of society, it's our responsibility to ensure we don't lag behind. Of course, violent street crime remains the top priority for most officers, as it should be. But with drug dealers, pedophiles and average street hoodlums going high-tech, it's no longer a question of chasing down nerdy hackers with overactive computer glands. Today, police officers must take advantage of training opportunities and develop an awareness of the enemy's high-tech tools and know how to defeat them.

DISCUSSION QUESTIONS

1. How do the media affect public perception of the crime rate and the incidence of violent crime in particular? Support or dispute the argument that increased use of community policing models can present more accurate views of crime than might be found in the media.

2. Rapid changes in technology make even comparatively recent information seem a few steps behind the times. What are some of the current crime problems associated with cyberspace and cellular phone technology (and any other high-tech areas with which you are familiar), and how do you think law enforcement should respond to these crimes? Should all police officers be trained to respond to high-tech crime, or should it be sufficient to assign just a few officers to a special unit? Explain your answer.

WEBSITES

www.fbi.gov/ucrpress.htm
Statistics in the Uniform Crime Reports can be reviewed at this site.
www.state.mn.us/ebranch/ag
This site, mentioned in McCauley's article, provides information about fraud cases on the Internet.
www.well.com/user/kfarrand/index.htm
Also mentioned in the McCauley article, this is the home page for a nonprofit group devoted to sharing information about computer crime.

CHAPTER 6: POLICE ISSUES

Some police officers have cynically suggested that "everyone hates cops—until they need one." While people in many occupations have more than their share of bad press (Heard any lawyer jokes recently?), police activities seem to make the headlines more often for negative than positive reasons. Despite police work in public education (e.g., Neighborhood Watch programs, self-defense training, D.A.R.E. classes), community support (e.g., police-sponsored athletic programs), and outright charitable activities (e.g., food drives and Christmas toy repair and delivery programs), the lead media stories are more likely to be about police brutality, corruption, racism, and favoritism.

Realistically, it cannot be in the best interest of any society to accept, without question or monitoring, the activities of those fellow citizens who have been assigned to maintain the social order. But it also seems that judgment of others' actions is best made with an understanding of the conditions and situations influencing those actions. As you can imagine, these issues deserve and receive considerable attention from police officials, politicians, academic researchers, policy makers, and the media. Our intent is to provide examples of both the conditions of police work and the problem of police misconduct.

One of the more enduring and troubling issues related to policing is the problem of police misconduct, ranging from accepting "freebies" like cups of coffee while on duty to instances of brutality and racism. In her article on police corruption, Sarah Glazer addresses the most serious categories of misconduct as she reports examples of brutality and racism in police departments. Of particular interest in this reading is Glazer's review of such techniques as community policing and civilian review boards, which law enforcement experts believe offer the most promising responses to police misconduct.

In her reading, Glazer asks whether police work breeds misconduct. Though many departments have a few officers who account for most complaints of misconduct, the climate set by other officers and by supervisors can either encourage or discourage that misconduct. The reading by Sam Quiñones reminds us that police misconduct is not limited to U.S. departments, forcing us to examine the inherent nature of police work—in any country—that may result in some officers engaging in corrupt activities.

The article by Marcus Laffey presents one police officer's view of the job. Nothing that he says, or that any other officer could say, can excuse the police misconduct that is discussed in the two following articles. However, it is important for citizens to be aware of how a "good cop" approaches police work. You may not always agree with the ways Laffey handles the situations he describes, but the reading should give you an appreciation of the frustrations and joys of being a cop. As you read Laffey's "diary," think about how the situations police officers deal with might affect their views about people.

READING 11
POLICE CORRUPTION

Sarah Glazer

In years past, police corruption typically took the form of bribery, but today it's often brutality or extortion—with innocent citizens the victims. Some experts contend that anticrime fervor has unleashed police without accountability to citizens. Others blame low pay and the lure of drug money. Police departments are experimenting with ways to reduce corruption. Sarah Glazer is a freelance writer in New York who specializes in social policy and health issues.

The Rodney King beating. Mark Fuhrman's racism. New Orleans policewoman and convicted murderer Antoinette Frank. Renegade cops in New York, Philadelphia and other cities. The 1990s have not been good years for law enforcement.

In fact, when future historians look back, 1995 will likely be viewed as the year that police misconduct reemerged as a major issue.

Americans could hardly ignore it. During the O.J. Simpson double-murder trial, television brought retired Los Angeles detective Fuhrman into the living rooms of millions. In taped interviews, Fuhrman repeatedly used the epithet "nigger" and boasted that he had beaten two suspects.

"We basically tortured them. . . . Their faces were just mush," he told a would-be screenwriter.[1]

Fuhrman's conversations inevitably recalled

Reprinted from Sarah Glazer, "Police Corruption: Can Brutality and Other Misconduct Be Rooted Out?" *CQ Researcher*, November 24, 1995, courtesy of the *CQ Researcher*.

the videotaped 1991 beating of King by four L.A. cops and prompted many Americans to ask once again: "Is this what cops are really like?"

"For many people in black neighborhoods, none of this is new," says Philadelphia City Council member Michael A. Nutter.

It remains unclear whether Fuhrman's tales of mayhem were empty boasts or true confessions. But his repeated use of "the N-word" was enough to give new credibility to long-standing complaints by citizens of police misconduct:

• In Philadelphia, more than 50 criminal cases have been thrown out of court [in 1995] involving arrests made by six renegade officers, and 1,400 cases are under review. The officers routinely abused career criminals and innocent citizens alike and have pleaded guilty to charges including robbery, obstruction of justice and civil rights violations, mostly against poor, black citizens.[2]

• In Atlanta, seven police officers [were] arrested [in 1995] on charges including stealing money during drug searches and extorting money from citizens in exchange for police protection. The arrests followed a two-year undercover operation aided by local and federal law enforcement agents.[3]

• In New Orleans, dozens of officers have been arrested since 1992 on charges that include murder, rape, drug dealing, bank robbery and auto theft. Frank was convicted of murdering a fellow police officer and two Vietnamese restaurant workers while she participated in the robbery of the family's restaurant. She was sentenced to death by lethal injection.

• In New York City, 16 officers implicated in a scandal that broke in 1994 in Harlem have pleaded guilty to charges including stealing cash from drug dealers, extortion of money from suspects and lying about arrests.

Some Causes of Police Misconduct

Historically, police corruption has been identified with bribery, where cops accepted money from gangsters or small-time criminals to overlook their offenses. But Mark H. Moore, professor of criminal justice at Harvard University's John F. Kennedy School of Government, says today's brand of corruption generally involves abuse of criminal suspects rather than collusion with them.

He blames the new trend on the harsh anticrime, punish-the-criminal rhetoric that has swept the nation recently. "The society as a whole is ambivalent about the use of excess force and extralegal justice," he observes. Police officers are operating "within the public's ambivalence" when they beat up a suspect, extort money or lie about an arrest in an attempt to get a conviction.

The idea that the "solution to the crime problem is to unleash the police is gaining ascendancy, and that's very dangerous," says Moore, if police are not held accountable for their actions. Drugs weave another thread into the latest scandals. "There's so much money—and the temptations are so prevalent—it's a wonder more cops aren't corrupt," says Samuel Walker, a criminal justice professor at the University of Nebraska, Omaha.

Harvey Schlossberg, a former director of psychological services for the New York City Police Department, says the problem is exacerbated by police officers' frustration over laws aimed at protecting the rights of criminal suspects: "When police see dealers with $300,000 in the back seat of their car and know that if they arrest them the court's going to turn them out anyway, it may seem a better form of justice to hit them in the pocketbook and take their money—especially if the policeman has a big mortgage."

But the root causes can be traced to a police department's failure to set high standards in hiring, training and supervision, says Neil Gallagher, who directed the FBI's undercover investigation of New Orleans' notoriously low-paid police. "When you put the lure of illegal profits from drugs before underpaid, ill-trained, poorly supervised officers," it became a recipe for corruption, says Gallagher, deputy assistant director in the bureau's Criminal Investigative Division.

Civil rights activists express frustration that it takes a Rodney King or Mark Fuhrman to focus public attention on police brutality.

The Christopher Commission, a blue ribbon panel appointed in the wake of the King incident, blamed the police department's failure to control brutal officers as the "heart of the problem." It issued over 100 recommendations ranging from tighter supervision and better screening of job applicants to racial sensitivity training.

But citizen activists say there's been little change in how police departments in Los Angeles—or elsewhere—do business since King was beaten after a high-speed chase. Of the 44 problem officers identified by the Christopher Commission for the high number of citizen complaints filed against them, 31 remain on the force.

"We think the response we saw nationwide to Rodney King is not unlike those to the Fuhrman tapes: namely, 'It can't happen here' from too many civic officials—that it 'only happens in L.A.' We think that's naive," says John M. Crew, director of the police practices project of the American Civil Liberties Union of Northern California.

"There's a tendency to get defensive and circle the wagons," Crew says. "There needs to be more than just words. There needs to be follow-through. If you look at the Christopher Commission report, most people would be shocked at how few of those recommendations have been implemented."

Tallahassee, Fla., Assistant Police Chief Walt McNeil likens the Fuhrman tapes, with their outspoken racism, to the 1963 news photos of police dogs attacking civil rights marchers in Birmingham, Ala.

"I think what has happened recently . . . validates the belief of a substantial number of

African-Americans that police are, in fact, not a part of the American democratic process, here to insure our liberties, but are part of the oppressive nature of the capitalist system," says McNeil. "If police organizations are going to succeed in changing this combative friction," McNeil warns, "chiefs are going to have to take a strong position in opposition to any form of racism. If we don't do that, this issue of distrust and friction will continue to fester, much like it did on the streets of L.A. with Rodney King."

While police officers say they've run across Fuhrman types before, they say he's not representative of most police officers. "In most police departments, there's a subculture of brutal cops. They find each other and form their own fraternity, which aids and supports all of their activities," says Bob Stewart, police chief in Ormond Beach, Fla., and an African-American.

That makes the message sent by those in the top ranks all the more important. "You have to create organizations that don't tolerate these sorts of behaviors," says Dennis Kenney, research director of the Police Executive Research Forum in Washington. D.C., which represents police chiefs.

The Los Angeles Police Department (LAPD) failed that test, according to the authors of a 1993 book on police brutality, who note that more than 20 LAPD officers witnessed the Rodney King beating. "Two cops can go berserk," they write, "but 20 cops embody a subculture of policing."[4]

As police officials, lawmakers and citizens wrestle with law enforcement problems, these are some of the questions being asked:

Does Police Work Breed Misconduct?

For decades, law enforcement officials have blamed instances of police corruption and brutality on a "few bad apples."[5]

"Overall, I think police agencies do a good job, but [officers] are going to fall through the cracks as Fuhrman did," says John Whetsel, police chief in Choctaw, Okla., and president of the Alexandria, Va.-based International Association of Chiefs of Police. "The only solution would be to do policing without using human beings. Unfortunately, we do use human beings, who reflect and come from the pool of citizens we serve."

But recently some criminologists have been arguing that in many cases the "barrel" is rotten—that individual police departments perpetuate a culture that either encourages or tolerates police misbehavior.

"Anyone who's read the Christopher Commission report is not the least bit surprised by the Fuhrman tapes," says criminologist Walker, co-author of *The Color of Justice,* a book on racial discrimination in the criminal justice system.[6] "The commission found evidence of a subculture that tolerated racist statements and failed to discipline officers guilty of misconduct.

"Fuhrman is an extreme case, but the important point is . . . he was never disciplined. Yes, he's a particularly rotten apple, but the management failure allowed the whole department to sink to a lower level than it should have."

Several studies of individual police departments have found that a few officers tend to be responsible for a high proportion of shootings, citizen suits or complaints of brutality.[7]

The Christopher Commission found that 10 percent of LAPD officers accounted for 28 percent of the complaints of excessive force or improper tactics from 1986–1990. Out of the 8,000-member force, citizen complaints of excessive force were filed against 1,800 officers. Over 1,400 had only one or two complaints against them. But 183 officers had four or more allegations. The 44 officers singled out by the commission as "problem officers" had six or more complaints.[8]

Some experts say these numbers just show the Fuhrman case has been blown out of proportion. After all, 44 problem officers comes to less than 1 percent of the department. Indeed, several studies have found that police officers use excessive force in only 1 percent of all observed encounters between police and citizens. In encounters with criminal suspects, the use of force tends to be higher—up to 5 percent.[9]

Walker believes that if police chiefs tracked officers with the most citizen complaints against them, they could catch future Fuhrmans. Another red flag, he says, is an officer who files numerous charges for resisting arrest. Such charges are typ-

How Race Colors Attitudes About Racism Among Police

Substantially larger percentages of blacks than whites felt they had been treated unfairly by police because of their race and that widespread racism among police officers is fairly or very common.

Have you personally ever felt treated unfairly by the police specifically because you are white/black?

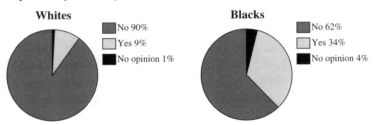

How widespread is racism against blacks among police officers?

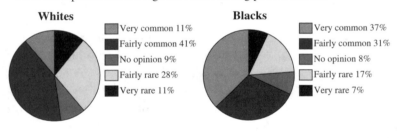

Source: The poll was conducted Oct. 5–7, 1995, by The Gallup Organization for CNN/*USA Today*.

ically used by rogue officers to explain why their suspects are brought in bruised or bleeding.

"The single most important thing we've learned since the Rodney King event is that a small percentage of officers were responsible for a huge percentage of complaints," Walker says. "I'm prepared to say this is a consistent pattern. You could walk into any police department and you could identify those officers."

But some cops would be unfairly targeted by this method, other police experts contend. "Officers in high-crime areas are going to have more events of use of force, but it doesn't mean that they're necessarily brutal," says Scott W. Allen, staff psychologist with the Metro-Dade Police Department in Miami.

A recent *Los Angeles Times* analysis of the 44 "problem officers" demonstrates the complexity of picking out bad cops. Complaints of excessive force or improper tactics against two of the offi-

cers who made the list were found to be without merit. Neither officer picked up a complaint of any kind from 1992–1994.

Cliff Ruff, president of the Los Angeles police officers' union, questioned how foolproof the method was. "If this list of 44 is such a problem, [how] did the Christopher Commission fail [to put] Mark Fuhrman on the list?" he asked.[10]

It's not so much the number of police officers engaging in misconduct that matters, other police experts contend, but how fellow officers treat them. Police "must stop using the 'few bad apples' defense to obscure the fact that the code of silence among honest cops is allowing crooked and racist cops to flourish," former San Jose Police Chief Joseph D. McNamara wrote after Fuhrman's racist boasts were broadcast.[11]

Numerous internal investigations of Fuhrman and interviews with police department psychologists had documented his racist attitudes, notes the ACLU's Crew. Yet Fuhrman testified he had not used the word "nigger" for the past 10 years. "We now know this was a man not terribly shy about expressing his racist sentiments," he says. "Yet no one in the police department stepped forward and said we saw a man commit an act of perjury."

Is There a Link Between Brutality and Corruption?

In 1993, the first big New York City Police Department scandal in 20 years was revealed by the Mollen Commission. Star witness Michael Dowd described how his "Loser's Club" of rogue cops extorted protection money from drug dealers and sold stolen cocaine to suburban Long Island teenagers.

Early in his career, Dowd testified, beating up

drug-dealer suspects in front of fellow cops became a test of officers' tolerance for further acts of corruption. "Brutality was, and is, the first kind of corruption," *New York Daily News* reporter Mike McAlary wrote in *Good Cop, Bad Cop,* his account of Dowd's seven years of wrongdoing.

"You kick some punk down the stairs in front of 10 cops and you have 10 friends, Dowd would say. Young officers . . . tested one another: How much bad could you be trusted to see, the old-timers wanted to know, before you ratted on another cop?"[12]

"One of the many indicators of potential problems is a police officer's involvement in minor police brutality or civil rights violations," concurs the FBI's Gallagher. "We're beginning to take a look at that as a signal of a person who will become involved in corrupt activities."

Gallagher headed the FBI's New Orleans office during "Shattered Shield," its year-long undercover investigation of the police department. "Some of the officers have multiple allegations of police misconduct in arrest procedures," Gallagher says.

The Mollen Commission found that police officers who engaged in the most egregious corruption, such as pocketing money from drug dealers, had started out by abusing and beating up defendants. The Kennedy School's Moore, who was a consultant to the commission, observes that beating a citizen, like bribery, is an abuse of authority. But does one necessarily lead to another?

"If you've done the minor offenses, the chances that you're going to do the major offenses go way up," says Moore. "It's also true that most [officers] who do the minor offenses"—like roughing up suspects or accepting a free lunch—"don't do the major offenses."

Police psychologist Ellen M. Scrivner of Washington, D.C., says the evidence that brutality leads to further corruption remains largely anecdotal. "Nobody's ever made that link" in the research, she says. Nevertheless, she says, there's reason to think that "brutality opens the door to other kinds of behavior that at one time you might have thought was horrifying."

Scrivner authored a study in 1994 for the Justice Department that examined psychological profiles of violence-prone officers. She concluded that a wide variety of individuals are at risk for using excessive violence, not just a few obvious "rotten apples." Scrivner's study notes that violence-prone officers typically fit one of the following profiles:

• young, "badge-happy," immature and impulsive;

• facing serious personal problems like divorce;

• suffering from burnout;

• troubled by enduring personality problems, such as abusive or paranoid tendencies; and

• old-line officers or "dinosaurs," who use a heavy-handed policing style to show they are in charge and are particularly sensitive to challenge and provocation.[13]

Scrivner suggests that police work's "focus on the dark side of life" can breed a cynicism and tolerance for violent acts that officers would once have condemned. "If you see a kid with his face shot off," she explains, "shoving someone in the course of an arrest isn't such a big thing, even if it's wrong."

Does Racism Play a Major Role in Police Misconduct?

"Police have two different faces," says Hubert Williams, president of the Police Foundation, a research organization in Washington. "In minority neighborhoods, it's law and order. In white neighborhoods, it's protect and serve. So it's not surprising we have this bifurcated way of seeing police in our society."

After hearings conducted around the nation in 1991 documented widespread police brutality, a NAACP report co-authored by Harvard Law School Professor Charles J. Ogletree Jr. concluded, "Racism is a central part of police misconduct." The report went on to say, "Police officers have increasingly come to rely on race as the primary indicator of both suspicious conduct and dangerousness."[14]

In a nationwide survey, the Police Foundation found that blacks represented 42 percent of citizen complaints of excessive force filed against large urban police departments in 1991. Yet blacks represented only 21 percent of big-city populations that year.[15]

Williams, an African-American and former police chief of Newark, N.J., sees police racism as a historical legacy. "Police have been the ones responsible for enforcing old laws of racial segregation and Jim Crow," he says. "There's a kind of unwritten law that police are expected to take whatever measures are necessary. There's a net thrown over people of color."

But the disparity in how blacks and whites are treated may not always be a matter of racial discrimination, according to a recent study. Incidents of excessive force "are concentrated among lower-class men and criminal suspects, which means they are disproportionately concentrated among racial and ethnic minorities," the authors of *The Color of Justice* conclude.[16]

In addition, co-author Walker notes, police departments have more contact with blacks because crime in most cities is concentrated in impoverished, black neighborhoods. Nevertheless, as incidents of police mistreatment accumulate over time, they create "a perception of systematic harassment" in the black community.[17]

According to a recent Sentencing Project report on blacks and the criminal justice system, one out of every three African-American males in their twenties is behind bars or on probation or parole.[18]

"Police target low-income communities for drug law enforcement much more so than other communities, in part because it's easier to do: There are serious problems there, there's more dense population and drug use is more likely to take place out on the streets," says Marc Mauer, co-author of the report. But "middle-class drug use doesn't come to the attention of police as much," because whites typically end up in treatment and don't buy their drugs in open-air drug markets.

In addition, under federal sentencing guidelines, crack use, the drug of choice among poor blacks, is punished more harshly than possession of powder cocaine, which is more common among whites.[19]

It's not clear how widespread police brutality is in minority communities, most experts say, because many citizens are afraid to complain. But one easily measurable form of police abuse that has long targeted black people—fatal shootings of citizens—has declined significantly. From 1975–1990, the disparity between the number of African-Americans and whites shot and killed by the police narrowed from about 7 to 1 to about 3 to 1. Walker calculates that at least 150 African American men were alive in 1990 who would have been shot by the police if the rates had remained at 1975 levels.

Many of the riots that took place in the 1960s in cities around the nation were precipitated by the fatal shooting of a black male by white police officers. Walker says the turning point in fatal shootings by urban police came in 1972, when New York Police Commissioner Patrick Murphy restricted use of deadly force to "defense of life" situations only. Previously, officers could shoot at any "fleeing felon." Over the next 15 years, the defense of life standard, along with requirements that police report any discharge of their gun, became standard in police departments.[20]

Civil rights groups like the NAACP have called on police departments to increase their hiring of minority officers. But that's not necessarily a panacea. The LAPD, widely criticized for tolerating racism, is 14 percent black, as is the city's population. (*See table.*)[21]

"There are black Mark Fuhrmans out there on police forces," says former police officer Gayle Fisher-Stewart, now a criminal justice instructor at the University of Maryland. Indeed, the Police Foundation study found that black officers were as likely to be targets of citizen complaints as white officers.

Nor has the presence of a majority black police force affected police discrimination against blacks in majority-black Washington, says Ronald Hampton, who retired last year after 23 years on the force. "Regardless of what color you are, after you go through that 20 to 24 weeks of training, when you come out, you perform in a way that will get you promoted, get you a good assignment and make people see you as a member of the team," says Hampton, executive director of the 35,000-

member National Black Police Association.

When Fisher-Stewart did random checks on cars as a police recruit in Washington, the cars stopped by her white supervisor always contained black drivers and passengers. When she took the wheel, Fisher-Stewart stopped a car with a white family, prompting a rebuke: "We don't stop whites." Says Fisher-Stewart, "Unfortunately, the police culture teaches us that we can treat people differently."

Ways to Reduce Misconduct

Law enforcement experts say the following techniques offer the best chances for identifying and eliminating police brutality, corruption and other forms of misconduct:

Community Policing Although it takes many different forms, the basic idea of community policing is to get officers out of their police cars, make them walk a beat and encourage them to become acquainted with neighborhood residents.

In fact, some police experts attribute Los Angeles' enduring problems with police brutality to its military-style philosophy. The LAPD traditionally stressed quick response times to crimes with patrol cars, the latest in armaments and relatively few officers on the beat. "There was a very high-technology, low-manpower style of policing, and many argue that what we're now seeing is the result of that aggressive approach," says Kenney of the Police Executive Research Forum.

If cops had more friendly contact with the residents of a neighborhood, community policing advocates argue, they would be less likely to abuse innocent people. In Charleston, S.C., police schedule foot patrols during the hours that neighborhood associations request, often switching from daytime to nighttime patrols. Beat officers attend all neighborhood association meetings and take complaints from residents. Before Charleston tried community policing in its public housing in 1988, says Capt. Ronald Hamilton, "police officers represented the enemy. The only times citizens used to see police was when there was a crime."

Residents used to hide the robbery and stabbing suspects he was chasing, Hamilton remem-

Blacks on Big City Police Forces
The percentage of black officers increased in each of the nation's 10 biggest police departments from 1983–92. Washington and Los Angeles were the only cities where the percentage of black officers matched or exceeded the percentage of blacks in the overall population.

| | Percentage of blacks | | | |
| | In police force | | In local population | |
	1983	1992	1983	1992
Washington	50.1%	67.8%	70.6%	65.8%
Los Angeles	9.4	14.1	17.1	14.1
Metro-Dade (Miami)	17.2	22.4	24.9	27.7
Detroit	30.7	53.3	62.7	76.1
Chicago	20.1	24.9	39.4	38.9
Philadelphia	16.5	25.7	37.5	40.2
Dallas	8.2	19.0	22.1	29.7
Houston	9.7	14.7	27.7	28.3
Baltimore	17.5	30.3	54.7	59.4
New York	10.2	11.4	25.5	28.5

Source: Samuel Walker and K.B. Turner, "A Decade of Modest Progress: Employment of Black and Hispanic Police Officers, 1983–1992," University of Nebraska, Omaha.

bers. Today, the residents will lead the police to suspects, Hamilton says. Although public housing residents account for 9 percent of Charleston's population, they account for only 1.7 percent of the crime, ranking public housing among the city's safest neighborhoods, he says.

In San Jose, the military-style police department was once known as a little LAPD. When McNamara became police chief, he instituted foot patrols and had officers attend meetings in minority neighborhoods. Gradually, he recalls, officers "began to realize that unless people reported crimes, provided evidence, served as witnesses and—when on juries—believed police testimony, criminals would not be convicted." After the reforms, he writes, "the police made more arrests than ever and crime decreased to the point that San Jose became one of the safest large cities in America, a city of minorities."[22]

But some experts worry that by giving officers free rein to roam the streets, community policing could actually intensify corruption and racism. They point to the most ambitious vision of community policing—officers solving social problems and preventing future crimes. A frequently cited example is the cop who sends an abusive husband into alcoholism treatment rather than arresting him for the tenth time.

"Telling street officers to be problem-solvers is an invitation to disaster," says Walker. "You're removing the controls essential to make sure that abuse is curbed." Where abuses like shooting suspects have been curbed, says Walker, success can be traced to strict guidelines from headquarters, not more freedom.

John J. DiIulio Jr., a professor of politics and public affairs at Princeton University, sees both positive and negative aspects. "You can't have community policing and at the same time hope some cops won't exercise renegade discretion to use power for corrupt ends, including abusing citizens' rights because of race."

But, Austin, Texas, Police Chief Elizabeth Watson retorts, "Clearly a person who holds that view operates under the myth that we control discretion—or ever did. It seems to make much better sense to guide the judgment by values, as opposed to strict reliance on rules and directives." Watson says she tries to convince officers that policing is about service to the citizen.

Watson, a former chief in Houston, says police relations with Houston's black community improved after she established regular meetings to hear grievances. "Many of the problems between citizens and police officers are rooted in misunderstandings," she says.

David H. Bayley, a professor at the School of Criminal Justice, State University of New York-Albany, thinks community policing might reduce brutality. But he notes that close contact with people in the community can further old-fashioned corruption. "Local citizens always want favors. If the cop is there all the time, the citizen can say, 'I want the delivery man to double park outside my business; what's it worth to you?'"

Conventional policing, which separated the cop from the community, was aimed in part at preventing old-style corruption like bribery, agrees Moore. But today's abuses—brutality and extortion—tend to be crimes directed against citizens, not carried out in collusion with them, he points out. That kind of mistreatment is less likely to occur, he believes, when the police officer actually knows the citizen.

Civilian Review Boards Citizen advocates like them. Police unions hate them. But no matter what each side thinks, citizen boards substantiate few citizen complaints.

"You investigate a complaint and you get to a stalemate because there's not enough evidence to call what happened one way or another," says Lawrence Sherman, a criminologist at the University of Maryland. "Ninety-five percent of brutality complaints are ruled unfounded simply because you don't have enough witnesses."

Mark Gissiner, who investigates police misconduct in Cincinnati, is president of the International Association for Civilian Oversight of Law Enforcement, which represents civilian review board personnel around the country. There are at least 90 such boards nationwide, according to Walker. Gissiner concedes that some boards are much weaker than others. But he argues that if a civilian board has independent investigative powers, it can have a strong deterrent effect on police brutality. As many as 30 boards have such powers, he estimates, but not all have full-time investigative staffs and only some use their powers aggressively to launch investigations.

Gissiner believes civilian oversight has helped reduce police brutality in Cincinnati. When he started in the city 10 years ago, he says, "It was pretty regular to see head injuries, broken bones. It's fairly rare for me to see complainants now with visible injuries. Now that police officers know there's another agency out there to review their conduct, I don't think police officers are willing to risk their jobs for the misconduct of another officer."

Unlike many civilian boards, which make recommendations to the police chief and then wait—sometimes interminably—for action, the

Cincinnati office reports to the city manager, who has the last word on whether an officer will be penalized. Cincinnati's civilian office substantiates about 18 percent of the complaints it investigates, considerably higher than the 3–9 percent rate for New York City's civilian board. One reason for the higher rate is that, unlike New York, Cincinnati's board only investigates major cases, such as those involving physical injuries, deaths in custody. The civilian office sends about 50–75 percent of the complaints it receives, such as lesser offenses like verbal abuse, to the police department to investigate and then audits the results.

From the citizens' view, the advantages of a civilian review board over a police agency seem obvious. In Los Angeles, for example, which has no civilian complaint board, the Christopher Commission found that officers at local police stations often discouraged people from filing complaints or threatened them with arrest.[23]

Yet even ardent advocates of civilian review boards have discovered that the reality can be discouraging. Civil rights activists cheered when New York's City Council overcame police union opposition to create a Citizen Complaint Review Board in 1993. New York Civil Liberties Union Executive Director Norman Siegel, who helped draft the legislation to make it as independent of the police department as possible, calls the results "disappointing." He has clients who have been waiting years for the board to rule on their complaints. "You need commitment from the police department; we don't have that," he says. "You need commitment from the mayor; we don't have that."

Training and Screening Police recruits spend much of their time learning how to use a gun during their six to nine months of training. But that's the wrong emphasis, says ex-cop Robert Leuci—whose undercover work blew the whistle on police corruption in New York in the 1970s. "A tiny percentage [of cops] will ever fire a gun. Everyone will deal with corruption from Day One. But no one [at the police academy] spends any time on it."

Critics of today's training say little time is spent on verbal communication or dealing with other races and cultures—skills more relevant to today's police work. "Early police officers were hired because they were big and strong and could mix it up on the street," says Barbara Raffel Price, dean of graduate studies at the John Jay School of Criminal Justice in New York City. "As racial and social class divisions become a more difficult problem for the country, the kind of policing we require has become more sophisticated."

But police academies have changed little to meet those social challenges, Price says. Hairdressers, she notes, train longer than the average police officer in New York.

"The power of being a police officer is corrupting," Price adds. "More education could contribute to the moral maturity one needs." Price advocates two years as a probationary officer instead of one—under the close observation of training officers. That would provide "an opportunity to root out people taking shortcuts," she says. She also advocates four years of college plus two years of police academy training rather than the typical half-year.

But other experts in the field downplay the importance of formal education. Though critics often focused on police officers' less-than-average educational levels several decades ago, police tend to have "above average" education today, according to Walker. It is standard at some police departments for officers to have two years of college, he says.

The police forum's Kenney agrees. "You're not going to train your way out of this one: [misconduct] is a cultural issue," he says. "If I join a police department and the informal norm is that I help myself to whatever's around or that I'm the macho guy who can rough suspects up, I'm going to subscribe to those behaviors because those are the behaviors my colleagues expect, and will reward me with friendship for doing."

Still others argue that the school of life is as important as formal education in recruiting an officer who will deal with people in a mature and honorable manner. Chief Stewart, in Ormond Beach, says he finds older recruits much more open to dealing sensitively with different races. "We're really hiring people at too early an age to handle the myriad and complex tasks of policing today."

In New York, for example, recruits continue to be dominated by young white males in their early 20s from predominantly white bedroom suburbs.[24] Typically, they have had relatively little contact with people from other races or social classes. The suburban social profile typified Dowd and many of his corrupt cronies.

Many young recruits have a "Rambo" fantasy of police work drawn from movies and TV, says psychologist Schlossberg. "There's a conflict between what's portrayed by the media and what the real role is. [On TV], they're all yelling, shouting or breaking laws. There's no real good solid investigative or intellectual type."

Schlossberg, a New York City resident and cop for 20 years, also thinks a residency requirement would provide cops more familiar with New York's melting pot of races. "To me, it's my neighborhood. I'll do things even if I'm off-duty because they affect my family. It's different than coming in as a paid mercenary. The British found that out when they hired the Hessians" during the Revolutionary War.

But how does a Mark Fuhrman or an Antoinette Frank get accepted by a police department in the first place? The publicity over such bad apples has put police department screening methods under the microscope. According to psychologist Scrivner, written tests are "geared more toward finding someone with some level of pathology," such as schizophrenia, rather than potential problem behaviors. And, she says, they usually do not explicitly "test for anything like racist attitudes."

"We're not looking at how people interact or their problem-solving capacity with those kinds of tests," she says. "If you give someone a pencil, you'll describe them in flattering terms. If you put them in a scenario, you'll learn more."

Some departments are experimenting with new approaches. In San Antonio, experienced officers interview candidates and evaluate them based on the behavior they think necessary for street patrolling. In Portland, Ore., citizen representatives from black neighborhoods participate in entry interviews and ask questions designed to elicit the candidates' level of racial tolerance.

Following the King beating, the Christopher Commission recommended periodic retesting of officers. More recently, questions have been raised about how Fuhrman stayed on the job after he requested a stress disability pension in 1983. Portland Police Chief Charles A. Moose, an African-American, says that Fuhrman prompted him to rethink how his department monitors the psychological state of its officers. "There was a gap between [reports of Fuhrman's] problems and the police department putting him back to work," Moose says.

Strong Supervision Professional, ethical supervision from the top down is the key, ultimately, to good policing, many experts say. "What you try to do is build a critical mass of people who always do what's right, who would not tolerate corruption or wrongdoing," says Walter Sirene, who teaches ethics at the FBI Academy.

Cops say they were struck by the total absence of that peer pressure to do the right thing among the more than 20 LAPD officers who stood around watching the Rodney King beating. "I'd seen vicious beatings, but I'd never seen anything like that in America," says David Whitfield, a retired New York City police lieutenant.

Law enforcement executives who take the FBI's special 11-week training course often assume that ethics is just common sense, and that it can't be taught, says Sirene. But "even a [police] culture that fosters racism can be changed," he says.

For example, Lee Brown banned racial jokes and slurs—even inside the station—when he became Houston's police chief. "That raised consciousness that it was an important issue," says Watson, then a member of the Houston force.

In Kansas City, Mo., Chief Steven C. Bishop sent an equally tough message in 1990, notes criminologist Sherman, when he fired officers for forcing a black minister to lie down on a sidewalk.

Anti-violence messages can be sent as well. In Charleston, S.C., Chief Reuben Greenberg requires a written report whenever an officer unholsters his gun. City police have only fired their weapons three times in the last 10 years of Greenberg's reign, according to Capt. Hamilton.

By contrast, most police departments require written reports only when the weapon is actually discharged, notes Scrivner, and that's too late. "If you have to fill out a report when you draw your gun," she says, "that's trying to change that behavior early on."

Some experts say that in order to stem corruption, police chiefs need to re-examine some of the most commonly accepted practices—like accepting free cups of coffee from local merchants. "It's not really free. The person in the store is buying you a present," observes former police officer Fisher-Stewart. "If we're going to talk about stopping corruption, we have to talk about stopping it all—including the police chiefs who get free hotel rooms for their Christmas parties. That sends a bad message to the troops."

Criminologist Sherman believes one of the most effective ways for a department executive to control police officers is through undercover cops posing as citizens or corrupt cops. But "most police departments wouldn't dream of doing that because they know police unions would be strongly opposed," he says.

To Price, the spying conducted in New York in the 1970s "was terribly demoralizing" to police officers. It's more important to develop cops who internalize ethical behavior, who "do the right thing because it's what you do when you're a police officer."

That's not likely to happen when rookie police officers get the wrong ethical signals from their superiors, starting with things as subtle as punitive language, she believes. "You can't scream at police during roll call and then expect them to go out and be nice to citizens," Price says.

Fisher-Stewart, an African-American, recalls that when she was a rookie in Washington, D.C., her sergeant would send his officers out every day with the exhortation to "put some meat on the table"—make felony arrests. "It got to the point where we didn't see people. We saw meat. And, when your steak is tough, you tenderize it. And so when the meat talked back, we tenderized it."

NOTES

1. Quoted in Gordon Witkin, "When the Bad Guys Are Cops," *U.S. News & World Report,* Sept. 11, 1995, p. 20.

2. "Nine Cases Tossed Out in Philadelphia Scandal," *The Washington Post,* Oct. 11, 1995, p. A22.

3. "Atlanta Holds Six Policemen in Crackdown," *The New York Times,* Sept. 7, 1995.

4. Jerome H. Skolnick and James J. Fyfe, *Above the Law* (1993), p. 13.

5. William A. Geller and Hans Toch, *And Justice for All: Understanding and Controlling Police Abuse of Force,* Police Executive Research Forum (1995), p. 142.

6. Samuel Walker et al., *The Color of Justice: Race, Ethnicity and Crime in America* (1996).

7. Geller and Toch, *op. cit.,* p. 143.

8. *Ibid.*

9. Walker et al., *op. cit.,* p. 96.

10. Alan Abrahamson, "What has Happened to the 'LAPD 44'?" *Los Angeles Times,* Oct. 15, 1995, p. A1.

11. Joseph D. McNamara, "Plague of Bad Cops," *Los Angeles Times,* Sept. 17, 1995.

12. Mike McAlary, *Good Cop, Bad Cop* (1994), p. 25.

13. Ellen M. Scrivner, *Controlling Police Use of Excessive Force: The Role of the Police Psychologist,* National Institute of Justice Research, October 1994. "What I have determined is there is no actual profile of the bad officers," Scrivner says. Excessive use of force, she concludes, "is a risk for all officers."

14. Charles J. Ogletree Jr., et al., *Beyond the Rodney King Story: An Investigation of Police Conduct in Minority Communities* (1994), pp. 21, 23.

15. Antony M. Pate and Lorie A. Fridell, *Police Use of Force: Official Reports, Citizen Complaints and Legal Consequences* (1993), p. 95.

16. Walker et al., *op. cit.,* p. 97.

17. *Ibid.,* p. 97.

18. Marc Mauer and Tracy Huling, *Young Black Americans and the Criminal Justice System: Five Years Later,* October 1995.

19. See *CQ Weekly Report,* Oct. 21, 1995, p. 3212. For background, see "Mandatory Sentencing," *The CQ Researcher,* May 26, 1995, pp. 465–488.

20. Samuel Walker, "Wars on Crime: Struggles for Justice," unpublished paper delivered to Stanford University Law School, Oct. 6–7, 1995. A 1985 Supreme Court decision, *Tennessee v. Garner,* ruled the "fleeing felon" rule unconstitutional.

21. Samuel Walker and K.B. Turner, "A Decade of Modest Progress: Employment of Black and Hispanic Officers, 1983–1992," October 1992 (unpublished paper).

22. Joseph D. McNamara, "Reinventing the LAPD," *Los Angeles Times,* Sept. 8, 1995.

23. Skolnick and Fyfe, *op. cit.,* p. 2.

24. Peter T. Kilborn, "Police Profile Stays Much the Same," *The New York Times,* Oct. 10, 1994, p. A1.

REFERENCES

1. Domanick, Joe, *To Protect and to Serve: The LAPD's Century of War in the City of Dreams,* Pocket Books, 1994. A journalist criticizes the military-style leadership of the Los Angeles Police Department, blaming the culture it created for the beating of Rodney King.

2. Maas, Peter, *Serpico,* Viking, 1973. This well-written biography of Frank Serpico, the New York City cop whose revelations of organized graft on the force led to the Knapp Commission's corruption hearings in the early 1970s, was made into a movie starring Al Pacino.

3. McAlary, Mike, *Good Cop, Bad Cop: Detective Joe Trimboli's Heroic Pursuit of NYPD Officer Michael Dowd,* Pocket Books, 1994. McAlary, a journalist at the *New York Daily News,* writes a fast-paced account of the wrong-doings—from beatings to drug dealing—of New York City cop Michael Dowd, who was at the center of the 1993 police corruption scandal.

4. Paley, Robert, *Prince of the City: The True Story of a Cop Who Knew Too Much,* Houghton Mifflin, 1978. This is the page-turning story, later made into a movie of the same name, of Robert Leuci, a New York City narcotics detective who took part in his division's widespread corruption in the 1960s. Leuci went undercover in 1970 and became the star witness in a series of federal cases that resulted in the arrests of dozens of police officers.

5. Skolnick, Jerome H., and James J. Fyfe, *Above the Law: Police and the Excessive Use of Force,* Free Press, 1993. Two distinguished criminologists discuss police brutality in America in light of the Rodney King beating, which they call the most visible atrocity in a police department that had become "aberrational." The authors also discuss the pros and cons of such remedies as civilian review boards and community policing.

6. Walker, Samuel et al., *The Color of Justice: Race, Ethnicity and Crime in America,* Wadsworth, 1996. In a balanced summary of the research, three academic experts ask whether America's criminal justice system—including police conduct—discriminates against racial minorities.

READING 12
LA CORRUPCIÓN POLICÍACA

Sam Quiñones

Corruption within the Mexican police force is being confronted by officers in Mexico City. The efforts of a valiant few are commendable, but the possibility of reform remains a long shot. Sam Quiñones is a freelance writer based in Mexico City.

It was that first day on the job that got Manuel Rodriguez off on the wrong foot.

That day 26 years ago, Rodriguez walked out onto Mexico City's streets proud to be a police officer, looking forward to a decent career. But that afternoon he returned to the stationhouse and walked headlong into the reality of Mexico's police system, in the person of his commander.

The commander asked him for the money. Rodriguez looked bewildered and admitted that he didn't know what the commander was talking about. "He cursed me," Rodriguez remembers. "He said, 'Tomorrow you have to bring something back for your bosses.'"

The experience, and what was to come, changed Rodriguez's cheery outlook.

Now a few years from retirement, Rodriguez has heart trouble and can no longer work the streets. His salary amounts to only a few hundred pesos a month. He worked a desk job for a while, but after a disagreement with a commander, he wound up cleaning bathrooms at the stationhouse.

Reprinted from Sam Quiñones, "La Corrupción Policíaca," *Police*, November 1994, by permission of *Police* magazine, Bobit Publishing, Torrance, California.

Now when the chief needs his Great Dane's private kennel cleaned, he calls Rodriguez. "The police officer has no right to live or eat," Rodriguez says. "The police officer has three options: the house, the street or the cemetery."

An Insider's View

Many people may have trouble feeling sorry for the street cops of Mexico City. After all, they're the ones most likely to stop tourists and citizens and take the infamous Mexican mordida—the "bite" or bribe.

But five officers interviewed for this report say behind that impression of the street cop rises a vast ladder of corruption where the officer is only the most public and exploited symbol.

These officers used their real names and agreed to a taped interview. During the interview, they offered a rare glimpse of the life of the street officer inside the city's police forces famous for their corruption and incompetence. While it's difficult to confirm some of the claims the officers made, each describes similar training and working conditions, though they work in different parts of the city.

In Mexico City, where the police number 24,000, street cops are either part of the traffic police corps or the patrol officer corps. Their mission is crime deterrence, though they also write tickets for infractions. They do not investigate crimes. Robberies, murders and assaults are considered state crimes and are investigated by the state judicial police. The federal judicial police are primarily charged with enforcing drug laws, merchandise piracy and counterfeiting.

A Pyramid Scheme

Street police officers are the foundation of a criminal justice–type pyramid scheme of enriching police commanders. "The ones who have promoted corruption are those who are in command," says Raúl Romero, who's been a patrol officer for 25 years. "They're the ones who have been the principal beneficiaries of corruption. They're the ones who have vacation houses, savings accounts, nice cars."

Because of this exploitation, these officers say their lives resemble that of the Southern sharecropper in the United States decades ago. They're poorly paid, yet are charged for their equipment. They work long hours, yet are paid no overtime. They live in constant danger and are badly trained—49 officers have been killed in the city so far this year and 619 have been injured. (Mexico keeps no statistics on the number of officers killed nationwide, but observers estimate it at 500). For backup, they must sometimes rely on colleagues who are alcoholics or drug addicts. They must occasionally act as the private employees of their chiefs. And after every shift, they must return to the stationhouse with enough bribe money to pay off their commanders or risk harassment or transfer to a job where they have to survive on their legal salary.

Leading the Reform

The five officers are part of a police reform movement, dubbed the "Dignity Movement," that is growing but so far remains small. By their estimates, approximately 50 officers in Mexico City are active, and many more share the ideas of the group but fear to do so publicly. The officers say they routinely face harassment, like having to pay for a day off. One chief who has tried to organize the dissidents was attacked and beaten by six men one recent night. Several officers have had death threats mailed to their stationhouses warning them to dissolve their movement or "the next meeting you'll have with Colosio," referring to the presidential candidate assassinated in Tijuana in March.

Their movement has been part of new calls for police reform, in Mexico City and across the country. "What we have today (in our police system) can best be described in one word: chaos," says Samuel Gonzalez, a law professor at Mexico's National Autonomous University. "We as citizens have to say, 'That's enough.'"

"What's required is a thorough professionalization of the police force, a Copernican Revolution that will stand present thinking on its head," says Luis de la Barreda, president of the city's Human Rights Commission. This group has spent much of its time investigating citizen complaints of police abuses, ranging from street bribes and selective enforcement of the law to extortion and beatings.

Barreda has proposed a national databank to keep track of police officers who are dismissed for criminal activity so they won't be re-hired by another police force. He also advocates revamping the forces, firing those who are corrupt over the next five or six years.

"Wholesale dismissals can be counterproductive," he says. "For a start, we don't have anyone to replace (fired officers). But we've also seen that fired officers form criminal gangs."

So it appears that for the moment, the dissidents within the police force must fend for themselves. Each officer interviewed insists he doesn't accept bribes. But to get by, they do admit to accepting "dadivas," tips of a few pesos given by citizens whom they've helped. Even so, none appears to be getting rich; only one has a telephone.

Money: The Root of All Evil

The root of the corruption pervading Mexico's police is the paltry salaries officers earn. To make their point, the officers eagerly pull out their two-week pay stubs. Their gross pay is between 600 and 700 pesos, roughly $175 to $200. Bus drivers make more. But that's just the gross pay. There are deductions as well. And frequently officers have to ask for advances. "When we ask for an advance, they deduct interest," says Eugenio Reyes, a patrol officer with 24 years of experience. "We have to pay interest on our own money. It's our money."

Take-home pay can be as little as 150 pesos for two weeks of work. Street vendors selling sweets usually make more. In Reyes' case, he and his family must make do with 250 pesos.

With salaries so low, bribe money has become an essential income supplement, especially to those officers with families. It's also necessary to keep bosses happy. "We ask for money from citizens. We give to the commander. The commander gives to the sector chief," Reyes says.

The amount each officer gives his bosses at the end of the shift depends on where he works. "We have to pay for where we work. If I want a good intersection, it's going to cost me 100 to 150 pesos a day," says Arturo Ostoa, a traffic officer with 18 years on the job. "Where there's circulation, there's more money."

Of course, it's the rare officer who stops with the daily cash his bosses demand. It is the general opinion of citizens that officers sometimes ignore calls for help because they're too busy shaking down motorists. Depending on how hard they work and where, as well as the events of the day, officers can pull in 500 to 1,000 pesos—roughly $150 to $300—daily.

Paying the High Price

That's necessary because back at the stationhouse the officers are charged more. They have to pay to maintain their patrol cars; tires, tune-ups and oil changes usually come out of the officer's pocket. If they don't pay, the next time an officer needs a set of tires, he may come away with a new gas tank instead. He'll have to return later. "Meanwhile, they put you guarding the holding cells or the reception. It's a way of harassing you," Ostoa says.

Those who don't support the pyramid are often assigned to details such as watching banks. Banks pay the city, which then assigns officers as security guards. Officers dread the detail. First, there's no opportunity to make the bribe money. Plus, working as a bank cop means many boring hours of being ordered around by civilians. "We're in there standing up. They don't feed us.

We can't go to the bathroom," Ostoa says. "They have parties—say it's the boss's birthday—and they leave the bank at 8 or 9 p.m. We have to stay until no one's left in the bank."

At times officers can take no more. Raúl Romero says he left the force twice, disgusted with the corruption.

"I returned because unfortunately to be a police officer here in Mexico carries a stigma. It's as if you've been a criminal," Romero says. "You can't find work anywhere. You go looking for work and they ask for your resumé. Then they won't give you work, except in the most exploited jobs. . . . And also, in some sense, one hopes that things will change."

Training Sorely Needed

Romero and the other officers spoke most vigorously about the need to raise police salaries and do away with daily quotas and paying for equipment. But they say that reforms in the police forces must also extend to training.

Police in Mexico have one of the highest death rates in all of Latin America. Much of that is due to a lack of proper training and equipment, says Arturo Diaz, a motorcycle officer who says his revolver was made in the 1940s. "What they teach in the academy is tactics to kill, not to defend. Shooting, shooting, shooting," he says.

"The lack of training causes violence," Ostoa says. Inadequately trained officers are more likely to resort to aggression than persuasion in their daily work, he says. Moreover, many officers have no idea how to accomplish routine tasks, such as cordoning off a block.

Recently, the incompetence has become painfully public, as has the people's unwillingness to put up with it any more. In five separate cases in June, officers ran over pedestrians. That wasn't new. What was new was that in each case mobs formed, and on several occasions they burned the patrol cars and beat the officers. "I've never seen people burn a patrol car. They'd just spit at us before," says Diaz.

In each case people believed the officers were drunk. "It's very probable . . . because it happens," says Romero. "Not just that, but drug use as well." Unlike the United States where many police officers come from the middle class, in Mexico the poor fill the police ranks. Many officers have little more than an elementary school education. And frequently the problems of the barrios follow these individuals to the police force, since officers go through only rudimentary psychological checks and no drug testing.

Substance abuse runs highest, the officers say, among the anti-riot forces and mounted police. But their superiors have balked at drug testing.

"They know if they had drug tests they'd be left with about half the police officers that they have now to repress those things," Romero says.

An Uncertain Future

The future of the police reform movement in Mexico City once seemed bright. Leading up to the recent national elections, presidential candidates took turns calling for massive changes in the way police forces were administered.

But the election results do not bode well for officers hoping for reform. The Institutional Revolutionary Party, which has been in power for 65 years, remains in control with a presidential victory and strong majority in the national legislature. The results would indicate there is little chance for meaningful reform in the country's criminal justice system. Old-line political bosses, many of them police administrators, seem disinclined to modernize the police force.

While reform-oriented officers hope to establish a union, that too may have little chance for success. Mexico City officials have used a law that forbids the unionization of armed forces to prevent law enforcement from doing so as well. The momentum that was building seems to have been reversed. "We're hopeful, but realistically it's going to be tough," Romero says. "There's not a strong consciousness among the rank and file."

READING 13
COP DIARY

Marcus Laffey

Anything can happen when a cop walks a beat. But even with the brawls, rapes, and hits it still has a way of feeling like a neighborhood. Marcus Laffey—a pseudonym—walks a beat in New York City.

Over the past year, more than a hundred people have worn my handcuffs. Not long ago, in a self-defense class, I wore them myself. There was a jolt of dissonance, like the perverse unfamiliarity at hearing your own voice on tape. Is this me? They were cold, and the metal edge pressed keenly against the bone if I moved, even when they were loose. The catch of the steel teeth as the cuffs tighten is austere and final, and never so much so as when it emanates from the small of your back. I thought, Hey, these things work. And then, Good thing. Because their intransigent grip means that, once they're on the correct pair of hands, no one should get hurt. Barring an unexpected kick or a bite, the story's over: no one's going to lose any teeth or blood, we're both going safely to jail, and at least one of us is going home tonight.

The handcuffs are a tool of the trade and an emblem of it, as are the gun and the nightstick. People—especially children whose eye level is at my equipment belt—stare at them, sometimes with a fearful look, but more often with fascination. Since I hold them from the other end, I regard them differently, just as surgeons don't feel uneasy, as I do, at the sight of a scalpel or a syringe. Police work can look ugly, especially when it's done well: you might see a man walking down the street, untroubled, untroubling, when two or ten cops rush up to him, shouting over sirens and screeching tires, with their guns drawn. You haven't seen the old man rocking on a stoop three blocks away with one eye swollen shut. You haven't heard his story, his description of the man being handcuffed: coat, color, height, the tattoo on his wrist.

The transformation from citizen to prisoner is terrible to behold, regardless of its justice. Unlike my sister the teacher or my brother the lawyer, I take prisoners, and to exercise that authority is to invoke a profound social trust. Each time a surgeon undertakes the responsibility of cutting open a human being, it should be awesome and new, no matter how necessary the operation, no matter how routine. A police officer who takes away someone's freedom bears a burden of at least equal gravity. Let me tell you, it's a pleasure sometimes.

My Beat

I walk a beat in a neighborhood of New York City that is a byword for slum. Even if the reality of places like the South Bronx, Brownsville, and Bed-Stuy no longer matches the reputation, and maybe never did, these bad neighborhoods are still bad. Children still walk through three different brands of crack vials in the building lobbies. People still shit in the stairwells. Gunshots in the night may have become less common in my precinct, but many people, young and old, can still distinguish that hard, sharp crack—like a broomstick snapped cleanly in half—from fireworks or a car backfiring.

The genuine surprise is how wholesome and ordinary this neighborhood sometimes seems, with its daily round of parents' getting kids ready for school, going to work, wondering if a car or a coat will make it through another winter. Life in the projects and the tenements can be just the way it is in suburbia, except that it takes place on busier streets and in smaller rooms. Sometimes it's better, in the way that city life, when it's good, is better than life anywhere else. In the summer, you can walk through the projects beneath shady aisles of sycamore and maple, past well-tended gardens and playgrounds teeming with children. There will be families having cookouts, old ladies reading Bibles on the benches, pensive pairs of men playing chess. Once, I went to the roof of a project and saw a hawk perched on the rail. Always, you can see Manhattan in the near distance, its towers and spires studded with lights, stately and slapdash, like the crazy geometry of rock crystal. There are many days when I feel sorry for people who work indoors.

The other revelation when I became a cop was how much people *like* cops. In safe neighborhoods, a cop is part of the scenery. I used to notice cops the way I noticed mailboxes, which is to say only when I needed one. But in bad neighborhoods I notice people noticing me, and especially certain classes of people—older people, young kids, single women, people dressed for work or church. They look at me with positive appreciation and relief. I am proof that tonight, on this walk home, no one's going to start with them. Sometimes they express that appreciation. The exceptions are groups of young guys on the street (older, if they're unemployed). Sometimes they're just hanging out, sometimes they're planning something more ambitious, and you're a sign that this wild night's not going to happen—not as they hoped, not here. Sometimes they express themselves, too.

When I'm working, I wear a Kevlar vest, and I carry a nightstick, pepper spray, a radio, a flashlight, two sets of handcuffs, and a gun with two extra fifteen-round magazines. A thick, leather-bound memo book has been squeezed into my back pocket, and leather gloves, rubber gloves, department forms, and binoculars are stuffed in various other pockets. When you chase someone in this outfit, it's like running in a suit of armor while carrying a bag of groceries. But I'm safe, and it's only very rarely that I feel otherwise. All the people I've fought with were trying to get away.

I walk around on patrol, keeping an eye out and talking to people until a job comes up on the radio. The radio is constant and chaotic, a montage of stray details, awful and comic facts:

"Respond to a woman cornered by a large rodent in her living room."

". . . supposed to be a one-year-old baby with its head split open."

"The perp is a male Hispanic, white T-shirt, bluejeans, possible mustache, repeat, possible mustache."

The appeal of patrol is its spontaneity and variety, its responsiveness to the rhythms of the street: there will be long lulls and then sudden convulsions as pickup jobs and radio runs propel you into a foot pursuit, a dispute, or a birth. When the action's over, the world can seem slow and small, drearily confined. And then you have to do the paperwork. . . .

Making Arrests

There are arrests that cops hope and train for like athletes, and in this felony Olympics, collars for homicides, pattern crimes, drugs by the kilo, and automatic weapons are considered gold medals. But the likelihood that things will go wrong with arrests seems to escalate with their importance: a baroque legal system, combined with the vagaries of chance, provides an inexhaustible source of misadventure. You feel like a diver on the platform who has just noticed that all the judges are Russian.

There was my rapist, a match for a pattern of sexual assaults on elderly women. My partner and I responded to a report that a suspicious person was lurking in the stairwell of a project, one floor up from the latest attack. When the man saw us, he ran, shouting, "Help me! Get a video camera!" We wrestled with him for what seemed like ages; he was limber and strong and sweat-soaked, as slippery as a live fish, and was chewing on a rolled-up dollar bill filled with cocaine. He looked just like the police sketch, and also had distinctive green eyes, which victims had described. He had been staying on that floor with his girlfriend until he beat her up and she threw him out, on the same day as the last attack. He was the rapist, beyond a doubt.

At the precinct, he collapsed, and he told the paramedics he'd ingested three grams of cocaine. At the hospital, his heart rate was two hundred and twenty beats per minute, and he was made to drink an electrolyte solution and eat activated charcoal, which caused him to drool black. He was handcuffed to a cot in the E.R. while the midnight pageant of medical catastrophes was brought in. There was an E.D.P. (an emotionally disturbed person) who had bitten clean through his tongue, clipping into it a precise impression of his upper teeth. Another E.D.P., an enormous drunk picked up from the streets, was writhing and thrashing as a diminutive Filipina nurse tried to draw blood: "Now I prick you! Now I just prick you!" An old man threw up, and another prisoner-patient, handcuffed to the cot next to him, kindly handed him the closest receptacle he could find—a plastic pitcher half filled with urine, which splashed back as he vomited, and made him vomit more.

I'd worked almost twenty-four hours by the time we got back to the precinct, when a detective from Special Victims called to say that my perp had already been taken in for a lineup, a few days before, and had not been identified as the rapist. This meant that we had to let him go. I'd felt nothing toward my suspect throughout our ordeal, even when I fought with him, although I believed he had done hideous, brutal things. But now, suddenly, I hated him, because he was no longer a magnificent and malignant catch—he was just some random asshole who had stolen an entire day of my life.

A few days later, I saw him on the street, and he said hello. I didn't. A few days after that, he beat up his girlfriend again, then disappeared. The rapes stopped.

Who Do You Believe?

Whaddaya got? This is what the boss—usually a sergeant—asks when he arrives at a scene, to make a decision or review one you've made. You tell him, I got a dispute, a matched pair of bloody noses, a shaky I.D. on a chain snatch; I got a lady with a stopped-up toilet who thinks I'm gonna help mop the bathroom; I got an order of protection that says I have to throw the husband out of the house, but he has custody of the three kids because she's a junkie and they have nowhere to go; I got twenty-seven facts in front of me, too many and not enough, in a broken heap like they fell off the back of a truck, which left yesterday.

When you arrive at the scene of an incident, you have a few seconds to take stock—to make a nearly instantaneous appraisal of a jumble of allegations concerning injuries, insults, histories, relationships between neighbors, brothers, lovers, ex-lovers, lovers again—all this with roots of enmity as tangled and deep as those among Balkan tribes. You say, "No, I just need to know what happened *today*." The outpouring of stories can move like a horse race—a hectic and headlong jostling for position, yet with everything moving in the same direction, toward the same end. Or it can turn out to be like a four-car crash at an intersection, where all the drivers sped up to lay triumphant claim to the right of way. Brawls often conclude with such a profusion of contradictory stories that you simply take the losers to the hospital and the winners to jail.

When we answered an emergency call from a woman whom I'll call Jocelyn (all the names in this piece, including my own, have been changed), her complaint seemed to be a simple case of assault; her assailant, George, who was the father of her infant daughter, had already left the scene. Jocelyn moved stiffly and was covered with scuffs and scratches, and one earlobe was notched where an earring had been pulled out. She was surrounded by a phalanx of female relatives who let out a steady stream of consolations and curses, all attesting to George's history of violence. I asked her about her earlobe, and she said, "Oh, that's old," and, looking closer, I saw that it was, and so were many of the marks on her. But then she lifted up her pant leg and showed me a fresh red scrape that covered most of the kneecap, and the course was clear. I asked for a detailed description and got one: "He's about five-eight and two hundred pounds, a lotta muscles and a bald head. Gonna take a lotta you cops to lock him up, 'cause he on parole for armed robbery and he say he ain't goin' back for nothin'!"

"Does he have a weapon now?"

"Wouldn't be surprised."

When my partner spotted him on the street, I called him over to us, and he came, without delay. "You George?" I asked, and he said that he was, in a clear, precise diction that was unusual for the street. He'd spent his time upstate well. I asked if he'd fought with Jocelyn, and he seemed mildly embarrassed, as if he had found out that they'd awakened the neighbor's baby. "Yeah, we did argue, over some stupid little thing."

"Tell you what," I said. "Take a walk with us up there. Let's straighten it out." The only matter to be straightened out was the "confirmatory identification," a procedural nicety in which I was glad to have his innocent coöperation. His lack of concern was disconcerting, and suggested either that her story was shaky or that his reflexes and instincts were wildly askew.

Upstairs, Jocelyn made the I.D. I discreetly put my location and condition—"Holding one"— over the air and gently asked George for a lengthy, time-killing version of events. Even when plentiful reinforcements arrived, and his alarm became evident, he didn't give up, but pulled back as someone tried, gently, to take his arm. Given his strength and the dimensions of the cinder-block hallway where we had gathered, no one wanted a brawl. He began to shake, and to bellow "I did not hit her!" and "I am not going back to prison!" We managed to coax him into restraints while he continued to shout, calling for neighbors to tell us what was really going on.

As we took George downstairs, he began to pitch his version of events: Jocelyn was a crackhead; he had custody of their infant daughter; he was angry at Jocelyn because she left the baby alone; her marks were from a fight she had yesterday; lots of people had seen her attack him earlier that day, and would testify that he had never raised a hand against her. On the street outside, one woman—who looked like a crackhead herself—said she had fought Jocelyn last night, and a man said he'd seen George endure Jocelyn's beating him without protest. Toni, whom George referred to as his fiancée, and who also had a child by him, happened by and joined in, shaking her head in disapproval of Jocelyn. But I still had a complainant, an I.D., a fresh injury, and no choice. And when George admitted that he "might have knocked her down" I didn't feel bad about bringing him in.

At the precinct, George alternated between brooding reveries on injustice and civil, reasonable explanations of his predicament. Then he suddenly assumed a soft-voiced and menacing tone, so that I couldn't tell if he was putting on a mask or dropping one. "I did time, man, time," he murmured urgently. "I know people who rob every day. I know people who sell guns, sell machine guns. I know people sell you a grenade, man, I could help you out."

Short of gunfire, nothing has as strong an effect on a cop as the word "gun." Guns are unique in their ability to change nobodies and wanna-bes into genuinely bad men in an instant. And while there is nothing more serious than apprehending a dangerous criminal, it also seems like boyhood itself when you can spend your days trying to get the bad guys. That was why, if I almost believed George when he told me about Jocelyn, I almost loved him when he told me about the guns.

I tried not to let it show, though. I didn't want to get greedy—to let the balance tip from buyer to seller. Not long before, a similar story—completely detailed, wholly plausible, legally sworn—had led me, along with thirty other cops, some equipped with full-body armor and shotguns, to raid an apartment where we expected to find a crate of semi-automatics but instead found a dildo and ten thousand roaches. I knew that if George meant it he'd say it more than once, and for his information to be useful he'd have to be willing to keep talking when he wasn't wearing my handcuffs. So I treated him with consideration—"You got change? I'll get you a soda"—and continued to process the arrest.

As it turned out, however, nothing came to pass. Jocelyn dropped the charges, and even came down to Central Booking to take George home. He was elated as he left, telling me, "Watch, I'm gonna get you a gun collar!" Laughing, I called after him, "Give me your number," and waited to see his reaction. He hesitated, then came back and gave me his beeper number. "I'm telling you," he said.

For a while after that, whenever I ran into George on the street, he would talk to me. The information was always good but never quite useful: he confirmed things I knew, and told me about witnesses to assaults and robberies who wouldn't come forward. I called him once or twice, and my call was never resumed.

The Cop as Hall Monitor

You often start with these cheesy collars: dice, blunts, trespass. It's not what you signed up for, being a glorified hall monitor, if "glorified" is the word. "Public urinator at two o'clock! Let's move in!" But it's part of the job, so you do it—preferably with the discretion you are empowered to exercise. If a group of guys are hanging out smoking marijuana and I'm walking by, one of two things tends to happen. Either I hear a rapid apology, the blunt is tossed—and if it's down a sewer there's no evidence to recover and no basis for a charge, you follow me, guys?—and the group gets a stern word of caution. Or someone decides to lock eyes with me and take a drag, and someone else calls out some cute remark, like "F—— the police!," and they decline to heed my word to the wise: "Break out, guys. Bounce!" No? And in seconds, or in a minute if I decide I want backup, they're all up against a wall. I start going into their pockets, taking names.

If someone has I.D., I might run a name over the air, and if there's no warrant out for this person's arrest he'll get a summons for Disorderly

Conduct at the scene. But most guys like these don't carry I.D., and you take them into the precinct to search them thoroughly, run the checks, and write the summonses. Often, someone will have drugs on him, or a stolen credit card. One in five will have an active warrant, in my experience, and fully half will come up on the computer as "Robbery Recidivist" or as "Target Narcotic Violator," which means that they have a number of convictions for mugging or dealing. Maybe they were just hanging out tonight, but, as far as I'm concerned, tonight they've lost their street-corner privileges. And now and then you find a prize, like a hard-core felon hiding behind a bottle of Bacardi.

For the most part, the time you spend with people you like and respect occurs at a low point in their lives: they've just been robbed, their child is missing, or their husband has collapsed from chest pains. You are less the bearer of bad news than the proof of it. More often, you become bound up in lives that are dismal and grim: parolees and their teen-age girlfriends, thugs, drunks, and junkies, E.D.P.s taking too much or too little for their pain. Other people you never get to know, even after you've spent some time with them.

The old man lived alone and died crumpled on the floor in a little alley between the bed and the wall. He was wearing a dirty shirt and no pants. His apartment was small and cluttered, and all his clothes were in old suitcases, or were stacked beside them, as if he were packing for a long trip. There were two televisions—one old, one brand-new. A manic kitten darted amid the piles of clothes and rubbish around the old man's body. Because he lived alone, we had to search for valuables, in the presence of a sergeant, and voucher them at the precinct. We found his military discharge papers, his false teeth, and stacks of pornography. The other cops left, and I stayed. It was my turn to sit on the D.O.A., waiting for the Medical Examiner to have a look, then for the morgue to take him away.

A man knocked at the door and said, "I took care of him. I'm his stepson. He wanted me to have the TV."

I told him to get some proof, and said that until then he should take the kitten. He left—without the kitten—and I turned on the television.

Less than an hour later, he returned with a lady friend. Both were completely drunk, and demanded in unison, "We loved him! We was his family! Let's have that TV!"

I closed the door on them and sat back down. There was a phone call. I waited, then picked it up, hoping that no one who cared for him would learn of his death by accident, from a stranger.

"Is Mr. Jones at home?"

"No, he isn't."

"Is this . . . Mrs. Jones?"

"No." But thanks for asking.

"When will he be available?"

"No time soon."

"When should I call back?"

"Can I ask who this is?"

"Mr. Jones had recently expressed an interest in our low-cost insurance policies, and—"

"He's not interested."

"And who, may I ask, is this?"

"The police. Mr. Jones is dead. That's why I'm here."

"Well, do you think—"

"Dead."

"There may be some—"

"Dead, dead, dead. He's stuck to the floor six feet away from me, guy. No sale."

"Have you considered whether you have all the coverage you need, Officer?"

I hung up and went back to watching television.

Who's the Victim?

Most of the time, the enforcement of the law follows a simple moral algorithm—the sum of what you should do and what you can. If the perp is there, you make an arrest; if he's not, you make a report. If he runs, you chase. If he shoots, you shoot back. The facts, rather than your feelings, dictate the course of action, but the close correspondence of the two is a satisfaction of the job. Sometimes, though, the victims are less sympathetic than the offenders, and an odd bond develops between cop and perp which can emotionally skew the equation.

One woman called to say that her thirteen-year-old son had locked her out of her house; she had obtained a Family Court order that allowed her to call the police whenever she couldn't control him. For over an hour, we knocked, reasoned, and threatened, and fiddled with the locks. We had ample time to find out about the family.

"Is there anyone—someone he isn't mad at—who could talk to him, get him to open the door?" I asked.

"Oh, he's not mad at me," she said. I let it go. "Maybe a friend from school?"

"I been tellin' him to go to school since last year," she said, adding that he stopped because the other kids beat him up. Asked why, she said that he wore makeup and women's clothes. My partner went to get a coat hanger, to see if he could work the door chain off. The woman went on about how the boy's father left her, how she worked, how the boy stayed out till dawn. She paused a moment, as if she'd just remembered, and said, "I had a three-year-old—she died. She was pretty." She paused again, then said, "I wish that faggot never was born."

My partner got the door open. The thirteen-year-old, a light-skinned black boy with hair dyed a sunny yellow, was dozing. I told him to get some things together, because he was going to a juvenile holding facility now and to court in the morning. By his bedside I saw a list of around twenty names—all men's, and all but a few with beeper rather than phone numbers. His mother picked up a skimpy pair of gold satin shorts, held them up to her substantial waist, and said, "Who wears these? Not me!"

What friendly or fatherly advice was there to offer? "I didn't peddle my ass when I was thirteen, young man, and now I have a cushy civil-service job"? We drove downtown without saying much, and I haven't seen him since.

Another day, on the street, I noticed that a middle-aged woman was staring at me, in the throes of indecision about whether to approach. I went over to her and asked if I could help. "My husband, he beats me, he beats me very bad," she said. I pressed her for details, telling her how, even if I couldn't make an arrest, she could get an order of protection, but she brushed me aside: "No, no, that's all no good. My daughter, she says she's just gonna get somebody to take care of him."

I told her that if he was beaten he'd probably take it out on her anyway, and again she saw I didn't get it. "I don't mean beat him up," she explained. "I mean take care of him. You know!" She raised her eyebrows, like she was letting me in on a sweet deal. "What do you think?"

"Lady, you noticed that I'm wearing a blue hat, badge, the rest? That I'm a cop? And you want to know what I think about having your husband murdered?"

Before she could ask me to quote a price, we parted, each convinced that the other had only a flimsy grasp of reality. A few hours later, another officer and I responded to a call of a "violent domestic dispute." A burly, middle-aged man answered the door and allowed us in. He was in his underwear and seemed at ease, smiling as he showed us around: there was no one else there, and no sign of a struggle of any kind. Even so, I didn't like him, and the female cop with me had the same reaction, but stronger: he had a corrupt and military air, as if he were an aide to some South American President for Life. As we left, I noticed a photograph of the woman I had spoken with earlier hanging on the wall. She was trying to win our argument, it seemed to me, saying, "Look at him. Look. If this one ended up dead, would you really come after me?"

I continued to have hopes for George. I didn't know if he was much more than a corner hoodlum, but the corners he favored were hot ones. And then he came to my attention again, formally, when he beat up his fiancée, Toni. The night before, she told me, George had knocked her down, shoved her against a wall, and confined her in a bedroom when she threatened to call the police. He'd slept at the door of the room, on the floor, to prevent her from escaping. The next morning, he went out and brought her back breakfast, drew her a bath, and then walked her up to her mother's house, where she called the cops.

When I came for George at his job, his rebuttal was as edgily eloquent and semi-plausible as

the last time: Yes, they argued, but, no, he didn't hit her ("Did you see a mark, a single mark on her?"), and if he shoved her once it was because she said she'd have him arrested if he ever left her. A cop witnessed that, he added, and we'd have to find him. He had a letter, in which she made that threat: we'd have to find it. I told him that I still had to take him in. He shrugged his acceptance, and we left for the precinct.

For the past year or so, it's been procedure to debrief every prisoner who comes into the precinct. Most perps won't talk, and many are as ignorant of the local underworld as they are of portfolio management. A detective asks, "Do you have information about robberies, homicides, guns, arson, hate crimes, chop shops, terrorism?" I've had people say, "Chop-chop? What chop-chop?" But when George's turn came he said, "Yes," "Yes," "Yes," "Yes," "No," "Yes," and "What was the last one?"

As it turned out, my prisoner was the Rosetta stone to scores of violent felonies, past and planned. George told us that people approached him to do hits and robberies almost every week. The narcotics king of Atlanta wanted to open night clubs in the city, for dancing and dealing, and had been asking George to run them. A robbery at a bodega was supposed to take place a few hours from now, and he knew the two guys who had planned it, what kind of gun they'd carry, how they knew the owner's brother, a pockmarked Dominican who carried a .357, and how he was the one to watch, to take out if he moved. One of the two had robbed a meat market a few months ago of five thousand dollars, with at least a grand in food stamps, which they moved through a Chinese restaurant. Most important, he knew about another planned hit—on a Brazilian man, a witness in a state case. He wouldn't say more.

It was as if George spread the deck and asked the detective to pick a card, any card—but only one. The detective chose the robbery planned for that night. The exchange was remarkably businesslike: if the bodega robbery occurred and arrests were made quickly, that would be good; if it could be prevented, that would be even better; and either result should be enough to secure

George freedom. Though it seemed shabby, and even dangerous, to bargain Toni's distress against the safety of a grocery store, it was just that—a bargain. What was left unmentioned was that George would, in all likelihood, be freed by the judge at his arraignment. Toni's case was weak, even terminal, and if history served as a guide the charges might well be dropped. (I had even found the cop who'd witnessed Toni's threats to have George arrested if he left her.) But George was back in the cage now, and he would do what he could to get out of it. It was a line of thought we encouraged.

As calls were made, and the hours passed, George explained that he had no problem giving up people who weren't close friends and who were going to hurt people. He had hurt people himself, and, while it didn't keep him up at night, he thought it a better thing if people didn't get hurt during jobs. George's efforts at moral understanding had a rote, calisthenic quality: "You think, What if it's your brother, your girl who gets shot in a holdup—how would you feel?" What really bothered him was that here he had information of great value, and he'd had to squander it on a domestic-violence charge. "I'm not gonna say all I know," he told me. "What if they grab me with a gun sometime, what am I gonna have left to give?"

It was after dark by now, and the bodega would be open for only a few more hours. There were countless reasons for the robbery not to take place then: a hangover, a date, the flu, an argument, a bad horoscope, or an arrest. The next night was Halloween, when the robbers could even wear masks without attracting notice. The detective passed the information to the borough robbery squad and sent us on our way to Central Booking.

The password had been spoken, but the gates remained shut. I hadn't quite expected that, and neither had George. This meant that he would have to spend the night with the losers, with their foul smells and sad stories, their tough-guy sneers and choked-back sobs. As I put him in the holding cell, George leaned close to me and whispered that he wanted to talk. "About the

Brazilian?" I asked. "About the Brazilian," he said. I loved that part; it was just like the movies. As they say, this is no job for a grownup.

There may be no crime more destructive to the criminal-justice system than a hit on a witness: if witnesses won't work, the system doesn't. For several hours, I pursued district attorneys and detectives to peddle my murder conspiracy, but there didn't seem to be a buyer. After midnight, I went home, determined to keep trying in the morning.

Let's Make a Deal

Toni arrived at court in the morning looking fresh and rested, and she remained resolute in her desire to press charges. When we were finished, I was taken aback at the vehemence of the assistant D.A.'s reaction. "Did you see that poor woman? I've never seen such fear!" she said. "I really want to put this guy away!" She had tears in her eyes.

Ordinarily, I would have been delighted with the response. Time after time, I've brought in assault cases, from domestic violence more often than not, and seen them dealt down to next to nothing. At last, I'd met a blazing champion of the downtrodden, and it couldn't have happened at a worse time. My peculiar mixture of motives made me uneasy, but I genuinely felt that her reaction was naïve and awry. There are times when my heart breaks for people; this wasn't one of them.

After Toni signed the complaint, I spoke to another supervising D.A., who sent me to another detective. This time, however, the detective reacted as I hoped, saying that we had to move, immediately, and do whatever possible to get to the Brazilian. But when I retrieved George from his holding cell, it looked as if the case had, again, fallen apart. He'd barely slept or eaten, and he was talking in crazy circles, saying that he could go back to jail and wouldn't care, and then that he'd never go back because he hadn't done anything. Once, he broke down—crying, with his face in his hands—and I thought we had lost him. We moved between paying him sympathetic attention and allowing him moments of privacy; we fed him; we let him call his sister to talk. "Think about your children!" I said. Let me tell you, we were ruthless. Finally, he came around and told us what he knew.

George didn't know if the Brazilian had testified or was scheduled to; if he was an informant or was just suspected of thinking about turning. The Brazilian ran narcotics for another dealer, who was in prison; the dealer suspected that his employee had betrayed him, and had ordered the hit. The fee would be six thousand dollars—half on agreement, half on completion. George also knew the name and address of the Brazilian, because he'd seen a video as a kind of prospectus for the hit: footage of the block, the apartment building, the apartment. In the last ten seconds, the Brazilian himself appeared in the video, stumbling unsuspectingly into the frame on his way home. All this George knew because he had been asked to do the hit.

Throughout the afternoon and into the evening, we worked on the deal. The D.A. wanted to know if anyone could I.D. the Brazilian as a witness or an informant; calls went back and forth between cops and prosecutors, word went up the chains of command, across agencies and jurisdictions. We were determined to prevent a murder, but the D.A., in particular, was terrified of another one, whose headline would read, "D.A. FREES PAROLEE, GIRLFRIEND SLAIN." He had Toni brought back in, to see for himself how she felt, how badly she was hurt, and if she was afraid.

George would not give the Brazilian's name without a promise from the D.A. that he himself would be out, today. The D.A. eventually agreed that it would be enough if the name checked out. George gave up the first name, which was all he remembered anyway—Kari. With this shred of evidence, the detectives started calling around and reporting back to us whatever they turned up.

"The D.E.A. has a Bosnian named Kiri, wants to know if it's your guy."

"F.B.I. has a Corio, from Naples."

"Naples, Florida, or Naples, Italy? Never mind, forget it, but keep taking anything close— Brazilian Kari might be Jamaican Kelly after how many guys are passing along the name."

By sundown, there had been no confirmation, but the D.A. agreed to let George out that night, in exchange for the Brazilian's address, with the stipulation that he accept the terms of the order of protection, enter a batterer's program, and agree to bring them the videotape the next morning. George gave an address in Manhattan, and a half hour later D.E.A. agents were on a cell phone from a car. No one was home, but neighbors confirmed that a Brazilian man lived there, and several said he was a drug dealer. They had a name. The Manhattan D.A. confirmed that he was a defendant in a drug case and a witness for the prosecution in a kidnapping: his own. The hit had been scheduled to take place that very night, it turned out, but the killers were spooked by the police presence.

And so it finally proved to be a good day's work, though not without its questions and compromises. A life was saved, by freeing the man who'd been asked to take it. The intended victim was the kind of person I'd just as soon arrest as rescue. But he was alive—at least for a little while longer—and George was his unlikely and reluctant savior.

George picked up his life more or less where he left off. Toni decided to drop the charges, and Jocelyn became pregnant by him again: "Gotta keep trying till I get a son," he said. Every week or so, I still run into George on the street, and we say hello. I like him, as far as it goes. The feeling is as mutual as it can be, I think, between two people who wouldn't hesitate to shoot each other. As he's a hit man and I'm a cop, the odds of such an occurrence are less remote than they might be otherwise.

The Importance of Family

It was near the end of my tour of duty, and I was headed back to the precinct when an aided case came over the air. Aideds are among the most frequent jobs, usually entailing an escort of E.M.S. workers to the scene of an illness or injury. When I arrived in the apartment, I could tell from the smell why someone had called. As I walked down the hall, past what seemed to be numerous, spacious rooms, the rank, ripe odor of decomposition grew stronger, and when an expressionless teen-age girl directed me to the last bedroom I was thrown less by the sight of the still, frail old Puerto Rican woman in bed than the four emergency medical technicians working around her. Two were crying.

The old woman was naked, lying face down, stuck to plastic sheets that made a crackling sound as she was unpeeled from them. She had once been a hefty woman but now looked less slimmed down than deflated: her breasts were empty, pressed against her chest, and the bones of her hips and thighs were plainly visible, draped with loose, lifeless skin. Maggots crawled on her, inchworming along, and popping off like broken watch springs. There was rodent excrement in the bed with her, and one E.M.T., examining her legs, said, with a horrified intake of breath, "Those are rat bites! Whoever did this to her should go to jail!"

The old woman let out a breathy moan as she was rolled over, feeling pain wherever her body was alive. This woman was dying; parts of her were already dead. And she didn't live alone. I turned away, and went to talk to the teenage girl: "Who takes care of this lady?"

"Well," she said, with a pouty, long-suffering tone, "I'm the one who does most of the work."

"Who lives here? How old are they?"

"Me and my sister and my grandmother. My sister's twenty-three, but she's out now."

"Can you tell me why you didn't feed her?"

"She said she wasn't hungry."

"Why didn't you call a doctor?"

"I'm the one that did."

"Before now, why didn't you call?"

"My mom said not to."

She said that her mother lived in another part of the city. I told her to call her and tell her to go to the hospital. I asked what they lived on, and she said her grandmother got checks and her sister cashed them to run the household. Ordinarily, E.M.S. prefers to have a relative ride in the ambulance with the aided, but when the teen-ager approached the door a no-longer-crying E.M.T. told her, curtly, "You want to visit Grandma? Take the bus."

Back at the precinct, it took some time to figure out how to write the complaint—for, while there are many laws regarding the care of children, the elderly are less explicitly protected. I found a misdemeanor in the Penal Law called "Endangering the welfare of an incompetent person," and named the adult sister and the mother as perpetrators. Since there were checks coming in, "Investigate larceny" was added. And that, I realized, without satisfaction, explained the family's nearly homicidal neglect. The old woman was the keystone of a tidy edifice of subsidies: a large apartment, Social Security, welfare for the teen-age girl. If she went to a hospital or a nursing home, all these benefits would vanish from their pockets. People talk about living from paycheck to paycheck; this family almost let a woman die that way.

War Stories

Every cop has his gripes and jokes, his epics and anecdotes about life on the job. I grew up hearing them. My great-grandfather was a sergeant, in Brooklyn: a dapper, dangerous figure from the Jazz Age who became Mayor Jimmy Walker's driver. My father was a police officer—briefly, before moving on to federal law enforcement, a law degree, and an M.B.A.—and his brother was a police officer for thirty-three years. My father died before I went on the job, but I think that my decision to become a cop would strike him as an affront to how far we've come from the hardscrabble west of Ireland and the docks of Hell's Kitchen. For the next generation to pound a beat might mean that his grandchildren would not try cases in the Supreme Court but instead make their livelihood digging potatoes with a stick by the crossroads outside Ballinrobe. Ah, acushla machree.

Now, after a few years on the job, I have my own war stories. On weekends, I'll sit back, lift up my feet, and tell my girlfriend, "I took a bullet out of a lady's living room. It must have been shot from Jersey. It went through the glass, and stopped on the sill. It landed there like a sparrow." Or "I talked a runaway into coming home. She was fourteen years old. All I had to do was tell her I'd lock up her boyfriend's whole family if she didn't." At times, the point of the job seems to be to make it home with an intact skin and a good story. The stories are a benefit, like the dental plan.

And you need them, like your handcuffs or your vest, to control events when you have to, and to cover your back. If you're a cop, you need a quick tongue, to tell the victim, the perp, the crowd, the sergeant, the D.A., the judge, and the jury what you're doing, what you did, and why. Are you ready to make a statement? No? Then you just did. You told me you weren't ready. "Police were unprepared to answer," says the lead in the morning paper. Or the gossip in the locker room, or the word on the street.

I also hear more than my share of stories. And so, aside from the odd Christmas party or fundraiser, I don't hang out with cops from the precinct. My friends who are cops were friends of mine before I went on the job. And most of the people I see regularly have nothing at all to do with police work. The job has enough of me. For five days a week, I stay off the streets unless I'm working them. And when I'm not in uniform I'd just as soon not see blue.

But I also notice that when I'm out on weekends and there's another cop there—at a wedding or a cookout or a club—I'll often spend most of the time talking with him. There are things you've done and places you've been that no one else has had to do or see in quite the same way.

136 PART 2: LAW ENFORCEMENT

DISCUSSION QUESTIONS

1. Of the techniques suggested in Sarah Glazer's reading for eliminating police misconduct (i.e., community policing, civilian review boards, training and screening, and strong supervision), which do you believe has the greatest likelihood for success? Why?

2. Given that police corruption exists in other countries, such as Mexico, defend or challenge the assertion that misconduct is an unfortunate but inevitable result whenever some citizens are given the authority to enforce the law against other citizens.

3. Marcus Laffey describes two personal revelations regarding police work, his pleased realization on being handcuffed in a training class that "these things work," and his surprise upon becoming a cop at how much people like cops. Given the negative press police often receive and the information about police misconduct in the other articles in this chapter, what evidence indicates that people really do like cops?

4. Laffey describes the deals made with "George" as an unfortunate but necessary aspect of police work. How much should effective policing rely on making deals with criminals in order to get information about other criminals? Who should decide, and what criteria should be used, when police make deals?

WEBSITES

www.ci.nyc.ny.us/html/nypd/finest.html

At the home page for the New York Police Department you can learn more about the department and the city described in Laffey's article.

www.echotech.com/quick.htm

The Fraud Information Center provides a "quick index" of police and law enforcement sites as well as other interesting links to crime stoppers and university police pages.

www.amnesty.org/ailib/aipub/1996/AMR/25103696.htm

Amnesty International's report on allegations of police misconduct in the New York Police Department.

wahoo.netrunner.net/pcc/

The Police Complaint Center is a national nonprofit organization that assists victims of police misconduct.

www.ci.mpls.mn.us/departments/other/cpra.html

The Minneapolis Civilian Police Review Authority, which is completely independent of the Minneapolis Police Department, investigates complaints of misconduct against Minneapolis police officers.

PART III

COURTS

CONTENTS

PART III. COURTS

CHAPTER 7: COURTROOM PERSONALITIES

The courtroom provides the formal setting for the second component of the criminal justice process. Lawyers may negotiate pleas in their offices and in courthouse hallways, and judges might decide questions of law in the privacy of their home or chambers, but it is in the courtroom that the process is made official. Courtrooms are often architectural showcases of their community, and it is not unusual—nor unintended—that citizens experience a sense of awe upon entering the sanctum. But despite the importance of the stage, the justice drama depends primarily on its legal actors. The key players will always include the defendant, the prosecutor, and the judge. Usually a defense attorney will also be present. The players gathered for an actual trial, as opposed to the simple formalization of an already established plea negotiation, might also include jurors and witnesses. All these people have interesting roles, but this chapter highlights just two types of players: lawyers and witnesses.

Lawyers are among the most maligned professionals in American society. In fact, an argument can be made that lawyers are considered at best a necessary evil in many countries. And this is not simply a contemporary point of view. You may recall Shakespeare's Dick the butcher's gleeful line, "The first thing we do, let's kill all the lawyers" (*Henry VI, Part II*). In colonial America the antagonism toward lawyers took the form of hostile legislation that, for example, stated it was neither necessary nor advisable to have judges learned in law. As a contrast to negative views about lawyers, the first reading in this chapter presents the profession in a more appealing light. Law professor Denis McLaughlin encourages law students to understand, appreciate, and practice the noble aspects of the legal profession. He refers to all types of lawyers, not just those practicing criminal law; thus the reading reminds us that defense attorneys, prosecutors, and judges play a unique and important role in our society. All of McLaughlin's points are worthy of further discussion, but pay particular attention to his comment about approaching the law with a critical eye. Is it the responsibility of lawyers to challenge a law as wrong—as Thurgood Marshall did before becoming a Supreme Court justice?

The second reading in this chapter reports on the research of psychologist Elizabeth Loftus, considered one of the most knowledgeable people in the world on the topic of eyewitness testimony. As you read about her skepticism of eyewitness testimony and the issue of repressed memory, ask yourself how trials might be changed if Loftus is correct. Should defendants be convicted on eyewitness testimony alone? Since child abuse almost always occurs in private settings, would placing restrictions on the evidentiary use of repressed memory to gain convictions be an inappropriate burden to place on prosecutors?

ON BECOMING A LAWYER

Denis F. McLaughlin

Denis F. McLaughlin is a professor of law at Seton Hall University School of Law. He delivered this speech to incoming students in the fall of 1993. In the speech, Professor McLaughlin stresses the importance of ethics, professionalism, and critical study to having a fulfilling career in law.

For the seventh and final time this morning, welcome to Seton Hall Law School. Having been greeted so many times this morning, you must know that my greeting is to serve some additional purpose. And it is. My purpose is to welcome you not only to the Seton Hall community, but to the community of lawyers of which you are now a part. For from this moment on, you must see yourself as a lawyer and as a member of the legal profession.

I want to speak to you this morning about two aspects of professional responsibility: the professional responsibility you owe to your profession and the professional responsibility you owe to yourself in becoming a lawyer.

Being Responsible to the Profession

You are an extremely select and privileged group. And I am not talking about LSAT scores and GPAs. I am talking about the privilege that your educational status has afforded you. Do you

Reprinted from Denis F. McLaughlin, "On Becoming a Lawyer," *Seton Hall Law Review*, vol. 26, pp. 505-11 (1996), by permission of the author and the *Seton Hall Law Review*.

know that less than 20% of the American population possesses a college degree? It's true. Our last census reported that only 19% of the American population age twenty and older have earned a college degree[1] and that only 1% of the population earns a doctorate level degree[2]—which is the degree you will earn here—the Juris Doctor degree. Because of your educational status, you will have the luxury of making life choices that other members of our society can only dream about. But with this privilege goes a special responsibility, especially in our role as lawyers.

The legal profession demands a lot of you. As lawyers, unlike other professionals, we are directly involved with the administration of justice. We are charged with upholding and preserving the rule of law, which forms the fabric of our society. Law touches every aspect of our lives and, without the continued confidence of the public in our system of justice and in its ability to dispense justice, our society cannot endure.

This is why in our professional ethics codes we are described as "guardians of the law"[3] and held to high standards of moral and ethical conduct. This is why the New Jersey and other state supreme courts refer to us as "ministers of justice."[4] But unfortunately that is not the public's perception of lawyers. More often than being called "ministers of justice," we are called mouthpieces, hired guns, hucksters, ambulance chasers. A survey released by the American Bar Association (ABA) shows that public confidence in the legal system and in lawyers is at an all-time low.[5] Sadly, it is the aberrational behavior of relatively few lawyers, and occasionally judges, that commands the headlines, and the enormous good done by lawyers goes largely ignored. It reminds me of the classic lament of the Peanuts character Charlie Brown—"When you're right, no one remembers—when you're wrong no one forgets."

In response to this survey, the ABA has launched a campaign to improve the image of lawyers and has hired a public relations specialist. Although this may help, I believe this is one campaign that will be won by actions rather than words. The best public relations ambassadors that the legal profession has are ourselves. The public perception will only change when each one of us sincerely embraces and accepts our role as a "minister of justice" and a "guardian of the law." The responsibility for transformation rests with each one of us. When each of us, in representing our clients, treats each client honestly and fairly and with a sense of humanity and dignity, the public perception will change. When lawyers keep foremost the sacred trust that has been given to us, public confidence will be restored.

We selected each of you because we believed that you possessed the moral character to serve the profession and the public honorably and with integrity. It will be some time before you begin your legal practices, but if you remember nothing else from the professional responsibility sessions of today and tomorrow, remember this—whenever any one of us falls from grace, we hurt not only ourselves, but every other member of the legal profession as well.

Being Responsible to Yourself

In emphasizing the responsibility you owe to your profession, we must not ignore the responsibility you owe to yourself in becoming a lawyer. It can be very difficult being a lawyer—balancing the demands of our obligations to our clients, the court, the bar, the public, as well as the pressure to meet a payroll. And we can sometimes become lost in the process.

As you start on the path of becoming a lawyer today, you must never forget that you are a person first and that you come to the legal profession with values, beliefs, and aspirations that are personal and unique to you. In learning how to be a lawyer, you cannot ignore this issue of personal identity. In making the transition from layperson to lawyer, you must begin to ask questions about yourself and your life that perhaps you have not asked before. You must begin the search for a unity of self and profession, a harmony of your values as a person and your role as an attorney.

The first step in this process of personal responsibility is to choose to become a lawyer because it is what you want for yourself. It would be a mistake and unfair to yourself if the only reason you were here was because it was what your parents, or your spouse, or some other person wanted for you. The law is a wonderful profession, but only if it is what you want for your life. Can you know for certain if the law is for you? No. You can have some idea, but you will not know for certain until you actually begin your practice, and even then it may take some time. You are taking a risk going to law school. But all we venture in life is a risk and life without risk is no life at all. I can tell you this, though—law is a risk well worth taking.

Law gives you the unique opportunity to be directly involved with the administration of justice. It gives you the tremendous opportunity to directly affect the quality of other people's lives for the better. I firmly believe that the opportunities for professional and personal fulfillment in the legal profession are unparalleled in any other. The law touches every aspect of our society, and whatever personal and professional interests you have, they may be blended beautifully with the law. Whether your interests are in the environment, the rights of the disabled, the rights of children, education, health law, employment discrimination, corporate and business, real estate, tax, family law, admiralty, patents, international law, criminal justice—whatever your interest—there is a place for you in the law.

You may also serve as a lawyer in so many different capacities. Some lawyers are courtroom litigators, while others never leave their offices. Some work in large, 100-member-plus firms, while others are solo practitioners. Lawyers work for all levels of government—federal, state, county, and municipal. Still others work as in-house counsel for large and small businesses, as well as for non-profit groups. Some become legislators, lobbyists, arbitrators, and some too become educators.

I do not know of any other profession that offers such a constellation of diversity and provides so many avenues for personal and professional fulfillment. I am now twenty years out of law school, and I do not regret for a minute my decision to become a lawyer.

Having made the decision to become a lawyer, the next step in your professional development is to see yourself as a lawyer from this moment on. I had a friend who attended medical school. On the first day of classes, the students went to a lab and a professor was there with a cadaver. The professor took a scalpel and cut the cadaver open. Three people fainted dead away. But after the session, all of the students understood its purpose—to make the students realize from day one that this was no longer college biology. This was medical school and they were there to become doctors. In the same way that these medical students are trained to see themselves as doctors, you must adopt this same mindset in seeing yourself as a lawyer.

You must strip away any notions that you have of yourself as a student. This is critical to your professional development. Remember, you did not come here to become a law student, you came here to become a lawyer. And you cannot practice law until you become competent in the law. When you see yourself as a lawyer, and not as a student, you will approach your studies with a perspective different from any other you have had in the past. You will realize that you now have a personal stake in each class, in each course, because this is now your profession. Each day you are learning the skills of your trade.

And do not think that your legal education ends at graduation. Lawyers, myself included, regularly attend trainings and lectures to keep current in the law. No one takes attendance, no credit is awarded, and no exam is required. Yet in any given week, hundreds of attorneys attend ICLE (Institute for Continuing Legal Education) seminars around the state. These are lawyers, practicing ten, twenty, and thirty years, who come for one reason and one reason only—to learn! They come as a matter of personal and professional pride because they know attendance will make them better lawyers. It is this same sense of personal and professional pride that you must adopt in your studies here.

Whatever you do not learn now will surely hurt you later on. Whether you remember the Freudian theories of personality disorder from college psychology may no longer be of particular detriment to you. But if you do not learn and understand the concept of promissory estoppel in Contracts or the theories of liability in Tort, you will surely suffer the consequences—most immediately when you sit for the bar exam, and most definitely when you practice law.

Remember your clients will not come to you with signs on saying "I am a Tort case" or "I am a Contract case." It will be up to you, the legal expert, to recognize the legal issues that your client's case presents. Your development of that legal expertise begins today.

Remember, that while your law school transcript may be of help to you in getting your first few jobs, it is only what you know that will enable you to represent your clients competently. Students study the same cases at Harvard that we study here. Lawyers do not enter the courtroom with their law school diplomas or their GPAs displayed on their chests. Judges have no idea where you went to law school, nor do they care. The success of your practice depends on one thing—your reputation for honest, competent, and quality representation. That quest for excellence and quality begins today.

The Importance of Being Critical

And when you study the law, study it critically—for the law is not static, but is ever-changing and evolving. Statutes and codes in force today may be amended or repealed in years to come. Even the United States Supreme Court, at times, reverses itself. Remember that laws are made by society to serve humankind. And while the law may not always achieve justice in every case, justice is nevertheless the goal of all law. Do not leave your common sense and your ideals of justice and fairness outside the classroom or the courtroom.

When you study the law, look to see what it is that we teach today that 25, 50 or 100 years from now people will ask: "How could they have believed that?"; "How could they have taught that?"; or "How could that have been the law?"

As a professor, I often think of the study of law in the first part of this century. Of how many professors dutifully assigned and how many students dutifully read the 1896 U.S. Supreme Court case of *Plessy v. Ferguson*,[6] which held that "separate but equal" facilities for people of different races was constitutionally permissible. Of how many students for years blindly recorded this case in their notes and incorporated it in their outlines. Until one person had the courage to stand up and say "No, it may be the law but it's wrong." To have the courage to stand up and argue the case of *Brown v. Topeka Board of Education*,[7] and change the course of American history. That was a person who studied the law critically. That person was Thurgood Marshall. Take a lesson in professional responsibility from this great jurist— and study the law critically. Be that spokesperson for justice.

And the final lesson in professional responsibility comes when you finish your studies here and are finally prepared to make the transition from becoming a lawyer to being a lawyer. You must then re-ask the questions we have talked about today—of what it is that you want for your life as a person and as an attorney—because you cannot separate the question of what kind of lawyer you want to be from the question of who you are as a person.

This process may take time. You may have to re-ask these questions at various turning points in your career. But eventually you will find your place. I did. The turning point in my life came when I decided to leave Philadelphia after realizing that the big-city, large-firm practice was not going to be for me. It was very difficult to leave everything that I had worked so long and so hard to achieve and to leave my colleagues, friends, and former classmates. But I knew in my heart that I needed a practice that would give me the opportunity to work more closely with people, to feel that I was making a difference. I came back to New Jersey and went to work for Legal Services—for those who do not know, legal services is the organization that represents poor people who cannot afford lawyers in civil cases. I worked as a volunteer attorney for six months before there was a paid opening. And when it was offered to me, I took it. I loved the work so much I stayed for ten years.

This is not to say that everyone should work for legal services. There are many paths to fulfillment in the law and you must find yours. If you want to be a tax lawyer, be one; if you want to be a corporate lawyer, be one. But be it because it is what you believe in for yourself as a person and as a lawyer. Be it because it best harmonizes your beliefs and values as a person with your vision of yourself as a lawyer.

And whatever kind of practice you eventually choose, make some time in your life to represent real people. In my years of practice, I estimate that I represented nearly 3,000 people. Nothing in my professional life ever compared to the satisfaction I felt on walking out of the courtroom with a client at the end of a case and having that person squeeze my hand and say "Thank you, thank you Mr. McLaughlin."

If you ever come to my office, you will not find awards or diplomas on the wall. You will see a bulletin board with pictures of my family. In the upper corner of that bulletin board you will see a four-leaf clover on a yellowing white card wrapped in plastic. A client I represented for three years gave that to me. She had been abandoned by her husband who left her with five children and a house in foreclosure after she developed cancer. She was Korean and had no family in America. But with all of her troubles, she had a marvelous green thumb and one day she saw that four-leaf clover in her garden. She said she wanted me to have it. And when she gave it to me she inscribed it with a cross and the words "God

Bless, Maria." I do not know what memories my friends have of their years of practice, but I know I will treasure that gift from Maria for the rest of my life.

I never earned what my friends in Philadelphia earned in the practice of law. But the law gave me something that money cannot buy. It gave me the satisfaction of knowing that in my own small way, I had made a difference in the lives of other people. And this is the true beauty of law. This is the wonderful opportunity that is before you today. It is yours to nurture and cherish as you choose.

And so I say to you: Study hard. Study to learn. Study for yourself as a matter of personal and professional pride. Study the law critically and do not be afraid to be the one who stands up and says "Yes, it may be the law, but it's wrong."

And when you finish your studies here and are ready to begin your practice, do not be afraid to follow your heart, even though others may tell you you are wrong. Do not be afraid to be the lawyer you feel you were meant to be. It is your life to live. You must decide how to live it.

REFERENCES

1. Bureau of the Census, Detailed Occupation and Other Characteristics from the EEO File for the United States (1990).

2. *Ibid.*

3. Model Code of Professional Responsibility Preamble (1981) ("Lawyers, as guardians of the law, play a vital role in the preservation of society.").

4. *In re* Joseph L. Nackson, 114 N.J. 572, 532, 555 A.2d 1101, 1103 (1989) (stating that the court views attorneys "as ministers of justice").

5. *See* Gary A. Hengstler, *Vox Populi: The Public Perception of Lawyers—An ABA Poll*, ABA J., Sept. 1993, at 60.

6. 163 U.S. 537 (1896).

7. 347 U.S. 483 (1954).

READING 15
THE PROBLEM OF EYEWITNESS AND REPRESSED MEMORY TESTIMONY

Jill Niemark

Psychologist Elizabeth Loftus's work on the fallibility of memory is controversial and has important consequences for the legal system. Jill Niemark, a journalist and novelist, explores what Loftus has discovered about memory and the resulting dispute among researchers.

She has been called a whore by a prosecutor in a courthouse hallway, assaulted by a passenger on an airplane shouting, "You're that woman!", and has occasionally required surveillance by plainclothes security guards at lectures. The war over memory is one of the great and perturbing stories of our time, and Elizabeth Loftus, an expert on memory's malleability, stands at the highly charged center of it.

Even in her field, opinion is divided between fury and admiration. "I have nothing good to say about Elizabeth Loftus," says Bessel van der Kolk, M.D., a psychiatrist at Harvard, who is an expert in dissociative disorders. "I have only the highest regard for Elizabeth Loftus's work," states Frederick Crews, former chair of the English department at the University of California

at Berkeley, and author of the most widely debated and discussed series of cover stories the *New York Review of Books* has ever published on the recovered-memory movement.

Loftus has spent most of her life steadily amassing a clear and brilliant body of work showing that memory is amazingly fragile and inventive. Her studies on more than 20,000 subjects are classics that have toppled some of our most cherished beliefs. She has shown that eyewitness testimony is often unreliable, that false memories can be triggered in up to 25 percent of individuals merely by suggestion, and that memory can be interfered with and altered by simply giving incorrect post-event information.

Because her work raises doubt about the validity of long-buried memories of repeated trauma in particular—though it in no way disproves them— she has found herself asked to testify in some of the more famous trials of our time. In fact, Loftus has been called as an expert witness in more than 200 trials, from that of mass murderer Ted Bundy to accused child-killer George Franklin; has appeared on countless talk and news shows, from *60 Minutes* to *Oprah*; has published 19 books and innumerable papers; and in 1995 received the Distinguished Contribution Award from the American Academy of Forensic Psychology.

Reprinted from Jill Niemark, "The Diva of Disclosure, Memory Researcher Elizabeth Loftus," *Psychology Today*, January 1, 1996, with permission from *Psychology Today* magazine. Copyright ©1996 (Sussex Publishers, Inc.).

Perhaps her voluminous mail says it best. One anonymous letter from an incest survivor concludes, "Please consider your work to be on the same level as those who deny the existence of the extermination camps during WWII." Another, from a jailed minister accused of mass child molestation, begins, "Your dedication and compassion for the innocent have earned my deepest admiration." Yet another, from a confused therapy patient, reads: "For the past two years I have done little else but try to remember. I have been told that my unconscious will release the memories in its own time and in its own way. . . . And I need to know if I am really remembering. The guessing has become unbearable."

Debating Memory

The war over memory is far from academic. In the mid-'80s an extravaganza of child-abuse cases swept this country, often directed at day-care workers, all of them based on testimony of children who often at first did not "remember" abuse, but when coached and asked suggestive questions, began to unravel a tapestry of magnificently horrific memories: preschoolers raped with knives, forced to drink urine, assaulted in networks of underground tunnels, tied naked to trees, and forced to watch their caretakers torture animals.

These notorious cases were quickly followed by a second wave, equally fantastic, involving adults who claimed they had recovered memories of sexual and/or satanic ritual abuse they had repressed during childhood. More than 800 lawsuits have been reported to date. Yet a third wave might have followed if we could prosecute extraterrestrials, for scores of Americans began to claim they had been abducted by UFOs and had long repressed *those* memories.

At the root of these claims is the belief that memory is always accurate, and that memories can be repressed—that one can bury traumatic experience in some crypt of the brain, forget it consciously, and then recover it in pristine form years or decades later. This two-pronged view of memory, imported (and distorted) from Freud into the popular culture, has been embraced by a whole

sector of America, from therapists to police detectives to the tens of thousands of adult women who read *The Courage To Heal,* often dubbed the bible of the recovered memory movement.

Uniquely, the war over memory has galvanized and mesmerized both high and low culture. It is the subject of earnest scientific research utilizing the most sophisticated tools of biology and psychology, and it is also battled out in lurid court cases covered intensively by the mass media. It is a war that has placed everyone from Roseanne to Cardinal Bernadin on the firing line. It has powerfully shaped and reshaped legislation, in a massive see-sawing of legal and public opinion.

To memory researchers like Loftus, who for years were quietly conducting their studies in academia, all this furor has been an incredible shock, as well as an unrivaled opportunity: "If I had known what my life would be like now—the frantic phone calls, the tearful confessions, the gruesome stories of sadistic sexual abuse, torture, even murder—would I have beaten a retreat back to the safety and security of my laboratory?" she asks in her recent book, *The Myth of Repressed Memory* (St. Martin's Press). "No. Never. For I am privileged to be at the center of an unfolding drama, a modern tale filled with such passion and anguish that it rivals an ancient Greek tragedy."

[In 1996 we entered] Act IV of the tragedy, for [in the previous year] convictions in mass-abuse cases [were] overturned with amazing rapidity and laws are changing once again. George Franklin, who was sent to jail in 1990 for first-degree murder in a 1969 incident that his daughter Eileen "remembered" 20 years later, was [eventually] set free, as were the accused in three cases where convictions for mass child molestation were overturned. And in May [of 1995], a New Hampshire judge barred prosecution based on repressed memories. Maryland, Minnesota, and California have [since] followed suit with similar rulings.

But Act V is yet to come, and may never end: for how do those innocently accused individuals put their lives back together? It is the theme that haunts Elizabeth Loftus. "I keep thinking of Oskar Schindler circling the lake with thousands of people," she says without a trace of irony, though she adds that she realizes people may misinterpret this statement as one of hubris. "If I could save one more person. . . ."

The Accused as Victim

The accused have been shot at, ostracized, imprisoned, interrogated, lost jobs and homes, and forced to fight lawsuits that have sometimes bankrupted them. In some of the cases, the charges seem entirely false. As *Wall Street Journal* writer Dorothy Rabinowitz writes of the notorious Amirault case, where three members of a family were accused of molesting the children in their model day-care center: "No reasonable person who looked at the trial transcript could doubt that three innocent citizens were sent to prison on the basis of some of the most fantastic claims ever presented to an American jury."

"It's shocking to me," says Loftus. "I feel as if some of these accusers are willing to blow up a 747 full of people because there might be one suspected child molester on board. They don't care that they're ripping the hearts out of families by their absolute insistence that this crime must be true, and that any attempt to cast doubt on that is backlash at best, and at worst the activities of some pedophile protector."

Though Beth Loftus is gregarious, warm, and (as one friend states) "always seems to be on a high without the aid of chemical infusion," she burst into tears twice in the first 20 minutes of our interview. We'd walked a few blocks back to her home from her favorite morning haunt, the Surrogate Hostess, pausing outside to lament with a neighbor over Loftus's "schizophrenic" tree, which wasn't growing properly. Her home is on a hill, comfortably furnished, with an eye for open space. Upstairs a loftlike, open-air bedroom offers a spectacular view of Lake Washington, set off with floor-to-ceiling bookshelves. Out in the garage is a cream-color sporty Mercedes, a quiet testament to the kind of money that can be earned as an expert witness (up to $400 an hour).

After a few minutes of chit-chat, I asked her about her mother's death by drowning when Loftus was 14. I was particularly curious because of an amazing anecdote she tells in her book: On her 44th birthday, at a family gathering, an uncle informed her that she had been the one to discover her mother's dead body. Until then, she remembered little about the death itself; suddenly the memories began to drift back, clear and vivid. A few days later her brother called to say her uncle realized he'd made a mistake, that Loftus's aunt had found the body, not Loftus. Therefore, those few days of "recovered" memories were utterly false. "My own experiment had inadvertently been performed on me!" she had written. "I was left with a sense of wonder at the inherent credulity of even my skeptical mind.". . .

The Beginning of Eyewitness Research

When she was growing up in Bel Air, California, Beth Fishman had no idea she was going to be one of the most famous psychologists in the world, that one day she would beat out B.F. Skinner when students at the University of Houston were given a choice between the two as guest lecturer. She was planning to be a high-school math teacher, "because math was the one thing my father and I could talk about." Two years after her mother's death, her father remarried. "Our stepmother had three children, and she was much nicer to her own kids. My two brothers and I became very close. We had all this history and tragedy and we bonded against our stepmother."

At UCLA she discovered psychology, graduated with a double major, and applied to graduate school at Stanford in mathematical psychology. There she met and in 1968 married Geoffrey Loftus. "I thought I'd take care of my husband's career just like my mother had, and then somehow in the third year of graduate school I got interested in long-term memory."

Fellowships and jobs kept the couple apart; even when they were both in New York, from the summer of 1971 to the summer of 1972, they lived in separate apartments. Finally, Geoff landed at the University of Washington and a year later Beth was offered assistant professorships at both Harvard and Washington.

He gave her 24 hours to decide, and suggested that if she went to Harvard they should divorce.

"I think he was hurt that I even had to think about it. I spent the next 24 hours on the phone with people. My advisors said, 'If you have to give up anything for Harvard don't do it, chances are you won't get tenured.' My friends said, 'If you have to give up anything for that odd marriage of yours, don't do it.' But I had to find out about Geoff. I really respected and cared about him." She moved to Washington, and not long after they bought the house she is living in now.

"Then I got a fellowship to Harvard. So we spent another year apart."

All this time, Loftus had been working seven days a week on yellow fruits: specifically, she was studying how the mind classifies and remembers information. In the early seventies, she began to reevaluate her direction. "I wanted my work to make a difference in people's lives." She asked herself, "What do I talk about when I have no other reason to be talking?" An impassioned conversation about a man who'd been convicted after killing someone in self-defense suggested the answer. Perhaps she could combine her interest in memory with her fascination with crime by looking at eyewitness accounts.

The Fragile Memory

Loftus obtained a grant to show people films of accidents and crimes and test their memory of such events. Thus the study of eyewitness testimony was born, a field she can literally claim as her own. At that time the world believed that eyewitness testimony was as reliable as a video camera. Loftus found that just the questions interviewers asked, and even the specific words they used, significantly influenced memory. "How fast were the two cars going when they hit each other?" will elicit slower estimates than ". . . when they smashed each other?"

Merely by careful questioning, Loftus could cause subjects to remember stop signs as yield signs, or place nonexistent barns in empty fields. Subsequent research has shown that violent events decrease the accuracy of memory: in fact, memory is weakest at both low (boredom, sleepiness) and high (stress, trauma) levels of arousal. The bottom line? Memory is fragile, suggestible, and can easily decay over time.

The implications for real life are obvious: witnesses of violent crimes questioned by police and detectives, who often have a bias, may not be reporting the truth. When Loftus published an article about her results in [Psychology Today] in 1974, she was suddenly hurtled from the safety of yellow fruits into the courtroom. She was called frequently to testify about the validity of eyewitness testimony for mass murderers like Bundy, Willie Mak, and Angelo Buono.

It was exciting and terrifying: "Eyewitnesses who point their finger at innocent defendants are not liars, for they genuinely believe in the truth of their testimony. . . . That's the frightening part—the truly horrifying idea that what we think we know, what we believe with all our hearts, is not necessarily the truth." Needless to say, her colleagues were bitterly divided about the appropriateness of her expert testimony. She was accused of exploiting trials to build her career; of taking research from windowless laboratories and applying it inappropriately to real life. . . .

What If the World Is Flat After All?

"Don't you ever worry that you're protecting pedophiles and molesters?" I ask her one afternoon, as we sit on her terrace. Her neighbors are gardening and have just invited her to a block party, the sun is shining, and we seem far removed, in this sylvan suburb, from the nightmare images of pederasts and butchered babies. "How do you make your judgment call?"

"You know, I've seen so many of these cases there's a cookie-cutter quality to them now. But I do wonder," she admits. "I have these moments when I think, What if I'm wrong about memory? What if people really do shove this collection of experiences into the subconscious and bury them there, and they leak and you can recover them in some accurate form and rely on it? I'm not saying it's impossible. Even the Hungerford case—where the daughter claimed her father raped her from the age of five until 23, including just days before her wedding, and then repressed all the memories until a few years later, when she entered therapy—even that I wouldn't say was impossible.

"When working on legal cases, in the end I can't say the abuse didn't happen. I can only say if these memories are false, here's how they may have developed. And I have this history—going way back—of worrying about the falsely accused. If there's one question I have about myself, one puzzle, it's that history." She has always worried about unfair punishment and has accepted almost every death penalty case offered. Her schedule is packed with flights to various cities to participate in court cases.

Scratch the surface and you discover how skeptical she is about the view of sexual abuse as the root of life-long trauma: she herself was molested by a baby-sitter when she was six and shrugs it off. "It's not that big a deal," she says candidly. When I mention award-winning poet Michael O'Ryan's recent memoir—in which he describes his childhood molestation as the cause of a tragic life centered around sexual addiction, which psychotherapy only belatedly began to heal—she gently scoffs and suggests that O'Ryan's therapy itself may have helped him create a revisionist view of his life, in which all of his troubles were traceable to that early experience.

The science of memory is itself contradictory, offering up evidence to both sides of the war—and both sides discount the other's arguments. Loftus's classic study, Lost in the Shopping Mall, showed that children and teenagers could be induced to remember the experience of being lost in a mall when young—even though it didn't happen—simply by being questioned about it. As time passed, the memories were embellished and became more vivid, much like traumatic "repressed" memories unearthed in therapy.

Since then, Loftus and colleagues have shown that even imagining a "false" (as opposed to real) event increases subjective confidence that the event happened, that subjects can confuse dreaming and waking events when presented with a list of them; that after being told they have tested with "high perceptual" ability and must have been exposed to spiral colored disks in their kindergarten classrooms, 50 percent of subjects can be induced to recall these nonexistent kindergarten "memories"; 63 percent can "recover"

nonexistent memories of being exposed to colored mobiles while in their hospital cribs—a literal impossibility since the nervous system is not developed enough to lay down explicit memories in the first few years of life.

Advocates of the phenomenon of memory repression claim that Loftus's work simply does not apply to abuse. "She doesn't study traumatic memory, she studies normal memory," asserts Judith Herman, M.D., a psychiatrist at Harvard Medical School. "During trauma, the explicit memory system fries," contends Connie Kristiansen, Ph.D., associate professor of psychology at Carlton University in Ontario.

Indeed, recent research shows that abuse may impact the master regulator of explicit memory—a tiny, seahorse-shaped organ called the hippocampus. Survivors of childhood abuse have a smaller hippocampus than normal. According to Daniel Siegel, Ph.D., a psychologist at UCLA, if the hippocampus malfunctions during trauma, while other components of memory carry on unabated, a memory may be laid down "implicitly," without conscious recall. In fact, the work of Joseph Ledoux, Ph.D., at New York University has shown that the amygdala, a tiny, almond-shaped organ in the brain, stores primitive emotional responses like fear independently of the hippocampus.

"The leap they're making, from implicit memory and Ledoux's work, is unconscionable," responds Frederick Crews, whose elegant essays in the *New York Review of Books* drew a direct and damning link between Freud and recovered memory. "We all know there's a wide area of mental activity that's implicit. When we drive our car down the street we are not consciously applying our skills. To say that the mere existence of implicit memory opens the door to the idea that multiple instances of incest can be completely forgotten is not only bad science, it's just flatly unethical."

"I've followed up on allegations of recovered memory made by patients in my practice," notes Richard Kluft, director of dissociative disorders at the Institute of Pennsylvania Hospital. He claims that 60.7 percent were able to document at least one episode of the abuse they had alleged in therapy. "In one case a father who had perpetrated incest and denied it gave a deathbed confession. He begged his daughter for forgiveness. She'd never accused him, never confronted him, and had not recalled the incest until she was in therapy."

Loftus doesn't buy it. "Just ask him for one documented, published case. Interview the fathers. Do not, do not, do not take a second-hand report of supposed confession without investigating." As for studies on the brain: "Genuine trauma may cause neurotransmitter change, maybe even brain volume changes. But can we rewrite laws based on such speculation? These findings are so far removed from actual repression of memories, and yet, sadly, so misused."

Says Kluft: "Loftus has done some brilliant work. Confabulation isn't new. The fact of the matter is, not only are there documentable recovered memories, there are also documentable false memories."

What's truly mystifying is that nearly every psychologist I spoke with acknowledged the possibility of truth on the other side—and yet the battle rages on, acrimonious as ever. Take Margaret Kelly Michaels—imprisoned for five years on charges of molesting children at the day care center where she worked. She's now free. But she still has eight civil suits pending against her; many parents are still convinced that she's guilty, and Michaels is filing a $10 million federal suit against the county, the state, and any individual involved in her prosecution. "I'm out to destroy a drooling, dark beast that never was," she has stated.

Red Licorice and Organ Donors

"I'm having an identity crisis," confesses Loftus over lunch one afternoon.

"You?" I stammer.

"I figure I have 25 years of good work left. And I'm wondering what to do next. Could I host a talk show? Could I be a columnist? Or should I start a think tank?"

She does not mean she would give up her work, just streamline it: "I could write four articles a year instead of eight, run two studies in-

stead of six." What she really means is she wonders how to better instigate social change, and how to enlist others in that cause. (Later, in an e-mail exchange, she writes me: "Yes, yes, you can live an unconventional life . . . that's the point of wanting to have a perch from which to educate people who think this is not possible.")

Walking back to campus, we chat idly about a colleague of hers who specializes in the study of alcoholism and is famed for his "bar" lab. He was at a faculty party the night before; like Loftus, he has been admired and decried for his research. At the party, he'd invited her to the 20th anniversary celebration of his marriage, where he planned to show a video of his wedding. She'd had a few glasses of wine, was teary and happy, and had put her arms around him, saying, "I'm so glad you're my colleague."

The conversation wanders from alcoholism to cirrhosis.

"I wonder if they could have given the liver Mickey Mantle got to someone else," she says. By now I've learned to recognize this kind of statement as archetypal Loftus: wouldn't that be efficient *and* you could save a life at the same time.

We talk of organ donors. A friend of mine is waiting for a kidney transplant and is quite ill. Loftus pulls out her wallet and shows me her driver's license. Organ donor. "I had to get past the idea that maybe they'd take my organs out before I was really dead."

At one point I simply asked her, "Why are you so nice to people?" Her response, quite Skinnerian and yet elusive: "I like myself afterwards."

On my last day, at a small party for some of her students in her home, someone brought a bag of red licorice. Loftus had been proudly showing off a kinetic sculpture by a Romanian named Constantin—a melange of sharp silvery pieces that, when they moved, looked both lethal and beautiful. The sculpture was her first major art purchase, but her real delight in it (of course) seemed to be the heroic story of Constantin, who walked across Romania for six nights (hiding by day) to reach the border and freedom.

She took the licorice and turned to me.

"One of the articles about me mentioned that I love red licorice, and ever since I've gotten bags of it from all over. I was thinking after our conversation about organ donors yesterday, that if you mention it, someone out there may become an organ donor, and if even one life is saved. . . ."

"I'll do it," I promise.

"You see," she continued, confident and pragmatic, lifting her glass of wine, "you can do something like that in every article you write, and that way you can change the world."

DISCUSSION QUESTIONS

1. Why, in your opinion, do lawyers so often have a negative image among citizens? What images of lawyers would you expect persons in the criminal justice system (e.g., police, probation officers, parole officers, corrections personnel) to have?

2. Citizens are often surprised to learn that prosecutors and defense attorneys are sometimes friends. Even more distressing might be the knowledge that during their careers many lawyers work as a prosecutor for several years before becoming a defense attorney. Both situations might support the image of lawyers as sly and deceptive, with the ability to serve both sides without reservation. Do you believe that these situations can compromise a competent defense or prosecution?

3. Elizabeth Loftus says that one of the most difficult aspects of eyewitness testimony is that the eyewitnesses who identify innocent defendants are not lying—they truly and honestly believe the defendant was the person they saw. This situation not only makes the eyewitness very believable to the jury, but also makes for very indignant eyewitnesses when their statements are challenged. What courtroom procedures might allow for eyewitness testimony that is accurate and disallow inaccurate eyewitness testimony?

4. Just in case Loftus is correct regarding the fallibility of repressed memory, should the maximum penalty be reduced for child abusers who are convicted solely on repressed memory testimony? Why or why not?

WEBSITES

www.ananet.org
www.hg.org
These websites for the American Bar Association and for Hieros Gamos are excellent places to find additional information about the study and practice of law.

weber.u.washington.edu/~eloftus
Elizabeth Loftus's home page with the University of Washington includes some of her articles on her memory research.

www.pbs.org/wgbh/pages/frontline/shows/dna
At this site is the transcript from a *Frontline* television show broadcast in 1997 by the Public Broadcasting System. The show includes information about eyewitness testimony and the use of DNA evidence.

CHAPTER 8: THE TRIAL

Of every one hundred typical felony arrests, only about eight will actually go to trial, even though for many Americans a courtroom trial is the predominant image of how the accused is "brought to justice." Likewise, while it is common for a defendant to be tried before a judge alone (called a bench trial; about half the cases going to trial are bench trials), most people equate trials with juries.

In this chapter's first reading, Robert Tarun helps us better understand the American trial process by contrasting it with trials in England. Interestingly, despite America's historical link to the English justice process, some distinct differences have developed in the way each country conducts a trial. Try to anticipate the points Tarun makes at the reading's end by determining on your own how the Old Bailey trial of M differs from what would occur in most American jurisdictions.

Tarun notes that jurors are selected differently in English and American trials. The voir dire process in American trials is not as convoluted and extended as the trials of O.J. Simpson and Timothy McVeigh would indicate. However, the selection for actual service on more typical juries is certainly more involved than Tarun observed at Old Bailey. Because both defense and prosecution usually are permitted to reject a certain number of potential jurors through the use of peremptory challenges, it is not unusual for persons with ties to law enforcement to find themselves dismissed by the defense, on the assumption that such persons are going to be predisposed toward the prosecution's argument. In his account of his own jury duty, former police captain Marshall Frank relates the unusual experience of an ex-cop on a jury in a criminal case. As you read, try to determine why the defense counsel did not dismiss Frank.

READING 16
COMPARING AMERICAN AND BRITISH TRIALS

Robert W. Tarun

An American lawyer highlights the significant differences between American and British criminal procedure. Robert W. Tarun, a former federal prosecutor in Chicago, watches the case of M, a manslaughter suspect in London.

Among the many hurdles that M faced on the first day of his manslaughter trial at the Old Bailey in 1990 were: a prior theft conviction; an excited utterance that he hit the deceased because he "felt like it"; an eyewitness who said the accused struck an unsuspecting C while his hands were in his pockets; two lengthy pre-trial interviews by Scotland Yard detectives; a barrister whom he first met on the day of the trial; a jury that was selected in two minutes; and a judge who directed his counsellor to proceed with the defence case that afternoon.

Despite the widespread assumption that American and British criminal procedures and trials are very similar, the reality is that there are many significant differences.

The Death of the Victim C

In September, 1989, two young women invited friends to a birthday party in the basement of a London pub. One of the invitees, M, then a 19-year-old labourer, brought his girlfriend L, her friend E and his sister N to the party. Although the

Reprinted from Robert W. Tarun, "An American Trial Lawyer's View of an Old Bailey Trial," *New Law Journal*, July 16, 1993, by permission of the author and the *New Law Journal*.

women had not received invitations, they remained with M at the party. After the pub closed at 11 pm, the four left the party and came across A, C's girlfriend, on a nearby road. She had an argument with M's guests over why they had not been invited to the party. In defence, A said that it was not her party and that she had had no input into who was invited. Seconds later (the defendant would later claim) C threw an errant punch at him, to which he reflexively countered with a right to the jaw which felled the deceased backwards where his skull thudded against the concrete pavement. C's girlfriend A dropped to her knees to gather his head and along with others, took him to his mother's home where he remained in what witnesses later alternatively described as a sleepy or unconscious condition. Alarmed that he remained unresponsive to those around him, C's friends summoned an ambulance at 4.30 am. Approximately seven hours later, he died at a nearby hospital. M was charged with C's murder, which charge was reduced to manslaughter.

The Trial of M

In 1990, the manslaughter trial of M was called at the Old Bailey. At the outset, both the barristers for the prosecution and the defence lamented to the judge that they had only received the M case and witness interview statements the night before. Although the court was somewhat annoyed at the apparent foul-up in the system, neither barrister asked for an adjournment—the denial of which in the American system of justice would have fostered an appellate issue.

The judge directed his usher to bring 15 potential jurors into the courtroom. The clerk of the court called the accused's name, and the short, stocky M, dressed in an ill-fitting double-breasted "trial suit," went into the dock with only a guard seated nearby. After reading aloud the formal charge, the clerk asked the defendant "Are you guilty or not guilty?" M, in a barely audible voice, responded "Not guilty." The court then assured the *venire* that the trial was likely to be finished by the following Tuesday. After the clerk had rattled off the names of 12 potential jurors, the court briskly asked the defendant whether he had any objections to the jury. Hearing no immediate objection, the clerk quickly swore in the 12 citizens. The jury selection process took less than two minutes. The judge informed the empaneled jury that the instant case involved the unfortunate and tragic death of one C and that the defendant was charged with striking the fatal blow outside a London pub on an evening in September 1989.

The Crown was then asked to proceed, and counsel gave a 10-minute opening statement which largely consisted of a recitation of witness statements. The prosecutor told the jury that there had been an invitation-only party on an evening in September of the year past, that some girls had had an argument over who had been invited and that "the defendant had without provocation struck one C, whose hands were stuffed in his pockets at the time of the blow." The force of the fist to C's jaw, the prosecutor stated, caused him to fall backwards and strike his head on a walkway, from which he never recovered. The prosecutor asked the usher to furnish the jurors with street diagrams and photographs of the scene of the crime which he briefly reviewed. The Crown's counsel then took his seat.

The Crown's Case

With no opportunity for an opening statement by defence counsel, the court directed the prosecution to present its witnesses. Following the brief testimony of one of the two party hostesses, eyewitness A, the deceased's girlfriend, recount-

ed the argument with M's friends outside the public house and the altercation shortly before midnight. She recalled that she saw M's fist "come around" after it had hit C and that she saw C fall backwards towards the ground where she heard his skull crack upon the pavement. She said that C had had his hands in his pockets that night as he frequently did and that she never saw him throw a punch towards M. In cross-examination, M's barrister carefully explored the distances between, and the location of, persons at the scene. However, neither A's relationship to the deceased nor her animosity towards the defendant was even mentioned. The prosecution next called an off-duty bartender, W, who said that on arrival at the scene of the altercation, he asked M why he had hit C. W vividly recalled M's succinct response: "I felt like it."

The court excused the jury for lunch shortly before 1 pm and asked the Crown how many more witnesses there were, strongly suggesting that there "must be a way for admissions" between the parties. The barrister for the Crown responded that he had an ambulance driver, a pathologist and one or two other minor witnesses. He apologised that the pathologist was not available until the following morning. The judge interjected that he thought the case was straightforward and simply involved the issue of self-defence. He could not see how post-incident events and medical opinion could have any bearing on the pivotal issue of self-defence.

Seizing the court's hint, the parties worked diligently over the lunch hour to stipulate to the testimony of the ambulance driver and pathologist.

In the afternoon, the Crown called a detective from Scotland Yard who related in verbatim question and answer format the entirety of two lengthy pretrial interviews of M. The defendant had been represented at both interviews by a solicitor who permitted his client to be fully examined. The inspector testified that in both interviews M said that on the night in question he had drunk five pints of lager and that he had struck C with a single blow which caused him to fall backwards striking his head. In each interview the defendant claimed that C had thrown a first, albeit unsuccessful, punch. The detective was not cross-examined. The Crown rested its case at three o'clock.

The Defence Case

M's barrister asked the court for an adjournment until the following morning, arguing that she had only received the file of this manslaughter case the evening before, that she had spent a total of less than two hours with her client and that she needed time to prepare him for direct and cross-examination. She also explained that she had expected the Crown's case to last until Friday and that she had no witnesses ready to testify. Although the judge again expressed puzzlement over the delay in files being provided to both counsel, he urged that the case was very simple, that the defendant knew the facts as he had certainly discussed them with his solicitor and that there was little to prepare him for in terms of cross-examination.

After the judge had made it clear to defence counsel that she could begin her case in 20 minutes, he adjourned for the mandatory afternoon tea. The barrister scurried up the steps of the dock to prepare her new client as courtroom personnel and spectators watched from below. While the jurors paced in an outer corridor of the Old Bailey, the usher in the courtroom whispered to observers that M had a bully's reputation in his neighbourhood and that he had been warned repeatedly by constables to stop picking fights.

The trial resumed 15 minutes later. A frightened young defendant took the stand, staring at his parents in the second floor visitor's gallery. The judge quickly admonished the soft-spoken defendant, saying he would do better to look at the jurors who would decide his fate, and to speak forcefully. The direct examination of M was an awkward exchange which included the defendant's plea to a theft charge two years earlier. The 5'5" defendant testified that the 6'1" C had inexplicably thrown a punch at him while the young women argued over why they had not been invited to the party. M was nervous and rather vague about ever responding to a passerby bartender's question as to why he had thrown a

punch. The defendant concluded his direct examination by offering his regret that C had died.

A stilted cross-examination began with a reminder that the defendant had consumed five pints of lager that night and the pointed question of whether he had been feeling "rather aggressive" under the influence. M responded that he had not felt aggressive and that five pints was not a large quantity for him to drink on a weekend night. In answer to a pugilistic point about why C had not adopted a protective stance following his alleged opening blow, the defendant conceded that his alleged aggressor had not been prepared for his "counter-punch." Although M was unprepared for this line of inquiry, he simply said he did not know why his "counter-punch" had been so effective or unanticipated.

In the final moments of cross-examination, counsel for the Crown submitted to the defendant: "I put to you that on the evening in question, you threw the first and only punch at C while he had his hands in his pockets?" The accused politely and not too surprisingly denied that that was so. There was no further direct examination of M. Throughout the trial, objections to opponents' evidence and questions were rare and when made, were often preceded by an apology such as "I'm sure my learned opponent did not intend to suggest by his question that . . . ." The judge begrudgingly adjourned the case until the following morning. At the end of the day the spectators seemed resigned to the likelihood that another defendant would be convicted at the Old Bailey. The next morning, M's counsel called L, the client's girlfriend, to recite the fateful roadside events. She testified that C threw a first punch which M ducked and then responded with a fist to C's jaw. Under cross-examination she was unable to explain why C would have started the fight. N, the defendant's sister, took the stand next, but her distance from the altercation made her a minor witness. However, she, like the Crown's witnesses, confirmed that her brother threw only one punch and did not strike the deceased more than once. The defence rested, and the Crown offered no rebuttal testimony.

At 11 am the court directed the parties to proceed with the final arguments. Counsel for the Crown gave, by American standards, a decidedly unemotional 15-minute closing which summarised the evidence and suggested that there was a clear basis in the evidence for the jurors to be "sure" that the defendant had unlawfully struck the fatal blow. The defence, in an equally passionless argument, stated that there was ample evidence of self-defence and explained that M was not on trial for the theft charge to which he had freely admitted his guilt. She also urged that his nervousness on the stand was understandable. To counter an effective prosecution argument that if C had been the aggressor he would have been prepared for a counter-punch, she reasoned that experienced fighters are knocked out all the time even though they are trained to expect follow-up or counter-punches. She concluded in quiet fashion that the jury should acquit her client. Little attention if any was directed during the arguments to the witnesses' motives or biases.

The Jury Charge and Summing Up

Without any jury instruction conference, the judge proceeded to instruct the jury on the law of manslaughter and self-defence and then summed up in detail the evidence presented at trial. He told the jury that although it was their duty to decide the facts and they could disregard his summary, he believed that the case boiled down to the simple issue of who struck the first blow. The court lamented that the death of C was an unnecessary tragic event which the jurors could not change and added that there was no question but that the defendant's punch had caused the victim's death. He argued that this was not a case about gate-crashers or a party, but simply about who threw the first punch outside a public house on an evening last September.

The judge, who had taken careful notes in laborious longhand, offered that the case basically involved "two young men out for the evening who have a few pints, and there was no evidence that M was the worse for drinking." In reviewing the eye-witness testimony of key Crown witness, A, the court remarked to the jury that "her attentions at the time of the altercation were focused on the source of her irritation—the women who by all evidence were not her friends of choice then nor today." In urging the jury to be careful, the court made an analogy between the trial testimony and a football game and penalties. Opposing fans, he explained, will not see the play from the same perspective. He cautioned that "people don't see everything, even if they're actually involved. In their mind's eyes they re-create. Before the event these people were not standing back saying 'I must take notes.'"

As to the burden of proof, the judge instructed the jury that if they were "sure" M threw the first punch, they should find him guilty. If they found that the defendant's testimony might reasonably be true, they should acquit him. The court urged the jury to try to reach a unanimous verdict and then directed the jury to retire and deliberate. The drained defendant left the dock to join his parents.

The Verdict

Within a half hour the jury sent a message to the usher that it had reached a verdict. The sullen defendant, the jury and counsel reassembled in the court, where the foreman announced a verdict of "Not Guilty," causing a cacophony of sighs in the balcony. Without so much as a glance towards his weary barrister below, M dashed out the rear of the dock to embrace his relieved parents in the hallway behind the courtroom. The judge, with no trace of disappointment at the verdict, thanked the jury for their service and hoped that they would not have to begin service anew, late on a Friday afternoon.

One is quite tempted to speculate unduly about the jury's decision and, in particular, the impact of the judge's synthesis of the facts and trial issue. Perhaps it is best to leave the M verdict with the words of the late Sir Sebag Shaw, an esteemed criminal barrister and later judge, who in opining that a jury is "the right kind of body to try criminal cases" observed:

> It [the jury] has the great merit and advantage of being anonymous and amorphous. Once the trial is over it's dissolved and there is no person responsible or answerable for the decision. It can therefore be much more indepen-

dent. It hasn't got to consider what people will think about it as an individual, as a judge might think about how the public will regard him as an individual, if he were to come to a wrong verdict.

Differences Between English and US Criminal Proceedings

The *M* trial highlighted some unexpected differences between the British and American criminal justice systems. Recognising the inherent risk of extrapolation from a single trial, the following distinctions were observed:[1]

• While solicitors for targets or defendants may permit their clients to be interrogated fully by detectives during a criminal investigation, their American counterparts would, in the absence of immunity or a clear promise of leniency, rarely permit such an interview of a client.

• While barristers are not permitted to meet or interview any witnesses prior to trial, American prosecutors would in any major case have spent hours and possibly days preparing key witnesses for trial. In most instances, these "government witnesses" would decline to be interviewed by defence counsel or investigators employed by the defence.

• While barristers regularly interchange the roles of prosecutor and defence counsel, American prosecutors are almost without exception full-time employees of the government.

• The American prosecutor is obliged to disclose to the defence all material which in his judgment tends to be exculpatory or which may be used to discredit or impeach government witnesses. In addition, the government must tender to the defence reports or statements of government witnesses after they have testified on direct examination. The statement or report must relate to the subject matter of the witness' direct testimony before it will be turned over. Signally, "unused statements" of the prosecution, such as reports of unsuccessful interviews, witnesses interviewed but not called at trial and investigative leads, are almost never disclosed to defence counsel in American courts.

• A request for a continuance to prepare for a manslaughter trial by defence counsel who had only had one day to confer with his client would be granted by most trial judges in America.

• While Crown and defence barristers are expected to review and resolve most evidentiary issues prior to trial, their American counterparts frequently do not, necessitating an often endless need for trial objections, sidebars and Court rulings.

• American jury selection is premised on impartiality, not randomness. The Sixth Amendment to the United States Constitution provides in part that "the trial by an impartial jury of the State and district wherein the crime shall have been committed . . . ." Jury selection in the US routinely takes an hour or more, and in a complex case days and occasionally weeks. To secure a fair and impartial jury, an American trial court will conduct a *voir dire* of prospective jurors sufficient to reveal any potential bias.

• Both the prosecution and defence have peremptory challenges in American federal courts, the number of which are dependent on the gravity of the offence. For offences punishable by death, the government and defendant are each allowed 20 peremptory challenges; for offences punishable by imprisonment for more than one year, the government is allowed six peremptory challenges and the defendant 10. For offences punishable by imprisonment of less than a year, the government and defendant are each allowed three.

• The civility between barristers and towards the court at the Old Bailey was extraordinary. Sadly, their American counterparts are often distrustful of each other and frequently are openly discourteous to their opponents.

• The conventional wisdom among defence lawyers in America is that defence lawyers should give an opening statement immediately after the government does so. The widespread belief is that unless the defence quickly counters with its theory of the case, the jury will make its mind up early and convict a defendant.

• An American defendant sits with his counsel during the trial (as opposed to in the dock) and is able to consult with counsel more effectively about the direct or cross-examination of witnesses as well as other trial strategy.

• If an American defence lawyer and client decide to have the client take the stand, the client will normally testify last so that the client will have had the opportunity to view the cross-examination style of the prosecutors and the benefit of complete knowledge of what defence witnesses have testified to.

• An American prosecutor would rarely ask a defendant the ultimate question or trial issue, for example "What I am putting to you, M, is that you threw the first and only punch at C while he had his hands in his pockets? Now isn't that really what happened?" The theory is that the accused's answer is predictable, self-serving and needless in view of his plea of not guilty.

• Closing arguments are much more theatrical and impassioned in America. Indeed, defence arguments occasionally border on the unruly.

• In the view of its burden of proof, a federal prosecutor in the US is permitted to reply in rebuttal to the defence closing argument.

• At the close of evidence any party in a federal trial in the US may file written requests that the court instruct the jury on the law as set forth in the requests. The court must inform counsel of its proposed actions upon the requests prior to the their arguments to the jury. Federal judges normally read verbatim instructions to the jury. Although there is no requirement that there be a jury instruction conference in a federal trial, such conferences are routinely conducted in chambers prior to closing arguments. Failure to hold such a conference may be a reversible error where the defendant demonstrates that he was prejudiced by such failure.

Many states have adopted "pattern jury instructions" for both civil and criminal cases—beginning in Illinois in 1961. This practice has made an enormous contribution to certainty and uniformity. There are also federal pattern jury instruction treatises which the courts and counsel alike look to for direction and specific instructions.

• The burden of proof is much more precisely and uniformly addressed in the US. The government must establish a defendant's guilt beyond a reasonable doubt. Rather than suggesting to the jurors that to convict the defendant, they should be "sure" that he committed the crime, an American federal court would most likely read a "reasonable doubt" instruction to a jury such as:

> In criminal cases, the government's proof must be more powerful than that. It must be beyond a reasonable doubt.
>
> Proof beyond a reasonable doubt is proof that leaves you firmly convinced of the defendant's guilt. There are very few things in this world that we know with absolute certainty, and in criminal cases the law does not require proof that overcomes every possible doubt. If, based on your consideration of the evidence, you are firmly convinced that the defendant is guilty of the crime charged, you must find him guilty. If on the other hand, you think there is a real possibility that he is not guilty, you must give him the benefit of the doubt and find him not guilty.[2]

The federal circuit courts in America are divided on the issue of whether a reasonable doubt instruction should be given. Some circuits have held that a jury should be instructed that "the government's burden of proof is beyond a reasonable doubt" and nothing more. Others have held that it may be a reversible error to fail to give an instruction, particularly if requested by counsel. The United States Supreme Court has held that the due process clause requires the government to prove "beyond a reasonable doubt" every element of the crime with which a defendant is charged. A defendant must be acquitted when the court defines reasonable doubt in a way that impermissibly eases the prosecution's burden of proof (trial court's equating "reasonable doubt" with "substantial doubt" violative of defendant's constitutional right).

• An American court does not routinely review in detail what it considers to be the main points of evidence for the jury. While a judge in a federal criminal trial has wide latitude to assist juries by explaining, summarising and commenting on the evidence, he is under a strict duty to direct the jury that they are the sole judges of fact and are not bound by the judge's comments. Few American judges would have treaded as far and perhaps as accurately as the *M* judge did in commenting upon the trial evidence.

• While a judge may permit a less than unanimous verdict in a felony trial in Britain, the United States Supreme Court has consistently recognised a defendant's right to a unanimous verdict in federal jury trials.

• Finally, the most obvious difference between the Old Bailey and American criminal courts remains the attire of the barristers. The wigs and robes in the hallowed halls of the Old Bailey lend a credence, majesty and respect for the law which few American courtrooms can duplicate.

NOTES

1. The US has a dual court system: each of the 50 states plus the District of Columbia has its own system as does the federal government. Unless otherwise indicated, the American law discussed in this section will be the applicable federal law.

2. *Pattern Criminal Jury Instructions* (Federal Judicial Center) No 21 Definition of Reasonable Doubt.

READING 17
AN EX-COP ON THE JURY

Marshall Frank

Retired police officer Marshall Frank spent thirty-one years fighting crime on the streets. In this selection he recalls his experience as a juror on a criminal trial.

For nearly 31 years I'd been exempt from jury duty. No more. This time when I received my summons I wouldn't be entitled to automatic exclusion as a law enforcement officer. Having just retired, I'd have to report.

Like most anyone, I dreaded the prospect of time away from home and responsibilities. There had to be a way out—I thought it would be simple. A hard-line cop to the core, I'd ascended to captain in the largest police department south of the Mason-Dixon line, Metro-Dade in Florida. A prosecutor's dream, a defense attorney's nightmare. I'd be home in no time.

I reported to the courthouse on a bright Monday morning and flashed my retiree's badge to the young woman in charge. "There's not a chance of being accepted," I explained. "So why waste my time and yours?"

"Sorry, please be seated."

Hmmmm.

My name became a number, UR1003, one of more than 300 exasperated men and women mustered in a huge assembly room listening to orientations about courtroom procedure and demeanor.

Reprinted from Marshall Frank, "Ex-cop on the Jury," *Police*, February 1995, by permission of *Police* magazine, Bobit Publishing, Torrance, California.

Old stuff. A long week stretched ahead.

First Impressions

At 2:30 p.m., my number was finally called. Thirty of us proceeded into a small, pristine courtroom nestled on the ninth floor. As we went to our seats I surveyed the scene. A young, blond judge presided. The lawyers, both white and immaculate, sat at their tables studying us. A black youth dressed in a rumpled black shirt and tie sat next to his lawyer. No one had to guess who the players were.

My prejudices began to surface. I'd seen it too many times. The defendant is probably charged with a major felony and knows the system. He has the public defender who's under pressure of a case load. The prosecutor looks confident. He's pro-cop. The other isn't.

I figure the guy's guilty. After all, it's rare that they're not. Just another dirtbag, a social parasite clogging the criminal justice system. That's my orientation, my background.

As the proceedings unfolded, my interest began to pique. This was a whole new adventure. What a great opportunity. Inwardly, I was hoping to be selected. But once they knew about me, I figured I'd be excused in a heartbeat.

Voir Dire

I listened carefully to the lawyers questioning each juror. They spent an inordinate amount of time trying to qualify the two blacks in the group of 30. They were both elderly, fragile and confused. Despite the good intentions of both sides, this jury was destined to be comprised of non-Hispanic, middle-class whites.

During the first round, everyone was asked if they were related to or knew anyone in law enforcement. Finally, at my turn I said, "I have hundreds. I'm a retired captain from the Metro-Dade Police Department in Miami."

There. That did it. The kid on trial cringed.

The prosecutor asked me no questions. I guess he figured I was with him. The gangly young defender waited until the end before posing one simple question about the concept of weighing evidence and defining reasonable doubt. Academic. No way this guy would be so stupid as to pick me.

The lawyers and judge huddled at the side bar and resumed with their selections. "Number one juror," announced the judge, "is Mr. Frank."

I would have been less surprised if a dozen dancing dolphins had performed in the courtroom. Here I was, an ex-cop by seven months being sworn in as a juror.

As the judge rambled through his speech I peered at the defendant, thinking of how often I had arrested punks like him. They were always guilty. Now I sat here in a position not of accusation but of final judgement, listening and evaluating only that information the judge would allow as appropriate for the jurors to hear. I knew there would be much information deemed inadmissible that we would never know about.

So often over the years I'd sat in a courtroom surveying a jury, speculating about how they'd think, feel, decide. I wanted to win! Now sure enough, sitting in the second spectator's row there I was: the polyester detective eyeballing all of us.

I was beginning to feel the metamorphosis that must take place when any citizen is sworn in as a juror. How fortunate I was to be able to play a part in another cog of the system's complicated wheel. My cynicism evolved into enthusiasm.

This was no jury of the defendant's peers. Four of us were carved right out of an Archie Bunker script—over 50 and fed up with government bu-

reaucracy, taxes and crime. The lone woman was a chain-smoking bleached blonde in her 60s. Of the two younger fellows, one was a rock musician and the other a jet ski enthusiast living on a houseboat.

The Case Unfolds

Sure enough, I was right. This defendant was a dirtbag. A 24-year-old, small-time dope pusher charged with robbing another dirtbag. A drug pusher. No wonder the public defender took this case all the way.

It was wonderful—lawyers standing before us, each eager to win. In my mind the courtroom was never a utopian forum where justice is truly dispensed, but an arena for legalistic combat. The prosecutor's aim: Convict the bastard. The defense's: Get him off, guilty or not. That's what it's all about.

I sat back and ate it up.

Next day, first witness. A too-well-dressed dude wearing gold-rimmed glasses saunters to the stand and takes an oath on behalf of the state. His name is Willie. He's 22 years old.

As soon as he opens his mouth I recognize the personality, the attitude. His character seeps through the phony facade. No matter how clean he is, or how he struggles to speak in middle class, he's just another street thief.

I catch myself drawing conclusions. I tell myself to listen to the facts. That's what counts here.

Willie was driving through his slum neighborhood one afternoon when the defendant, Reggie, approached him walking his bike. The two were lifelong chums; they'd grown up on the same street in Ft. Lauderdale.

Willie testifies that Reggie pointed an automatic through the driver's window and demanded his neck chain and some money. Reggie reached into the car and opened the door so that Willie could stand up to get the money out of his pocket. Reggie then pedaled away on his Schwinn and made his escape.

Irate, Willie hurried to a girlfriend's apartment to get his gun. Why? Of course, to look for a cop to make a robbery report. The gun was for "self-protection" in case he saw Reggie. Yeah.

But before Willie could find a pay phone, along came a police officer who noticed that the gun was lying on the car seat. Willie then not only got his chance to report the robbery, but he was arrested on a firearms charge and carted off to jail.

Trying hard to portray himself as "Joe America," Willie was artfully exposed by the defense attorney as a three-time felon convicted for drug dealing and other offenses.

My old investigator's adrenaline kicked in with the urge to leap across the jury box and fire off about 80 questions myself. On cross, the public defender was polite, almost too nice.

Next witness for the state: Mongo, the robbery detective's nickname.

A detective for eight years, Mongo knew the street people better than he knew his own family. He was notified about the robbery that afternoon but went home anyway. Never said why.

Four days later, Mongo took a statement from Willie. Four days! At that point Mongo had probable cause to go after Reggie and arrest him, but he didn't. Never said why.

Nine days later, Reggie received a minor gunshot wound. When he was released from the hospital, Mongo was there to finally make the collar.

In a taped statement played before the jury, Reggie never admitted to robbing Willie. He said he "asked" Willie for the chain, and Willie gave it to him. The so-called "confession" was one of the sloppiest I'd ever heard. I used to teach the subject.

Finally, one more witness: Willie's girlfriend. Until today neither attorney has ever met her. Now suddenly overwhelmed with a sense of civic duty, she testifies that she stood outside her place and witnessed the entire robbery. She accuses Reggie.

Again, I'm squirming in the jury box. Nail her, I think to myself. No way she could have seen the robbery from her vantage point. Her testimony is full of holes.

The state rests.

To his credit, Reggie takes the stand. It's no surprise he admits being a small-time drug pusher and thief. With a glazed stare, he speaks almost unintelligibly.

"This," he says, "is nothing more than a debt."

Street stuff. Willie owed him money and Reggie took collateral. Yes, he might have intimidated Willie, but he never robbed him with a gun—not someone he's known all his life. Who are we to believe?

The Jury's Decision

The trial was short. We retired to the jury room and, not ironically, I was elected foreman. Then we tried to put the pieces together. Where was the cop who arrested Willie? How could Reggie hold a gun in one hand and open Willie's car door with the other, all while holding his bike? Why did Mongo wait so long to act? The girlfriend's testimony was discredited.

Within minutes we were all on the same track. No one needed my analysis. Some had trepidation about setting Reggie free—another menace back on the streets. But that wasn't the issue here. We not only had reasonable doubt, we were certain it never happened the way it was portrayed.

We were out in 15 minutes. When the verdict was read Reggie's face uncontrollably cringed, weeping. He clutched his lawyer's hands and bowed his head in tears. I choked a bit myself. For some reason, I felt a pang of sympathy for this dirtbag.

So, the young defense attorney wasn't so stupid after all.

DISCUSSION QUESTIONS

1. Robert Tarun quotes a British barrister who contends that the jury has the advantage of anonymity and need not be concerned about what people will think of it. In the two trials of police officers accused of beating Rodney King and the two trials of O.J. Simpson for the deaths of Nicole Brown Simpson and Ronald Goldman, we see examples of juries who may be concerned about the public perception of them as "individual" juries. Do you think the federal jury in the King case and the civil jury in the Simpson case were influenced by the previous jury's decision in each case? If so, in what ways? If the verdict in each of the first cases did influence the verdicts in the second cases, is that necessarily bad? Do juries lose their independence when they lose their anonymity? Why?

2. Which of the many points Tarun notes as distinctions between English and American trials do you see as the most important? Why?

3. Marshall Frank concludes his account of jury duty by suggesting the young defense attorney wasn't so stupid after all. What do you think the attorney was counting on? Was the state's evidence so weak that even an ex-cop wouldn't find enough to convict? Were the procedures used by the police so poor that an ex-cop would see how badly the police had screwed up?

4. Regarding jury qualifications in general, should jurors be knowledgeable in such areas as police work, forensics, science, the law, and so on? Would "justice" be more likely accomplished if jurors were directly involved in, or very knowledgeable about, the specific issues involved in trials?

WEBSITES

www.ajs.org

The American Judicature Society is an organization concerned with such issues as ethics in the courts, judicial selection, the jury, court administration, and public understanding of the justice system. At its website you can gather more information about juries and other aspects of the trial.

www.inlink.com/~aasgaard/memes/juror-handbook.html

This hypertext version of the *Jurors' Handbook: A Citizens Guide to Jury Duty* highlights the powers, rights, and duties of jurors.

www.criminaljustice.org

This site for the National Association of Criminal Defense Lawyers provides information about the practice of criminal law.

CHAPTER 9: SENTENCING

The sentences pronounced on convicted offenders can be as varied as their crimes. At one end of the punishment continuum are sentences involving probation, restitution, and fines. In the middle range are sentences of institutional confinement. Certainly the most punitive end of the continuum is the sentence of death. Readings in chapter 10 address some sentences that rely on community sanctions. Chapters 11 and 12 consider sanctions that more clearly involve deprivation of liberty. This chapter presents readings on two controversial punishments: the death penalty and corporal punishment.

Most writers on capital punishment hold and argue either a pro or con position; a single selection rarely presents both sides of the debate. The American Bar Association provides a very welcome alternative in its scholarly forum on the death penalty. Before reading this article, clearly formulate (maybe even commit to writing) your personal ideas about whether (1) the death penalty is imposed arbitrarily, (2) the death penalty is applied in a racist or discriminatory fashion, and (3) what purposes are served by the death penalty. Then, compare your opinions on these issues with those of the scholars discussing the topics in this reading.

After the caning of American Michael Fay by Singapore officials in 1994, and the return of chain gangs to some southern states, arguments were made that the American public in the mid-1990s was ready to accept a resumption of corporal punishment for some criminal offenders. The selection by Dennis J. Wiechman provides an interesting overview of crime and punishment in Singapore. As you read his comments ask yourself if a policy that works in one country would necessarily work in another.

READING 18
THE DEATH PENALTY: A SCHOLARLY FORUM

James Acker et al.

Eight scholars of law, the social sciences, and the humanities discuss and debate capital punishment as a matter of scholarship, public policy, and classroom teaching for the American Bar Association. The participants in the debate, moderated by the editor of the ABA Journal Focus on Law Studies, *are: James Acker, associate professor of criminal justice, SUNY Albany; Dane Archer, professor of sociology, University of California, Santa Cruz; David Baldus, professor of law, University of Iowa; Leigh Bienen, senior lecturer, Northwestern University School of Law; James Coleman, professor of law, Duke University; Shari Diamond, professor of psychology, University of Illinois at Chicago; John McAdams, associate professor of political science, Marquette University; and Austin Sarat, professor and chair of the Department of Law, Jurisprudence and Social Thought, Amherst College.*

EDITOR: *Why has the death penalty attracted so much scholarly attention from such a wide variety of disciplines?*

AUSTIN SARAT: I'm not so sure how broad the disciplinary representation in study of the death penalty is, but I have the sense that death penalty research has often been quite narrow in its focus. As Zimring pointed out in the *Law & Society Review* in 1993 (Vol. 27, No. 1), most death penal-

ty research is advocacy or policy oriented. That work is important, but I think it is also important to connect work on the death penalty to broader questions about the nature of law, the connection between law and violence, and the cultural meaning and significance of punishment.

LEIGH BIENEN: The persistence and pervasiveness of the general philosophical interest in punishment, retribution, evil, and justice means that the discourse often seems to be very broad, but that discourse is frequently very superficial, repeating the same old cliches on both sides. Then there is the whole tradition of counting: counting the number of people on death row, the number of executions, the time between executions, etc. We count because we are looking for patterns and try to understand what is happening. The death penalty has attracted so much attention from scholars, but also from the public, the popular press, and popular culture because it directly implicates death and dying. Since the death penalty necessarily involves juries, judges, courts, statutes, the United States Congress, state legislatures, and other institutions of legal interpretation and authority, it is surprising there is not more discussion of the death penalty as a matter of public policy.

JAMES ACKER: No one discipline has a monopoly on the kinds of information or reasoning that can respond adequately. A law regulating this area would be soul-less without ethical underpinnings, rootless without history, mindless without empirical foundation, and otherwise lacking without the religious, political, psychological, and sociological dimensions that are associated with capital punishment. The death penalty attracts so much attention because it is about life and death, civil liberty and order, individual and state, crime and justice, race and power, evil and redemption, and other matters that are timeless and important. As scholars, we hope that our enthusiasm for the issues is tempered by scientific and other constraints that are supposed to form a part of scholarship, but I think it would be regrettable to attempt to dampen the zest that fuels at least some scholarship in this area. It is rewarding to participate in a quest for knowledge and a debate about policy that involve issues that really seem to matter.

DANE ARCHER: In the case of the United States, at least, concern is no doubt spurred by the imminent prospect of thousands of executions. For the rest of the industrial world, the issue has scholarly appeal, but may lack some of the urgency generated by the issue here in the United States. Unlike all other democratic societies, the U.S. is re-embracing the death penalty as appropriate punishment and, indeed, we Americans are expanding the lists of offenses for which execution is merited. For many American scholars, the scientific curiosity involves the nature and merit of the kinds of evidence or other factors that apparently convince the general public that the death penalty is warranted, even as all other industrial nations embrace the abolition of this form of state killing. The death penalty therefore appears to be another example of "American exceptionalism."

LEIGH BIENEN: There are many countries outside of western Europe—e.g., China and other parts of Asia, where the government cheerfully executes people and there is no public policy debate. Not that there is much of a public policy debate in the U.S., for all the news items which appear on the media. I would argue that a good bit of the public and news interest in the death penalty is rather ghoulish, people's fascination with executions and death, and that little of what you see in the media is "discussion" or even a consideration of the public policy or legal issues.

SHARI DIAMOND: Researchers aren't very different from the general population, which used to turn out in large numbers for executions in the days of public hangings. When you couple that with the obvious horror of an irrevocable error, and the more modern concern with racial discrimination, it's hard to imagine a more compelling research topic. The imposition of the death penalty is still a relatively rare event, but we need only look to the huge research literature on the jury trial to recognize that low frequency generally does not deter the research community. The fascination with the jury may be due to the shadows it casts, and the same could be said for the death penalty. It speaks to philosophers and social scientists about the meaning of justice.

Arbitrariness and the Death Penalty

EDITOR: *Twenty-five years ago, the U.S. Supreme Court—in the case of* Furman v. Georgia *(1972)—temporarily curbed the death penalty, because its application was arbitrary and capricious ("wantonly and so freakishly imposed," to quote Justice Potter Stewart in a concurring opinion). Is the use of the death penalty today more consistent and less arbitrary?*

AUSTIN SARAT: The death penalty today is, I think, no less inconsistent, no less arbitrary. *Gregg* (1976) didn't eliminate arbitrariness; it just narrowed the range of cases in which arbitrariness could occur. *McCleskey* (1987) provided the best evidence that the problems that concerned the Supreme Court in 1972 were alive and well in the late 1980s. The recent de-funding of death penalty resource centers and limitations on *habeas* have not helped to produce greater fairness.

DAVID BALDUS: The issue of arbitrariness, in the sense of comparative excessiveness, does not appear to be a matter of public concern. *Furman* and *Godfrey v. Georgia* (1980) are the last Supreme Court decisions that expressed any concern about whether it is possible to distinguish death cases, in any meaningful way, from the great bulk of similar cases that result in less severe punishments. *Pulley v. Harris* (1984) took the issue off the screen, so far as the Eighth Amendment is concerned.

JAMES COLEMAN: An argument can be made that application of the death penalty today is more arbitrary and more inconsistent. And I am not sure that the range of cases in which it is available really is that much narrower. The Court's decision in *Gregg* essentially reached the same conclusion that Justice Harlan had reached in *McGautha* (1971)—that there is no practical way to guide a jury's ultimate decision whether to impose the death penalty. In the end, the only thing that can be done is to give each defendant facing the death penalty an opportunity to plead for mercy. That was the upshot of *Lockett v. Ohio* (1978). But *Gregg* went beyond *McGautha* and erected the complex guided discretion systems that now exist, imposing super due process requirements, ostensibly for the purpose of limiting or guiding the jury's (or other sentencer's) discretion. Rather than fairness, the result primarily has been complexity. In *Furman*, for example, Justice White posed the question whether one could make a meaningful distinction between the cases in which the death penalty was imposed and those in which the defendant was eligible for the death penalty but it was not imposed. The answer was "no," and that was proof that the sentence was arbitrary. The answer, in my view, is still "no," despite Justice White's later change of judicial mind.

SHARI DIAMOND: Harlan may have been right in *McGautha,* when he wrote that it was "beyond present human ability" to identify in advance those characteristics of the defendant or the crime that call for the death penalty. Even if he was wrong—and it *would* be possible—we certainly haven't done it. Although we've taken rape off the table (unless it accompanies a homicide), prosecutorial, judicial, and jury discretion are remarkably wide. The labyrinthine sentencing instructions provide little guidance, leaving juries to rely on their own devices rather than to be guided by legal standards (such as they are). The instructions also create new sources for disparity—two triers of fact can easily arrive at different decisions on the same defendant if they find different meanings in the instructions, even if they are making every effort to adhere to them.

Whether intentional or unintentional, curable or incurable, the structure currently in place offers no serious support for consistency in judgment. It is interesting to ask whether a "twister" is more arbitrary than a lightning bolt.

LEIGH BIENEN: It seems there is more uniformity in rhetoric than there is uniformity across jurisdictions. The huge discrepancies in the number of death sentences imposed and the number of executions across state jurisdictions indicate to me that arbitrariness has not decreased. The culture of the death penalty is very different in Texas and Alabama than it is in New Jersey or New York. But more importantly, a court which has affirmed many death sentences (e.g., the Pennsylvania Supreme Court, or the Texas Court of Criminal Appeals) is going to have a very different attitude toward capital appeals than a court where a death sentence is a relatively rare event. Some courts now treat the affirming of death sentences as routine.

JAMES ACKER: The relative lack of data concerning the administration of the death penalty in pre-*Furman* days makes comparative assessment of the pre- and post-*Furman* levels of arbitrariness difficult. However, perhaps we can make some inferences from post-*Furman* statutes. Two structural legislative changes occurred post-*Furman*. First, some crimes—rape, burglary, kidnap, robbery—were eliminated as capital offenses. Theoretically (but probably not so much in practice), the death penalty also was limited to a narrower class of criminal homicides. Second, capital trials became bifurcated (guilt v. punishment) in all jurisdictions. But the post-*Furman* legislative reforms accomplished little else. The schemes purport to regulate only sentencing discretion; they do not even aspire to control charging discretion, which remains a major source of arbitrariness. The class of death penalty–eligible murders remains quite broad. Statutes give minimal guidance about how sentences should be imposed, and the evidence suggests that sentencers simply ignore the statutory guidelines. *Prima facie,* then, there is little reason to expect that the level of arbitrariness has changed much over time. In short, with the notable exception that rape (of adults) has been eliminated as a capital offense, it's hard to conclude that we have more or less arbitrariness now than in pre-*Furman* times. But I do think it is relatively easy to conclude that the amount of arbitrariness now remains unacceptably high.

DAVID BALDUS: It is difficult to know whether there is more or less arbitrariness than pre-*Furman*, primarily because there is so little data available on which to base such judgments (*see Acker above*). Our Georgia research (Baldus, Woodworth and Pulaski) examined this issue with a comparison of 240 pre-*Furman* with 600 post-*Furman* cases, and we saw some improvement. The post-*Furman* cases continued, nevertheless, to reveal a lot of excessiveness, none of which was explicitly corrected by the Georgia Supreme Court. [Speaking nationally], the problem is aggravated by the decline—to nearly zero—in the use of executive clemency, which formerly set to life many of the least aggravated cases. This has been offset, in part, by the more active intervention of some state [appellate] courts which reverse 25–35% of death sentences on legal grounds.

LEIGH BIENEN: I don't think the arbitrariness can ever be eliminated unless prosecutorial discretion is abolished, and that will never happen. Since whether you are sentenced to death is hugely affected by the economic resources available to the defendant, that raises fundamental questions about justice. I don't think the death penalty can ever be administered justly, although it can certainly be administered more justly than it is at present.

JAMES COLEMAN: One still cannot explain in case after case in which the defendant is eligible for the death penalty, why the prosecutor seeks it in one but not the other, or why the jury imposes it in one but not the other. That is the definition of arbitrary that the Supreme Court had in mind back in *Furman*.

AUSTIN SARAT: I think that Justice Blackmun was right—the problems with the death penalty cannot be remedied; we cannot have a punishment which is individualized and yet one which is consistent. In the end I don't think that the

structure of capital punishment can be brought within the Constitution.

EDITOR: *For the most part, juries play no role in criminal sentencing, except in death penalty cases where our system of justice has created a "people's voice" to legitimize or reach better decisions on life and death. Would we be better off if only judges decided the life or death question? Can judges be more easily constrained by the rule of law and structured guidelines than twelve citizens?*

JAMES ACKER: I don't think we would be better off [if only judges decided], because any advances that might be made in achieving greater consistency through judge sentencing would be more than offset by sacrificing the collective sentiment of the jury about the justice of a life or death sentence. Notwithstanding the imperfections of the jury system, and the capital jury in particular, I remain convinced that juries are to be preferred over judges in rendering decisions that have the moral dimension that is at the heart of capital sentencing decisions. Reliance on juries might contribute to inconsistencies in life/death sentencing decisions, but my guess is that the greater consistency through reliance on judicial sentencing might result in more death sentences. That more death sentences would be imposed does not prove that those sentences would be unjust. But since there is no agreement on what justice demands in this context, I would rather trust my lot to twelve people tried and true. Maybe the optimal combination would be to give judges a one-way corrective power; they could reduce jury death sentences to life if they perceived improper considerations motivating the sentence, but they would not be empowered to override a jury's decision to impose a life sentence. I would prefer to err on the side of erroneous exercises of mercy than arbitrary sentences of death.

LEIGH BIENEN: I am in agreement with Acker. Judges have always been subject to these [electoral and political] pressures, which is why juries were conceived of to begin with. I notice the trend in the legislatures is towards more judicial control over death sentencing. The purpose behind these enactments, as I see it, is to increase the number of death sentences and make legislators feel that they are being "tough on crime." But if you believe, as I do, that disparities are inevitable, what is the benefit of having more death sentences and executions? I don't think the criminal justice system would benefit from more executions, more death sentences, more people on death row, or more media attention or catering to the public's hunger for sensational news about death sentences and executions.

EDITOR: *There seems to be some consensus that the application of the death penalty is still highly arbitrary. If so, what can be accomplished by the American Bar Association's recent (February 1997) and highly publicized call for a moratorium on executions until greater consistency and fairness can be achieved?*

SHARI DIAMOND: I don't know the history of the ABA's recent resolution, but it wouldn't surprise me if multiple groups within the ABA with differing agendas contributed to it. It would be well justified, however, if it were based solely on concerns about arbitrariness and/or discrimination. Note that Justice Blackmun initially supported the death penalty in *Furman* and *Gregg,* but after a twenty-year struggle "to develop procedural and substantive rules that would lend more than the mere appearance of fairness to the death penalty endeavor," he gave up, and in *Callins v. Collins* (1994) declared that he could no longer support the death penalty.

JAMES ACKER: I haven't had the chance to see the ABA proposal for a moratorium, but given the vast distance that lies between what is "fair" and what the system presently looks like, there certainly is an opportunity to make the system "fairer" or "less arbitrary" than it is now, without altogether eliminating the death penalty. For example, enactment of the Racial Justice Act would help in the policing of race discrimination. Seriously narrowing the range of death penalty– eligible crimes (such as to murders with multiple aggravators) would reduce the opportunity for abuses of discretion. Providing well-qualified and adequately funded attorneys to accused and convicted capital offenders would help, as would insisting on charging guidelines and a system for enforcing those guidelines.

JAMES COLEMAN: The perception that the system lacks fairness is what motivated the ABA to adopt its moratorium resolution. Twenty of the past twenty-four presidents of the ABA supported this resolution. I doubt anyone would argue that these nineteen men and one woman are radical people out to abolish the death penalty. Rather, I think we do our duty as lawyers, when we bring to the public's attention potential problems and concerns about the justice system that might undermine public confidence.

JOHN MCADAMS: Invoking the ABA's call for a moratorium is simply an appeal to authority. It's been quite obvious in recent years that the internal politics of the ABA has become increasingly dominated by liberal political activists. ABA positions on abortion, affirmative action, family leave, gay rights, and health care make this perfectly obvious.

DAVID BALDUS: The ABA could contribute to the goal of better understanding the problems of excessiveness, if it would support research designed to assess the scope of the problem and what may be done to ameliorate it.

EDITOR: *One factor motivating the ABA moratorium is a concern over executing innocent people due to a lack of procedural safeguards.*

LEIGH BIENEN: There seems to be a new and curious cynicism regarding the execution of the innocent these days. That innocent people will be executed is not given much weight in arguments against capital punishment. There seems to be public acceptance of the fact, perhaps because of the new attention given to assuming the risk and the inevitability of risk for any policy, including seat belts, air bags, cancer and cigarettes, etc.

JOHN MCADAMS: What Bienen describes as "cynicism regarding execution of the innocent" I would regard simply as realism about public policy. There is no such thing as a risk-free public policy. The best evidence supports the view that execution of innocents is extremely rare. Ironically, two scholars who oppose the death penalty have provided this evidence. Bedau and Radelet found, among 7,000 people executed in the United States in the 20th century, 23 people whom they *claim* to have been innocent, not a number to be taken as the literal truth, given sparse historical records, the need for subjective analysis of data, and their own biases.

Race and the Death Penalty

EDITOR: *Is the death penalty an area of our criminal justice system that, today, can be called racist or discriminatory?*

JAMES COLEMAN: This is a big subject. I believe that the criminal justice system is racist and discriminatory, but not in the sense that it violates the Equal Protection Clause. Consider, for example, a case that I have handled since 1983 (*Booker v. Singletary, FL*), where the prosecutor filed a sentencing recommendation that the death penalty ought to be imposed. The prosecutor, defense lawyer, judge and victim all were white. In arguing that the crime was heinous, the prosecutor wrote: "The injuries to this lady's innocent body are numerous . . . degrading rape by a young male of the opposite race, *prior* to fatal stab wound." Neither the judge nor the defense counsel objected to this argument; nor did the Florida Supreme Court notice it in its review. This direct appeal to race, in other words, was unremarkable. I don't think that the prosecutor who wrote the memo thought he was being racist. He was just expressing an attitude that prevailed at the time, that was accepted as normal.

In capital cases, prosecutors routinely move to exclude all black jurors, on the ground that such jurors would be sympathetic to the black defendant. This can be traced to the legacy of our antebellum criminal system, in which slaves and free blacks were not considered equals and in which more severe punishment was accepted as normal. I think the country still believes that black defendants deserve more severe punishment, because they are more threatening, especially when the victim of the crime is white. The criminal justice system will never be fair or nondiscriminatory until it is administered by both black and white citizens, until prosecutors and jurors are forced routinely to deal with the experiences of black people and to factor those experiences into their decisions. There is no such thing

as a race-neutral decision in the criminal justice system, when it affects black people and when their voice is not part of the discussion leading to the decision.

JOHN MCADAMS: This is not an easy question to approach empirically. For example, it is clearly the case that blacks who murder whites are treated more harshly than are blacks who murder blacks. This looks like racial disparity *if* you assume that the circumstances are similar in the two cases. Unfortunately, it's vastly unlikely that they are. Most murders are among people who know each other. Murders done by strangers are much more likely to be regarded as heinous than are murders growing out of domestic quarrels, drug deals gone wrong, and such. It might seem reasonable to compare the punishment received by blacks who murder whites with the treatment received by whites who murder blacks. Unfortunately, while black on white crime is relatively rare, white on black crime is even rarer. There simply isn't an adequate statistical base to allow us to generalize about whites who murder blacks, which pretty much leaves us to compare the way the system treats blacks who murder blacks with the way it treats whites who murder whites. When we do this, we find some fairly solid-looking evidence that the system is unfairly tough on white murderers—or if you prefer, unfairly lenient on black murderers. But even this finding is one we have to be skeptical about. Is the average black on black murder quite similar to the average white on white murder? Or are there systematic differences?

LEIGH BIENEN: The criminal justice system is controlled and dominated by whites, although the recipients of punishment, including the death penalty, are disproportionately black. The death penalty is a symbol of state control and white control over blacks. Black males who present a threatening and defiant persona are the favorites of those administering the punishment, including the overwhelmingly middle-aged white, male prosecutors who—in running for election or re-election—find nothing gets them more votes than demonizing young black men. The reasons for this have much more to do with the larger politics of the country than with the death penalty. I would also argue that the class and economic discrimination affecting the death penalty are "worse," in the sense of being more unjust, than the racial elements.

JAMES ACKER: There is considerable evidence that the output of capital punishment systems in several states is influenced by race. The race effects may not reflect overt, intentional invidious discrimination. The influences may work more subtly. The media may publicize white victim homicides much more intensely, for example, which in turn puts pressure on prosecutors to do something in response, by seeking a capital sentence. Likewise, prosecutors choose cases in which they will seek death very cautiously. They may assess that the odds are higher of gaining a death sentence, when the homicide victim is white. Generally speaking, African-Americans are less likely to serve on capital juries, because a higher percentage of African-Americans do not survive the death-qualification process. For these reasons, the capital punishment process in several states has yet to be purged of race discrimination.

DAVID BALDUS: Much of the debate on the race issue naturally turns on the interpretation of the data concerning the frequency with which death is sought and imposed on different racial groups. It is useful to distinguish between gross unadjusted racial disparities, on the one hand, and adjusted disparities that control for the presence of aggravating and mitigating factors that clearly influence the decisions and that may also be correlated with race. A failure to adjust introduces a significant risk of an erroneous inference about the influence of race. For this reason, gross disparities, especially based on the entire nation, are suspect. At best, these data are suggestive, and experience indicates that when the disparities in death sentencing rates are adjusted for legitimate case characteristics, unadjusted race disparities usually, but not always, decline.

[With these important methodological issues as background], what do the data tell us about differences in discrimination in the pre- and post-*Furman* periods? There are significant differences in race effects, both across and within states. There are differences in the magnitude of race effects at different decisionmaking levels in the states—i.e., prosecutorial decisions to seek the death penalty and jury decisions to impose death. There are also differences that correlate with culpability. The risk of race effects was very low in the most aggravated capital cases; however, in the *mid-range* cases, where the "correct" sentence was less clear, and the room for exercise of discretion much broader, the race disparities are much stronger. Whereas the overall average disparity for the two groups (black v. white) tends to be 6–8 percentage points, in the mid-range cases the disparities are typically two to three times that large.

JOHN MCADAMS: David Baldus' discussion of the literature on racial inequity is highly useful. I agree entirely with his characterization of what the data show. The studies don't show discrimination consistently. Studies in some jurisdictions show it, and studies in others do not. This could be the result of *genuine* differences across jurisdictions, or it could be the result of a weak general pattern, which happens, by statistical accidents, to be "significant" in some studies but not in others. When we add all this up, I think the system does discriminate against black *victims* in at least some decisions in some jurisdictions. This is wrong. But it's not the politically correct fantasy of a system massively discriminating against black offenders. It's not at all clear that racial inequity is worse in the administration of the death penalty than for other punishments. Now, the question for death penalty opponents: Is the degree of racial inequity that Baldus describes such that it renders capital punishment unacceptable?

JAMES COLEMAN: There is a difficulty we have talking about race that makes empirical evidence less useful than perhaps in other areas of research. One of the things that always interested me was whether Baldus et al. looked at the racial composition of juries in their study. In *McCleskey*, the jury was composed of 11 whites and 1 black man, a retired county worker. In the early jury cases (*Strauder v. West Virginia*, 1879; *Virginia v. Rives*, 1880, etc.), the Court made quite clear that it was recognizing *only* the right of black people to be considered for jury service, not a right actually to serve. By implication, the Court was saying that a racially neutral decision could be made to exclude particular black jurors (or all of them) and that the administration of justice would not be affected. I question this premise. In the 11th Circuit's decision in *Jackson v. Herring* (1995), the court held that although the defendant had established a *Batson* violation, the error was harmless because the defendant could not show that the decision of a racially mixed jury would have been different. That result seems compelled by neutral principles, but it ignores reality. Do any of us believe that having black people participate in the decision whether to impose the death penalty on a black person would not make a difference in the deliberations? I think it is impossible to administer a criminal justice system without *including* in the decision-making the experiences of all segments of the community, at least the significant ones.

AUSTIN SARAT: I think that we are all pretty reliant on the Baldus study, which seems to say that race of the victim is key. The race of the victim and defendant influences invisible decisions about whom to charge and prosecute for capital murder. And class can't be left out—research suggests that the quality of defense counsel makes a huge difference. If you can afford quality counsel, then your chances of "surviving" a capital charge improve immeasurably.

DAVID BALDUS: There is much anecdotal evidence from lawyers who represent capital defendants. Many of them seriously question the validity of statistical studies that do not reveal disparities based upon the race of the defendant. It is possible that there is such discrimination, but that it is not sufficiently large and systematic to be picked up by the data.

Victims and the Death Penalty

JOHN MCADAMS: I want to strongly insist that when we consider the racial equity of the death penalty, or indeed any other issue in criminal justice, that we give priority to the interests of the *victims* of crime, to law-abiding citizens. Politi-

cally correct attitudes make this difficult. A key element of political correctness is the conviction that blacks are victims of white racism. All issues are assumed to pit blacks against whites. Naturally, one should side with blacks, the historical victims of oppression. This has all sorts of perverse consequences. Thus, it sometimes seems that people concerned with racial injustice are unhappy that while guilty white offenders go free, equally guilty black offenders get imprisoned. Fair enough. But then they seem to want to address the injustice by letting more guilty blacks go free.

JAMES ACKER: It is difficult for me to dismiss the constitutional principle of "equal justice under law" as political correctness. If the real concern is to be directed toward the victims of crime, as [Harvard law professor] Randall Kennedy has pointed out, then the anger of those who believe in capital punishment—as a deterrent or as retribution—should be redoubled when evidence suggests that homicides involving African-American victims are treated as less serious events by actors in the criminal justice system. Under these circumstances, African-Americans reap none of the presumed benefits of the capital punishment system, yet the capital sanction is sought and delivered with comparatively great regularity in white victim homicides, especially those committed by African-American offenders. The debate hardly involves arguments that guilty people should go free. Severe alternative sanctions are available to capital punishment, including life imprisonment without parole in many jurisdictions. Sometimes, the erroneous assumption is made that opponents of capital punishment are not concerned about victims of crime, or that they somehow denigrate the seriousness of murder. If the execution of murderers is all that can be offered to crime victims, then maybe it's time to regroup and think a bit harder.

JOHN MCADAMS: I'm not "dismissing constitutional principles." What I said is that political correctness inclines many people to adopt an offender-centered approach to racial inequity, rather than a victim-centered approach. I find it difficult to understand the absence of concern for victims—who are disproportionately black and poor—in discussions of the death penalty.

LEIGH BIENEN: Those who worry about constitutional issues and criminal defendants do so because that is what the Constitution directs us to. It isn't a lack of concern for victims, but the Constitution isn't concerned with victims. That may be unfortunate or unwise public policy, but constitutional rights are preponderantly for criminal defendants. There is a reason for this: persons who are accused of crimes or commit crimes have few supporters, and as a society we believe that fair adjudication is a primary value.

JOHN MCADAMS: It's certainly correct, to a certain extent, that the Constitution or, rather, the Bill of Rights, isn't concerned with victims. Other parts of the federal and state constitutions that give governments the powers necessary to establish police forces and punish criminals do show a concern for the victims. This concern is never explicit, because at the time of the writing of the Constitution, it wasn't controversial that government had the right to punish criminals.

JAMES COLEMAN: I don't understand the current resort to the victim in response to almost any criticism of the criminal justice system. It is as if the end—the interests of the innocent victim—justifies the means, a system that is unfair and discriminatory. But none of that deals with questions of fairness in the imposition of a sentence. A death sentence can be warranted in the particular case and still be unfair. The Supreme Court in *Gregg* and *McCleskey* made the point that a defendant who "deserves" the death penalty is in no position to complain that others equally deserving are shown mercy. The problem with this position is that it ignores how the system contributes to the inconsistent results. I go back to Justice Brennan. If the death penalty is not used to punish offenders generally, or if it is not being used to protect all communities equally, then the punishment is being imposed unfairly. Calling a position "politically correct" does not confront its merits. Some who oppose the death penalty or are indifferent to its use also care about how the criminal justice system functions.

JOHN MCADAMS: In fact, the interests of the victim *may* justify a system that is unfair and discriminatory, if the choices are to continue the system or dismantle it. The harm that follows from dismantling the system may exceed the harm involved in the unfairness. My point was that the failure to properly punish criminals disproportionally harms black people. Nobody would argue that racial inequity in punishing robbers means we have to stop punishing robbers. Nobody would argue that if we find that white neighborhoods have better police protection than black neighborhoods, we address the inequity by withdrawing police protection from *all* neighborhoods. Yet people make arguments exactly like this where capital punishment is concerned.

JAMES COLEMAN: John McAdams misstates the choice. It is not whether to punish or not to punish. Of course, we don't stop punishing black robbers because white robbers are permitted to go free—*unless* the evidence is that "taking money by force" generally is not a crime unless it is committed by black people. In that case, we have a system more akin to the slave code, which created special crimes for slaves and free blacks, which were not crimes if committed by white people. I think it is well established that equal protection requires that people be punished similarly for similar criminal conduct. The issue, therefore, is whether the death penalty is reserved to punish only certain disfavored groups, while criminals from other groups are not subjected to such punishment, even when their conduct makes them eligible.

Purposes of the Death Penalty

DANE ARCHER: In addition to the issues surrounding fairness and racial differences, should we not also be asking questions about the purpose of the death penalty?

AUSTIN SARAT: I think that the moral and ethical claims [for abolition] are still there. But the "new" abolition presents itself as a form of legal conservatism—emphasizing fairness (due process) and equality (equal protection).

DANE ARCHER: The U.S. increasingly appears to be the deviant case with respect to use of the death penalty. Virtually all Western, democratic, industrial societies have embraced abolition and—if one can safely judge from international media—citizens of those nations increasingly regard as barbaric America's renewed enthusiasm for executions. More important, the abolitionist nations seem to regard the death penalty as lacking an ethical purpose. Beginning in the 1950s, when abolition swept much of Europe, people began asking if there was any serious evidence that the death penalty accomplished anything other than the death of the executed. In *Violence and Crime in Cross-National Perspective* (Yale University Press, 1987), my co-author Rosemary Gartner and I searched our archive of international data for any evidence that the presence or abolition of the death penalty had an effect on homicide rates. We concluded that there was no evidence for any form of a deterrence effect. Is it, therefore, time to ask whether the European perspective is valid? Other than vengeance—not, perhaps, the most laudable basis for law and public policy—what then is the *purpose* of the death penalty? This is the question asked of us by other democratic nations. Are we going to avoid answering it?

JOHN MCADAMS: The notion of the U.S. as the deviant case is interesting. When used by opponents of the death penalty, this is simply a variety of the *argumentum ad populum*. If a majority of nations have ended the death penalty, it must be a bad thing. Ironically, proponents of the death penalty can use the same argument form to claim that since an overwhelming majority of U.S. citizens favor the death penalty, it must be a good thing. Both arguments, obviously, are fallacious. The whole notion of "American exceptionalism" is one saturated with ideological double standards. Among liberals, American exceptionalism in regard to government funding of religious schools, the rights of people accused with crimes, and the activist role of the courts have been applauded. American exceptionalism in regard to gun control, socialized medicine, and the death penalty have been deplored. Among conservatives, of course, the positions have been reversed.

DANE ARCHER: John McAdams's reply is well stated, but I worry that I must not have stated my question clearly, for he misses the main point. The issue is *not* whether an opinion "head count" shows more nations opposed to the death penalty than in favor of it. The *real* issue is an empirical question: Where is the evidence that the death penalty deters homicide specifically or violent crime generally? Surely it is incumbent on those who favor executions to show that they are effective, accomplish deterrence, etc.? The burden of empirical proof would seem to lie with the pro–death penalty scholar. In the absence of any consistent evidence for deterrence, are we really satisfied using the death penalty in the U.S. for some reason—at present unclear to me—other than deterrence? If so, what is that other reason?

JOHN MCADAMS: I'm a bit surprised to find Dane Archer, in the context of the question of whether the death penalty deters murder, claim that "the burden of empirical proof would seem to lie with the pro–death penalty scholar." If we execute murderers and there is in fact no deterrent effect, we have killed a bunch of murderers. If we *fail* to execute murderers, and doing so would in fact have deterred other murders, we have allowed the killing of a bunch of innocent victims. I would much rather risk the former. This, to me, is not a tough call.

Teaching About the Death Penalty

EDITOR: *I'd like to turn the discussion toward pedagogy, as we wind down toward the end of our talk. Teaching and student learning is one of the special missions of the ABA's College and University Program and* Focus on Law Studies, *in particular. How do you teach about the death penalty? What are the opportunities and pitfalls?*

LEIGH BIENEN: I think the death penalty is a very rich topic for teaching in law and the social sciences and the humanities, because it is truly a crosscutting issue. The legal issues are technical, complicated, and involve statutes, cases, rules, federal and state law, and everything else. The social science questions are profound, and the philosophical and humanitarian issues are very sharp on both sides.

JOHN MCADAMS: Whether the death penalty has any deterrent effect is a classic one for any course on social science research methods. All the issues are there. First, how does one define the variable "death penalty" (on the books versus actual use)? Second, how do we deal with simultaneous causality (i.e., the death penalty's impact on the murder rate versus the impact of the murder rate on demand for the death penalty)? Third, can we sort out the influence of confounding variables (multivariate analysis helps, but it often ignores cultural differences)? Finally, what about lack of variance in the key variable (death penalty rarely has been imposed)? All these compelling questions and accompanying measurement problems can be explored in a research methods course.

JAMES ACKER: I have found it rewarding to teach semester-length classes on the death penalty. One of the challenges is to capitalize on the emotions that typically drive students' initial views, by channeling them into more systematic lines of inquiry. I think it would be a mistake, and probably futile, to try to squelch these sentiments. Death penalty classes usually succeed precisely because they are comprised of groups of individuals with sharply different views, anchored by others who pose equally challenging questions and represent unique points of view.

JAMES COLEMAN: Like Acker, I also teach a semester-long seminar (which I have taught since 1989). My law students at Duke University come with many different views on capital punishment. Over the course of the semester, all of the students find themselves revisiting things they began the semester firmly convinced of. For the last two years, I have added a very successful clinical component to the seminar, co-taught by a colleague. Students on all sides of the death penalty agree that working with an actual defendant on real issues brings alive what we discuss in class.

DANE ARCHER: I have included capital punishment in a course on violence and crime. In one part of the course, students have a chance to meet violent offenders from a nearby California Youth Authority facility. Many initially "progressive" students find themselves unexpectedly embracing the penal goals of incarceration and incapacitation, even if they are not persuaded that prisons

are otherwise effective (e.g., rehabilitation). When we then examine the debates regarding the death penalty, I have the students break into small discussion groups to try to identify the *different* purposes that are (or might be) served by executions—specific deterrence, general deterrence, retaliation, economics, psychological respite for the victims, etc. I find that this approach sensitizes students to the underlying issues surrounding the purposes that can be served by punishment in general, and the death penalty in particular.

LEIGH BIENEN: In my Homicide course, I spend a good bit of time on the capital punishment statutes, especially the statutory aggravating and mitigating factors and their use of language. I find this a useful teaching device. In my Persuasion course, I ask the students to look at capital punishment opinions as if they were literary texts, in terms of the persuasive aspects of the opinion. One problem with teaching capital punishment is how to deal with the negative materials—the brutality, the indifference of the judicial system, the pervasive violence, the tolerance for injustice, characteristics of the criminal justice system that are magnified in capital punishment.

EDITOR: *How do students respond in the classroom? Are their views fixed or fluid? Do their attitudes get in the way of the topic?*

JAMES ACKER: Students who start out firmly in the pro–death penalty camp often become troubled by the issue of executing innocent people, or by evidence of race discrimination, or by the quality of lawyering in some cases, or by the Supreme Court's apparent retreat from meaningful policing of death penalty systems. Students who are strongly against the death penalty often are given pause when they confront the brutal case facts involved in capital murders, or issues of serial killers or life term prisoners who kill, or when asked to contemplate alternative punishments that strike the right combination of justice and social utility. Students who find themselves without strong convictions perpetually agonize, probably more deeply than the strong pro– and anti–death penalty students. I find very few to be indifferent. Some minds are hopelessly closed and will not entertain diverse perspectives or struggle with evidence contrary to their beliefs, but by and large the discussions that evolve over the course of a semester, and the growth that many students do evidence, give me confidence that most students are willing and able to test their views and to think about the issues in academically rigorous fashion. I would be less optimistic about unsettling preconceived notions about the death penalty, if only a class or two is devoted to the subject.

JOHN MCADAMS: I teach the death penalty in about two weeks of a broader Public Policy course, where expecting students to fully examine and reconsider their own views is simply too ambitious. I try to convey a few points, to which students seem quite open: (1) the issue is more complex than they think; (2) the empirical evidence is unclear; and (3) there are real possibilities of unintended consequences. Students are not resistant to these points, probably because none of them challenge students on the basic social values that determine their views of the death penalty. I don't ask students to express an opinion pro or con on the death penalty, and I very much doubt that any students change their minds. What I hope for is a bit more subtle and nuanced opinions, but not different opinions.

DANE ARCHER: I encourage students to examine their own views about the death penalty to learn what *kind* of pro-executionist or abolitionist they are. *Why* do they support the death penalty, and what purposes do they believe it serves? *Why* do they oppose the death penalty, and what harm do they believe it causes? In either case, I encourage students to articulate what kinds of empirical *evidence* would provide support for their views.

JAMES COLEMAN: Our students feel comfortable disagreeing with each other about issues we discuss. I think that is critical to a successful seminar. Students who favor the death penalty do not feel reticent about expressing their views, and those who oppose the death penalty try to deal with the legal issues on the merits, rather than resort to moral or politically correct positions.

EDITOR: *How do your own beliefs and attitudes about the death penalty influence your teaching?*

JAMES ACKER: From a teaching perspective, I continuously am reminded that reasonable people can and do disagree about capital punishment on all levels, from emotional to intellectual. These reminders make it difficult to get lazy, or even entirely comfortable with the treatment of given issues. Because the issues can be supercharged, I find myself playing—more than usual—the role of devil's advocate, in an attempt to not let people (or myself) rest easy with the last statement made.

JAMES COLEMAN: Like Acker, I also play the devil's advocate, but students know what my position is on the death penalty. We all try not to let our personal views prevent us from discussing the issues and respecting and listening to each other's views.

LEIGH BIENEN: I always tell students that I spent fifteen years working for the public defender actively engaged in litigation challenging the reimposition of the death penalty [in New Jersey]. But I certainly don't expect students to agree with me; most of them are in favor of capital punishment.

EDITOR: *What are 2 or 3 of the best books for teaching about the death penalty? Why are they particularly effective with students?*

JAMES ACKER: My top three books for teaching are: (1) Coyne & Entzeroth, *Capital Punishment and the Judicial Process* (Carolina Academic Press, 1994). This is the only casebook, to my knowledge, that covers the death penalty. It presents major cases and has interesting discussion notes. (2) Victor Streib (ed.) *A Capital Punishment Anthology* (Anderson Press, 1993). This edited collection presents excerpts from numerous law review articles, which cover the range of law, philosophy, and empirical aspects of the death penalty. The recent editions of this book now come with a disk, on which Streib presents edited cases and other materials, an invaluable addition for those who use electronic teaching materials. (3) Hugo Bedau (ed.), *The Death Penalty in America: Current Controversies* (Oxford University Press, 1997) is an excellent current collection of historical, legal, and empirical articles about the death penalty, with a few edited cases. There are many more books that might be appropriate for classes with different objectives.

SHARI DIAMOND: Greenhaven Press recently published a book on the death penalty as part of its "opposing viewpoints" series, which would be useful as a supplement in courses not specifically focused on capital punishment. *Death Penalty* (Paul Winters, ed.) is a collection of short essays by researchers, judges and journalists on issues from deterrence to equity. Though short on the social scientist's point of view, the book is great for setting out the various positions that this controversial topic has stimulated.

LEIGH BIENEN: In my Persuasion course, I am currently teaching Mikal Gilmore's *Shot in the Heart* (Doubleday/Anchor Books, 1994) as my death penalty book. I find it a very powerful, well-written book that describes the family background and institutional history of Gary Gilmore. I have also used Helen Prejean's *Dead Man Walking* (Vintage Press, 1993), which is very good in showing law students a side of the death penalty that most of them had not considered (the popularity of this book and the movie have made that less true in 1997 than in 1995).

SHARI DIAMOND: I would be inclined to assign *Dead Man Walking* as one of the readings, even though some students may have "seen the movie."

The book includes a great deal of information about research on the death penalty, packaged along with a compelling story that addresses all of those touched by the capital crime, including the victims' survivors. As good as the movie is, the book is better.

AUSTIN SARAT: One of the best books for teaching about the death penalty is Truman Capote's *In Cold Blood* (Random House, 1965). It gives a deep and rich sense of who the killers are and why they did what they did, as well as a nice portrait of their trials, their lives on death row, and their execution. Another good book for teaching purposes is Lesser's *Pictures at an Execution* (Harvard University Press, 1993). This book picks up the important question of how, if at all, the death penalty differs from murder. It provides a nice overview of literary treatments of capital punishment while focusing on the Harris execution, California's first post-*Furman*.

EDITOR: *I wish to thank all of the contributors for a stimulating, informative, and frank exchange of perspectives on the death penalty across a wide range of topics. It is clear from the forum that there are not just two, but many, points of view on capital punishment as a matter of scholarship, public policy and teaching.*

READING 19
CANING AND CORPORAL PUNISHMENT

Dennis J. Wiechman

Singapore has one of the most severe penal codes in the world. Mandatory caning is incorporated in the penal code for such offenses as theft or robbery and is imposed in addition to imprisonment. Dennis J. Wiechman, professor of criminal justice at the University of Evansville in Indiana, looks at the application of caning in the Singapore criminal justice system and addresses some of the misperceptions this type of punishment has garnered in the Western media.

Singapore has received much negative media publicity concerning the issue of caning and its justice system in general. It does have a harsh penal code by Western standards, but its system of justice does work under the leadership of Prime Minister Lee. In 1994, media attention was focused upon Michael Fay, a native of Kettering, Ohio, who attended a private preparatory school in Singapore. Mr. Fay, who was eighteen years old at the time, was detained by Singapore for defacing automobiles with spray paint and other acts of vandalism. Mr. Fay was to be caned with six lashes after a four-month prison sentence. Singapore reduced the number from six to four lashes and carried out the punishment in May 1994.

Some in the Western media distorted Singapore and its government. The distortions carried

Reprinted from Dennis J. Wiechman, "Caning and Corporal Punishment: Viewpoint," *CJ International*, vol. 10, no. 5, September/October 1994, with permission of the Office of International Criminal Justice, University of Illinois at Chicago.

over to Michael Fay and his families in Singapore and Ohio. The issues of caning and crime were also debated in many U.S. forums from talk shows to taverns. One proposed St. Louis, Missouri, city ordinance that failed would have made caning a public punishment for graffiti artists.

The Western media have shown demonstrations of martial arts experts using a cane on a number of objects, and flesh was even torn from a side of beef. The Singapore government responded that the flogger need not be a martial arts person, but only in good shape. It also disputed the stories of "flesh tearing" and said that the cane leaves only bruises or marks. The prison department reported that a doctor will stop the caning if the prisoner is incapable of continuing. Several Western media outlets reported that the caning would be public but the Singapore government said that all its caning is done in private. There have been many inaccuracies reported, and this commentary will try to correct a few of them.

Singapore is a nation currently under scrutiny and review by modern media. Singapore has been condemned by some in the press as "barbaric and backward," and not in touch with modern and enlightened penal practices. The current controversy surrounds Michael Fay, who was in a preparatory school in Singapore. Allegedly this teenager and several friends spray painted several cars and did some other acts of vandalism in Singapore. He was given a short-term sentence and the government of Singapore "caned" this young man as an example to all who damage and deface other people's property. The controversy involved diplomatic requests for clemency. President Clinton made formal requests for the young man from Ohio. Most of the controversy focused on the caning issue and the fact that this foreign nation used it on a young citizen of the United States.

Some in the media have been very quick to condemn Singapore for such a practice. Some in the contemporary media have not been truthful in their descriptions and portrayals of the justice system in Singapore. One example of the misleading information is a report that cited Singapore as an "Islamic nation" that uses whipping and lashing. "That's why they use a cane to whip its people into compliance." The label of Islamic nation could not be further from the truth. Suzanne M. Bonds, who wrote an excellent article on Singapore justice, concludes, "The ethnic division is approximately 76.4% Chinese, 14.9% Malay, 6.4% Indian, and 2.3% other. The majority of Chinese are Buddhists or atheists; the Malays are nearly all Muslims" (pp. 11–12). How do you go from 15% Malaysian-Muslim to an entire "Muslim nation"? Singapore is not a "Muslim nation." This label was a total fabrication, and did an injustice to all.

Justice in Singapore—It Works!

There is agreement between the modern media and many scholarly writers. "Justice in Singapore, It Really Does Work." Many T.V. news magazine shows accurately portrayed how well the government runs and how little crime there is in this "city-state." All the contemporary media do agree: there is very little crime in Singapore. There is not complete agreement as to why that system works so well. This narrative will explore briefly some of the reasons why it does work. The scientific community also cites the "nation-state" with very low crime rates (Bonds, p. 16). John Andrade, author of *World Police* (1985, p. 177) explains why the crime rates are so low in Singapore.

> The severe attitude to crime adopted by the government of Singapore has been remarkably successful. The Republic is one of the most orderly countries in the world, sharply contrasting with other South Asian areas. Police powers are comprehensive (the CID includes a Prosecution Branch). Courts deal harshly with habitual offenders, regardless of their nationality; and corruption in high places, historically common in Asia, is noticeably absent.

Crime Rates in Singapore

Does Singapore have low crime rates or is this another inaccuracy in the media? The crime rates in Singapore have been reported for 1960 to 1983. Quah and Chey list the entire Singapore crime rates in a United Nations publication (1989). The Singapore rates are reported in crimes per 100,000 population, the same as the United States crime rates. When one compares the Singapore overall crime rates with the U.S. rates one finds some significant differences.

1. 1980 382% higher for the United States
2. 1981 254% higher for the United States
3. 1982 250% higher for the United States
4. 1983 216% higher for the United States

The overall crime rates of the United States run between 200% and 380% higher than Singapore. One must keep in mind that these rates are not exact and precise. (Crime rates in Singapore are not formulated the same way as in the U.S.) The United States has significantly higher overall crime rates.

What about violent crimes in Singapore; are there any measures? Quah and Chey (1989, p. 266) also report the Singapore "Crimes Against Persons Index" which contains *all* crimes against people. The U.S. "Violent Crime Index" is the closest indicator, but only contains four serious crimes against people (murder, rape, robbery, assault). When one compares these two crime indices for ten years (1974–1983) one finds some astounding results. For the ten-year period, the United States had violent crime rates between 749% to 1405% higher than Singapore. The U.S. only measures four crimes and Singapore measures *all* crimes and the U.S. still had significantly higher violent crime rates for a ten-year period.

Corporal Punishment

Some in the Western media condemned Singapore for its barbaric use of caning and "corporal punishment." They feel the use of such punishment is cruel and unusual and outdated in any modern and civilized nation. On one local talk show, the person called for an end to trade between the U.S. and Singapore, as long as Singapore continues the use of caning and corporal punishment.

Again, the popular media have not been exercising full disclosure. Some call the practice of corporal punishment barbaric and inhumane, but they fail to point out that the United States Supreme Court upheld the practice of corporal punishment in schools by teachers and administrators. The Supreme Court concluded that it is all right to use corporal punishment as a *last* resort when all other methods have failed. Many states prohibit corporal punishment under state law, but some still practice its use even today. The media do not cry foul and yell "barbaric" each time a child is spanked in the U.S. If we have to end trading with Singapore because of corporal punishment, then how are we going to punish ourselves for the same policy and practice? I would be the first to agree that caning as I know it in Singapore is much more severe and painful, but it is still corporal punishment. We do not have the moral superiority to condemn Singapore for our same practices.

Age of Accountability

In the United States the age of accountability varies greatly by states (twelve to eighteen years) and the crimes for which juveniles are punished. The U.S. Supreme Court set the age of accountability "at the time of the crime" for juvenile executions at sixteen years of age. The U.S. Court made those rulings in the 1980s and clarified them in the 1990s. South Carolina executed George Stinney at age fourteen, the youngest during the 1900s.

Islamic law sets the age of accountability at *puberty,* not at a fixed year for all. It recognizes differences among children and their differing maturation periods. Bonds (p. 16) explains the issue of age in Singapore.

> In the Singapore penal system, a young offender is considered to be juvenile up to the age of 16. Male juvenile offenders can be sent to approved schools by the courts; female juvenile offenders can be sent to approved homes.

Some of the media criticized Singapore for caning a juvenile who is certainly older than sixteen years of age. I do not hear the same outrage when the United States asks for a death penalty for a juvenile who is sixteen years old. Caning appears to be minor when compared to the *execution* of a juvenile. The United States has also signed treaties in the United Nations which limit the age of accountability for executions at eighteen years of age (Streib, 1987). Where do the U.S. media have the right to tell Singapore, "You are wrong," when the U.S. uses the same age standard for juvenile executions?

Ignorance of the Law

One idea put forth by the media is that Fay "did not know what the laws of Singapore were"; therefore, he should not be punished. This is known in popular legal terms as "ignorance of the law." The legal systems of both the U.S. and Singapore are based on the English system of common law. Most English-speaking nations of the world share the same historical common law roots and legal doctrines. All of these nations are bound by a common law concept, which is "ignorance of the law is no excuse." Great Britain, the United States, and Singapore *all* share this legal doctrine. One cannot simply go to court and say, "I did not know it was wrong, so you can't punish me." The courts hold all people equally accountable in all common law nations. In the United States, one is presumed to know all the federal laws as well as the laws of each state, county, and city where one lives or travels. No one knows all the laws of one state, let alone the federal, city, and county ordinances. But this legal fiction still holds everyone accountable to the same standard. Michael Fay had lived in Singapore for several years and was not a tourist or newly arrived visitor.

A few in the media were quick to condemn Singapore for caning and label the nation as "inhumane" and out of touch with contemporary thought. Some writers went even a step further to label the nation and people as barbarians and sadistic creatures. These impressions were harmful and inaccurate. Most of these inaccuracies were from people who have not studied the history of the nation or its political and economic importance in a modern society. This same group failed to explore the people of Singapore, their culture, customs, and views on issues of importance. The greatest of all faults is that they condemned a nation's legal and criminal justice system without any knowledge of how well it works. These same people cannot explain why Singapore police have almost no corruption or engage in little physical abuse of its citizens. These factors would be much more important than one simple fact of "they use a cane in their punishment, therefore, they are wrong and barbaric in all areas."

Personal Observations and Opinions

I personally would not want to be caned. The demonstrations provided by the media show it as a very painful experience. I also would not want my children to be caned. I understand and grieve with the parents of Michael Fay. It is normal for all parents to try and protect and shield their children from any harm.

I am personally opposed to corporal punishment in our schools. I do not agree with some that corporal punishment or caning would act as a deterrent in the United States. My personal opinion on this issue is one of "Deweyism and pragmatism." Singapore has a system that works for Singapore. Its citizens are safe and relatively crime free. We, in the United States, do not have a right to condemn it for its use of a punishment that we also use in different degrees. We do not have a right to tell Singapore that it is wrong when we have the highest crime rates of any industrialized nation in the world. We do not have a right to correct Singapore as long as we continue to incarcerate more people per capita than any other nation in the world. We do not have an excellent track record on rehabilitation of offenders. I am not advocating caning in the United States—I am arguing that we do not have the moral superiority to tell others they are wrong!

REFERENCES

Andrade, John. *World Police and Paramilitary Forces.* New York: Stockton Press, 1985.

Bonds, Suzanne M. "The 'Big' Little Nation-State." *CJ International.* Vol. 7, No. 2 (March–April. 1991), pp. 11–18.

Quah, Jon S.T. and Ong Seng Chey. "Singapore." Chapter in *Urban Crime: Global Trends and Policies.* Found in Buendia, Hernando Gomez, editor. Tokyo: The United Nations University, 1989, pp. 257–290.

Streib, Victor L. *The Death Penalty for Juveniles.* Bloomington: Indiana University Press, 1987.

DISCUSSION QUESTIONS

1. Disregarding your personal opinion on capital punishment, what do you believe is the strongest argument supporting the use of the death penalty? What is the strongest argument supporting the abolition of the death penalty?

2. In what has come to be called the Marshall hypothesis, Supreme Court Justice Thurgood Marshall reasoned (*Furman v. Georgia*, 1972) that public support for the death penalty is a function of lack of knowledge about the subject. If citizens were provided with information about the death penalty, he reasoned, they would conclude that it is immoral and unconstitutional. What, if any, points addressed in the death penalty reading could be considered the kind of information that might make citizens pro-abolitionist?

3. Dennis J. Wiechman believes that no country has the right to tell other countries how they should go about punishing their criminals—especially if the country giving advice isn't doing a particularly effective job of controlling its own crime rate. At its most general level, this position addresses the topic of cultural relativism. Are there times and situations (and if there are, how do we recognize them?) in which it is appropriate, maybe even mandatory, that one or several countries force another country to change its policies and procedures? For example, what should the "civilized" nations of the world "do" about restrictions on free speech in the People's Republic of China, circumcision of female genitalia in Africa, beheading in Saudi Arabia, or lethal injection in the United States?

4. If corporal punishment should be used in the United States, what form should it take (e.g., whipping, electric shock) and for what crimes should it be applied?

WEBSITES

www.essential.org/dpic

The Death Penalty Information Center, an abolitionist organization, has one of the best Internet sites for information about the death penalty.

dpa.state.ky.us:80/~rwheeler/deathpen.htm

This page from the Kentucky Department of Public Advocacy's website has a remarkably complete list of Internet links on the death penalty.

www.infidels.org/library/historical/robert_ingersoll/corporal_punishment.html

This paper by Robert Ingersoll, written in 1891, reminds us that issues relevant to corporal punishment are very much the same today as they were over a century ago.

PART IV

CORRECTIONS

Contents

PART IV. CORRECTIONS

CHAPTER 10: COMMUNITY AND INTERMEDIATE SANCTIONS

For many years the primary sentencing options for convicted felons were either standard probation or imprisonment. Under probation the offender is allowed to remain at liberty in the community, although under specified conditions. Imprisonment, on the other hand, is deprivation of liberty, usually by secure confinement in a jail or prison. Since the 1980s state jurisdictions have increasingly recognized a need for criminal penalties that fall between standard probation and imprisonment. These "intermediate sanctions" include some that are community based (e.g., intensive supervision probation (ISP), home confinement, community service) and some that require residential confinement at a facility other than jail or prison (e.g., halfway houses, residential treatment centers).

One of the first problems officials faced in creating intermediate sanctions was devising community-based penalties that correspond in severity to imprisonment. With retribution and deterrence as the main contemporary goals of punishment, sanctions must be viewed by both the public and the offender as punitive. In the first reading, Joan Petersilia and Elizabeth Deschenes are concerned with the offenders' point of view. Using rankings provided by male inmates, the authors found that, for example, inmates consider one year on ISP to be equivalent in punitive value to six months in jail, three years on standard probation, or a $500 fine. Interestingly, five years on ISP was deemed harsher than one year in prison but less harsh than three years in prison. As you read this article, ask yourself what it is about sanctions like ISP that would lead some offenders to prefer imprisonment.

We learn from Petersilia and Deschenes that probation is considered punitive by some offenders. In the next reading, six federal probation officers help us understand why. Using the "day in the life" approach, these probation officers provide a fascinating portrayal of the variety of people and problems they encounter. As you read each officer's account, think about the skills a successful probation officer must have.

While some persons believe the correct goals of criminal punishment should be retribution or deterrence, others hope that the sanctions will help offenders become law-abiding citizens. The goal of rehabilitation requires us to evaluate penalties on their potential to improve the offender—no matter how punitive the public or offenders believe the punishment to be. This effect is difficult to measure. The reading by Russ Immarigeon helps accomplish the task by reviewing some recent research findings that suggest there are some correctional programs that "work." Particular attention is paid to a community service program in New York, programs geared specifically toward the female offender, and how the concept of restorative justice is being used to balance the concerns and needs of offender, victim, and community.

WHAT INMATES VIEW AS PUNISHMENT

Joan Petersilia and Elizabeth Piper Deschenes

Are there intermediate sanctions that equate, in terms of punitiveness, with prison? The authors report on a study in which prisoners in Minnesota were asked to rank the severity of various criminal sanctions and which particular sanctions they judged equivalent in punitiveness. The authors also explore how inmates rank the difficulty of commonly imposed probation conditions and which offender background characteristics are associated with perceptions of sanction severity. Joan Petersilia is an associate professor in the School of Social Ecology at the University of California, Irvine, and director of RAND's Criminal Justice Program. Elizabeth Deschenes is a researcher in RAND's Criminal Justice Program.

The intermediate sanctions movement of the 1980's was predicated on the assumption that the two extremes of punishment—imprisonment and probation—are both used excessively, with a near vacuum of useful punishments in between. According to Morris and Tonry (1990), a more comprehensive sentencing strategy that relies on a range of "intermediate" punishments—including fines, community service, intensive probation, and electronic monitoring—would better meet the needs of the penal system, convicted offenders, and the community than the current polarized

Reprinted from Joan Petersilia and Elizabeth Piper Deschenes, "What Punishes? Inmates Rank the Severity of Prison vs. Intermediate Sanctions," *Federal Probation*, March 1994, a publication of the Administrative Office of the United States Courts.

choice. The central thesis of the Morris and Tonry proposal is that there are "equivalencies" of punishment and that, at some level of intensity, community-based punishments are as severe as prison terms (i.e., have roughly the same punitive "bite"). They encouraged states to identify these roughly equivalent punishments (or "exchange rates") and allow judges to choose among sentences of rough punitive equivalence. They predicted that in many instances judges would choose to substitute restrictive, intermediate punishments in lieu of a prison term.

Implementing intermediate sanction *programs* within states' broad-based sentencing structure (particularly in states with sentencing guidelines) has proven much easier than developing the comprehensive sentencing *system* that Morris and Tonry envisioned. A major stumbling block has been reaching consensus on the relative severity of different community-based punishments (e.g., house arrest versus community service) and, more importantly, on *which* intermediate sanctions, in what dosage, can be substituted for prison. When the choice was simply prison versus standard probation, most everyone agreed that prison was more severe. But with the emergence of highly restrictive community-based punishments—which often require drug testing, employment, and curfews—it is no longer obvious.

Most law-abiding citizens probably still believe that no matter what conditions probation or parole impose, remaining in the community is categorically preferable to imprisonment, but evidence suggests that offenders might not share this view. When Oregon implemented an intensive supervision probation (ISP) program in 1989 and offenders were given the choice of serving a prison term or participating in ISP (which incorporated drug testing, employment, and frequent home visits by the probation officer), about a third of the offenders chose prison instead of ISP (Petersilia, 1990).

The Offenders' Perspective

It may also be that prison is losing some of its punitive sting. For example, Skolnick (1990) reported that, for certain California youth, having a prison record was no longer seen as stigmatizing, and the prison experience not particularly isolating, since they usually encountered family and friends there. If prison is not judged as severe as we presume it is, this may have important implications for sentencing policy. Since the major purposes of the criminal law are retribution and deterrence, this means that sanctions must be viewed as punitive to fulfill their goals. And, as Crouch (1993, p. 68) has noted, "Theoretically, for prison to have the punitive and deterrent effect on offenders that the public desires, a fundamental assumption must be met: that offenders generally share the state's punitiveness in the ranking of criminal sanctions."

The unanswered question is, "do they?" If they don't, and if community-based punishments can be designed so that they are seen as equally punitive by offenders, then perhaps policymakers—who say they are imprisoning such a large number of offenders because of the public's desire to get tough with crime—might be convinced that there are other means besides prison to exact punishment.

Despite the importance of the offenders' perspective as noted by Crouch (1993), there have been only three prior attempts to survey the opinions of criminal offenders regarding the perceived severity of sanctions (McClelland & Alpert, 1985; Apospori & Alpert, 1993; Crouch, 1993), and none of these studies included the newer intermediate sanctions (e.g., intensive probation). In ad-

dition, most prior research on sanction severity has used either paired comparisons or magnitude estimation to measure judgments, and both techniques have methodological or analytical flaws.[1]

McClelland and Alpert (1985) surveyed 152 arrestees in a midsize western city, following the example of Erickson and Gibbs (1979) who used magnitude estimation techniques to survey policemen and adults in households. Respondents were given a list of penalties (randomly ordered), including different levels of fines, probation, jail, and prison, and instructed to assign a number to each penalty based on the standard of 100 for 1 year in jail. They found that persons who had more experience with the criminal justice system (e.g., more prior convictions) minimized the seriousness of prison in comparison to other punishments. And in later research, Apospori and Alpert (1993) suggested that as the threat of the legal sanction became realized, arrestees raised their perceptions of the severity of sanctions. In a survey of 1,027 incoming prisoners at a Texas institution who were asked if they would prefer probation or prison, Crouch (1993) found that the majority of inmates preferred prison to probation, believing probation was stricter. In addition, Crouch found that those who were married preferred probation to prison, yet minorities and older inmates preferred prison.

This article presents the results of an exploratory study undertaken in cooperation with the Minnesota Department of Corrections and the Minnesota Sentencing Guidelines Commission and funded by the National Institute of Justice to explore these issues. The study developed an instrument and methodology for measuring offender perceptions of sanction severity and, using that method, collected data on the following questions:

1) How do inmates rank the severity of criminal sanctions, and which sanctions are judged equivalent in punitiveness?

2) What background characteristics are associated with variations in the perception of sanction severity?

3) How do inmates rank the difficulty of probation/parole conditions, and how does this affect their ranking of sanctions?

Our research attempted to build upon prior research by adding the newer intermediate sanctions to the survey and including both magnitude estimation and rank ordering scaling techniques. The simpler technique of rank ordering is likely to give a more accurate model of the ratings of various punishments, since offenders may not have the mathematical skills necessary for the magnitude estimation judgment of severity. Besides increasing the simplicity of the task, the use of ordered logistic regression to model the underlying latent scale of sanction severity and test for differences between individuals allowed greater flexibility in the analysis (Agresti, 1990). The basic model being tested assumes that each individual has an underlying scale of the severity of different sanctions. Ordered logistic regression allows us to more easily test whether various sanctions are indeed equivalent with less rigid assumptions about the data.[2] For these reasons, the rank ordering analysis is preferred and this article focuses on those results.

Study Design and Results

Sample Selection The sample selection criteria were designed to identify offenders who would likely be targeted for intermediate sanctions and therefore whose perceptions about the severity of such sanctions are particularly relevant. We used the same criteria to identify our sample that had been outlined by the Minnesota Legislature in deciding which inmates qualified for the state's Intensive Community Supervision (ICS) program. To be eligible for ICS, offenders must be either a probation violator or a new court commitment with less than a 27-month prison sentence to serve. Offenders with prior convictions for murder, manslaughter, or rape are ineligible. The sample was drawn from incoming inmates who met the ICS eligibility criteria at the two main receiving facilities in Minnesota, St. Cloud and Stillwater. Forty-eight male inmates were so identified during the months of April–July 1992, and all agreed to participate in the study.

The sample of inmates were 50 percent white, and the majority of nonwhites were Afro-American; the average age at the time of the current offense was 26. Inmates tended to be unemployed prior to prison, and about half had less than a high school education. Inmates were serving, on average, prison terms of 17 months, and most had been convicted of property offenses. Inmates averaged seven prior arrests and two prior felony convictions, and one-third had previously served time in prison.

Data Collection RAND staff coded various demographic and criminal history data from each inmate's official corrections file. Interviews were administered with those who agreed to participate in the study, and respondents received $20 for participating. The interview took about an hour to administer and was divided into four sections:

1) *The Magnitude Estimation Task.* Fifteen legal sanctions were selected for the study (see table 1). Each sanction description was printed separately on a 3×5-inch card and presented one by one to the respondent in a random order. Respondents were instructed to compare each of the sanctions to the standard of 1 year in jail, which was equivalent to 100 points.

2) *Offender Background Interview.* About 25 open-ended questions were asked offenders requesting information on employment, housing arrangements, family relationships, present prison experiences, and their perceptions of prison versus community-based sentencing.

3) *The Ranking of Probation Conditions.* Inmates were asked to estimate "the difficulty you would probably experience in trying to meet the (specified) condition." They were asked about 13 commonly imposed conditions and directed to place each "condition card" next to one of five responses (ranging from not difficult at all to very difficult).

4) *The Rank Ordering Task.* To rank order the sanctions, inmates were given a stack of 4×6-inch cards (randomly ordered). Each card had printed on it one of the 15 sanctions (see table 1). Inmates were instructed to simply place the cards on the table, from left to right, in order from least severe to most severe.

Inmate Rankings and Equivalencies of the Severity of Criminal Sanctions The means and standard deviations for the rank orders of the 15

Table 1. Inmates' Rank Ordering of Criminal Sanctions

Criminal Sanctions	Mean	Standard Deviation	Median Rank Order
Fines			
$100	1.3	1.1	1
$1,000	4.5	3.4	3
$5,000	7.6	3.6	7
Probation			
1 year	4.2	2.0	4
3 years	6.8	2.7	6
5 years	9.8	2.8	10
Intensive Probation			
1 year	7.1	2.2	7
3 years	9.5	2.2	10
5 years	11.4	2.6	11.5
Jail			
3 months	4.6	3.1	3.5
6 months	6.4	2.9	6
1 year	9.6	2.8	10
Prison			
1 year	9.7	3.2	11
3 years	13.0	2.0	14
5 years	14.5	1.5	15

sanctions presented in table 1 suggest that inmate consensus is greatest at the lowest and highest levels—i.e., $100 fine and 5 years in prison. The larger values for the standard deviations on other sanctions suggest there is some variation between individuals, particularly on the ratings of a $5,000 fine, 3 months in jail, and 1 year in prison. Nonetheless, the means and medians provide similar results in the overall rank ordering of the various sanctions. For example, there appear to be "clusters" of sanctions—5 years probation, 3 years intensive probation, and 1 year in jail all have a median rank of 10. To statistically test for significant differences in the rank ordering of various sanctions, further analysis was necessary.

The data were analyzed using ordered logistic regression to model the ordered categorical responses as a function of the type of sanction. In the simplest case the model is of the form:

$$ranking = f(sum\ \beta(i)*sanction(i))$$

The results of this type of analysis are a collection of parameter estimates or "betas," one for each sanction in the simplest case. The estimated coefficients in this model form a latent variable scale yielding an interval valued "score" for the various sanctions. The betas represent ranking of the sanctions and standard errors for the sanction's position on the latent scale. The statistical test of the difference between the ranking of the sanction and the ranking of the omitted category is a chi-square test with 1 degree of freedom.

The first model tested using ordered logistic regression compared all other sanctions to 1 year of intensive supervision. For this model, the parameter estimate for 1 year ISP was set to zero, and as shown in table 2, sanctions that are not statistically different from 1 year intensive probation include 6 months jail, 3 years probation, and a $500 fine. The parameter estimates for the other sanctions show results that are consistent with the simple comparison of the median rank orders.

To test for equivalencies in the ratings of the sanctions, the ordered logistic regression analysis was repeated, each time omitting a different sanction, and chi-square tests performed, comparing sanction to the omitted category. The results of this analysis can be used to devise formulas for the substitution of incarceration for community-based punishments as shown in table 2.

A number of things are worth noting. First, inmates judged 1 year spent in jail as equivalent to 1 year spent in prison. In fact, in the open-ended interviews, several inmates stated that prison time was easier to do because there were more activities to occupy their time and conditions were generally better. Inmates also ranked 5 years of intensive probation supervision as harsher than 1 year in prison but not as harsh as 3 years in prison. Five years in prison was judged more severe than any other sanction and had no equivalent in terms of the intermediate sanctions measured here. Similarly, a $100 fine was judged as significantly less severe than any other sanction measured here, having no other statistical equivalent.

Differences Between Individuals To test for differences between individuals, ordered logistic regression was used and various models com-

Table 2. Inmates' Perceived Severity of Criminal Sanctions

Criminal Sanctions	Parameter Estimate	Standard Error	Chi-Square
$100 fine	−7.42	.68	118.3*
$1,000 fine	−2.14	.38	32.4*
3 months jail	−1.85	.36	25.8*
1 year probation	−1.80	.35	26.5*
6 months jail	−0.49	.34	2.1
3 years probation	−0.15	.34	0.2
1 year intensive probation	0.00		
$5,000 fine	0.24	.36	0.4
3 years intensive probation	1.25	.33	14.2*
1 year jail	1.35	.34	15.4*
5 years probation	1.45	.35	17.4*
1 year prison	1.56	.35	19.5*
5 years intensive probation	2.49	.36	47.9*
3 years prison	4.17	.39	113.1*
5 years prison	7.38	.56	175.1*

*Chi-square test of difference between this parameter estimate and the estimate for the omitted category (1 year ISP) is significantly different at $p < .05$.

pared by using the chi-square differences from likelihood ratio tests. Only two of the background variables were significantly related to the perceptions of sanction severity: (1) inmates who were married and/or had children tended to rank prison and jail confinement as more severe than those who were single; and (2) inmates who were single tended to rank financial penalties (e.g., fines, restitution) as more severe than inmates who were married. We found no differences in the rankings of sanction severity by race, prior prison experience, employment history, drug dependency, or how safe the inmate felt in prison. It is possible that the sample was too small to detect differences or the characteristics of our sample too homogeneous. On the other hand, it may be that the differences noted in earlier studies reflect the clearer distinctions in the offenders' mind between prison and probation, which because of the inclusion of intermediate sanctions, was not as pronounced in our study as in earlier research.

Rating the Difficulty of Complying with Various Probation Conditions We were interested in learning how inmates varied in their perception of the difficulty of complying with various probation conditions and whether this perception affected their rankings of different sanctions. Figure 1 presents the results, with the responses averaged over all inmates.

Inmates generally felt they would have little difficulty in complying with various restrictions. The overall rating for the 13 probation conditions was 2.1, which is "relatively easy." They judged the easiest conditions to be payment of a $100 fine and 10 hours per week of community service and the most difficult conditions to be house arrest with 24-hour electronic monitoring and the payment of a $20-per-week probation/parole supervision fee.

It might seem contrary that inmates who judged certain intermediate sanctions as equivalent to prison in harshness would also judge the individual conditions making up those sanctions as rather easy to comply with. Information offered by inmates during the interviews suggests that while each individual condition might be easy to comply with, when conditions are stacked together—*particularly over longer time periods*—they become much more difficult. House arrest sentences are often for periods of 6 months to 1 year, and intensive probation is usually for 1–2 years.

We analyzed the relationship between background characteristics and inmate ratings of probation conditions and found only one significant difference: Those with no history of drug or alcohol use (as noted on their official prison records) reported finding it more difficult to attend a weekly outpatient treatment program than did the users. We also tested whether the inmates' overall rating score on probation conditions was related to the ranking of the severity of the overall criminal sanctions but found no significant differences between those who rated the probation conditions as easy to comply with and those who rated the conditions as more difficult.

Figure 1. Inmate Perceptions of the Difficulty of Probation Conditions

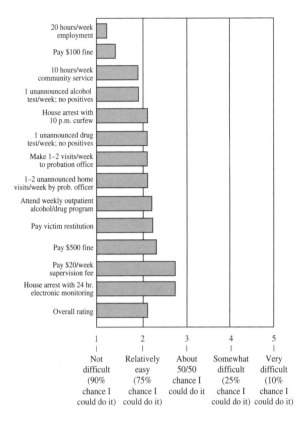

Discussion and Policy Implications

Our results provide empirical evidence to support what many have suggested: that it is no longer necessary to equate criminal punishment solely with prison. The balance of sanctions between probation and prison appears to have shifted, and at some level of intensity and length, intensive probation is the more dreaded penalty.

These findings have a number of research and policy implications. For one, the clusters of sanctions identified as "equivalent" in severity should be useful to sentencing commissions attempting to incorporate alternatives into sentencing guidelines and to devise formulas showing the equivalency of alternative sanctions to imprisonment.

Ideally, one wants to devise an intermediate sanction that includes enough conditions (but not more than necessary) to exact punishment and protect the public. But since little knowledge ex-

ists about how many conditions, or what type, are necessary to achieve those goals, jurisdictions continue to add conditions, thus negating one of the major purposes of intermediate sanctions, which is to provide suitable punishment at less cost than prison. Inmate judgments on punitive equivalence could be useful in setting some boundaries on what types of conditions, imposed for how long, are required to mete out "tough" probation sentences and to suggest some rough ordering that might be used to create a continuum of punishments—from fines through community service, standard probation, intensive probation and house arrest, then moving on to jail, and finally prison.

The study results also have implications for sentencing and deterrence research. Sentencing studies routinely build mathematical models of punishment that treat anything other than prison as "zero" and assign positive values only to increments of imprisonment. Similarly, deterrence studies assign numerical ranks reflecting sanction seriousness and then analyze whether there is a relationship between the severity rankings and some post-treatment outcome (e.g., usually recidivism). Both types of studies rely on scales of sanction severity, which our study suggests are in need of refinement. At a minimum, sentencing studies need to recognize different levels of probation supervision (i.e., not code all probation sentences identically) and that probation terms do not equate to "zero," which implies no sanction at all.

Our findings also have implications for sentencing policy more generally. It is argued by some that the United States has failed to develop a sufficient range of criminal sanctions because the dialogue is often cast as punishment (prison) or not, with other sanctions being seen as "letting off" or a "slap on the wrist." The results of this study show that certain community-based sanctions are not a "slap on the wrist" and are judged quite punitive. This should give justice officials pause, particularly those who state they are imprisoning such a large number of offenders to get "tough on crime." Our results suggest that, in the minds of offenders, community-based sanctions can be severe, and it can no longer be said that incarceration is preferred simply because, as Fogel (1975) stated, "we have not found another satisfactory severe punishment."

NOTES

1. For example, one problem with magnitude estimation is that the validity depends on the adequacy of subjects' mathematical skill, since it requires subjects to rate various stimuli in comparison to the standard numerical value. Although used in numerous psychological experiments on subjects with varying skills, research has shown that the use of magnitude estimation techniques among naive or poorly educated subjects is questionable (Jones & Shorter 1972).

2. Ordered logistic regression does not depend on the use of an interval level of measurement, as does the magnitude estimation techniques.

REFERENCES

Agresti, A. (1990). *Categorical data analysis.* New York: John Wiley and Sons.

Apospori, E., & Alpert, G. (1993). Research note: The role of differential experience with the criminal justice system in changes in perceptions of severity of legal sanctions over time. *Crime and Delinquency* 39(2), 184–194.

Crouch, B.M. (1993). Is incarceration really worse? Analysis of offenders' preferences for prison over probation. *Justice Quarterly, 10*(1), 67–88.

Erickson, M.L., & Gibbs, J.P. (1979). On the perceived severity of legal penalties. *Journal of Criminal Law & Criminology, 70*(1), 102–116.

Fogel, D. (1975). *". . . We are the living proof . . ." The justice model for corrections.* Cincinnati: W.H. Anderson Co.

Jones, B.C., & Shorter, R. (1972). The ratio measurement of social status: Some cross-cultural comparisons. *Social Forces, 50,* 499–511.

McClelland, K.A., & Alpert, G.P. (1985). Factor analysis applied to magnitude estimates of punishment seriousness: Patterns of individual differences. *Journal of Quantitative Criminology, 1*(3), 307–318.

Morris, N., & Tonry, M. (1990). *Between prison and probation: Intermediate punishments in a rational sentencing system.* New York: Oxford University Press.

Petersilia, J. (1990). When probation becomes more dreaded than prison. *Federal Probation, 54*(1), 23–27.

Skolnick, J.H. (1990). Gangs and crime old as time: But drugs change gang culture. *Crime and Delinquency in California, 1980–1989.* Sacramento, CA: Bureau of Criminal Justice Statistics, State of California, pp. 171–179.

READING 21
A DAY IN THE LIFE OF A FEDERAL PROBATION OFFICER

E. Jane Pierson et al.

Six U.S. probation officers describe a typical workday. The authors, all of whom serve in specialist positions, offer commentaries on their work that range from philosophical to highly creative. Any names used for probationers are fictitious. Although the circumstances depicted reflect real-life situations, they have been altered for the sake of confidentiality.

Enhanced Supervision— Not Necessarily "Tail 'Em, Nail 'Em, and Jail 'Em"

By E. Jane Pierson, *Senior United States Probation Officer, Eastern District of California*

Not so long ago, probation officers made home contacts based on a predetermined schedule, whether or not there were any issues to address in that particular case. The "classification" of the case, not the issues, determined the officer's contacts. So when the time came for a "visit" the officer got in his or her car and drove to the residence. Then, the officer would proceed to talk

Reprinted from E. Jane Pierson, Thomas L. Densmore, John M. Shevlin, Omar Madruga, Jay F. Meyer, Terry D. Childers, "A Day in the Life of a Federal Probation Officer—Revisited," *Federal Probation*, December 1992, a publication of the Administrative Office of the United States Courts.

with the "client" about that person's children, spouse, job, school, the weather, or whatever, while leaning against his or her car, "kicking the tire." In those cases, there were no real issues to be addressed.

The above scenario is not likely to be repeated with the implementation of "enhanced supervision." Meaningless "tire kicking" or "quota system" contacts as well as the "monthly reporting ritual" or "assembly line," as this officer referred to it, have been abandoned for a more common-sense approach to supervision. Enhanced supervision is grounded in statutory authority which mandates that the probation officer accomplish certain objectives. Enhanced supervision provides for the officer's professional judgment as to where and how his or her time is best utilized based on the officer's evaluation and re-evaluation of issues in each individual case. Issues to be addressed rather than a quota to meet now occupy the officer's day. And occupied, it is!

Verification Verification appears to be a key word in enhanced supervision, but then it always has been or, at least, should have been. Verification of the offender's residence; employment and specific job duties; finances; roommates; new charges, disposition of old charges; fine, restitution, and penalty assessment payments; travel requests; attendance at counseling sessions; performance of community service hours; and so on, all have their place in a day's work. Verification by the officer equates to accountability of the offender. Officer verification and offender accountability do not necessarily equate to "tail 'em, nail 'em, and jail 'em," as it may superficially appear. Verification is consistent with this officer's statutory duty to "keep informed . . . as to the conduct and condition of a probationer or a person on supervised release" (title 18, section 3603(2)).

Verification and more verification proved essential in one particular case in which a female, convicted of bank embezzlement, obtained employment as a receptionist. The sentencing judge had imposed a special condition that she must disclose her conviction to her employer if she handled cash or negotiables. The offender did not notify her employer because her job duties, she claimed, did not include the handling of cash or negotiables. Employment was verified in the usual ways—pay stubs, phone calls, and contact at the job site. Her employment seemed in order until this officer requested a copy of the offender's most recent employee evaluation, wherein it was noted that she was progressing well in payroll training! Following this officer's near coronary at learning this bit of information, direct contact with the employer revealed that the offender's payroll training consisted of her learning how to input employee work hours into a computer only. The offender did not lose her job, and she has since confided that she feels more comfortable and secure in her employment now that her employer is aware of her conviction.

By demanding accountability from the offender via verification, officers enforce the conditions and thus protect the community, but an officer is also charged with aiding the offender. How, you say, since we, as enhanced supervision officers, obviously have no trust in the offender? Yet, we do trust the offender—it is simply his or her creditability we must verify. We aid the offender in much the same way we always have—by referral and by providing services ourselves. Referrals are for employment services; vocational rehabilitation; education; parenting classes; marital/family

counseling; credit counseling; food and/or clothing from social service agencies and/or churches; Alcoholics Anonymous; Narcotics Anonymous; contract drug aftercare providers; residential treatment programs. And we follow up to ensure that services were provided or additional referrals made to assist the offender and to enforce the conditions—although it was somewhat perplexing, yet humorous, when I received a letter from a destitute and homeless offender I had modified into a community corrections center, to see that it was addressed to the attention of "Mrs. Prison."

Noncompliance When noncompliance is detected, a violator's warrant is not automatically requested; in the majority of cases, interim sanctions are applied. If this strategy is not successful, then the offender meets with the supervising officer and supervising U.S. probation officer for a nonjudicial compliance hearing. Usually additional sanctions are imposed on the offender. Every effort is made by the officer to bring the offender into compliance prior to court or Parole Commission action. One nonjudicial compliance hearing ended with the offender indicating that he understood his responsibilities much clearer, and he made the comment, "You people are really serious about this." To date, he remains in compliance.

When all else fails, the violator's warrant is requested and issued. The offender is then taken into custody, which seems to provide the most pathetic and the most humorous of situations. For example, a parolee, who was arrested early one morning while still in his underwear, very irately stated, "You are treating me like a common criminal." Another parolee who came into the office asked, "How much trouble am I in?" And upon seeing the deputy U.S. marshals answered his own question, "Big trouble."

And the last but certainly not the least aspect of our job is keeping the court and the United States Parole Commission informed of the offender's behavior or, in most cases, his misbehavior and what has been done in attempts to correct noncompliance. Paperwork can easily be deemed the probation officer's nemesis.

My day consists of any combination of, and

occasionally it seems all of, the above and more (i.e., surveillance, search, home confinement/electronic monitoring, modifications, community corrections center referrals, court appearances, and the demon telephone—I have a *lot* of co-dependent offenders). The list is by no means complete. Overall, the day of an enhanced supervision officer is stressful, frustrating, and too long with too many things to do, but it is also challenging, exhilarating, and humorous. There is little that is more professionally rewarding than knowing that you have been instrumental in helping to prevent another victim statistic or in helping an individual overcome his or her self-defeating behavior simply by doing your job.

We, as enhanced supervision officers, are Jacks and Janes (no pun intended) of all trades and specialists in each separate aspect that comprises supervision. Enhanced supervision has provided us supervision proponents with the validity and legitimacy that had for too long taken second place in the order of importance of the duties of a probation officer. I, for one, say it was about time for supervision to quit being the stepchild of the system.

One Hot Day at a Time: Daily Meditations of a Drug Specialist

By Thomas L. Densmore, *Senior United States Probation Officer, Northern District of Texas*

Is it hot—104 in the shade! But then, it's always hot here. Heat never stops the duties of a drug specialist in the United States Probation Office. Being about the Government's business in the cause of therapy does not succumb to the weather. "Neither rain, nor snow, nor sleet . . . nor heat."

The only concession you make to the heat is to work early in the day or late at night. In the middle of the day, find shade. I start early enough today to see "Tony" before he goes to work. He is 35, recently released from 6 months in treatment, on his own for the first time, working his first real job at a grocery store. He is having a hard time figuring out how to be a clean and sober 35-year-old. He last saw life sober at age 10. He's missed a lot since then, such as basic survival skills. We do a budget. He spends $17 a week on cigarettes; $13 on food; $7 on incidentals. I persuade him to let the rest go into the credit union so that he can pay his rent, phone, and lights at the end of the month. He agrees. Relapse can be brought on by something as simple as the thought: "It's not fair that I don't make enough money to even pay my rent." He'll entertain himself by going to an AA group and playing dominoes after group. Tony gives me a urine specimen to prove his sobriety.

A quick call to the office. "Ken" is avoiding treatment. He missed a urine call last night. He is already at work. I leave a message with his wife ("Tell Ken to be ready to give me a u/a when he gets home tonight."). I sweat through a couple more stops. No one is home. Everyone is already at work. I need to find some coolness in a productive way.

I guess I'll take a few hours to check on the five clients at our residential program. The counselor fills me in on each client's progress. "Fawn" doesn't want to be here. "Lee" has just written a letter to the judge saying, "I'm trapped in treatment. Please send help." Interesting, since the judge sent him here. "Terri" is moving into a new phase of treatment which requires that she give her life story, an eye-opening event for her. "Ernest" is looking for treatment support in the community. "Amado" is ready to graduate. I talk with each client. Fawn decides to try it for one more week. Lee changes his mind that treatment is worse than prison. Terri explains how frightening it is to see your life without being high. She is overwhelmed by how much she has lost, especially time. Ernest is encouraged that he can find people who care for him outside of treatment. Amado is excited/scared about his graduation next week.

We have just finished hiring our contract counselors for next year. We did real good. We got great counselors. So now I can pretend that I'm a counselor/line officer again. This is fun. I love working the field, even in the heat. I might not even check into the office.

It's still hot outside. Guess I'll go to the office,

do paperwork, hope it's cool. At the office, my secretary has been working hard. She has all of the therapy bills for June ready for me to check and sign. After paying the bills, I begin the age-old game of phone tag. I return eight messages. I talk to three recording machines and five people. I will have to testify next Thursday that high blood pressure and hemorrhoid medications can't combine to result in a u/a positive for cocaine. The defense will have a doctor to testify that in this defendant's body, these medications create cocaine metabolite. Where do they find these doctors anyway? I also agree to do: a training session for new counseling staff; a speech at a networking meeting for counselors; and an audit trip to West Texas. One counselor wants to complain that I deducted too much from his last bill. I should have stayed in the field and sweltered.

Despite the heat, I head on out. All strapped up and ready to go, the boss gives me the latest from Washington. Somebody messed up. Washington needs $24 million to pay for defense attorneys. Every district has to contribute what they can from their current drug therapy budget. In the middle of this heat, everything is frozen. No new treatment. Everything is cut back until further notice. Get the word out. Hold the drug budget for fiscal 1993. So much for the rest of this day.

Another 10 calls. Dallas will do a "freeze group" and Saturday workshops. Arlington will do only the Saturday workshops. Fort Worth will do a group and get free therapy for new clients. Lubbock will get free therapy until the freeze is over. The West Texas people will use AA until the "Freeze of 92" thaws. The heat and the field are forgotten. Let's figure this out. How much money do we have left for counseling? How much can I risk sending back? Will the clients relapse? I hope not. I am whipped. I'm going home. This day started out with such promise. Just a nice day of seeing people, driving around, acting important, and sweating. This "freeze in July" is going to make things "hot" for us until Christmas.

One more stop to get that u/a from Ken and then I'm done. He'd better be ready.

Finally, home. Oh, no! I forgot the u/a's in my car. They must be boiling by now. I either have to mail them tonight after this terrible hot day or keep them cold in our refrigerator. ("Honey, I have some u/a's I forgot to mail. I have to keep them cold until I can mail them tomorrow. I vote for our refrigerator. How do you vote?")

Just one more stop at the post office and THEN I'm done.

A Special Offender Specialist Hits the Road

By John M. Shevlin, *Supervising United States Probation Officer, Southern District of Florida* and Omar Madruga, *Senior United States Probation Officer, Southern District of Florida*

It is 7 a.m. on Monday, and I am where we park the Government cars. I will be spending the day in the field with my supervisor. He periodically rides in the field with me as he does with the other officers assigned to the Special Offender Unit in the United States Probation Office in Miami, Florida. Our unit supervises offenders involved in violent crimes, major drug conspiracies, racketeering, money laundering, and major frauds. We also supervise offenders associated with criminal organizations, public corruption, and other sensitive cases.

Our first stop of the day is with an individual relocated to our district, an offender who formerly cooperated with the Government. We have gotten an early start so that we can see this offender at home before he leaves for work. He is a difficult case to supervise for many reasons. Based upon his cooperation with the Government, he feels that he need not follow the conditions of supervision like any other offender. Also, he frequently suggests that it would be in his best interest to return to the district in which he was sentenced. After questioning him in reference to residence, employment, and other personal circumstances, I once again persuade him to discard any thought of returning to the district of his sentencing.

Our next stop is at a car dealership where Mr. Udall is a salesman. He is a criminal who has made a career out of defrauding the public. He has sold fraudulent oil leases, rare coins, precious stones, and vacation time-shares. In those few instances where delivery was actually made to a customer, the product was incredibly overpriced. Once again, Mr. Udall makes his usual request to enter into a self-employment situation. Once again, I deny him permission to do so. He appeals to the supervisor who also indicates that he may not enter into a self-employment situation. As we depart the car dealership, I comment to my supervisor that Mr. Udall will no doubt return to some sort of criminal activity the day after he gets off supervision. In his case, a term of probation is truly protecting the public from additional criminal activity.

Before our next stop, I do a "drive by" of the area. I do this because Mr. Rodriguez is an active confidential informant for the Government. He has been approached by some narcotic traffickers to utilize his place of business, a building supply corporation, to launder narcotic proceeds. Unbeknown to the narcotic traffickers, the offender is involved with the Government in a "sting" operation. After driving by the business, I see an automobile which I do not recognize. Using the cellular phone, I conduct a check of the license plate. The vehicle is registered to Mr. Rodriguez' wife. As the car appears to be brand new, I assume that Mr. Rodriguez has driven the car to work himself. Once again using the cellular phone, I call Mr. Rodriguez at his place of business. He confirms my finding that the vehicle is his, and then my supervisor and I go into the business. As there are no customers in the business at the moment, Mr. Rodriguez is able to discuss freely his confidential informant activities. Because he speaks only Spanish, I translate for my supervisor who speaks only English. We review his confidential informant activities, and all appears to be in order. Due to the sensitive nature of the case, Mr. Rodriguez is only seen at his place of residence or employment. I do not have him report to the office.

Mr. Francois is our next stop. I go to his residence, and he is once again at home. Based upon his cooperation with the Government, he received a term of probation as opposed to the mandatory 5-year term of incarceration that he was facing. The issue as to his unemployment is once again addressed. I have been repeatedly instructing him to secure employment, and he has been repeatedly doing everything in his power to avoid securing employment. Mr. Francois then requests permission to travel to the Turks and Caicos Islands. These islands, located in the Caribbean, are known as a haven for drug trafficking and money laundering. His request to travel to this area is denied. I explained to Mr. Francois that this denial is based upon the fact that he has been convicted of importation of cocaine, he has a history of criminal activity associated with importing cocaine, and he is in technical violation of his supervision by not being employed. He becomes extremely irate and states that he intends to have his attorney file a motion with the court. I explain to Mr. Francois that he can file anything with the court that he wants. However, I give him an employment search log and instruct him to fill out the log. Also, based upon the fact that he is unemployed, he is to report on a weekly basis. Mr. Francois will make good on his threat to file a motion with the court. After leaving, my supervisor and I discuss what our response to the judge will be.

Mr. Perez is our next stop. He has an extremely lengthy prior record. If he is once again convicted of drug trafficking, he will be classified as a career offender. He is now working at a construction site as a painter. After briefly reviewing his situation, I take a urine sample from him. He has had a history of drug use. Nevertheless, this has not been a problem as of late.

We then stop at "calle ocho" in an area of Miami known as Little Havana. Once again, I translate for my supervisor as we order our Cuban lunch. At the conclusion of lunch, we use the cellular telephone to check with the office to see if there are any messages. I am advised that Mr. Francois' attorney has left two messages: one for me and one for my supervisor. After finishing lunch with some cafe Cubano, we resume our field day.

Yesterday, I had organized an itinerary to make the best use of the day. Our next stop is at the Federal Bureau of Investigation office where I locate Agent Kennedy. I explain to him that I have received a copy of a travel permit from the Southern District of New York in reference to a well-known organized crime figure. My special offender colleague in the Southern District of New York always advises me when this individual travels to Miami. The organized crime figure owns an expensive condominium in a prestigious apartment building located on Biscayne Bay. Agent Kennedy thanks me for the information and indicates that he will advise other law enforcement officials who may want to know about the presence of this individual in our district.

Mrs. Marcus is our next contact. She is the wife of a former attorney who is under my supervision. He was one of several attorneys involved in a scheme to bribe state court judges. He is now on a term of supervised release after having received a sentence of incarceration and a large fine. Payment of the fine has been a major issue for Mr. Marcus. He has repeatedly indicated that he does not have enough assets to pay the fine. Mr. and Mrs. Marcus are presently involved in a hotly contested divorce trial. She called yesterday to advise me that she has some financial information that may prove of interest to the probation office. I thank Mrs. Marcus for the documentation and indicate to my supervisor that this documentation will prove interesting to compare to the Personal Financial Statement that Mr. Marcus gave me last month.

Our next three stops do not result in personal contacts with offenders. A former police officer convicted of providing protection to narcotic traffickers has called in sick to the hotel where he is now employed as a chef. Mr. Gonzalez, convicted of unlawfully exporting military armaments, is not at his place of business, a company that sells cellular phones and beepers. His employment has been a problem since his release from prison. In his next office interview, I will suggest to him that he secure another job.

The last stop of the day is with Mr. Adler. Like many of the offenders in the Special Offender Unit, he takes issue with employment. He is a career offender who throughout his life has held virtually no legitimate employment. He is not at the residence, and Mrs. Adler indicates to me that he is out looking for work. Sure, Mrs. Adler! In any event, I ask Mrs. Adler to have her husband call me tomorrow morning at 9 a.m. My supervisor and I then return to the area where the Government cars are parked. While doing the paperwork for the field day, I staff some of the cases with my supervisor. He and I agree on courses of action in reference to several of the stops made today. It has been a typical day in working with the offenders I supervise. It is challenging work, work I enjoy.

Guideline Specialist: An Advocate for Accuracy

By Jay F. Meyer, *Senior United States Probation Officer, District of Minnesota*

Not long after I started with U.S. Probation in 1984, Congress passed the Sentencing Reform Act. During the next several years, while the U.S. Sentencing Commission debated the monumental issues inherent to guideline sentencing, my colleagues and I often debated the advantages and flaws of a system that would eliminate parole and devise a determinate sentencing system comprised of stringent guidelines. Out of a basic fear of change, and some philosophical misgivings, I hoped for a legislative delay in the enactment date. It was not to be, for on November 1, 1987, the Federal sentencing guidelines became compulsory for all crimes committed after that date.

I recall my attendance at the original training program our office had on the guidelines in 1987. Between the sighs and murmurs we tried to comprehend the big "white book" that listed an infinite flow of guidelines with peculiar codes and curious page numbers. Then, as we attempted to discern the scope of each guideline, we followed the big "brown book," with its abundant commentary, instructions, and examples; it was a formidable day, both for the trainers and the trainees.

Well, my knowledge of the sentencing guidelines and, in particular, the significance of amendments, has grown steadily over the past 5 years. It was enhanced by a 1-month temporary duty at the Sentencing Commission in 1988 and bolstered substantially by a 2-year immersion at the Sentencing Commission where I was the training coordinator from 1989 to 1991. I returned to the U.S. Probation Office in Minnesota and was named sentencing guideline specialist in May 1991.

As guideline specialist, I function as the district's principal resource on sentencing guidelines and sentencing-related issues. As such, I develop materials and train probation officers, law clerks, and case agents on guideline application. Additionally, I am responsible for updating staff on new amendments and developments related to the sentencing process. I regularly consult with colleagues on application issues and also field questions from prosecutors and private counsel on topics related to guideline application and the implications of proposed plea agreements. On occasion, I assist a judge with a particular project related to sentencing guidelines. I also prepare presentence reports.

One of the privileges of my position has been the opportunity to assist the Sentencing Commission and the Federal Judicial Center with training programs. As a trainer for the new officer orientation programs and train-the-trainer programs, I have had an easier time staying abreast of changes generated by the Administrative Office of the U.S. Courts and the Sentencing Commission. Through these programs I have also had the occasion to learn from other districts' practices and bring back new ideas to our office. These training opportunities have kept my training skills active and allowed me to be a more informed and prepared trainer for staff in my district.

Unquestionably, the most visible facet of my position is to assist officers with their guideline application questions and to ensure that they are cognizant of the impact of new guideline amendments and case law. As case law develops regularly and amendments are made to the guidelines annually in November, I need to be on the front line to explain the modifications and their ramifications. To be effective in this capacity, I must re-main informed of changes in the sentencing guidelines and developments with case law and how the changes are integrated with local policy. With the frequency of new amendments over the past 5 years, it has been a challenge to keep abreast of the changes and to sufficiently apprise officers of them.

My responsibilities as guideline specialist are made easier because our district has specialized units. It is simpler to explain procedural and guideline changes to a smaller pool of officers and to ascertain whether they grasp the big picture issues and the narrower application principles. Naturally, a full-time presentence investigator requires less time to become proficient in sentencing guideline and sentencing law application because of the volume of reports prepared.

Another feature of my position is to assure presentence investigators that no matter what the level of competence in guideline application, they will always encounter arguable areas and witness conversations where reasonable minds disagree. While the sentencing guidelines have vastly reduced the large expanse of discretion in sentencing, they have also introduced a new realm of discretion, which ranges from the analysis of offense behavior to the recommendation of maximum end of the imprisonment range to the court.

Perhaps my most significant task as guideline specialist is to stress how fundamentally crucial accuracy is in the presentence investigation process. Over the past 5 years I have learned how vital it is for a presentence investigation to correctly represent the facts of the offense and characteristics of the offender. Whether it be the facts surrounding an offense or the application of specific offense characteristics to the offense itself, accuracy must steer the process. To become more accurate, one must not only comprehend the guidelines, but come to discern the intent and scope of the guidelines. This can be accomplished by carefully reading application notes and commentary in the guideline manual and by calling the Sentencing Commission's "hotline" when questions arise in the office that those who are most adept in guideline application cannot answer.

Although practitioners continue to debate the virtues and inequities of the Federal sentencing guidelines, I believe that as guideline specialist, my primary obligation is to support the U.S. probation officer who, according to Rule 32(c)(2) of the Rules of Criminal Procedure, is to apply the guidelines as he or she "believes to be applicable to the defendant's case. . . ." While I assist the probation officer in his or her role, I will continue to stress the importance of education and accuracy. As we proceed, we should not lose sight of the fact that we have been charged with the responsibility to prepare a presentence report with our best judgment, backed up by facts whenever possible. In the end, the more we strive to be accurate, the more precise the measurement will be of whether the goals of the Sentencing Reform Act have been achieved.

A Mental Health Specialist's Day in the Field

By Terry D. Childers, *Senior United States Probation Officer, Northern District of Illinois*

Donald "WHO IS IT?" The voice boomed from behind the closed door in response to my insistent knocking.

"Federal Probation Officer."

Silence.

Then, "WHADDYA WANT?"

"I'd like to speak to Donald Jones, please."

"WHO?"

"Donald Jones."

"NOBODY NAMED THAT LIVE HERE!"

I couldn't believe that I had the wrong address. Not that I couldn't be mistaken. It's rather difficult to find an address in some sections of Chicago's West Side because few of the buildings are numbered. I don't know whether it's the result of intent or neglect, but most of the addresses have obviously been ripped from the structures. The numbering section in Chicago is such that all even numbered addresses are on the north or south side of the streets, and all the odd numbered addresses are on the west or east side of the streets. So, you could usually find a particular address just using that system. Unfortunately, there are so many empty lots on the West Side (resulting from burned-out buildings) that it is still quite difficult to know if you have found the correct address. There was always some guesswork involved, but I was confident I was in the right building.

"Is this 3524 W. Crenshaw?" I asked the disembodied voice.

"YEAH!"

"Is this the third floor?"

"YEAH!"

"And is this the only apartment on this floor?"

"YEAH!"

"But Donald Jones doesn't live here?"

"RIGHT!"

"Well, do you *know* anybody named Donald Jones?"

"UH UH!"

I seemed to be at a dead end. I stepped away from the door and glanced at my field book. The card for Donald Jones revealed that I was at the correct building and on the right floor. I was about to turn around and leave when I noticed that there was an alias for Donald on the field card: "Snatch." This was probably a name that Donald had used during his days of running afoul of the law. I figured that I should at least give it a chance.

"Is Snatch there?"

"WELL YEAH, SNATCH'S HERE," the voice answered in a tone suggesting I had asked is grass green, water wet, or the Pope Catholic. "WHY DON'T YOU JUST ASK FOR SNATCH, MAN?" he yelled. "YOU CONFUSE ME!"

"Sorry," I apologized, "my mistake. Could you just tell Donald that his PO is here to see him please?"

The voice mumbled something and then bellowed, "HEY, SNATCH, YOUR PO'S HERE, MAN!" I wondered if this guy ever said anything in a moderate voice.

A few moments passed, and then I heard the beginning of the sound that almost always welcomes a person to any closed door on the West Side. It was the litany of locks unlocking, latches unlatching, and chains unchaining. Clink, clink.

Clank, clank. Clack, clack. Then the door opened and Donald's smiling face peered out at me. "Hey, Mr. Childers! How you doin'?"

"I'm fine, Donald. How are you?" I answered. We were still separated by a steel security gate covering the entire door, and as Donald struggled with the huge padlock, I studied his composure. He looked calm, alert. His hands trembled slightly, but I had seen him when he couldn't even hold a coffee cup without spilling the contents all over himself. From a cursory glance, he looked pretty good.

I gazed behind Donald into the apartment. It appeared disheveled and messy, and there seemed to be people sleeping in chairs, on sofas, and on the floor. I had never been to this apartment before. Donald had only moved there last week. Like many others on my caseload, Donald never really *lived* anyplace; he just *stayed* places. He tells me that the people he lives with are his cousins, but if this is true, Donald's aunts and uncles were incredibly procreant people. From the way he talks, one out of every three people on the West Side is Donald's cousin.

He finally removed the padlock from the security gate and pulled it aside to let me in. As I had never been to this apartment before, I asked Donald to give me a brief tour. It didn't take long, as the apartment was quite small. I walked through the various rooms, gingerly stepping over the sleeping forms, and finished the tour in the tiny kitchen where Donald and I both sat down at the green formica table. I noticed only one other person moving around in the apartment, a young man who I presumed to be "the voice." He was scurrying around the apartment, emptying the contents of all the ashtrays into a shopping bag, intent upon his task. I doubted that he was embarrassed about cigarette butts. Subtle fellow.

I asked Donald to bring me all of the medication he was taking. He left and shortly returned with several bottles of medicine. I noted the dates of the prescriptions, as well as the dosages, physician's name, address, and telephone number, and number of pills. I asked Donald if he was taking his medication, and he said he was. Until recently, he was taking Thorazine, an antipsy-

chotic medication. Donald responded well to Thorazine, but developed severe side effects, including tardive dyskenisia, uncontrolled spasms of the facial muscles. He was given Cogentin and other medication to ease the side effects, but they were not effective. I had discussed this with his psychiatrist some weeks before, and the doctor suggested substituting the Thorazine with Haldol, another antipsychotic major tranquilizer that did not seem to cause the same kind of irritating side effects. I was extremely concerned about this, as Donald had a tendency to stop taking his medication if he felt the least bit uncomfortable.

"How's the new medication, Donald?" I asked.

"Oh, oh, it's good Mr. Childers. Yeah, yeah, real good. That other stuff, that was just too strong, you know? It made me all tense and all tired at the same time. And it gave me the twitches. I hate the twitches, man. Yeah. I walk down the street and people look at me twitchin' and they think I'm crazy, you know? So yeah, yeah, this is much better. Yeah. Absolutely."

"And how are the voices, Donald?" I asked. Donald often suffered auditory hallucinations when he stopped taking his medication.

"Oh better, better, much better," he answered. "Like they're not telling me to do things no more, you know? Yeah, really. It's like they're hardly voices anymore. Just a kind of buzzing. No words. Just buzzzzzzzzzzz. And I can watch TV again! Don't think that Dan Rather's talkin' special to me anymore, you know? Can listen to the news and not be in it. Yeah, yeah, like that news."

As I listened to him, I emptied his bottle of Haldol and carefully counted all the tablets. It was immediately apparent that there were twice as many tablets as there should be. I could only surmise that Donald was not taking the medication as he was supposed to. I confronted him with my conclusion, and he replied that it was true. He was not taking the medication at the dose it was prescribed. He was supposed to take one 2 mg tablet in the morning and another 2 mg tablet at bedtime. He was only taking the one before bed. I explained to him my concern about this, recalling how this pattern had previously led to severe decompensation, and told Donald that I expected him to take the medication as prescribed. He responded that taking the tablet in the morning made him groggy and sluggish for the rest of the day, and I replied that he should discuss this with his psychiatrist at their next meeting. But, in the meantime, I expected him to take the medication as ordered. I also told Donald that I was going to go to the clinic where he receives treatment and talk to his social worker about his progress. Donald had a pervasive pattern in which he would stop taking his medication, become depressed and anxious, use cocaine (to self-medicate), become paranoid, decompensate further, and then be hospitalized. It is a pattern shared by many of the offenders on my caseload.

I was always concerned about drug use. Donald assured me that he was clean, and all of the results of his urinalysis tests supported this. However, I was now troubled by his new living situation and the possibility that somebody who lived there might be using drugs. The ashtray emptier had left an impression on me. Donald responded that, to his knowledge, his cousin did not use drugs, and if any other people were to use drugs in the apartment, they would be reminded of Donald's parole status and told to leave. I asked him who all of the other people sleeping in the apartment were, and he said that they were all friends of his cousin. I obtained all the ID information on the cousin and would run a name check with NCIC and the Chicago Police Department within the next week.

I left Donald's numberless building and drove directly to the mental health clinic about a mile away. I spoke to his social worker for some time, sharing my concerns that Donald might relapse to his old pattern of not taking his medication and begin using drugs. She suggested that within the next week we all meet together and explain to Donald our expectations and possible consequences for not following them. We agreed that it was essential that all of us—me, Donald, the social worker, the psychiatrist, and the nurse—attend this meeting. A date was established, and the social worker assured me that she would monitor the situation closely.

Sheila I left the clinic and headed to my next appointment, which was on the South Side of Chicago. It's a curious thing, but it seems that the South Side has a much worse reputation than it deserves. I often hear visitors to Chicago express fear and trepidation about venturing into the South Side, and some of that is justified if you don't know the city very well. But in reality, the West Side is far worse. The closest thing that I have ever seen to Chicago's West Side is the South Bronx in New York. All of the West Side is dangerous, but there are pockets on the South Side that are really very nice. Unfortunately, the person who I was now about to visit did not live in one of those pockets.

I parked in front of Sheila Bond's house, surveyed the block to see if there was any suspicious activity around, and walked up to her porch. I have known Sheila for over 6 years and have violated her parole three times, always for drug use. She had most recently been reparoled 10 months ago and so far had exhibited no signs of abuse.

I knocked on the door and Sheila opened it. She had on a nightgown. Nothing else. No robe, no housedress, just a nightgown. This is not unusual. Sheila *always* has on a nightgown. For the 6 years that I have been making visits to her home, Sheila has never answered the door dressed in anything else but a nightgown. Regardless of the time of day, regardless of the season or weather, Sheila has had on a nightgown. It might be 7 a.m. or 7 p.m., it might be a sweltering 96 degrees or a frigid 10 below zero, and Sheila has on a nightgown. We always go through the same ritual. She answers the door in her nightgown. She murmurs "just a minute," disappears for a few seconds, and reappears in different apparel. Sometimes a robe, sometimes a housedress, sometimes slacks and a shirt, but it is always evident that the nightgown is still on underneath.

There is nothing seductive about any of this. Sheila is hardly a seductive woman. Weighing over 260 pounds, she cares little about her appearance and less about her aroma. Her personal hygiene is dismal.

Sheila rarely frowns. She rarely smiles. Her

face is, if you can imagine, without expression. It is what clinicians would describe as "flat" or "shallow" affect. She is a psychiatric phenomenon and has been in and out of mental institutions since the age of 13. She has been labeled with almost every psychiatric disorder found in DSM-III-R, the psychiatric bible: schizophrenia, schizophreniform, schizo-affective, delusional disorder, manic-depressive, major depression, dysthemia, borderline personality disorder, schizoid personality disorder, and even suggestion of some obsessive-compulsive disorders. She has been in every kind of psychiatric program imaginable and has been maintained on a variety of psychotropic medications. She's a real mess.

Her mother hates her. I do not say this lightly. I am fully aware of the impact of words, and I realize that "hate" is subjective and laden with philosophical and even theological overtones. It should probably not even be in my vocabulary, either as a clinician or as a law enforcement official. But it is the only word that conveys the intensity of the relationship of this mother and daughter. Sheila's mother has done things to her that have been so destructive, so malicious, and so purposefully intentful, as to be almost beyond comprehension. This woman makes Sybil's mother look like Saint Anne. Countless efforts have been made over the years by psychiatrists, social workers, and others to involve this woman in treatment, but she has always resisted it. Worse, she sabotages any gains that Sheila makes in treatment. Sheila's mother hates her, but she has never been able to leave her.

As I'm musing about this hateful situation, Sheila returns in more appropriate attire, shorts and a blouse, the nightgown stuffed haphazardly into the shorts. I follow her into the house, a single family home that Sheila shares with her mother and, occasionally, other relatives. Entering this house is like walking into a den of hate. The air is heavy with it, a presence that makes you feel tired and old, that makes you want to flee to the air and light outside. In all the years that I have known Sheila, in all the times I have been in this house, I have never witnessed a kind word, seen a gentle touch, or heard genial laughter.

I went through the same routine with Sheila as I had with Donald. I counted the number of tablets of all of her medications, determined that she was probably taking them as she was supposed to, and told her that I was in weekly contact with her counselor and was aware that so far she had been making all of her therapy appointments. Sheila responded to any of my statements with a series of murmurs or grunts, which was the norm for her. I told her to be in my office for an appointment 2 weeks from today, and she walked me to the door. Just before I entered my car I glanced back at her house and Sheila was standing motionless on her porch, staring at a spot somewhere just above my head, still neither smiling nor frowning, one of the saddest creatures I have ever known.

Jim I left Sheila's neighborhood behind and drove north on Lake Shore Drive to a far more fashionable neighborhood on the North Side. I was there to meet with a sex offender who was procrastinating about submitting to a psychological evaluation. In addition to supervising offenders who have very serious psychiatric problems, I am also responsible for the supervision of most of the sex offenders in my district. They almost always live in better areas than my psychiatric cases; they almost always have more going for them in terms of finances and employment; and they almost always cause more human pain than any other kind of offender with whom I have ever dealt. Jim Anderson, at whose apartment I had just arrived, has caused more pain than most.

I buzzed his apartment and his voice responded over the intercom system, "Yes, who is it?" The voice was controlled, modulated, almost a whisper.

"Terry Childers."

"You're 10 minutes late, Mr. Childers. I just called your office to see if you had forgotten about me. You *know* this is my lunch hour, and you *promised* me you'd be on time. Now it's almost time for me to go back. Are you trying to get me in trouble?"

"Look, Jim," I answered, "I really don't want to stand here in the hallway having a discussion with the intercom, so just buzz me in, OK?" The door buzzed, and I let myself into the mirror-covered corridor leading to the elevators. Jim lived on the fifth floor in a 20-story building, and I entered the bank of elevators that serviced the first 10 floors. I exited the elevator, walked to his apartment, #505, and knocked on the door.

"Who is it?"

"Give me a break, Jim. It's Childers. Would you just open the door, please?"

The door cracked open and Jim's face, a dark, hard, but rather handsome face, peered out. The chain was still on the door.

"Are you by yourself?"

"Yes, Jim, I'm by myself. Were you expecting me not to be?"

"You can just never be too careful, that's all," he uttered, releasing the chain and opening the door.

I entered an apartment that was so neat, it was eerie. It wasn't that everything was clean and fresh and sparkling, though it all was. It was more like everything had its own exact place. I moved a magazine that was on the kitchen table to set down my briefcase. Jim lifted up my briefcase, placed it on one of the kitchen chairs, and put the magazine back to its original location—*exactly*.

It was time to get down to business. "Jim, the last time we talked, I gave you the name of the psychologist to call for the evaluation. Have you talked to him yet?

"Yes, I talked to him, and I think there's a problem."

"And what might that be?" I queried.

"Well, he has an office at The University of Chicago, and he wants me to meet him there."

"And what's the problem with that?"

"It's just too far!" he cried.

"Jim, it's 15 minutes away from your front door! You live practically next to Lake Shore Drive, and that takes you straight there."

"But that's not the only problem," he whined. "It's also in a dangerous neighborhood. If I go down there I might get hurt. I just can't do it."

"Hyde Park (where The University of Chicago is located) is one of the safest areas on the South Side. I simply don't buy your argument about it

not being safe. The bottom line is you must get this evaluation in order to comply with the conditions of your parole, and I expect you to do it."

"There's also another problem," he said.

Why was I not surprised? "OK, what other problem?"

"This psychologist expects me to talk to him about all that stuff that happened years ago, when I got in trouble. And he wants to talk to me about my sex life and stuff, and I see no need to do that."

Feeling that we had finally arrived at the real issue, I answered as carefully as I could. "Jim, you were convicted of a sexual offense against a child. The purpose of this evaluation is to see if there has been a change in your basic sexual orientation and patterns of arousal. It is what we expect anybody convicted of a similar offense to have."

"I was not convicted of a sexual offense," he answered.

"What?" I asked, incredulous.

"I was convicted of kidnapping."

"Well, that might be true, but the kidnapping involved you taking a 6-year-old child against his will, holding him captive for over 12 hours, and repeatedly sexually attacking him. I'd say that was a sexual offense."

"I don't want to talk about that! It makes me painful! It makes me painful! You have no right to try and make me talk about things that make me painful!"

"Are you telling me that you refuse to cooperate with this evaluation?" I demanded.

"No," he responded. "I am willing and even welcome the chance to talk to somebody who is sympathetic to me and will help me with some of my problems, but I see no need for this kind of testing."

"Well, this is the kind of testing that we are going to suggest that you have, Jim."

"I've already talked to my attorney, and he told me not to do anything without talking to him first."

"You may certainly talk to your attorney if you wish, but neither you nor your attorney are going to be the ones who determine what kind of testing or counseling you receive. I know that the psychologist is in his office today. I expect you to call him and make an appointment today and to call me tomorrow and let me know when that appointment is. Understand?"

"This is harassment," he spat.

"I don't think so," I replied. "I'll be in my office tomorrow by 8:30. I expect to hear from you by 9:00."

"I have to talk to my attorney first."

"9:00," I repeated, and let myself out of the apartment.

I felt a certain sense of relief when I walked out of the apartment building onto the street. Things were definitely getting a little tense in Jim's apartment. I again reminded myself to discuss with my supervisor the idea of joining up with another U.S. probation officer when visiting the more dangerous and volatile offenders on my caseload like Jim Anderson.

I proceeded to the Special Investigations Unit of the Chicago Police Department located in Cook County Juvenile Court. This is the specialized unit that investigates child sexual abuse cases. I had established an excellent relationship with the unit, as I had with other Federal and local law enforcement agencies that focus on this issue. I spoke to the sergeant for some time, who acknowledged that all of the offenders that we shared in common were not suspects in any cases at this time. After I left there, I made several other stops, some to offenders' homes, some to mental health clinics, and then prepared for my last visit of the day. It would be very different from most of the visits I make in the field. It would be with a victim.

John I have on my caseload an offender named John Smith. John had been convicted of a child pornography offense and had recently been released to parole supervision following a 2-year period of incarceration. There was a special condition for mental health aftercare, and I had referred him to a clinic specializing in the evaluation and treatment of sex offenders.

John was convicted for receiving child pornography through the mail. However, when the agents searched his apartment, they found a number of homemade videotapes depicting John having sex with what appeared to be a young teenage girl. As it turned out, the girl was his stepdaughter, Brigid. He was never charged, federally or locally, for this behavior. He acknowledged that the girl on the tapes was his stepdaughter, but at the time the tapes were discovered by the agents, the girl was no longer a minor.

Of course, one of the first things I asked John when he was released from prison was if he had any contact with Brigid anymore. Although he continues to live with the girl's mother, he assured me that he never has any contact of any kind with Brigid and that he does not plan to. He was unsure of where she might live, but thought that it might be in Blue Island, a southern suburb of Chicago.

The problem now was that John was telling the psychologist doing his evaluation that Brigid had been an active and willing participant in their sexual encounters. He states that she was in no way coerced or manipulated and, as a matter of fact, initiated the sexual relationship herself. According to the psychologist, it was crucial to know the degree to which the girl's participation was voluntary or coerced. John had given us both written permission to speak to Brigid. The trouble was finding her. There was no longer any communication between the girl and her mother.

A check through the phone book for Blue Island had been unsuccessful, as had been directory information. There was no one by the name of Brigid Johnson listed. So I decided to check with the Blue Island Police Department to see if they might have any information on this girl. As it turned out there was no criminal history for a Brigid Johnson, but there had been some traffic violations issued to a person by that name. The identification information revealed Brigid to be a 21-year-old white female, which fit the description of the Brigid I was looking for. I proceeded to the address on the ID card and walked up to the modest apartment building. There were no names on the mailboxes or doorbells. I rang the bell for the first-floor apartment. A young blonde woman, dressed in a Grateful Dead T-shirt and blue sweatpants, opened the door.

"Brigid?" I asked.

"Yes?"

I showed her my badge and ID. "Federal probation officer. May I speak to you a moment, please?"

"What's this about?" she asked. I could see the worry on her face.

"John Smith," I answered.

The worried expression on her face changed to something else. Anger? Fear? I couldn't be sure. She looked at me hard for several seconds and then, without a word, opened the door and let me in. She gestured for me to sit down on the sofa in the tiny living room, and she took a chair opposite me.

"I knew he was out," she said.

I nodded.

"I haven't seen him in years. Or my mother either. But I still hear stuff about them, you know?" She was silent for a while, staring intently at the carpet. "He doesn't know where I live, does he? I don't want him to know where I live. Or her either."

"He told me that he heard you lived here in Blue Island. He said he didn't know the exact address. I won't tell him where you live, I can promise you that." I explained to her how I obtained her address and also explained to her the purpose of my visit. I took my time doing so, making sure that she understood that she was in no way bound to do any of this if she didn't want to.

"So the bottom line," I concluded, "is that the psychologist would like to talk to you about what happened between you and John—about the stuff that is on the videotape. It could be done by telephone. You wouldn't even have to leave the house. Or if you don't want to talk to the psychologist about it, you could talk to me, and I would relay the information to her. But it's entirely up to you."

She stood up and went to the window. She crossed her arms across her chest and hugged her shoulders. She was completely silent. Finally, she turned around to face me.

"No," she said. "I can't do it. I won't do it. It happened a long time ago and it's taken me a long time to get my life back together. Things are finally going OK for me. I'm engaged now. I'm supposed to get married next year. My fiancé doesn't know anything about this. Can you imagine what might happen if he found out? If anybody found out? Nobody in my life now knows anything about this, and that's the way I want it to stay. It's my own dirty little secret, one that I have to live with every day of my life, one that I still cry about, but only when I'm alone. The memories are not dead yet, but they're buried in a place and nobody but me knows about them. No. I won't do it. I won't talk about it. Not to the psychologist. Not to you. Not to anybody. Not ever."

She had begun to cry, her body quaking with silent sobs. She bent down toward me, her hands making a pleading gesture.

"I was just a little girl!" she moaned. "Just a little girl."

I was beginning to feel like an ogre. I was afraid that I had opened up old wounds that had never really begun to heal. "Look," I said, "I'm sorry that I've upset you, which I obviously have, but I can't help but think from your reaction that you might still have a lot of unresolved issues about all of this. There are counselors that specialize in this kind of thing, you know, victims of child sexual abuse. I would be more than happy to give you some of their names and—"

"NO!" she shouted. "It's over. It's dead. It's buried. I just want to make it go away and never come back. No counselors. No help. Nothing. I just want it to go away."

She was silent for a while, again staring out the window, and then addressed me in what sounded like a defeated, listless voice. "I'm sorry. I can't help you. I hope you understand."

"It's OK. I do understand." I took one of my business cards out of my badge case and handed it to her. "Here, this is one of my cards. If you should change your mind, or if there's anything I can help you with, just call me. And if John ever contacts you or begins to bother or harass you in anyway, call me and we'll take care of it."

"Thank you," she said, taking the card without looking at it.

I let myself out the door and was almost to my car, when I heard her call out behind me.

"Hey, Mister?"

I turned around. She was leaning out of the open door.

"Don't let him hurt anyone else, OK? Don't let him hurt anyone else."

Before I could answer, she closed the door.

My field day was over. As I drove home, I pondered Brigid's request. "Don't let him hurt any-one else." How many similar requests I have heard in the past 16 years. Don't let him rob another bank, don't let him sell another drug, don't let him steal another check, and on and on. I sometimes wonder, as all probation officers do, if anything I do really ever makes a difference. Do I ever do anything that prevents a man from being murdered, a child from being abused, a woman from being raped? I don't know. I can probably *never* know. I can only hope.

WHAT WORKS?

Russ Immarigeon

As penal populations and community corrections cases grew during the 1980s and 1990s, researchers and policy makers increasingly asked, "What works?" The answer is that some correctional interventions do work, if applied wisely. Russ Immarigeon writes on criminal justice and child welfare issues. He coedits the SUNY Press series Women, Crime and Criminology.

The 1990s are restless, often despairing times in criminal justice. Sensational newspaper and television stories can topple promising innovations. Misleading headlines can also give impetus to political movements that hamper meaningful criminal justice operations. The specter of unsupervised parolees committing horrendous crimes or allegations that prison inmates are lounging in luxury at taxpayers' expense are never helpful to rational criminal justice policy-making.

Political leaders routinely fight one another to see who is the toughest on crime. Little media attention is given to how criminal justice agencies actually operate or what they need to accomplish their mission. Instead, piecemeal, ill-considered "remedies" are imposed on criminal justice systems; systems then adapt to these mandates.

Academic and popular commentary on the state of criminal justice in America is eerily congruent. Sociologist Herbert Gans argues that the threat of

Reprinted from Russ Immarigeon, "What Works?" an insert from the U.S. Department of Justice in the December 1995 issue of *Corrections Today* magazine.

crime in our communities has created, among the lower and working classes as well as the middle class, a public mood that supports increasingly punitive criminal sanctions that promise little more than criminal displacement or isolation.

David C. Anderson, former editorial page writer for the *New York Times* and the *Wall Street Journal,* is decidedly more despondent about the public mood. Anderson argues that expressive justice ("laws, policies, and practices that are designed more to vent communal outrage than to reduce crime") has grasped control of criminal justice in the United States. Another journalist, Wendy Kaminer, agrees that, as far as crime policy and practice are concerned, substance seems irrelevant.

Searching for What Works

"There ain't no success stories in prison," says an inmate in Jerome Washington's *Iron House: Stories from the Yard.* That also can be the case for most of the men and women sentenced to incarceration or community corrections in the United States. Yet, how many success stories emerge from these confined or otherwise often punitive experiences? Almost 20 years ago, a research group hired by the New York State legislature claimed that Washington's maxim holds as true for intervention programs as for inmates. Robert Martinson, one member of the research team, boldly stated that "Nothing works!"

Martinson's salvo gave the media a mask to hide behind when it failed to examine firsthand the workings of correctional rehabilitation programs, and it abetted the political retrenchment of public funds from rehabilitation programs behind as well as beyond prison walls. It also propelled the correctional research community into action. Several researchers, with Stuart Adams and Ted Palmer leading the counterattack, issued important challenges to Martinson's imprecise assertion. Within several years, Martinson himself would retreat from his original statement. Later, Francis Cullen and Karen Gilbert would argue that rehabilitation is valuable because it is the only justification for humane state intervention, its purpose is supported regularly by public opinion polls and it counters harsher approaches to criminal sanctioning.

But the damage was done. Thereafter, little attention was given to the question, "What works?" Throughout the 1980s and early 1990s, however, as penal populations and community corrections caseloads grew, the "What works?" question attracted increasing attention from researchers and policymakers alike. An impressive literature has been published by Canadians such as Don Andrews, James Bonta and Paul Gendreau and by Americans such as Alan Harland, Phil Harris and Peter Jones. New Zealander Kaye McLaren has examined extensively the characteristics of programs that reduce reoffending. [In 1994], National Development and Research Institutes (NDRI), a New York City–based research group, began a three-year project to complete a comprehensive review of all evaluations conducted since 1968 assessing the effectiveness of jail, prison and community corrections interventions. In short, NDRI will review what has happened since Martinson's exaggerated assault on correctional programming.

What We Know

The "What works?" literature is quite extensive and is growing at a rapid pace. Generally, more meta-analysis of the existing research literature is occurring than original research on the impact of particular program or penalty interventions. Recent literature reviews, however, are extremely relevant for program development, and

practitioners and policymakers are, at best, neglectful if they do not consider the findings of these reviews. Often, they reveal that much of current correctional policy is simply headed in the wrong—and ultimately costly—direction.

Kaye McLaren's and Paul Gendreau's research indicates some of what is known about what works in correctional interventions. McLaren, a policy and research analyst with the New Zealand Department of Justice, reports that "there is a significant body of evidence for the existence of a small but significant group of correctional interventions which have been effective in reducing re-offending." Successful interventions, she says, "share certain common components, and together these components form a set of principles of effectiveness which can be applied to many types of intervention." These principles, she adds, are useful in community and residential settings.

McLaren identifies "principles of effectiveness" that include the following factors:

• a social learning approach that assumes attitudes and behavior can change if noncriminal attitudes and behaviors are introduced and reinforced;

• clear, consistent rules and sanctions to make legal sanctions certain and understandable;

• illustration of and support for noncriminal attitudes and behaviors;

• practical problem-solving skills;

• positive links between community and program resources;

• relationships between staff and offenders that are open, emphatic, warm, trusting and encouraging of noncriminal attitudes and behaviors;

• advocacy for offenders and brokerage with community resources;

• use of ex-offenders as positive role models;

• offenders' involvement with the design of specific interventions;

• staff focus on strengthening pro-social and noncriminal behavior rather than stopping antisocial and criminal behavior;

• offender peer groups directed toward reinforcing antisocial and noncriminal behavior;

• sound theoretical knowledge and adequate resources to apply appropriate principles of effectiveness;

• multiple methods of intervention rather than reliance on narrowly based interventions;

• emphasis on relapse prevention and self-efficacy; and

• matching individual offenders with specific interventions.

McLaren notes that none of these principles are set in stone, yet they do provide direction for program design that is based on experience and has passed some evaluative muster. Understanding of what works is evolving and, in fact, the ability of a program to reevaluate and revise its forms of intervention also is critical for program success.

Paul Gendreau, a professor of psychology at the University of New Brunswick, also has reviewed the literature and, like McLaren, he adds that it is as important to identify what does not work as it is to clarify what does work, at least in certain circumstances.

Gendreau agrees with McLaren about the positive influence of directing intensive services to high-risk offenders, the matching of offenders and interventions, the importance of disrupting criminal networks and providing relapse prevention, and the value of advocacy and brokerage services. However, Gendreau also identifies "principles of ineffective intervention," which include traditional psychodynamic therapies, non-directive relationship-oriented therapies, radical non-intervention and traditional medical model approaches, the use of intensive services with low-risk offenders, and clinical approaches that encourage externalizing blame to parents and others, venting anger or ignoring the impact of their crimes on the victims.

Significantly, Gendreau finds that many of the so-called "punishing smarter" strategies do not work. Such interventions include boot camps, electronic monitoring, longer periods of incarceration, urinalysis, humiliation and shock incarceration. Many of these options are politically popular and more likely to receive scarce state or federal funding, but Gendreau's findings, which are supported by other research, colorfully illustrate the frustration of many observers that programs receive political support more for the appearance than the reality of working.

"When it comes to putting offenders in programs," says McLaren, "it's a case of one size doesn't fit all." McLaren recommends three approaches to offender placement—"put offenders in programs that address problems they actually have, put offenders with more severe problems into more intensive programs, and choose programs that fit into what's known about the most effective way to impact a given problem."

Making Things Work

Certainly, measuring recidivism is important. Offenders who do not recidivate commit no further crimes, or at least no detected crimes. However, measurements of recidivism too frequently assume that the interventions they assess were properly designed, skillfully implemented or actually determined behavioral change. Design, implementation and causal factors suggest that it is important to look beyond recidivism to qualitative aspects of the processes that produce behavioral change. Indeed, it is important to look beyond criminal justice interventions to see whether any other life-course events were responsible for the changed behavior.

The factors for what makes programs work outlined by McLaren, Gendreau and others can be found in interventions associated with correctional options programs. In the following pages: (1) a New York community service program illustrates the effectiveness of limiting correctional intervention to clear and concise requirements that staff and offenders can work together to achieve; (2) a review of programming for female offenders suggests the utility of matching individual offender needs with specific program interventions; and (3) a review of two states' approaches to restorative justice demonstrates that victim, offender and community involvement in criminal justice decision-making helps create a strong, supportive environment for the use and growth of correctional options.

Community Service

Community service sentences are options that impose unpaid hours of labor on offenders who work for government or private, not-for-profit community or neighborhood groups. In the United States, community service sentences were first used in 1968 for offenders convicted of driving violations. More than 25 years later, no statistics are available in this country that give an accurate overview of the extent and nature of use of these penalties. Moreover, the use of community service usually is enmeshed in poorly focused or overly optimistic statements of purpose. Little evaluation has been done to see what impact community service sentences have on the offenders serving them, the communities obtaining free penal labor or the criminal justice systems that increasingly impose them.

Community service sentences initially were viewed with caution as well as with enthusiasm. Critics were as likely to support the option as they were to raise questions about its application. Some critics claimed that community service was a form of penal servitude; others worried, with good reason as it turns out, that community service sentences were widening the net of social control. More recently, critics have raised questions about the utility of community service as a method of achieving offender accountability, a concept that is rarely defined with much cogency. Also, critics say that the term "community service" is a misnomer that belittles the voluntary community service performed by millions of Americans not involved with the criminal justice system. In other words, community service should be restricted to the worthy, not the unworthy, among us. Community service has nonetheless become a routine judicial sentencing option in most jurisdictions.

The Center for Alternative Sentencing and Employment Services (CASES) in New York City runs one of the country's best-known community service programs, the Community Service Sentencing Project (CSSP). CASES was founded in 1989 when community service and court employment programs operated and evaluated by the Vera Institute of Justice merged to form the new agency. CASES handles lower-end felons who complete 70 hours of community service over two-week periods at work sites throughout the City. Most of these sentences were imposed in lieu of 30 to 90 days of jail time.

The CSSP, cited in *USA Today* as "a model of the way it ought to be run," is distinguished by its concise use of community sentence work and the clarity of its operations. Unlike most community service penalties or programs, CSSP manages and supervises the same 70-hour work period for all clients in the program. Throughout the program's history, supervisors have regularly informed judges about the program's selection criteria, supervision process and enforcement mechanisms. The program takes a "just deserts" approach, matching a specific penalty to a particular goal, reducing the incarceration of petty, persistent property offenders.

"In order to maintain the integrity of the sanction," says Joseph Singleton, an associate director at CASES, "CSSP's intake criteria is selective and the sentence is enforced through compliance activities, a warrant execution capacity and re-sentencing procedures." What makes this program work is a combination of formal and informal operating procedures.

The CSSP places court representatives in courtrooms in four boroughs of New York City. Each day, these representatives size up the daily court docket, looking for eligible offenders. After offenders are identified, they are interviewed briefly. Then, the court representative appears at sentencing to let the court know the program is willing to accept offenders sentenced to 70 hours of community service. The program does not accept clients with other formal conditions of probation.

"Compliance monitors start each day at the same time our enforcement officers start," Singleton says. "They call all participants in the program at seven o'clock in the morning, wake them up, remind them of their obligations and make sure there are no problems hindering their arriving at their work site."

"It doesn't take too much for many of them to not go in," Singleton observes, mindful of the limited work habits and histories of program participants. The program provides offenders with bus or subway tokens to travel to and from the work site each day, and the program has an 800 number for participants to call if problems arise or they cannot appear. If offenders have substance abuse, housing, child care or other problems that put them at risk of not showing up, support service coordinators ask them what they need and bring them to where they can get help.

Correctional Options for Female Offenders

Several years ago, Meda Chesney-Lind and the author reviewed available statistics, program descriptions and research evaluations for a report, "Women's Prisons: Overcrowded and Overused," published by the National Council on Crime and Delinquency. What we found then holds regrettably true [in 1995]: The population in women's prisons is rising at a rate greater than increases in the male population, most of the new women entering prisons are nonviolent property and drug crime offenders, and relatively few programs are available in the community to effectively divert women from incarceration. We also found, with a few exceptions, that women offenders receive little attention from probation and parole agencies, corrections departments, and legislative or judicial review committees when it comes to developing community-based sanctioning programs or prison overcrowding remedies.

A major step in developing programs that work for female offenders is recognizing the need for such programming. One stumbling block is the lack of empirical evaluations of the few programs that are working with female offenders and their families. The author spoke to a half dozen leading practitioners and researchers, and all expressed concern about the paucity of evaluation in the field of female offender programming.

A second important step is understanding why it is useful to establish female-specific programming. Nearly all practitioners who work with female offenders say that one fault of many of these programs is that they are based on models that are used with men. Often this is done because administrators, perhaps leery of an equal protection lawsuit, mistake difference for discrimination, equity with equality. A key lesson, program oper-

ators assert, is that women are different from men and require different forms of programming that address their needs and situations. Programs must know who they are working with and design interventions that directly address their individual situations.

Barbara Bloom, a California-based criminal justice consultant and author of *Why Punish the Children?*, reports that programs for female offenders often fail because they do not conduct assessment studies to identify the needs of these women and the services that are available to them. Programs that address perceived rather than real needs may be gender-specific, she says, but they are not individually specific; therefore, they run the risk of being duplicative, irrelevant or otherwise unnecessary.

Lessons learned from specific programs often can be helpful to others. Bloom notes, for instance, that if programs have insufficient autonomy over such matters as which offenders can be selected for their treatment intervention and which behaviors will be defined as rule violations, then these programs likely will lose sight of their original goals and objectives. Parenting and other programs for women located in women's prisons run the risk, she says, of being identified by female offenders as part of prison management, thereby erecting a significant barrier to the desired delivery of services.

Creating the opportunity structure for interventions that work with and for female offenders requires a supportive policy environment and carefully designed programs. [In 1993], Sherry Haller, executive director of a Hartford, Conn., advocacy and public policy group, pulled together six practitioners and policy analysts to identify "the critical experiences of the female offender population (particularly as victims of sexual abuse and domestic violence), and the relationship between these experiences [and] their criminal behaviors, addictions, and abilities to serve as the primary caregivers to their children." In an unpublished report, Haller and her colleagues identify not only a continuum of sanctions for female offenders, but also an array of supportive roles that can be played by policymakers, criminal justice administrators, municipal leaders, citizens and social service providers.

Finally, and perhaps most important, programs designed for female offenders must confront a conundrum rarely faced squarely: Women often are physically and mentally healthier and safer inside prison than they are in the community. But women are not imprisoned for protection; their incarceration is meted out as punishment. And punishment, studies by Gendreau and others seem to show, is what works least, especially for women. So, the challenge for program designers is to create community-based programs that address the myriad needs of female offenders in a safe and nurturing environment.

Restorative Justice

Restorative justice is rapidly paving paths into the mainstream of not only sanctioning theory, but sanctioning practice, as well. Restorative justice practices, such as victim-offender reconciliation, the use of community boards and restitution programming, originate in biblical traditions. In recent years, however, religion-based organizations such as the Mennonite Central Committee Office of Criminal Justice and the Justice Fellowship have written extensively about the foundations of restorative justice, and they have managed programs based on restorative justice principles, the most notable of which are victim-offender reconciliation programs.

A central dynamic of restorative justice is that most punishment-oriented practices—the widespread use of imprisonment, for example—have failed because they do not meaningfully include victims and offenders in making decisions about criminal sentences. In essence, restorative justice builds on several principles of effective intervention, including self-management and control, problem-solving and attitude changes.

"Restorative justice," notes Kay Pranis, the Minnesota Department of Corrections' restorative justice planner, "is not a program or a specific set of programs. It is a way of thinking about how to approach the problem of responding to crime, a set of values which guides decisions on policy, programs, and practice. Restorative jus-

tice is based on a re-definition of crime as injury to the victim and community rather than affront to the power of the state. The primary purpose of the criminal justice system in the restorative justice model is to repair the harm of the crime to the degree possible."

Mark Umbreit, among others, has conducted important research on restorative justice interventions. Specifically, in juvenile offender cases, Umbreit found that victim-offender mediation was experienced as a demanding sanction, satisfying to victim and offender alike. Use of this sanction seemed to reduce victims' fears and, at least slightly, reduce offender recidivism within one year of the victim-offender meeting.

Communities are now organizing around restorative justice in two states. In Minnesota, the Department of Corrections has a restorative justice planner who is working with communities, victims groups and corrections managers to inform them about the nature and implementation of restorative justice. In Vermont, with support from a Correctional Options grant, the Department of Corrections is implementing statewide use of reparative sanctions.

In 1990, the Minnesota Citizens Council on Crime and Justice and several religious groups organized a conference to explore the restorative justice concept. Shortly thereafter, the council conducted a public opinion survey that found sizeable support for reparative sanctions. A public education campaign reached out to inform key community leaders. Independently, the Minnesota Department of Corrections also was examining restorative justice. In 1991, the Department of Corrections and the Citizens Council joined together in their efforts. Late in 1992, a statewide conference drew the attention of many middle-level correctional managers. Feedback from this conference encouraged further state pursuit of restorative justice options.

The Vermont Department of Corrections restructured its mission to increase community participation in the development and operation of sentencing options. A major tenet of this restructuring is that the role of state government is to serve and support local communities, and local communities, in turn, are to serve and support individuals and families. Restorative justice, through the work of community reparative boards, is intended to act as the linchpin of this significant reform.

Reparative probation brings offenders face to face with community members at a meeting that is designed to establish a negotiated agreement detailing a plan for offenders to repay victims and the community. A public opinion survey laid a firm foundation for the program: 75 percent of those surveyed wanted an overhauling of the criminal justice system; 92 percent wanted property offenders to repay their victims; strong support was evident for giving community work assignments instead of jail time for drunk drivers, drug users, shoplifters and others; strong support also existed for using community reparation boards to monitor such sentences; and support was even evident for using community sanctions with repeat offenders.

"Vermonters want to be actively involved," says Project Director Michael J. Dooley. "They want punishment to focus on opportunities and means for offenders to repair injuries and damages they caused."

Reparative probation is one method Vermont has designed to sanction low-risk offenders who commit crimes of lesser severity. Whereas high-risk, violent offenders are channeled into a risk-management track that incorporates intensive interventions, reparative probation is designed to "repair the damage done to victims." Once adjudicated guilty, offenders in this program are given a probation sentence that is suspended using an administrative probation order that imposes the condition of completing the Reparative Probation program. Offenders appear before community reparation boards, which are composed of five local citizens, Together, the board and the offender devise a plan to restore and make whole the victims of crime, make amends to the community, learn about the impact of crime on victims and communities, and learn ways of avoiding new offenses. Aspects of these plans can include community service work, restitution, victim-offender mediation, decision-making programs, skills development and others. All conditions must be completed within 90 days, when the board can discharge successfully completed cases.

Despite seemingly utopian brush strokes, restorative justice options are susceptible to both monitoring and evaluation. The Minnesota effort, for example, has already identified "benchmarks" for the effective use of restorative justice intervention. These benchmarks include the degree of available victim services, the opportunities for victim and offender participation, the encouragement of offenders to take personal responsibility for their actions, the extent of community involvement in decision-making and the development of connections between citizens and criminal justice professionals. Some care must be given to the forms of monitoring and the methods of evaluation, but restorative justice interventions can nonetheless be measured and reviewed in an accountable fashion.

Conclusion

Correctional options programs offer the promise of a broad range of alternatives for criminal justice systems historically lacking choices among the penalties they mete out to criminal offenders. However, concentration on politically popular options is short-sighted unless greater attention is given to a broader conceptualization of not just the range of available alternatives, but also the use of specific forms of intervention with individual offenders. No intervention, however well designed and implemented, is appropriate for everyone. Moreover, as research shows, it is frequently the case that less restrictive interventions are more effective than sanctions that sound tougher and more punitive.

Two points require emphasis. First, no effort to establish effective programs or sanctions can thrive without meaningful assessment and evaluation research. Research is necessary not only to determine specific outcome measures, but also to design program services and determine who is eligible for particular programs. The Vera Institute of Justice regularly compiled and reviewed arrest history and other data on jail-bound offenders in New York City before it opened the doors to its community-service program. Research continued as the program was implemented, and program administrators were given up-to-date information on such matters as the average number of prior offenses held by offenders before they are given jail time. This information determines the program's selection criteria.

Finally, a policy development process is essential if a jurisdiction hopes to maximize its use of correctional options by creating a supportive environment for these programs. In Vermont, Gov. Howard Dean told a gathering of corrections professionals of his concern that one bad experience with an offender in a community-based program could destroy the state's entire reparative justice initiative.

The Center for Effective Public Policy has pioneered an intermediate sanctions process that includes creating a group of high-level policymakers; establishing educational, data-gathering and decision-making processes to guide the group's deliberations; emphasizing the use of local resources to meet specific policy objectives; and implementing determined policies and sanctions. Crucial to this process, the center affirms, is the commitment of policymakers to become and remain a part of the decision-making and implementation, and the availability of the staff, time and fiscal resources to properly support the actions and agenda of the policy group. Whether states follow these guidelines or they inform all concerned constituencies before implementing programs and policies, as Vermont has done, there are clear-cut ways to ensure that correctional options not only can work but that they also can be allowed to improve over time.

REFERENCES

Anderson, David C. 1995. *Crime and the politics of hysteria: How the Willie Horton story changed American justice.* New York: Times Books.

Cullen, Francis and Karen Gilbert. 1982. *Reaffirming rehabilitation.* Cincinnati: Anderson Publishing Co.

Gans, Herbert. 1995. *The war against the poor: The underclass and antipoverty policy.* New York: BasicBooks.

Kaminer, Wendy. 1995. *It's all the rage: Crime and culture.* Reading, Mass.: Addison-Wesley.

McKnight, John. 1995. *The careless society: Community and its counterfeits.* New York: BasicBooks.

Washington, Jerome. 1994. *Iron house: Stories from the yard.* Fort Bragg, Calif.: QED Press.

DISCUSSION QUESTIONS

1. Joan Petersilia and Elizabeth Deschenes, reporting on Skolnick's study, suggest that one reason imprisonment may be losing its punitive sting is that some offenders no longer see prison as stigmatizing. Moreover, the prison experience is less often isolating, since inmates often have family and friends in the same institution. Do you agree that factors like these can make imprisonment less punitive? Why or why not? What could be done to make imprisonment more punitive? Would your suggestions meet constitutional prohibitions against cruel and unusual punishment?

2. Discuss the merits of Petersilia and Deschenes's suggestion that community-based penalties can be as punitive as imprisonment. How difficult would their suggestion be to carry out?

3. Were the types of people and problems that probation officers encounter ones that you expected or did some surprise you? In Terry Childers's account, his meetings with four clients are described in wonderful detail. Discuss which of the techniques Childers used with Jones, Bonds, Anderson, and Smith you particularly liked or disliked.

4. How aware do you think the public is of research that shows some correctional programs "work"? How much public support would there be for community-based programs that may change offenders for the better, but are not especially punitive?

5. Discuss the merits of female-specific correctional programs.

WEBSITES

www.ncjrs.org/corrdocs.htm

This is the page within the National Criminal Justice Reference Service to find documents related to corrections. All of the articles can be read online or downloaded for later viewing or printing. The site is frequently updated with new research and statistics concerning state and federal prisons and all types of corrections programs.

www.rand.org

The RAND Corporation is actively involved in criminal justice research and has produced particularly interesting publications in the area of intermediate sanctions.

www.csg.org/appa

The American Probation and Parole Association provides information about the organization and corrections issues in general.

CHAPTER 11: PRISON LIFE

The conditions and dynamics of prison life have been the subject of film and television, books and journalism, and scientific studies. Motivation for the public's interest in prison life ranges from morbid curiosity to human compassion. The topic is important to researchers and corrections officials because the physical, psychological, and social situations of prisoners will affect such practical concerns as staff and inmate safety, facility security, and the likelihood of achieving such correctional goals as rehabilitation, retribution, incapacitation, and deterrence. Because of widespread interest in this topic there are abundant possible readings for this chapter. The two that follow were selected because they present contrasting views—that of an inmate and that of a student intern.

In the first reading, Pennsylvania prisoner Victor Hassine describes his transition to the role of convict. This process of "prisonization" requires new inmates to learn the norms and values of their new environment. The transition to "convict" might not be especially difficult or traumatic if the new inmate's life outside prison was not so different from the prison experience. In some cases, like Hassine's, the prison presents such an alien setting that the new inmate has no idea what others expect of him or what he can expect of others. As you read Hassine's impressions of his first weeks at the prison, think about how prison officials might arrange a more helpful classification process. In light of Hassine's realization that sleeping too much or having too much "stuff" in your cell is dangerous, think about other everyday behaviors on the outside that would have to be modified upon entering prison.

Amanda Larsen's recollection of her internship at an Illinois prison provides an interesting contrast to Hassine's experience. Of course, we cannot expect an intern or employee to have the same view of prison life as does an inmate, but how far apart should the experiences be?

READING 23
HOW I BECAME A CONVICT

Victor Hassine

Victor Hassine was convicted of first degree murder in 1981 and sentenced to life imprisonment. He donates royalties from the book to the organization Families of Murder Victims.

Graterford State Prison, Pennsylvania's largest and most violent penal institution, was built in the early 1930s to hold all of the state's most violent prisoners. On June 14, 1981, while it could not contain all 8,000 or more of the state's most wanted, it certainly had enough room to hold me. Its steel-reinforced concrete wall measures four feet thick by 32 feet tall and encloses over 65 acres of land. Originally designed to hold eight separate cell blocks within its perimeter, Graterford ended up with only five. But these cell blocks are huge constructions, each containing 400 cells.

Everything inside appears as huge and massive as the wall itself. Each housing unit is a rectangular structure, measuring about 45 feet wide by three stories tall by 820 feet long (over twice the length of a football field), perpendicularly attached to a quarter-mile-long main corridor which measures about 20 feet wide by two stories high.

I knew none of this as I sat handcuffed and shackled in the back seat of the sheriff's car, waiting to be taken inside to begin serving my life-without-parole sentence. All I could see was a blur of dirty, grainy whiteness from the giant

wall that dominated the landscape before me. It made me feel very small and insignificant, and very frightened.

A giant steel gate rose up to allow the sheriff's car to drive into Graterford's cavernous sallyport area, a fortified enclosure designed to control traffic. Once the gate fell shut, I was immediately hustled out of the car by some very large, serious-looking corrections officers. I knew I would have to submit to a cavity search, but it wasn't the strip search that dominated my memory of this event. It was the *noise*.

Since concrete and steel do not absorb sound, the clamor and voices from within just bounced around, crashing into each other to create a hollow, booming echo that never ended. It sounded as if someone had put a microphone inside a crowded locker room with the volume pumped up, broadcasting the noise all around the sallyport. It was this deafening background noise that would lull me to sleep at night and greet me in the morning for the next five years. Though I have been out of Graterford for many years now, its constant din still echoes in my ears.

The prison guards finished their search and escorted me up Graterford's main corridor, a dim, gloomy, 20-foot-wide by over 1500-foot-long stretch. The lack of natural light and the damp, dungeon-like air in this place was oppressive. As I took one tentative step after another, I promised myself never to take bright and sunny places for granted again. Having just left the Courthouse hours before, I was so disoriented that I lost track of how far I had been walking.

Things changed with sudden permanence once I reached the central corridor gate that separated the administrative section from the prison proper. This was the first time I saw the faces, shapes, and shadows of the men who would become my future friends, enemies, and neighbors. They stared at me and I stared back, as scared as I had ever been in my entire life.

Once inside, I was walked through a gauntlet of desperate men. Their hot smell in the muggy corridor was as foul as their appearance. Most of them were wearing their "Graterford Tan," an ashen gray pallor. The discoloration of these distorted human forms represented the prison landscape. At Graterford you work, eat, sleep, and idle indoors. You never have to go outdoors unless you want to risk the sometimes deadly yard. Many inmates served their time like cave dwellers, never leaving Graterford's concrete and steel shelter.

My first impression was that most of these men brandished their scars and deformities like badges of honor. None of them seemed to have a full set of front teeth. Many bore prominently displayed tattoos of skulls or demons. They all seemed either too tall or too small, but none seemed right. Eyes were buggy, beady, squinted, or staring, but none were caring. Heads were too big, too small, pointed, swollen, or oblong, some with jutting foreheads, twisted noses, massive jaws, and gnarled hands. But none seemed human.

One could argue whether it was the look of these men that led them to prison or whether it was the prison that gave them their look. What tales of suffering their bodies told seemed to be of no concern to them. They were content to wear their scars openly like a warning, the way farmers use scarecrows to keep menacing birds away. Today I feel pity and compassion for those who have had to suffer so much pain and tragedy in one lifetime. But on that hot June day, all I wanted was to get away from these ugly creatures as quickly as possible. Just looking at them made me fear for my life. There was no pity or compassion in my heart then, because their grotesqueness made me forget they were human.

Now when I watch a new arrival walking "the gauntlet of desperate men," I can always sense his hopelessness. I know my staring is as horrifying to him as it was for me on my first day, and I know what I must look like to him.

Getting Classified

Toward the end of the main corridor I was shepherded into the shadowy expanse of yet another corridor. This led to the Clothing Room, a cold, damp place equipped with a tile-walled shower and an adjoining room where endless rows of mothballed clothes hung on racks like mismatched goods in a thrift shop.

My escort guard ordered me to "get naked" and surrender my personal effects to an inmate dressed in brown prison garb. I was still wearing my nice suit and tie from the Courthouse. As I stripped down, I handed the silent inmate the last vestiges of my social identity. He tossed them impatiently into an old cardboard box. After the guard conducted another "bend-over-and-stretch-'em" search, I was given delousing shampoo and ordered to shower.

As I stood naked and shivering after my shower, I was assigned two pairs of navy blue pants, two blue shirts, three T-shirts, three pairs of boxer shorts, three pairs of socks, a blue winter coat, a blue summer jacket, two towels, and a pair of brown shoes. Everything but the shoes and socks had "AM4737" boldly stamped in black. This number was my new, permanent identity.

Once I had dressed, I was taken to be fingerprinted and photographed, then escorted to E-Block, officially known as the Eastern Diagnostic and Classification Center (EDCC). Though Graterford had five cell blocks, only A- through D-Blocks were considered part of the prison. E-Block was treated as a separate facility, which inmates and staff called "Quarantine." Because all new receptions to Quarantine were issued blue prison uniforms, they were labeled "Blues." The general population inmates who wore brown uniforms were referred to as "Browns." Contact between Blues and Browns was strictly forbidden.

Soon I found myself before the E-Block Sergeant's desk, wearing my new blue uniform, cradling my belongings, and waiting for whatever came next. The Sergeant walked me to a room full of bedding. There another inmate in brown dropped a rolled-up mattress on my shoulder. Inside it were stuffed a blanket, pillow, metal cup, plastic knife, fork, and spoon, a pack of rolling tobacco, soap, toothbrush, toothpaste, and a disposable razor.

Awkwardly balancing the mattress roll on my shoulder with one arm and carrying my prison-issued clothes with the other, I followed the Sergeant down a flight of stairs to my cell on one of the bottom ranges. The moment I twisted my body and cargo sideways into the dark, narrow cell, the Sergeant slid the door shut and disappeared from sight.

The next two days were spent in the prison's infirmary for shots and a complete medical examination. While it was a doctor who examined me, it was an inmate who drew my blood and wrote down my medical history. Since the infirmary was also used by Browns from general population, a guard followed me and the other receptions everywhere we went. This constant surveillance had me wondering why we were so heavily guarded.

I later learned that any exposure of Browns to Blues was closely watched by the staff. One reason was that, since they had more liberties than the new arrivals, Browns often tried to barter privileges with Blues. For example, a pack of cigarettes could buy extra phone time or a library pass; and for a pack a day, you could rent a TV or a radio. Also, some Browns were homosexuals and would exploit weaker Blues. Almost all of them were point men for prison gangs, who reported back on the new prospects among Blues for possible gang membership or future victimization.

After I completed the medical examination process, there were about two weeks of idleness. Finally I was taken to an Examination Room on the block for a series of written psychological and literacy tests. There was no supervision in this room, and the testing process took about two days.

Two months of more idleness followed as I waited to be interviewed by my counselor. There were over 400 inmates on E-Block and many

fights. It seemed as if every time the block was let out into the yard, a fight would break out somewhere. From my experience, when convicts are let loose after being locked up for long periods of time, aggressive behavior is an immediate and natural consequence.

To occupy time, people played cards and worked out. It was during these idle days in classification that longstanding friendships and alliances were made and when inmates distinguished the weak from the strong—predators from victims.

The first impressions I made on others during classification have stayed with me in prison ever since. Since I was not a career criminal, I was initially viewed as a "square john": a middle-class outsider with no experience of the social world of inmates. To both my advantage and disadvantage, I was seeing everything through the eyes of a foreigner, making many foolish mistakes yet gaining just as many unique insights into their world.

When I was finally called in for my interview, the counselor examined my test results and asked me a minimum of questions about my conviction and sentence. The interview took only ten to 15 minutes.

Two weeks later, I was summoned to appear before the Classification Committee. Sitting before a counselor, the block Sergeant, and a Major of the Guards, I was asked what prison I wanted to go to and why. I could only suggest Graterford since I didn't think other prisons would be any better or worse. Then I waited outside while they reviewed my file. Within a few minutes, I was called back and informed that I had been classified to Graterford. Just before I left, the Major added in a pleasant voice, "You'll be working for me."

At the time I didn't consider the significance of my job assignment. I was too relieved to know that the tortuous classification ordeal was finally over. A few days later, I traded in my blues for browns and moved off Quarantine into the general population.

To me and most of the others, as I later discovered, classification was a total waste of time. While different prisons in Pennsylvania purportedly provided different types of rehabilitation programs meant to serve the needs of various kinds of offenders, in reality it seemed that only three considerations were used to determine a convict's ultimate destination: (1) race, (2) hometown, and (3) availability of cell space. At the time, most of the minority inmates in the state were classified to Graterford or Western Penitentiary. The other seven prisons consisted of mostly white inmates under an all-white civilian staff.

From the inmate point of view, the testing was an utter sham. For one thing, the written tests were given to everyone without even determining who could read or write. The written tests I took were in an unsupervised room with about 30 other men, most of whom just picked answers at random or copied them from someone else.

Because the tests were given so irrelevantly, inmates tended to see their results only as a tool of manipulation. Under this assumption, many men had developed theories on how to answer the test questions. Some felt it was best to copy from the brightest men in order to improve their chances at getting a clerk's job over kitchen or laundry duty. Others felt they should give lunatic answers so they could be medically released from work altogether. Still others gave no answers at all and faked illiteracy. Such men reasoned that they could enroll in school and appear to do extremely well, thereby fooling the parole board into believing they had worked hard to make a positive change in their lives. All these connivances were based on the inmates' understanding that they were being conned as much as they were doing the conning.

Getting Dug In

Inmates serving long sentences preferred to lock at Graterford because, even though it was violent, it afforded them the most personal liberty. This was so because the more violent a prison is, the more reluctant guards are to enforce petty rules for fear of being assaulted.

Once I was classified to Graterford, I had to move my belongings, along with my mattress, blanket, and pillow, to B-Block. This was a working block, reserved only for those inmates who had been assigned a job. My assignment turned out to be a fortuitous clerical job in the Major of the Guards' office. All my belongings were fit into a single shopping bag which I carried in one hand, while my rolled-up mattress was once again toted on my shoulder. I walked down the long main corridor to B-Block, my new home. Though it mirrored the design of E-Block, it was considerably less crowded and noisy. Comparatively, this hell seemed more like heaven to me.

The first thing I noticed was that the men on B-Block were much older than most of those on the classification block. These were the "Old Heads" of the prison, inmates who had done a long stretch. When I arrived at my assigned cell, I quickly signed in at the Block Sergeant's desk and requested cleaning supplies. Then I spent the morning scrubbing down every inch of my cell. By noon count I was able to lie down on my bed, smoke a cigarette, and consider what I was going to do next.

My cell measured about six feet by 12 with a ten-foot high ceiling, from which dangled a single light bulb with a drawstring switch. For furniture, I had a flat, hard steel bed and a steel desk and chair which had been assembled as one unit. The mandatory toilet afforded a sink directly above it with a steel medicine cabinet above that. High over the toilet was a rusty radiator which served as my only source of heat in the winter. Finally, I had a flimsy wooden foot locker with a hasp that could be locked with a commissary-bought combination lock.

My cell entrance was a solid steel sliding door with a fixed glass window on the top quarter. On the opposite wall was a window that could be manually opened and closed, just a little. The concrete walls were painted a dingy off-white and adorned with graffiti and cigarette stains.

Despite the grim accommodations, this was my home. I was due to report to work the next morning and I could feel myself getting dug in. In prison it doesn't take much to make a man happy: food, some quiet, a good book, a job, and enough heat in the winter. That day I was happy just to be able to lie on that hard bed with a 70-

watt light bulb glaring in my face. I felt the worst was over. I could now begin to serve my time.

Escape from Reality

Like most first-time arrivals to Graterford, I was only preoccupied with survival and how to avoid becoming the victim of violence. This sudden refocusing of attention led me to change my habits, my personality, and even my values. With these changes came a new way of viewing the world as a place of unrelenting fear.

If I made eye contact with a stranger, I would feel threatened. An unexpected smile could mean trouble. A man in uniform was not a friend. Being kind was a weakness. Viciousness and recklessness were to be respected and admired. Oddly enough, these changes were in some way comforting. In the struggle to survive, it was easier to distrust everyone than to believe in their inherent goodness.

Danger became a determining factor of the changes in my attitude and personality. When there was general movement in the prison, for example, the main corridor would fill with hundreds of inmates in transit. This made the corridor an extremely dangerous place to be. I was more likely to see a stabbing than a guard on duty.

The cell blocks were just as insecure. A guard at one end of a cell block could not identify anyone at the other end; the distance of 700 feet was just too great. Because of their fear of being assaulted where no one could see them, many block guards never patrolled the inner perimeter and spent most of their time avoiding conflicts at all cost, even turning the other way.

By the time I had settled in, however, I found myself feeling safe enough to think beyond the moment. This was something I had not been able to do since my arrest. Unfortunately, this new sense of security brought with it the "sleeping phase." I began to sleep 12 to 14 hours a day. My whole life consisted of eating, working, and sleeping. I never dreamed. I only tried to stay unconscious for as long as I possibly could.

Though I had no way of knowing it at the time, I had entered a very common prison-adjustment phase. So common, in fact, that walking in on a newcomer while he sleeps is the most practiced technique of cell thieves and rapists. In Graterford, a man who spends too much time in bed sends the same signal as that of a bleeding fish in shark-infested waters.

"You can't be sleeping all the time," cautioned my chess partner one day, waking me to play a game. "You can't sleep away your sentence. You have to stay awake to stay alive in here."

Keeping Busy

He was right, and I knew it. So I resolved to keep myself busy. I took up reading and painting as hobbies. I was allowed to buy almost as many books, magazines, and newspapers as I wanted, as well as canvasses, brushes, and paints. Self-help was encouraged so long as you could pay for it yourself.

Soon I was reading everything I could get my hands on and painting well into the wee hours of the morning. My cell became crowded with books, magazines, canvasses, newspapers, and even an easel. I went so far as to rig up extra lighting, hang pictures, and buy throw rugs for the cement floor. I had successfully transformed my cell into a cluttered boarding-house room.

Like some literary critic and master artist, I was so deeply submerged in my hobbies that I became as obsessed as a man digging his way to freedom. But I was no literary critic and certainly no artist. 1 was just another lifer trying to escape the real world.

"You have to spend more time out of that cell, Victor," insisted my chess mate and only friend at that time. "It's not healthy to do a 'bit' [time] like that. Look at your cell, you have junk everywhere. You even have lights on your wall that look like they belong in a room somewhere else."

"I'm just getting dug in," I replied in defense, annoyed that my efforts at avoiding reality had been detected.

"This isn't getting dug in, this is foolishness. You're in a penitentiary—a tough one. You should never try to forget that. Never try to make yourself believe you're somewhere else. Do you know what a lit match could do to this cell?"

His words struck an unnerving chord. Only a

few months earlier, I had watched a man whose cell across the way had been deliberately set on fire. He had screamed and banged helplessly on his locked door, flames dancing around him, biting at his flesh. Through his cell window, I could see billowing black smoke envelope his pleading, twisted, horrified face until he disappeared. It had taken some time before guards responded to his screams.

The very next day I gave away my books, magazines, newspapers, art supplies, and my easel. I knew I had to fight as hard for my safety as I did for my sanity.

THE JOLIET CORRECTIONAL CENTER: AN INTERNSHIP TO REMEMBER

Amanda Larsen

Amanda Larsen recalls her experiences as an intern at the Joliet Correctional Center, learning about the facilities, inmates, and herself. Larsen graduated from the University of Illinois at Chicago in 1996 and is currently working as a police officer in suburban Chicago.

As I approached the building, I found the architecture to be comparable to that of a medieval castle. It was a beautiful tan-colored brick structure covering approximately 30 acres. The irony of the building was visible to the naked eye and included the following: posted signs reading "Do not pick up hitchhikers," the six towers occupied by armed officers, and the tall metal fence topped with barbed wire. I was at the Joliet Correctional Center in Joliet, Illinois. This was my first day of "on the job training" in the world of corrections.

I began my internship at the Joliet Correctional Center in the spring of 1996. I was completing my last semester before graduating with a bachelor's degree in criminal justice at the University of Illinois at Chicago. The internship was to be

Reprinted from Amanda Larsen, "Joliet Correctional Center: An Internship to Remember," *The Keepers' Voice*, Fall 1996, by permission of *The Keepers' Voice*, a publication of The International Association of Correctional Officers.

the stepping stone that I needed to determine my future as a dedicated employee in the Department of Corrections.

The Joliet Correctional Center

The Joliet Correctional Center is one of four maximum security facilities for men in the state of Illinois. However, Joliet serves a special function as the Reception and Classification unit for the Northern part of Illinois. There are two separate cellhouses in this prison. One cellhouse houses approximately 550 inmates who are serving their sentences at Joliet. In the other cellhouse, there are more than 600 inmates at any time who are received from all of the Northern Illinois counties. These men stay for approximately seven to ten days during which they are tested and classified for transfer and permanent assignment to one of the other 25 adult correctional centers in the state.

I first started working in the administrative building in the Field Services office. This office is basically responsible for the paroling of inmates, which occurs on a day-to-day basis. This office is also in charge of the administrative processes involved with work-release for inmates. These are the Field Services duties in a nutshell, but it is a continuous, complex job which I came to realize very quickly. I became familiar with the many tasks that are involved in the process including: contacting inmates for parole information, verifying the information, contacting and informing prestart zones of potential inmates, and completing the many forms involved in the parole process. I was taught and guided by Mr. Mike Allen, Correctional Counselor II, who is in charge of this office. Although I did not have a lot of contact with the inmates and other prison premises while working in the Field Services office, I found it to be a valuable, critical experience.

Learning About the Prison and the Inmates

After familiarizing myself with the numerous components of this office, as well as some of the others, I gradually began to enter into the inmates' home, the cellhouse. Although often encountering the permanent population in the West Cellhouse, I was assigned to the East Cellhouse, which is directed by Superintendent Sheila Burford. This is where the transient population, the reception and classification of inmates, is housed. The Clinical Services supervisor, Samantha Franklin, arranged for me to accompany a correctional counselor into the cellhouse. Here, I was able to interact with many different actors involved in the prison system. I became acquainted with those involved in maintaining security and custody of the inmates, the correctional officers, sergeants, and lieutenants.

I was received with smiles, compliments, and occasional hoots and hollers by the inmates. They seemed to be just as curious about me as I was about them. The correctional counselor, Diane Sternisha, would simply introduce me as an intern who was assisting her with her work on the galleries.

The cellhouse was a whole new experience for me. The architecture spoke for itself with its cement floors, heavy metal bars, and individual cells housing up to two inmates. The most notable aspect of the cellhouse, as well as the general prison premises, was the numerous locks located everywhere. Upon my first trip onto the gallery, I felt like I was being locked in. A correctional officer would unlock the gallery door, let us in, and close and lock the door behind us. Shortly thereafter, I realized that being locked on the gallery was basic freedom compared to living in a locked cell. I understood the need for security, not only for the employees, but for the inmates as well.

I played the silent observer for the first few adventures into the cellhouse. Counselor Sternisha and I would go up and down the galleries, sometimes interviewing specific inmates for processing purposes, but more often just answering questions that anyone had. This was the most educational aspect of the internship. I was learning all of the necessary information needed to become a solid correctional counselor from an expert. I took many pages of notes on security classifications, institutional assignments, transfer information, and calculating approximate outdates. Once I felt I had acquired enough knowledge to respond to the inmates' questions, I began to "counsel" the inmates myself with Counselor Sternisha's guidance.

Learning About Myself

But learning about the IDOC rules was not the only important part of my internship. I also learned about the moral obligation that any IDOC employee has to treating inmates with respect as human beings. I like to believe that I am a compassionate person without any prejudicial views, who treats all people equally. Working with inmates in a maximum security facility, who have committed various crimes from D.U.I. to murder, put my beliefs and morality to the test. The following two incidents are prime examples of the morality issue I faced while working at the prison.

One particular day in the cellhouse tested my ability to be an objective counselor working with other humans who have committed some very heinous crimes. In one day I met four men who were serving their sentences at Joliet for murder, one serial rapist, and one child molester. I was unaware of their backgrounds while conversing with them and another counselor. I would never have believed them to be any sort of criminal at all. After learning of their convictions, I became enraged. I was angry at them for perpetrating these crimes on other innocent humans. And yet, if we had not been in a prison cellhouse, where they had been sent as punishment for these acts, I would not have treated them any differently than I would any other person I met.

Another unforgettable incident tested my ability to remain detached from my personal feelings. I was in one of the cellhouses with a different counselor talking with some inmates, when we were called over by one particular man. He had some questions for the counselor, and we answered them, but also got into a conversation with him about the situation surrounding his crime. He went on to proclaim that he was wrongly imprisoned and that he had acted in self-defense during the homicide for which he was convicted. He portrayed himself as the victim of abuse and that he chose his only alternative in the situation, murder. As I walked away from this man, I began to feel sorry for him and a bit confused. The counselor recognized the look upon my face. She then asked, "So, do you believe that one?" I replied with, "I am not sure what to believe or how to feel."

Later that day she changed my feelings of confusion and sympathy concerning this man to feelings of anger and rage. This man had raped and killed a young woman. He was hardly the victim of abuse, nor did he act in self-defense. He had been responsible for the brutal sexual assault and murder of an innocent victim. I was very upset and angry with this man. I hoped that I did not have to see him again that day or in the near future. I was afraid of how I might react knowing the circumstances of his crime. That night, I thought deeply about myself and the world we live in. I did not try to understand why there is such heinous crimes as the one I had learned about that day; rather, I realized the need to detach myself from my "job" at the prison, in order to complete it without anger and prejudice towards any inmate, regardless of his criminal history.

I found out on this day that I needed to know myself better than any one else in order to conduct myself properly in this sort of environment. I felt good about myself and the kind of person I was, and I wanted others to be aware of it also.

But, I knew that in order to perform a job where I was constantly in contact with other people who may or may not possess the qualities I respect in a person, I had to respect and know myself. This is a concept that I learned in a criminal justice Corrections course: you must look in the mirror and into yourself and be comfortable and secure with what you see, then you will be able to work in the field of corrections.

Opportunities for Those Wanting Them

After completing my internship, I was able to give a more educated perspective on the whole prison system. Many people have called prisons a place of little or no possibility. The question then arises: how can a place of little or no possibility have possibilities? I was very fortunate to work in the controlled environment of Joliet Correctional Center. I feel that this facility does present the men with possibilities if they choose to partake. One of the most important programs offered at most of these facilities is drug education and rehabilitation classes. They also offer educational courses up to the second year in college. They have training for certain trades within the facility. The inmates are able to work in a desired field, if their behavior record allows, to enhance their ability within that trade. There are a variety of religious ceremonies offered, and several different religious leaders are available to give guidance to the men. These are some of the steps that must be taken for a person to improve their future after becoming involved in the criminal way of life. The facilities may offer these types of programs, but the person must choose to participate. Making the choice to participate in any one of these programs is making the choice to make a change in oneself. This is the most critical point in the life of a criminal, to change their ways. A correctional facility can offer intervention programs to make it a place of possibility, but the individuals must want the opportunities for themselves, in order to benefit from them. Without wanting a brighter future, all of the possibilities offered to a person are of no use. Therefore, it is up to each individual to seek out possibilities and use them to their fullest potential.

I was only the fourth college intern to take on the daring feat of working at Joliet. The staff was somewhat apprehensive about my position as a student learning the rules and regulations of a maximum security prison. But, I quickly adjusted and the staff grew to think of me as one of their fellow employees who was just new to the world of corrections. I met a lot of very nice people who were willing to guide me, a neophyte penologist, and to teach me the ropes. I appreciate all of the planning and preparations that were done by the prison staff and my sponsor from U.I.C., Dr. Jess Maghan. I feel that this internship was of great value to my education, as well as my future. I hope to one day be back at Joliet or another correctional facility as a true member of the Correctional Counseling staff.

DISCUSSION QUESTIONS

1. Victor Hassine describes the classification process as "a total waste of time" since the final decision about the prison to which a new inmate is sent comes down to race, hometown, and availability of cells. Corrections officials in Pennsylvania and elsewhere are likely to disagree with this assessment. They would claim that classification decisions are based on inmate needs (e.g., education, treatment, medical), institutional needs (e.g., work assignments must be filled for the prison to operate), and community safety (e.g., the escape potential of the inmate). Discuss what criteria you believe should be used in deciding the prison an inmate should go to, the cell and work assignment the prisoner should get, and the treatment program designed for the inmate.

2. Much of what Hassine learned about life in prison was initially provided by his chess partner. In light of genuine safety issues (e.g., sleeping inmates being raped and cells with too much "stuff" getting torched), should new inmates have to rely on the kindness of strangers to learn about prison life? Discuss whether prison officials should take some responsibility for informing new inmates about some aspects of the prison subculture.

3. Amanda Larsen notes that her internship provided instruction about the prison rules, but there is no indication that she learned the inmate rules. That is, if Hassine is correct, new inmates must learn to follow not only the official (prison) rules but also the rules of the inmate subculture. Assume for a moment that Larsen's experience was comparable to that of a new prison employee. Discuss whether employees, like inmates, should learn both the official rules governing the prison and the unofficial rules governing the inmates' interaction with prison staff and other inmates. If you believe employees should become familiar with the inmate rules, how could that be accomplished?

WEBSITES

www.wco.com/~aerick/links.htm

Attorney Arnold Erickson provides what may be the most complete listing of links to prison and corrections topics you will find anywhere.

www.synapse.net/~arrakis/jpp/jpp.html

This electronic version of back issues of the *Journal of Prisoners on Prison* provides an alternative to articles on crime and punishment written by academics, journalists, and criminal justice professionals.

www.acsp.uic.edu/iaco/about.htm

The *Keepers' Voice* is a newsletter of the International Association of Correctional Officers; the electronic version of the printed publication is found at this address.

CHAPTER 12: CORRECTIONS POLICY

Deciding what principles should guide corrections agencies, and what procedures should be used in accord with those principles, is a topic of corrections policy. Are corrections programs supposed to deter, rehabilitate, provide retribution, or simply incapacitate? How do probation, prison, parole, community service, etc., achieve these distinct goals? Citizens, politicians, scholars, and corrections officials around the world have been debating these issues since the establishment of formal systems of criminal justice. It seems that consensus is as elusive today as it has been in the past. The readings in this chapter address topics related to corrections policy and help us appreciate their complexity.

The first selection, the comments of four journalists, highlights key policy questions including what we do with our aging inmate population, the appropriateness of long-term imprisonment, and the consequences of prison expansion. As you read the journalists' comments you will notice that each mentions, in some manner, the important topic of deciding which criminals, and for which crimes, really should be in prison. That point is elaborated upon in this chapter's second selection, in which William DiMascio provides information about why prison populations are increasing and who is ending up in prison. You might find it interesting to provide your own answer to the question considered in this selection, then compare your answer to the facts as given in the reading: Why are inmate populations up?

READING 25

OUTSIDE LOOKING IN: FOUR JOURNALISTS EXAMINE CRIMINAL JUSTICE ISSUES

Ted Gest, Julia Cass, Dan Morain, and Michael Isikoff

Four journalists who cover criminal justice issues were asked for their impressions of the state of corrections today. Their observations hone in on some of corrections' most pressing problems—aging inmates, a rising prison population, and the consequences of stiff penalties for drug offenses.

Fighting Crime and Cutting Budgets

Ted Gest is National News Editor and has covered legal affairs for *U.S. News & World Report* since 1981.

"An alarming trend, folks," warned the lecturer, pointing to a population chart. "By 3000 A.D., all Americans will be retired or in prison." This recent *Wall Street Journal* cartoon reflected a grim reality for correctional officers. For more than a decade now, budget watchers have been warning that state prison spending will outpace allocations for higher education and other important government functions.

The direst predictions have not come to pass, but we at *U.S. News & World Report* have been tracking the trend. In our July 3, 1995 issue, we

published a five-page package featuring a story headlined "Crime and Punishment" that dissected the conflict between fighting crime and cutting budgets. It was accompanied by "The View From Inside the Wall"—an on-scene account describing the impact of the imprisonment boom on staffers in the Oklahoma prison system.

The corrections story in America is hardly a simple one. On one level are many anticrime activists and their sympathizers among the politicians who make public policy demanding "get-tough-on-crime" remedies; on another are fiscal realities dictating that government can't build its way out of the crime problem. Although federal policies that appear to take both tacks simultaneously naturally receive the most attention from the national news media, we know that the toughest decisions on correctional policy are hammered out in state capitals.

Our *U.S. News* roundup cited Oklahoma as a case study. Gov. Frank Keating had been elected after waging a get-tough campaign, but he was forced to release 500 convicts early amid lawsuits over prison conditions and skepticism among state legislators about sharply increasing correctional budgets. Readers of *Corrections Today* are well aware of such scenarios in many states, but the dilemmas usually are not apparent to a national audience.

When states consider punishment options, a threshold question must ask how the imprisonment rate affects the crime rate. Obviously, those behind bars don't commit robberies while they're incarcerated—at least on the street—so some offenses are prevented every year that a convict remains in custody. Despite many attempts by experts at linking imprisonment policies to crime levels, the impact of adding cells on the extent of violence is far from clear. Our article compared the numbers of Americans under all kinds of correctional supervision with the violent-crime totals as measured by the federal victimization survey, and found no consistent pattern. We also showed how incarceration levels vary widely by state.

Much of the story was devoted to describing a variety of corrections approaches being tried around the country, including the building boom in Texas, parole's end in Virginia, North Carolina's sentencing-grid scheme and "intermediate sanctions" programs such as drug courts, boot camps and neighborhood probation supervision. We wanted to expose readers to the idea that the public need not always choose between long prison terms and outright release. While not advocating any particular program, we cited a survey we had taken showing that when confronted with a choice of anticrime strategies, Americans chose prevention over punishment, 45 to 38 percent—hardly the impression one might get from speeches on the campaign trail.

We concluded the article by mentioning some of the federal policies that likely will have an impact in the coming years, including the "truth in sentencing" provisions of the 1994 crime law and the then-pending legislation to restrict litigation over prison and jail conditions. Neither of these developments had played out as 1997 began. We believe that our article helped give readers a comprehensive picture of the major debates on correctional issues today. The account went far beyond typical news media reporting of the latest prison disturbances and admissions or releases of notorious inmates.

Fundamental shifts in criminal justice come slowly. The cartoon figure's year 3000 prediction probably is exaggerated, but it may be well into the next century before the most cost-effective punishment practices are worked out. In the meantime, as correctional populations seemingly rise without end, our reporting should help alert Americans to the public-policy tradeoffs that typically are lost in the shrill election-year rhetoric over crime and punishment.

Dysfunctional Prisons

Julia Cass, a reporter for the *Philadelphia Inquirer*, has covered prisons since 1993. She is coauthor of a 1990 book about race in the South.

As I write this, I am thinking of a story I just completed about Pennsylvania's first nursing home prison—a geriatric and long-term medical care wing that's part of a new prison being retrofitted from a former state mental hospital.

Imprisoned there are people whose actions once made the front page, but who now lie helpless on hospital beds or hobble down hallways on crutches. When I visited, I was especially struck by a man from suburban Philadelphia who'd attempted to shoot his ex-wife in a company parking lot. He missed her, but killed her co-worker, then turned the gun on himself. Instead of dying, he made himself a quadriplegic.

I interviewed a 77-year-old inmate at a different institution who wants to go to this new prison. Except for eight years of freedom in the 1970s, he's been imprisoned since 1945. He killed his mother-in-law during a drunken argument. Then, after his release 24 years later, he was convicted of shooting and wounding a woman in a bar. He said he didn't do this second crime. I looked into the case a bit, and he may have been correct. But, it's all academic, and since he's so institutionalized, he doesn't want to be released. He's got arthritis and asthma and a bad heart, and he fears being robbed if he's out on his own.

Obviously, this story reflects the graying of our prisons as offenders serve longer and mandatory sentences. It also reflects another pervasive reality of criminal justice in America today—our lack of imagination about what to do with offenders besides punishing them. Punishment seems to be the only response we can think of to express our abhorrence of crime and to feel we are maintaining control.

In my interview with the elderly inmate, who'd grown up in a Georgia sharecropping family, I asked if he felt his life had a purpose. He said he really didn't know. "I'm confused." Then, he went on to say that he honestly felt his life had been worthless. I don't know his whole story, but I gathered from my interview that he'd been a hard-working man with a bad temper and a drinking problem. But, was he so evil and dangerous as to require lifelong incarceration?

Several years ago, I did a story on an inmate with a life sentence who was making very worthwhile use of his time. He has since tried for a commutation and has not made it. (In Pennsylvania, a life sentence means life without parole.) Almost none do now. In the course of researching that story, I met other lifers who were equally impressive.

I've spent enough time visiting prisons to know these inmates aren't the norm. But, there are more of them than I'd expected, and it is these decent people who probably will never get out who I cannot erase from my thoughts. I guess meeting them made it necessary to question the standard portrait of inmates—dehumanized, defined solely by their crimes, expected to respond only to punishment.

I think we've gone punishment/prison crazy. It's the pill for every offender—the vicious, dangerous ones, the manipulative ones, the ones who were always decent people and remain so, the rehabilitated ones, the elderly ones, even the quadriplegics. There's so little attention given to sorting them and seriously considering alternatives that it's no wonder prisons are so crowded and dysfunctional.

At the ACA convention here in Philadelphia, I was struck by the contrast between going to workshops on, say, "The Role of Corrections in Addressing the Problems of Violence in Juveniles" and "What Works"—and going inside a crowded prison, where the sheer numbers overwhelm the best of our professional intentions.

People may debate whether prisons should be about rehabilitation, deterrence or incapacitation, but the reality inside looks more like crisis management and damage control.

The main argument I hear against putting so many people in prison with longer sentences is money: It costs too much. We need the money for other things, like prevention and education. Only in the African American community do you hear anything said about the human cost of keeping so many people behind bars.

I don't hear many corrections professionals speaking in these terms, especially not in recent years. So, why should the public care how long inmates are incarcerated or believe anything can be done to put any of them on a different path? Obviously, discounting any worth or potential in those million plus in prisons and jails underpins our willingness to see them warehoused—and warehousing certainly looks like the future of corrections.

Managing a Growing Prison System

Dan Morain is a staff writer for the *Los Angeles Times*. He has been covering criminal justice issues periodically since 1980.

It was not James Gomez's best day. Gov. Pete Wilson had just called for a criminal investigation of Corcoran State Prison, and Atty. Gen. Dan Lungren agreed to open the probe. Seven inmates had been fatally shot by correctional officers since the prison had opened less than a decade ago.

Gomez, then director of the California Department of Corrections, had called some journalists together a few days before Thanksgiving to address the issues.

"My goal is to reduce violence and to reduce death," Gomez said.

Gomez was entirely believable. He strikes me as a decent, sincere, honest man. Certainly, he is an accomplished manager, one well-skilled at negotiating his way through the legislature and the rest of state government.

But in California, it may be that one man in Sacramento cannot manage the state's prisons. To the extent that California's experience foreshadows what happens in the rest of the country, let this be a cautionary tale. Two years ago, I was the lead writer of a four-part series in the *Los Angeles Times* detailing the largest prison construction program in the nation's history, and analyzing reasons for the voracious expansion of California's prison budget.

Since that series ran, hell has broken out, or at least its equivalent for a guy like Gomez.

At that time, the California prison system included 28 prisons, and 130,000 inmates. Now there are 32. As this is being written, there are 145,000 inmates, but population rises by about 1,000 each month. California prisons cost $3.1 billion then. Now, the prison budget is $4 billion.

In *The Times'* series, there were plenty of examples that politicians should have taken as red flags: the $550 milkshake-makers for the staff cafeteria; the land deal for a new prison that nicely enriched some local politicians; the Capitol lobbyists and Wall Street bond dealers who make good money from the prison building industry; the astonishing statistics that as many as 20 percent of the inmates are mentally ill.

Since that series ran, problems have only continued. Besides the stories of substandard care from mentally and physically ill inmates, inmates have been in running battles with one another at several institutions. Any of a number of issues could have been, and still could be, the focus of legislature hearings and rational discussion, and maybe even consensus.

But as I found in 1994, there was little oversight of prison expansion. Key legislators ceded much of their responsibilities because they were confident the Department of Corrections operated efficiently.

This has changed somewhat. Now, politicians realize that they can get attention by bashing prisons. They cuffed around Gomez in hearings. But they haven't held a single hearing into the shootings that have resulted in 40 inmate deaths in the past 11 years, more than all other states combined. They have stayed away from any inquiry into Corcoran.

As I found in 1994, lawmakers in Sacramento are far more interested in appearing to be tough on crime than on understanding what happens to criminals once they arrive in prison. In the 1994 election year, the California Legislature passed and Wilson signed 104 bills lengthening criminal sentences, including the nation's harshest—by far—three strikes sentencing law. They approved a similar number in 1996.

It doesn't matter that California could save $160 million a year by eliminating prison terms for people convicted of the crimes of petty theft with a prior, repeat drunken driving, drug possession, marijuana offenses, forgery or fraud. Indeed, California has more than 4,000 prison inmates—enough to fill one prison—on the charge of petty theft, generally shoplifting, with a prior. There will be no Willie Hortons on these lawmakers' watches.

Consensus about how to deal with prisons is lacking. Liberals want "alternative" placements. Conservatives want inmates piled up. No one wants to build another prison. It may be, perhaps two years from now, that a federal judge will declare California prisons too crowded, and real decisions will have to be made.

But Gomez was left to struggle to keep the system together. On the day that Wilson called for the investigation, Gomez was focusing on one problem at the prison. He was a little like the Dutch boy and dike. He had locked down the security housing unit at Corcoran, after correctional officers had fired wooden bullets from gas guns 63 times to break up fights at Corcoran's yards in less than a 30-day period. He was reviewing one policy that placed rival gang members on the yards with one another, to determine if that was the root of new violence.

"These are some of the most violent, difficult offenders," Gomez said. "No matter who you put them with, there are problems."

Indeed, California has 145,000 problems, and another 1,000 arriving each month. Just before Christmas, Gomez got another job and announced his resignation.

The Problem with Getting Tough on Drugs

Michael Isikoff is a correspondent for the Washington, D.C., bureau of *Newsweek*. He has covered criminal justice issues for the past ten years.

Few developments in recent years have had a more disturbing impact on America's criminal justice system than the war on drugs. A series of mandatory sentencing laws—enacted during the height of antidrug hysteria in the mid-1980s—has caused the nation's prison population to explode. Aggressive crackdowns by federal and state law enforcement agencies—using everything from undercover "buy-bust" stings to the use of drug courier "profiles"—have led to dismaying abuses of civil liberties. As a criminal justice reporter, I have watched and written about many of these problems as they have unfolded over the past decade. But, two cases in particular I have reported on . . . have reminded me just how seriously the judicial system has been distorted by the zeal to "get tough" on the drug trade.

One involves Manuel Antonio Noriega. At first blush, that may sound incongruous: it is likely that no single figure from the recent past personifies the perceived evil of the global drug trade more than Panama's one-time tyrannical dictator. Yet, when I covered Noriega's trial in 1991, I was amazed at the flimsy quality of the evidence against him: it was based almost exclusively on the uncorroborated testimony of convicted drug dealers. As a journalist, I don't pay for interviews; the view of mainstream news organizations such as mine is that the exchange of money to would-be sources inevitably taints whatever the source might say in return. Yet, here was the U.S. government purchasing testimony with a commodity infinitely more valuable than cash. Drug felons facing literally decades in prison were provided years off their sentences, and in some cases their freedom, in exchange for saying precisely what federal prosecutors wanted them to say.

It turns out I didn't know the half of it. In late 1995, new evidence in Noriega's case surfaced that showed even more questionable prosecutorial abuse. To obtain the testimony of one of its most crucial witnesses—a major Panamanian cocaine trafficker named Ricardo Bilonick—the U.S. government had cut a secret deal with the leaders of Colombia's Cali drug cartel. Private correspondence and unsealed court transcripts demonstrated conclusively that federal prosecutors in Miami had negotiated with U.S. lawyers representing the leaders of the cartel. Under the resulting deal, one of Cali's biggest traffickers—the brother of cartel baron Jose Santacruz Londono—had his sentence slashed. In exchange, the cartel agreed to help "persuade" Bilonick to voluntarily fly to the United States to testify. The story I wrote for *Newsweek* on Oct. 30, 1995, documented the deal and suggested just how the cartel chieftains in Colombia managed this "persuasion": They paid him $1.2 million, coupling the bribe (implicitly sanctioned by the U.S. government) with some suggestive hints about possible misfortunes that might befall members of his family if he chose not to comply. The case remains a powerful example of the lengths to which federal prosecutors will go to obtain politically popular convictions—and a disturbing reminder of the hypocrisy that underlies so much of the government's crusade against drug abuse.

Another story I wrote for *Newsweek* involved a far less notorious defendant—Derrick Curry, a 22-year-old product of the Washington suburbs. The son of a college professor, Curry had been a local high school basketball star; at the time of his arrest for conspiring to sell crack cocaine, he also was a first-time offender with no history of violence. Yet, under drug war mandatory sentencing laws, his punishment was severe: 19 and one-half years in federal prison with no possibility of parole. That's longer than the average prison term for convicted rapists and armed robbers. It's also far harsher than the sentence Curry would have gotten had he been selling powder cocaine rather than crack. More than a year ago, the U.S. Sentencing Commission concluded the disparity between crack and cocaine sentences was inherently discriminatory. The two drugs are essentially the same product. Yet one—crack—is used largely by inner city blacks while the other—powder cocaine—is far more likely to be consumed by suburban whites. The inequity was so glaring that Attorney General Janet Reno had privately denounced it to her staff as "outrageous." But, by the time the Sentencing Commission report was being considered, the country was on the eve of an election and modifying crack sentences would leave the Clinton administration vulnerable to the charge of being "soft" on drugs. So, Reno and her Justice Department acquiesced in congressional legislation overturning the Sentencing Commission's recommendation to equalize sentences. One more opportunity to introduce sanity into drug laws was squandered. The consequences—in building prison populations and more wasted lives like that of Derrick Curry—will be felt for years to come.

WHY INMATE POPULATIONS ARE UP

William M. DiMascio

Today, more than 5 million people in the United States are under the supervision of the criminal justice system; more than 1.6 million are in prisons or jails and the rest are on probation or parole. William DiMascio analyzes the factors that have led to a significant rise in the prison population over the past two decades. DiMascio is executive director of DiMascio and Associates, a communications firm in Bala Cynwyd, Pennsylvania.

MYTH

Prisons have a revolving door, and inmates are now serving far shorter prison terms than before.

FACT

Since 1923, the average prison term served by inmates in the U.S. has remained constant at about two years. State prisoners are still serving average sentences of two years in length. Federal inmates, however, have been serving longer sentences since the passage of the Sentencing Reform Act of 1984 and the adoption of mandatory sentencing laws. The Act introduced truth in sentencing into federal courts, which mandates that offenders serve a minimum of 85 percent of their sentences. For example, inmates convicted of a violent offense who were released from federal prisons in 1992 served average terms of 56 months, compared to 50 months served by violent offenders released in 1986. Federal drug offenders released in 1992 served an average of 33 months, compared to 22 months served by those released in 1986.[1]

For the better part of this century, incarceration rates remained relatively constant. Then a dramatic change began in the 1970s, when huge increases in inmate populations were recorded across the country. Clearly, policy changes aimed at taking a bite out of crime—largely in response to the public's fear of violence and the "war on drugs"—were what drove the influx of new inmates.

The phrase of the day became "lock 'em up and throw away the key." This attitude, coupled with large increases in spending on law enforcement, mandatory sentencing laws and more and longer sentences, especially for drug offenses, led to larger prison populations.

It is extremely difficult to draw a connection between increases in incarceration and fluctuating crime rates. Putting offenders behind bars may keep them from committing more crimes while they are there, but no significant overall deterrent effect has yet been proven. Furthermore, some experts believe that factors such as shifting demographics—into and out of the crime-prone years—changing patterns of drug use and the drug trade, and changes in police tactics may have an even greater influence on crime rates.

The Crime Rate and Public Fear

Fear of crime, rather than rising crime itself, is one factor that has fueled the nation's rising incarceration rates. Interpretation of crime statistics is complex, however, and conflicting inferences can be drawn from the data.

Crime rates are calculated in two ways. The National Crime Victimization Survey (NCVS), conducted by the U.S. Bureau of the Census, gathers information from a sample of households and businesses, asking respondents whether they have been victims of crime over the past year. According to this survey, the rate of violent crime—rape, robbery and assault (murder and manslaughter obviously cannot be self-reported)—went down by 3.6 percent from 1980 to 1992. The rate of property crime against households—burglary and larceny—dropped by 33.1 percent over the 12-year period. The rate of property crime against individuals—theft without force or threat of force—declined by 28.7 percent.[2]

The second widely used measure of crime is the Uniform Crime Reports (UCR), compiled by the Federal Bureau of Investigation from crimes reported to or by the police. Unlike NCVS, UCR makes no distinction between crimes against individuals and crimes against households. These reports indicate that the rate of violent crime—including murder/non-negligent manslaughter, rape, robbery and aggravated assault—increased by 40 percent between 1985 and 1994.[3]

Almost all of the increase over the nine-year period is in the category of aggravated assault, which involves serious injury and includes all assaults or threats of injury with a deadly or dangerous weapon. Many criminologists attribute this increase to changes in reporting and not necessarily to higher levels of crime.

The rate of property crime—burglary, arson, theft and auto theft—decreased by 8.4 percent over the 1980–92 period as measured by the UCR.[4]

The National Academy of Sciences Panel on the Understanding and Control of Violent Behavior concluded that greater gun availability leads to an increase in the percent of murders and felonies where guns are used, but does not affect general violence levels. In 1989, some 12,000 people—60 percent of all murder victims in the U.S.—were killed with firearms, and another 70,000 were injured. The risk is especially acute for teenagers and young adults, particularly minorities. The firearm murder rate in 1989 for black males ages 15 to 19 was 105.3 per 100,000 compared to 9.7 per 100,000 for whites in the same age group.[5]

While more murders are being committed with firearms, the murder rate in the U.S., which ranks very high when compared to other industrialized nations, did not fluctuate very much over the past two decades. The murder rate in 1994 was 9.0 per 100,000 people, compared to 9.4 in 1973 and 10.2 in 1980.[6]

Neither the NCVS nor the UCR focus on crimes such as drug possession and trafficking. Yet arrests involving some aspect of illegal drug possession or sales increased by 126 percent from 1980 to 1992;[7] this may be largely due to changes in enforcement priorities, rather than an increase in the number of drug crimes.

Other factors, such as demographics, also complicate the interpretation of crime statistics. Criminologists James Q. Wilson and Richard Herrnstein, authors of *Crime and Human Nature,* argue that "criminal behavior depends as much or more on age as any other demographic characteristic." Almost 60 percent of the people who were arrested and charged with crimes in 1994, for example, were between the ages of 13 and 29.[8] Because the young are high-rate offenders, changes in the proportion of the population that falls within this age group will have an impact on the national crime rate.

Wilson and Herrnstein explain: "Shifts toward a more youthful population, such as during the 'baby boom' years after World War II, would be expected to produce increasing crime rates as the babies grew into adolescence." Current projections indicate there will be a 25 percent increase in the number of teens in the 15 to 19 age range by the year 2005.[9]

A final challenge to understanding crime statistics is that crime rates generally do not rise or fall steadily. Snapshots of trends can be misleading. For example, according to the UCR, the overall crime rate decreased by 2.2 percent from 1980 to 1990, but data from the same source indicate that the overall crime rate increased by 11.8 percent from 1985 to 1990.[10]

Some policy analysts who draw primarily on NCVS data argue that recent declines in the country's crime rate are the result of increases in our imprisonment rate. They maintain that increases in incarceration have caused decreases in the crime rate. But government crime reports are sometimes contradictory and, depending on the reporting techniques, the offense and the time frames selected, it is possible to draw varied conclusions about the impact of the policy decisions of the past decade. In fact, when viewed graphically, historic changes in rates for particular offenses and the increase in incarceration show there is no clear-cut relationship between imprisonment and crime rates.

Despite the complexity of statistical interpretation, a small dip in overall violent crime was noticeable by 1994, with a 3 percent decrease in violent crime nationally compared to the previous year; a decline was even more pronounced in some of the nation's major cities.[11] According to preliminary UCR reports for 1996, the trend was even more pronounced, with record declines in the murder rate in 1996. Overall violent crime decreased 7 percent in 1996: homicides were down 11 percent; robbery, down 8 percent; aggravated assault, down 6 percent; and forcible rape, down 3 percent.[12]

Criminologists continue to debate the reasons for the decline in crime, citing a range of factors, including more aggressive police tactics, community-based programs, gun control laws, stabilization of the drug trade, and more offenders in prisons. Experts are reluctant to predict that the trend is permanent, however, pointing out that the homicide rate among juveniles remains high and that the population of teenagers, those who are in their most crime-prone years, will increase dramatically over the next decade.[13]

One factor contributing to the atmosphere in which public policy is made is media coverage of crime. A study by the Center for Media and Public Affairs found that even though crime rates had remained essentially unchanged between 1992 and 1993, television coverage of crime and violence on the evening news doubled during this period.[14]

Policymakers maintain that they have taken a hard line against lawbreakers in response to the public's fear of crime, although public opinion surveys do not always support this argument. The public and corrections officials agree on the need to imprison violent offenders. However, when citizens are informed about possible alternatives, they often favor a range of sanctions for nonviolent offenders. The findings of a number of public opinion studies have encouraged leaders around the country to take a closer look at alternatives to incarceration.

Mandatory Sentencing

Mandatory sentencing laws require prison terms for certain offenses, and most stipulate a minimum number of years the offender must serve behind bars. Such laws have had an enormous impact on prison populations nationwide, as these examples illustrate:

• All 50 states have established mandatory sentencing laws covering a range of crimes, including violent and gun-related crimes, drug offenses, drunk driving and property theft.[15]

• Thirty-four states have "habitual offender" laws requiring enhanced prison terms for repeat felony offenders, in some cases regardless of the seriousness of the crime.[16]

• Alabama has a two-year minimum sentence for drug sales; five years are added to this sentence if the sale is made within three miles of a school or housing project, and an additional five years is imposed if it occurs within three miles of both. This means an offender could receive a 12-year sentence for selling any amount of drugs almost anywhere in an urban area such as Birmingham.

Such mandatory sentencing laws deny judges their traditional powers of discretion. Judges cannot reduce the term for offenses that carry prescribed mandatory minimum sentences, and they are restricted from imposing alternative sen-

State and Federal Prison Population, 1980–1996

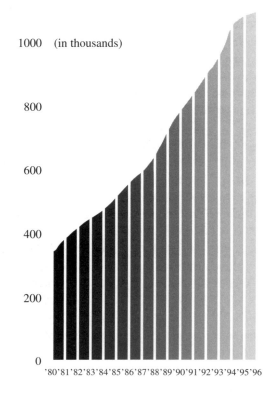

Source: Bureau of Justice Statistics

tences no matter what mitigating circumstances may be involved. In theory, lawmakers enact mandatory sentencing laws so that punishments will be meted out consistently; in practice, however, mandatory sentencing policies have enhanced the significance of the discretionary power of prosecutors who decide what charges to file against defendants.

• A 1994 study by the Department of Justice found that more than one-third of all federal prisoners incarcerated under mandatory laws for drug offenses were considered low-level offenders. These low-level offenders constituted 21 percent of the overall federal prison population.[17]

• Recent research indicates that mandatory sentencing laws have either short-lived or no deterrent effects. A 1992 study of mandatory drug sentencing laws in Delaware showed a significant rise in the prison population, but no reduction in drug arrests, trafficking, or use.[18]

• According to a 1991 U.S. Sentencing Commission study, "A greater proportion of black defendants received sentences at or above the indicated mandatory minimum (67.7 percent), followed by Hispanics (57.1 percent) and whites (54 percent)."[19]

Legislators who pass mandatory laws often do not realize that the decision to increase the penalty for a crime is also a decision to spend millions of additional dollars on corrections. But some legislators are beginning to examine the financial consequences of sentencing laws. In Louisiana, each mandatory sentencing bill must be accompanied by an impact statement that assesses how the bill would affect plea bargaining, jury trials, the prison population and the corrections budget. Such an impact statement allows legislators to make informed judgements about the costs and other effects of a proposed law.

In response to growing concern about the impact of mandatory sentencing, Congress included a "safety valve" provision in the 1994 crime bill to give federal judges greater discretion in sentencing drug offenders who have minor criminal records and no history of violence.[20]

"Three Strikes and You're Out" Laws

Public concern with violent crime has led to citizens' initiatives and legislation in many states for lengthy mandatory sentences, including policies to lock up three-time felons for life without parole. Since 1993, 22 states and the federal government have adopted some form of the "three strikes and you're out" law.

Georgia went further and implemented a "two strikes" law. And California's "three strikes" law has a twist: it provides for doubling of sentences on a second felony conviction.[21]

The expected impact of these laws varies from state to state, depending on how broadly the statutes are written and how they are to be implemented. Much of the impact on prisons won't be seen for 10 to 15 years because most of the offenders sentenced under these provisions would have received lengthy prison terms under prior laws.

In the state of Washington, where such legislation was first passed in 1993, the initial year of the law's implementation resulted in only three dozen prosecutions for a third strike.[22]

In contrast, California is expecting huge increases in its prison population as a result of its "three strikes" law, which requires a sentence of 25 years to life upon conviction of a third felony. The state's Department of Corrections predicts the prison population will grow 70 percent by 1999 resulting in a 256 percent capacity rate. To keep capacity at its current level, the state will have to build 15 new prisons in the next five years at a cost of $4.5 billion. Without new prisons, three inmates will be housed in space designed for one.[23]

Furthermore, since many "third-strike" law defendants feel they have nothing to lose by going to trial, there is far less plea bargaining, resulting in a sharp increase in trial rates; estimates range from 144 percent in Los Angeles County to almost 200 percent in Santa Clara County in the first full year of implementation. Other consequences of fewer plea bargains include increases in jail overcrowding as three-strike defendants awaiting trial occupy limited jail space and the diversion of court resources away from civil cases. In Los Angeles County, it is expected that 60 of the 120 judges handling civil cases will be transferred to criminal cases.[24]

While the California law stipulates that the first two offenses must be violent or serious to implement it, the third strike can be one of 500 felonies.[25] In March 1996, the Center on Juvenile and Criminal Justice reported that more than twice as many marijuana possessors had been sentenced for second and third strikes in California as for murder, rape, and kidnaping combined.[26] In all, 85 percent of those sentenced under the law were convicted of nonviolent offenses as their final strike.[27] For example, Jerry Williams of Redondo Beach, California was convicted of a third strike for stealing a slice of pizza. Because the 27-year-old had two prior robbery convictions, he was sentenced to 25 years to life under the new law.[28]

Longer Prison Terms

Since 1923, the average prison term served nationwide has been about two years, though the length of the average sentence imposed and prison time served varies from state to state.[29] In recent years, however, with the adoption of "truth in sentencing" practices, the length of sentences served by inmates in some states, and particularly by inmates in the federal system, has been increasing.

• Federal drug offenders released in 1992 had served terms 54 percent longer than those of federal drug offenders released in 1985.[30]

• Nationally, inmates released from prison in 1990 had served an average of 22 months, but offenders admitted to prison that year were expected to serve 25 months behind bars, a 14 percent increase.[31]

Many people feel, however, that offenders are serving a lower percentage of their sentence. But reports claiming that prisons now have "revolving doors" and that offenders stay behind bars for shorter and shorter periods are misleading. The figures quoted for average length of stay in prisons are, by definition, for inmates who are released and, therefore, include proportionally fewer inmates serving long sentences. Also as prisons become overcrowded, authorities release inmates with less serious crimes and shorter sentences, often in significant numbers. These early release mechanisms can further skew data on the average length of incarceration.

The Aging Inmate Population

Longer sentences have had some unexpected results. "The long sentences being handed down are building a large number of geriatrics into the penal system," says Anthony Travisono, former executive director of the American Correctional Association. Older inmates are one of the fastest growing segments of the prison population.

• Largely due to the impact of the "three strikes" law in California, it is estimated that within ten years, the number of inmates in the state prison system over age 50 will increase from about 5,000 to 51,000. By the year 2020, it is projected that fully 20 percent of the state's prison population will be over age 50.[32]

• In 1994, federal and state prisons held 27,674 inmates over the age of 55, and 701 inmates over 75 years of age.[33]

With many more inmates growing old in prison due to the nationwide trend toward longer sentences, corrections officials face a new set of challenges. To accommodate an older population, they must provide long-term health care, wheelchair accessible facilities and menus to fit special diets. The estimated average annual expense of medical care and maintenance per inmate over 60 is $69,000, three times the norm.[34]

Anti-Drug Efforts

The nation's war on drugs is a major cause of the increase in our prison population. Almost two-thirds of the $12 billion annual federal anti-drug budget is spent on law enforcement, pulling thousands of drug offenders into the criminal justice system each year.[35] Furthermore, the federal anti-drug budget is just a fraction of state and local anti-drug spending on both law enforcement and criminal justice.

According to the Bureau of Justice Statistics:

• The number of adults in prison nationwide for drug offenses more than tripled from 1986 to 1991.[36]

• Between 1980 and 1994, the number of drug offenders incarcerated in federal prisons rose from 4,749 to 46,499.[37]

• In 1994, 61 percent of all offenders in federal prison were convicted of drug crimes, compared with 45 percent in 1988 and 25 percent in 1980.[38]

• The increase in prisoners sentenced for drug offenses accounted for almost half of the growth of new commitments to state prisons from 1980 to 1992.[39] Many of these inmates are not powerful drug dealers, but low-level drug offenders who sell small quantities of drugs on the street in order to support their own drug habit.

• Offenders convicted of drug crimes are also serving longer sentences. For example, the average time served by drug offenders sentenced to federal prison rose from 22 months in 1986 to almost 33 months by 1992.[40]

Since 1980, much of the growth in the prison population has resulted from a doubling of the number of arrests for drug law violations and a tripling of the rate of incarceration for convicted drug offenders.[41]

Sex Offenders

Increased prosecution and conviction of sex offenders, as well as longer and harsher sentences, have contributed significantly to prison population growth.

From 1988 to 1992, state and federal prisons experienced a 37 percent increase in admissions of sex offenders. The *Corrections Compendium* reported that in 1988 state and federal prisons held some 62,000 sex offenders, which comprised 9.8 percent of the inmate population. In 1992, these facilities had 98,000 sex offenders, accounting for 11.5 percent of the overall population. California, with 16,000 inmates convicted of sex offenses, had the largest group, and North Dakota, with 93, the smallest.[42]

The actual crimes span a wide range of behaviors, including the most violent sexual assaults, rape and child molestation, as well as consensual acts, such as statutory rape, and non-contact offenses such as exhibitionism. While some of these offenders are violent and need to be incarcerated, legislative mandates and judicial decisions often have resulted in longer sentences for all sex-related crimes.

New York Governor George E. Pataki signed an executive order in the spring of 1995 to prohibit all sex offenders from participating in new, highly intensive probation programs for nonviolent felons.[43]

Earlier, Washington State adopted its groundbreaking "sexual predator" law which provides for indefinite confinement of child molesters and rapists deemed too dangerous for release at the end of their court imposed sentences. New Jersey, Wisconsin and Kansas have adopted similar laws.[44]

The Mentally Ill

Local jails, and to some extent prisons, also have been affected by the rising number of people released from facilities for the mentally ill who are now in custody for minor criminal offenses. In his book *Nowhere to Go: The Tragic Odyssey of the Mentally Ill*, psychiatrist E. Fuller Torrey writes that in 1988 there were 100,000 people in jails who required treatment for serious mental illnesses. According to the National Coalition for the Mentally Ill in the Criminal Justice System, there are about 33 percent more mentally ill individuals in jails than in mental hospitals.[45] In addition, 60 percent of those in the juvenile justice system have a diagnosable mental health problem.[46] A California study found that 8 percent of the state prison population had one of four major mental disorders; an additional 17 percent had less severe but serious mental illnesses.[47]

"Jails have become the dumping ground for the mentally ill," Ray Coleman, former president of the American Jail Association, told members of Congress at a briefing in January 1991. "Mentally ill individuals sometimes spend three to four months in jail without a trial for a misdemeanor such as a 'dine-and-dash,' sometimes while judges try without success to get them into a treatment situation. If they were not mentally ill, they'd be released on [their own] recognizance. These individuals are seriously ill. They are not serious criminals."

Tough Parole Policies

Most states have parole boards that may exercise discretionary authority to release prisoners to community supervision after they have served their minimum sentence, for example, eight years of an eight-to-twelve-year sentence. (If inmates serve their maximum term, they are generally released to the community without control or supervision of any kind.) Some states offer time off the minimum for good behavior, further reducing the prison term. But parole boards throughout the country have tightened release criteria, often in response to political pressure. Inmates who would have been paroled in the past are now being held for longer terms, thus contributing to prison growth.

In Virginia, the 1993 gubernatorial campaign was waged and won by George Allen who promised to abolish parole, a pledge that was later made into a state policy. Along with other changes made in the state, this policy is expected to contribute to a doubling of the prison population in ten years as prisoners serve longer sentences. By 1995, 11 states had abolished parole.[48]

In recent years, parolees have been returned to prison in record numbers for violating the conditions of their parole. Violators who test positive for drugs, for example, or who leave town without permission or fail to report to their parole officer often are reincarcerated instead of facing increased supervision in the community or receiving drug treatment, job training or other services to help them comply with their release conditions.

• According to a 1995 report, 40 percent of all parolees in California are returned to prison for technical violations of parole.[49]

• Nationally, from 1980 to 1991, the number of parole violators who were returned to prison quadrupled, increasing from 28,800 to 142,100.[50]

• A study of all prison admissions in 1987, conducted by the National Council on Crime and Delinquency, showed that 15 percent of admissions were for technical violations of parole conditions such as failure to participate in programs, evidence of illegal drug use, or noncompliance with curfews.[51]

• From 1987 to 1991, Oregon tracked parolees being released for the first time and observed that over periods of three years, they were returned to prison at rates ranging from 38.9 percent to 46.7 percent. Approximately half of these were returned for technical violations of parole.[52]

Truth in Sentencing

Truth in sentencing practices have been enacted by states in response to public concern that offenders are often released before their full sentences have been served. The concern is fueled, in part, by the public's misunderstanding of parole release, which gives the impression that offenders are being released from supervision early. In fact, judges establish their sentences knowing that they probably will not be served entirely behind bars but recognizing the importance in many cases of supervising offenders during the initial periods of re-entry to society. In some instances, however, inmates have been released early to make room for other prisoners since space and resources are becoming increasingly scarce, especially when states are under court order to limit prison population growth.

Truth in sentencing usually mandates that the actual sentence served by the inmate is a substantial percentage, often 85 percent, of the maximum time imposed by the sentencing judge. That is a considerable increase from the average 48 percent of a sentence that violent offenders served in 1992.[53]

In adopting truth in sentencing, policymakers must come to grips with the politically sensitive issue of adjusting the lengths of prison sentences or face explosive growth from significantly longer sentences. For example, without truth in sentencing, an offender sentenced to four years for burglary might expect to serve less than half that sentence and then be released on parole. Under truth in sentencing practices, however, that offender would be required to serve perhaps 85 percent of the sentence imposed, or 3.4 years in this case.

The phrase "truth in sentencing" is sometimes used more generically to refer to consistency in sentencing as promoted by sentencing guidelines, which are discussed below.

A Possible Response: Sentencing Guidelines

Sentencing guidelines are another tool for implementing sentencing policy with an emphasis on making punishments for particular crimes more certain. This concept grew out of a general perception that sentencing practices were inconsistent, that the same or similar crimes could result in vastly different punishments. Guidelines set forth clear and uniform standards for punishment that take into consideration the offender's prior criminal record as well as the gravity of the offense and permit a measure of judicial discretion in atypical cases. Punishments include prison, as well as noncustodial penalties. By 1994, guidelines were in use in 14 states and the federal courts.

Guidelines are drafted by or for legislative bodies and generally reflect the philosophical and political leanings of elected officials. Experience with sentencing guidelines demonstrates that these mechanisms can lead to less or more

imprisonment. They simply ensure that whatever policies are chosen by the drafters will be followed by judges fairly closely.

Where policymakers have incorporated into their guidelines concerns about the growth of inmate populations, states have done a better job of controlling prison growth than states where this concern has gone unaddressed. In 1993, North Carolina adopted sentencing guidelines, one goal of which was to control the growth of its prison population. The guidelines target low-risk offenders for community-based punishments where appropriate and ensure that prison space is available for violent offenders. Federal sentencing guidelines, adopted in 1988, on the other hand, do not take prison capacity into consideration and have contributed to the increase in federal inmates.

SOURCES

1. Bureau of Justice Statistics, "Prisoners in 1994," 1995.

2. Bureau of Justice Statistics, "Criminal Victimization in the United States, 1992," October 1993.

3. Federal Bureau of Investigation, *Uniform Crime Reports 1994*, 1995.

4. Federal Bureau of Investigation, *Uniform Crime Reports 1992*, 1993.

5. Jeffrey A. Roth, "Firearms and Violence," National Institute of Justice, February 1994.

6. Federal Bureau of Investigation, *Uniform Crime Reports 1994*, 1995; and the National Center for Health Statistics.

7. Bureau of Justice Statistics, "Drugs and Crime Facts, 1990," 1991; and "Drugs and Crime Facts, 1993," 1994.

8. Federal Bureau of Investigation, *Uniform Crime Reports 1994*, 1995; and the National Center for Health Statistics.

9. Malcolm Cladwell, "Baby Boom's Urban Cradle Braces for Future Rocked by Crime," *Washington Post*, May 26, 1994.

10. Federal Bureau of Investigation, *Uniform Crime Reports 1992*, 1993.

11. Federal Bureau of Investigation, *Uniform Crime Reports 1994*, 1995.

12. "The Complete Preliminary Annual Uniform Crime Report," U.S. Department of Justice, Federal Bureau of Investigation, June 1, 1997.

13. Fox Butterfield, "Homicides Plunge 11 Percent in U.S., F.B.I. Report Says," *New York Times*, June 2, 1997.

14. "Crime Down, Media Coverage Up," *Overcrowded Times*, April 1994.

15. National Council on Crime and Delinquency, "National Assessment of Structured Sentencing Final Report," January 1995.

16. "Why '3 Strikes and You're Out' Won't Reduce Crime," The Sentencing Project, 1994.

17. Department of Justice, "An Analysis of Non-Violent Drug Offenders with Minimal Criminal Histories," February 4, 1994.

18. John P. O'Connell, Jr., "Throwing Away the Key (and State Money)," *Spectrum,* Winter 1995.

19. U.S. Sentencing Commission, *Mandatory Minimum Penalties in the Federal Criminal Justice System*, August 1991.

20. Violent Crime Control and Law Enforcement Act of 1994.

21. Alan Karpelowitz, "Three Strikes Sentencing Legislation Update," National Conference of State Legislatures, November 1994.

22. Jack Hopkins, "Heavy Hitters Not Striking Out," *Seattle Post-Intelligencer,* December 2, 1994.

23. "The Bill Comes Due for 'Three Strikes' Law," *The San Francisco Chronicle,* January 22, 1995.

24. California Legislative Analyst's Office, "The 'Three Strikes and You're Out' Law: A Preliminary Assessment," January 6, 1995.

25. California Legislative Analyst's Office, "The 'Three Strikes and You're Out' Law: A Preliminary Assessment," January 6, 1995.

26. Greg Krikorian, "Wilson Hails Result of '3 Strikes,'" *Los Angeles Times*, March 7, 1996.

27. "Three Strikes Law Targets Pot Smokers," *Wisconsin State Journal,* March 7, 1996.

28. Eric Slater, "Pizza Thief Gets 25 Years to Life," *Los Angeles Times,* March 3, 1995.

29. Bureau of Justice Statistics, "Historical Corrections Statistics in the United States, 1850–1984," December 1986.

30. Bureau of Justice Statistics, "Federal Drug Case Processing, 1985–91," March 1994.

31. Bureau of Justice Statistics, *National Corrections Reporting Program 1992*, October 1994.

32. Philip G. Zimbardo, "Transforming California's Prisons into Expensive Old Age Homes: Enormous Hidden Costs and Consequences for California's Taxpayers," Center for Juvenile and Criminal Justice, November 1994.

33. American Correctional Association, *1995 Directory of Juvenile and Adult Correctional Departments, Institutions, Agencies, and Paroling Authorities,* 1995 .

34. Philip G. Zimbardo, "Transforming California's Prisons into Expensive Old Age Homes: Enormous Hidden Costs and Consequences for California's Taxpayers," Center for Juvenile and Criminal Justice, November 1994.

35. Office of National Drug Control Policy, *National Drug Control Strategy 1994*, 1994.

36. Bureau of Justice Statistics, "Survey of State Prison Inmates, 1991," March 1993.

37. Federal Bureau of Prisons, Office of Research and Evaluation.

38. Federal Bureau of Prisons, Office of Research and Evaluation.

39. Bureau of Justice Statistics, "Prisoners in 1993," 1993.

40. Bureau of Justice Statistics, "Prisoners in 1994," 1995.

41. Bureau of Justice Statistics, "Drugs and Crime Facts, 1990," 1991.

42. CEGA Services, Inc., "Incarcerated Sex Offenders Total Nearly 100,000," *Corrections Compendium,* November 1993.

43. James Dao, "Pataki Bars Sexual Offenders from New Probation Program for Nonviolent Felons," *New York Times*, May 1, 1995.

44. Barry Meier, "'Sexual Predators' Finding Sentence May Last Past Jail," *New York Times*, February 27, 1995.

45. National Coalition for the Mentally Ill in the Criminal Justice System.

46. National Coalition for the Mentally Ill in the Criminal Justice System, "Responding to Mental Health Needs of Youths in the Juvenile Justice System," 1993.

47. Donald Specter, "Mentally Ill in Prison: A Cruel and Unusual Punishment," *Forum*, December 1994.

48. Peggy B. Burke, "Abolishing Parole: Why the Emperor Has No Clothes," American Probation and Parole Association and Association of Paroling Authorities International, 1995.

49. Center for Juvenile and Criminal Justice, 1995.

50. Bureau of Justice Statistics, *Sourcebook of Criminal Justice Statistics—1993*, 1994.

51. James Austin and John Irwin, "Who Goes to Prison?" National Council on Crime and Delinquency, 1990.

52. Oregon Department of Corrections.

53. Bureau of Justice Statistics, "Prison Sentences and Time Served for Violence," 1995.

DISCUSSION QUESTIONS

1. Journalist Ted Gest says the American public may not be as punishment-minded as the politicians seem to think. Dan Morain suggests lawmakers are more interested in appearing tough on crime than on understanding what happens to criminals arriving in prison. Discuss how well you believe the contemporary correctional policy of getting tough on crime (e.g., longer and more frequently imposed prison sentences) accurately reflects the American public's attitude toward criminals.

2. Are the "right" criminals being sent to prison? Several journalists seem to believe we are imprisoning more offenders than we really need to for purposes of public safety. Based on information from William DiMascio's reading, do you agree? What if the purpose for sending people to prison is retribution instead of incapacitation—does it make any difference if the offender is a danger to society in that case?

3. Journalists Julia Cass and Dan Morain write that "People may debate whether prisons should be about rehabilitation, deterrence or incapacitation, but the reality inside looks more like crisis management and damage control" (Cass), and that "Gomez [director of California's Department of Corrections] was left to struggle to keep the system together" (Morain). Discuss how, or even if, prison officials can address policy issues like rehabilitation, deterrence, or incapacitation, when their time must be spent responding to daily crises. Are overcrowded prisons the culprit, or would prison officials have little time for broader questions like the goal of imprisonment even with fewer prisoners?

WEBSITES

www.bop.gov

At the home page for the federal Bureau of Prisons you will find information about the federal prison system and can get the most recent prisoner statistics.

www.corrections.com

From this site you can find interesting information about all aspects of corrections and link to the most important professional organizations in the field (e.g., the American Correctional Association and the American Jail Association).

PART V

OTHER ISSUES

CONTENTS

CHAPTER 13: JUVENILE JUSTICE

Two hundred years ago no distinction was made in the way juveniles and adults were processed in the criminal justice system. As long as the accused had reached the age of criminal responsibility—often age ten—the police, courts, and corrections agencies pretty much handled all cases alike. The situation began to change with the establishment of the nation's first juvenile court in Chicago in 1899. Juveniles were to be viewed as less responsible for their actions and more in need of rehabilitation than punishment. As the twentieth century draws to a close, some have returned to the belief that some juveniles should be subject to the same courts and punishments that adults face. The readings in this chapter consider the issue of how to respond to juvenile offenders.

Fox Butterfield's article provides a brief history of the development of the juvenile court. This reading highlights reasons both for abolishing the juvenile court and for reforming it—it seems that few people favor the status quo. As you read the selection, think about how you believe society should respond to juvenile offenders. In what ways are juveniles and adults different? Should those differences be considered when responding to misbehavior by each?

You may have heard about the Scared Straight program first established at Rahway Prison in New Jersey, based on the common-sense notion that youths who see what prison is really like would avoid any behavior that might get them there. Scared Straight's mission was to scare juveniles into a law-abiding lifestyle by having prisoners show them, in a prison setting, the realities of prison life. Although there is disagreement about the effectiveness of the Scared Straight program, it served as a base from which other "show the realities" programs developed. The reading by Lane Nelson describes a program at the Louisiana State Penitentiary at Angola that uses personal testimonies, skits, one-on-one talks, and group discussions to get young people to understand where their behavior may take them.

Do you think America's problems with delinquency are shared with other countries? The reading by Josine Junger-Tas suggests that delinquency is a widespread problem among Western nations. Of course the fact that a problem is widespread does not reduce its importance. However, the research reported by Junger-Tas also notes that there are similarities in more than just the occurrence of delinquent behavior. Despite cultural differences boys are always more delinquent than girls, and families in all societies play an important role with respect to delinquent behavior. As you read this selection think about why the occurrence and characteristics of delinquency are so similar among Western countries.

READING 27
IS THIS THE END FOR JUVENILE COURTS?

Fox Butterfield

Fox Butterfield uses the Chicago juvenile court system to illustrate why many are calling to restructure, if not abolish, the juvenile court. Overcrowding and insufficient resources have combined to leave the system in chaos and fuel the trend to try juveniles as adults. Butterfield is a New York Times *correspondent and author of the book,* All God's Children: The Bosket Family and the American Tradition of Violence *(1995), a story of violence transmitted through culture and family.*

The nation's juvenile courts, long a troubled backwater of the criminal justice system, have been so overwhelmed by the increase in violent teen-age crime and the breakdown of the family that judges and politicians are debating a solution that was once unthinkable: abolishing the system and trying most minors as adults.

The crisis began building a decade ago, when prosecutors responded to the growth in high-profile youth crime by pushing for the trial of greater numbers of children, dramatically raising caseloads.

But the courts have become so choked that by all accounts they are even less effective than before, with more juveniles prosecuted but fewer convicted and no evidence of a drop in rearrest rates for those who go to prison.

The resulting situation angers people across the political spectrum, from those who believe the juvenile court is too lenient, to those who feel it fails to prevent troubled children from becoming ensnared in a life of crime.

In interviews around the country, judges, probation officers, prosecutors and defense lawyers described a juvenile court system in perhaps the worst chaos of its history.

In Chicago, where the first juvenile court was created in 1899, judges today preside over assembly-line justice, hearing an average of 60 cases a day, about six minutes per case. In New Orleans, public defenders have to represent their poor clients with no office, no telephone, no court records and little chance to discuss the case before trial. In New York, where the [1997] case of Malcolm Shabazz—who admitted setting the fire that killed his grandmother, Malcolm X's widow—focused new attention on Family Court, some officials say it is time to junk the system.

Almost everywhere, with juvenile courts starved for money, record-keeping is so primitive that often the judge, the prosecutor and the defense attorney have different records on the same defendant, making an accurate assessment of the case impossible. And because the courts cannot afford their own warrant squads, young defendants sometimes fail to show up for trial or simply skip out of the courtroom with virtual impunity.

Despite calls for tougher justice, the overcrowding and lack of resources mean that only a small percentage of the young people who move through the juvenile justice system are imprisoned, although there are other forms of punishment, the most common of which is probation.

Of the 1,555,200 delinquency cases referred by the police to prosecutors nationwide in 1994, 855,200, or just over half, resulted in what in adult criminal courts would be called indictments, said Jeffrey Butts, at the National Center for Juvenile Justice. Of these, Butts said, 495,000 defendants were found guilty.

In turn, 141,300 of these cases resulted in a juvenile's being incarcerated. That is 9 percent of those originally sent to prosecutors by the police.

By contrast, in adult criminal court, which is explicitly intended to be punitive, 90 percent to 95 percent of defendants who have been indicted plead guilty in a plea bargain, often as a way to win a lighter punishment. The philosophy of juvenile court traditionally was to rehabilitate rather than punish young offenders, a premise that has come under attack in recent years.

Congress is poised to pass legislation, backed by President Clinton, that would provide federal grants to states that sharply increase the number of young people they try in adult court.

The legislation, already passed by the House and likely to be adopted soon by the Senate, would further undermine the authority of the juvenile court at a time when many specialists predict there will be a new wave of youth crime, as the number of teen-agers increases by 15 percent in the [first] decade [of the 21st century].

"The Family Court is bankrupt," said Peter Reinharz, chief of New York City's juvenile prosecution unit. "It's time to sell everything off and start over."

Reinharz is a longtime critic of the juvenile court, but even its staunchest defenders are now troubled by what they see.

"It is no longer just the chronic problems that have long plagued the court, like overcrowding and making do with less," said Bart Lubow, a senior associate of the Annie E. Casey Foundation who has studied juvenile courts around the nation. "Now there's a crisis of confidence, since the very notion that has been its cornerstone, that

children are different from adults and therefore need to be treated differently, is in question."

Important Issues

Among the issues swirling in the nation's 3,000 juvenile courts are the following:

• As pressure to get tough on young criminals has increased, the number of juveniles arrested who are prosecuted in court has climbed to 55 percent in 1994 from 45 percent in 1985. But the percentage of young people convicted has not kept pace, rising to 33 percent in 1994 from 31 percent a decade earlier.

In Chicago, the figures show an even more dramatic effect of overloading the system. The Cook County state's attorney has increased the number of juveniles he prosecutes to 85 percent of all those sent to him by the police, but about 70 percent of these cases are dismissed for lack of evidence or the failure of witnesses to appear, according to a new study by the Children and Family Justice Center of the Northwestern University School of Law.

"This is the dirty little secret of Cook County," said David Reed, the lead author of the report. "You have lots more cases but almost the same number of judges and prosecutors, and they can only do so much work and prove a certain number guilty. So all these kids are brought in on criminal charges and then most are let go. It fosters cynicism about the court, makes the public and crime victims mad and teaches young people that justice is a joke."

• With an angry public demanding harsher punishments, it is becoming increasingly difficult for judges to differentiate between defendants who may have committed a youthful indiscretion and those who are on their way to a lifetime of crime. The distinction is critical. Almost 60 percent of those teen-agers sent to juvenile court for the first time never return. But every time a young person is sent back to court, his likelihood of being arrested again increases until recidivism rates reach 75 percent by a fifth appearance, said Howard Snyder, of the National Center for Juvenile Justice.

• Despite a rush by legislators in all 50 states

over the past decade to pass laws trying young people in adult court, there is no evidence that being convicted in adult court or sentenced to adult prison is more effective in reducing youth crime than the juvenile justice route. A new study of 5,476 juvenile criminals in Florida, which followed them from their arrest in 1987 through 1994, concluded that those tried as adults committed new crimes sooner after their release from prison, and perpetrated more serious and violent crimes, than those tried as juveniles.

Charles Frazier, a sociology professor at the University of Florida and a co-author of the report, said that keeping young people in the juvenile justice system works better because juvenile institutions provide more education and psychological treatment for inmates, helping offenders rehabilitate themselves. By contrast, adult prisons now are more punitive and have largely abandoned trying to change criminals' behavior.

"Ultimately, you are going to release all these people back into the community, and the juvenile justice system does a better job of reclaiming them," Frazier said.

Juvenile Court

The criticism of the juvenile court misses a fundamental point, some specialists believe. With the breakdown of the family, can any court system, juvenile or adult, do the job society once did: instill discipline and values in children, punish them if they are bad and then help redeem them?

"The juvenile court was set up 100 years ago, in a very different America, to help cure kids of immigrant families with manageable problems, like truancy, petty thefts and fighting," said Jeffrey Fagan, the director of the Center for Violence Research and Prevention at Columbia University.

As envisioned by pioneering social worker Jane Addams, the juvenile court was to be a surrogate parent and the judge a kindly doctor, seeking to understand the social conditions that had led the child astray, the way a doctor would study a disease. This paternalism was reflected in the informality of the courtroom, with the judge sitting at an ordinary table, not behind a bench, and wearing only street clothes, not a robe.

The court's guiding principle was to do what was "in the best interest of the child," not to protect the community or ensure the child's constitutional rights. So punishments were kept light, since children were thought to still be in the process of forming their personalities, and thus more amenable to reform than adults. And all proceedings and records were kept confidential.

An antiseptic nomenclature was even invented to avoid stigmatizing children. A boy was "taken into custody," not arrested. He had a "petition of delinquency" drawn against him, rather than being charged. And there were no convictions, only "adjudications," and no sentences, only "placements."

But today, poverty, joblessness and violent teen-age crime seem far worse than they were in the 1890s, often making the court's customs appear quaintly anachronistic.

Also, as a result, Fagan said, "The juvenile court can no longer do what it was set up to do. It certainly can't do what the public expects it to do, control juvenile crime."

Statistics only hint at the magnitude of the troubles the court is asked to resolve.

Since 1960, the number of delinquency cases handled by juvenile courts nationwide has risen almost four times, to 1.55 million in 1994. During the same period, the number of cases involving abused or neglected children, which are also handled by juvenile courts, has increased five times faster than even the delinquency cases, said Butts of the National Center for Juvenile Justice. And these abused and neglected children are often the very ones who become delinquents.

Among delinquency cases, violent crimes are rising the fastest. From 1985 to 1994, juvenile crimes involving weapons soared 156 percent, murders jumped 144 percent and aggravated assaults were up 134 percent. Property crimes were up 25 percent.

A Case Example

Perhaps the most revealing place to see the troubles is in Chicago, home to the nation's oldest and largest juvenile court. The Chicago court is not the best; that may be in Louisville, Ky., San Jose, Calif., or Oakland, Calif., where the judges command wide respect. Nor is it the most beleaguered; that distinction may belong to Baltimore or New Orleans. Cook County is just a good example of what goes on in a high-volume juvenile court.

A tiny 13-year-old defendant, so short he could barely see Judge William Hibbler seated behind the bench, was on trial for murder.

The defendant—who will remain unidentified in accordance with the court's rules of confidentiality—was wearing an Atlanta Braves baseball jacket, and he looked more like a team mascot than a hardened criminal. But the teen-ager was charged with first-degree murder for shooting a man who was trying to buy crack cocaine.

At an even younger age, he was arrested for armed robbery and burglary, though without being sent to prison. This time, after his arrest for murder, he had been and allowed to return home because the court had failed to give him a hearing within the 36-hour limit specified for juveniles.

While free awaiting trial for murder, he had stolen a car.

Neither his mother nor father was in court. His father had died of alcohol poisoning; his mother, a crack addict, was in a boot camp on a drug charge.

Hibbler, the presiding judge of the delinquency division of the Cook County Juvenile Court, wore a black robe, a small sign of how the court has shifted from its original informality and evolved, in the judge's phrase, into more of a "mini criminal court."

The courtroom is inside the Cook County Juvenile Center, a modern structure a block long and eight stories high that from the outside looks more like an office building than a courthouse with a juvenile jail attached. The building was recently reconstructed as part of an effort to reverse the turmoil overtaking juvenile court.

Inside, however, the waiting rooms are still painted a dingy brown and are jammed with largely black and Hispanic families, with many people holding crying babies. In the men's rooms the toilets are broken and the metal mirrors are scrawled with graffiti.

These dilapidated conditions, said Lubow of the Casey Foundation, "basically say to the families and kids who come to juvenile court that we don't take them seriously, that we value them less as people."

Now, after talking with his lawyer, the youth begrudgingly confessed to murder as part of a plea bargain. Hibbler then solemnly ordered that he "be committed to the Illinois Department of Corrections, Juvenile Division, till 21 years of age."

The boy smirked. He knew he had beaten the system again. He could be free in as little as five years. Without the plea bargain, he could have been transferred to adult court and faced a minimum sentence of 20 years.

It was the kind of case that infuriates conservatives and others, suggesting that juvenile court is little more than a revolving door.

But it was also the kind of case that makes children's rights advocates argue that juvenile court is failing to help young people from troubled families by intervening early enough to prevent them from becoming ensnared in a life of crime.

Even many judges themselves, who are often the only defenders of the juvenile court, concur that the court is foundering. But the judges tend to blame the politicians who have passed laws to try more teen-agers in adult courts.

"There is a crisis," Hibbler acknowledged. But, he contended, "Children don't stop being children just because they commit a crime, and calling for an end of the juvenile court is the same as saying we should do away with grammar schools and junior high schools and just put everyone in college."

Clogging the Courts

In the traditional juvenile court, probation officers played a key role.

They presided at what is still widely called "intake," or arraignment in adult terms. After the police decided which juveniles to send to court—about half were dismissed with the equivalent of a parking ticket—the probation officers would screen out children whose crimes were petty or who had no record. Nationwide, they filtered out about half the cases referred by the police.

But in Chicago in the late 1980s, in response to the epidemic of crack cocaine and the rise of teen-age gun violence, Richard M. Daley, then the Cook County state's attorney, wrestled this power away from the court probation department. To appear tough on crime, he began prosecuting 97 percent of the cases forwarded to him by the police, according to an analysis by the *Chicago Sun-Times*.

Daley is now mayor of Chicago, and that figure is down to 85 percent, the state's attorney's office says.

But Bernardine Dohrn, the director of the Children and Family Justice Center at Northwestern University, said that prosecuting such a high proportion of cases has overwhelmed the court, resulting in about 70 percent of the cases filed by the state's attorney being dropped before trial.

A new study by Ms. Dohrn's center has found that while the number of delinquency cases heard each month has more than tripled in the last decade, the number of convictions has remained almost flat.

"They are clogging the system," Ms. Dohrn said, "and when you do this wholesale, you drive kids into the system who don't belong there, and you don't find the kids who aren't in school and are getting into serious trouble. They are able to pass through for a long time without being stopped. So it's a double whammy, and dangerous."

Probation officers are also supposed to enforce the most commonly used punishment in juvenile court, probation—a court order requiring a young person to go to school or find a job and obey a home curfew the rest of the day.

But no one likes probation: not judges, who want more innovative alternatives, not the offenders, who chafe at the loss of freedom, and not the police or prosecutors, who regard probation as a farce. Worst of all, probation further undercuts the credibility of the court.

For judges, probation is part of a terrible dilemma. "I really have only two major choices," said Glenda Hatchett, the presiding judge of the Fulton County Juvenile Court in Atlanta.

"I can place these kids in incarceration, where they will learn to become better criminals, or I can send them home on probation, back to where they got in trouble in the first place," Hatchett said.

Because governments have always regarded the juvenile court as a "poor stepchild" of the criminal justice system, Hatchett said, there isn't money for the kinds of programs she believes would help, by reaching at-risk children and their parents when the children are 4, 5 or 6 years old.

Shifting Roles: Probation Officers Become Enforcers

Laura Donnelly is a Chicago probation officer with a master's degree in social work.

That makes her part of a vanishing breed, because today more and more probation officers have degrees in criminal justice. The change reflects the transition of the juvenile court from its origins in social welfare, treating the best interests of the child, to a criminal justice agency.

Ms. Donnelly has a caseload of 45 youths whom she visits a few times a month at home, school or at work to make sure they are where they are supposed to be. Three of her clients have disappeared completely. She is confident she could find them, if she had enough time, but she does not.

She could also get a court-ordered arrest warrant, but the juvenile court cannot afford its own warrant squad, and police officers she knows are reluctant to spend time looking for children on warrants, unless the person is arrested on a new charge.

"A lot of officers don't want to waste their time on kiddie court when the judge is going to release the kid anyway," she said.

Ms. Donnelly stopped by a house on Chicago's South Side where one of her clients lived with his grandmother and 13 cousins, since his mother, a crack addict, couldn't be found. A husky 16-year-old, the boy was on probation for selling crack and was confined to his home 24 hours a day unless accompanied by his grandmother.

A charge of auto theft had been dropped when he repeatedly failed to appear for trial and the witnesses in the case tired of going to court without any result. That is a common way for young defendants to win.

Ms. Donnelly reminded the boy that he had another court date in two days, relating to a charge of theft and battery incurred while he was supposed to have been confined to home. He had forgotten about the appearance.

It was another day's work for Ms. Donnelly. "These kids have had nothing but chaos in their lives," she said. "That's what we have to overcome, to give them as much structure and consistency as we can."

"But how," she asked, "do you replace the absence of the family?" Sometimes she thinks the only answer is to move in herself. But she knows that would not work either.

A Move for Change: Young Suspects in Adult Courts

All these troubles have sparked a growing movement to drastically restructure and perhaps abolish the juvenile court.

Leading the charge are conservative politicians who have passed laws in all 50 states allowing juveniles to be tried in adult court and sent to adult prison.

In Illinois, a person under 17 may be tried in adult court for crimes including murder, carjacking and armed robbery as well as possession of drugs or weapons within 1,000 feet of a school or housing project, a provision that disproportionately affects minorities. Illinois also has a version for juveniles of the "three strikes and you're out" law.

Congress [was] poised [in 1997] to pass the most Draconian law yet, with provisions for $1.5 billion in federal grants to states that try larger numbers of young people in adult court and making 14-year-olds subject to trial in federal court if they commit certain felonies.

"It's the end of the juvenile court," said Ira Schwartz, dean of the School of Social Work at the University of Pennsylvania. "All you would have left is a court for larceny." Such a truncated court would not be financially viable and would probably be scrapped, he suggested.

At the same time, some left-wing legal scholars have also called for abolishing the juvenile court, though for very different reasons. Barry Feld, a professor of law at the University of Minnesota, believes that young people often fail to get adequate legal representation in juvenile court and would fare better in adult court, where they would be more likely to be assigned decent lawyers.

Under his plan, as a further protective measure, juveniles in adult court would be given a "youth discount," or lighter sentences, depending on their age.

Some children's advocates who in the past championed the juvenile court have begun urging still another solution—that the court scale back its judicial role and transfer its functions to community groups or social service agencies that would provide better treatment for young people in trouble.

In the rush to try juveniles in adult courts, some critical questions go unasked. For example, are 13- and 14-year-olds really competent to stand trial like adults?

Often such young defendants cannot tell a coherent story to help defend themselves, said Thomas Grisso, a psychiatry professor at the University of Massachusetts Medical Center. What then should the court do? Wait till they are more mature?

As a result of all this ferment, Schwartz said, "What we have right now in the juvenile court is chaos, with every state moving piecemeal on its own." A century after the creation of the juvenile court, he said, "Unless we take it more seriously, what we are headed for is its abolition by default."

ANGOLA'S JUVENILE AWARENESS PROGRAM

Lane Nelson

Lane Nelson summarizes the history of the Juvenile Awareness Program at Louisiana State Prison at Angola and members' efforts—through early intervention and education—to help young people at risk. Nelson is a staff writer for the Angolite, *a magazine produced by inmates at Angola.*

In 1990, Kenneth Hill and a group of his fellow students toured the Louisiana State Penitentiary on a field trip. They saw the execution chamber, the cemetery, and prisoners working in the fields under armed guard. "Some took it seriously, but most of us joked around and had fun," remembered Hill. The group also stopped by KLSP—the prison radio station—where they were lectured by an inmate disc jockey. "He told us about prison life and what goes on here. Then he pointed at me and said: 'You'll be back. You're loaded on drugs right now, I can tell.' I was high," admitted the 24-year-old Jefferson Parish native, "but I denied it because my teachers were there." He paused a few moments before adding, "Sometimes I think I bad-lucked myself by coming on that tour."

Three months later Hill was involved in an after-school fight with youngsters from another neighborhood. The confrontation turned deadly when one teen was shot and killed. Hill was arrested for the shooting, convicted of second degree murder and given life without parole. The

Reprinted, with permission, from Lane Nelson, "In the Loop," *The Angolite*, September/October 1996.

place he joked about six years ago is now his home, forever. "I never dreamed I'd be in this situation," he told a group of juveniles from the Jefferson Parish Diversion Program this past summer. "I had a scholarship to Southern [University] for music. I was like a role model to a lot of the kids at my school."

Now it is Hill who speaks to teenagers that tour Angola. He is part of the 27-member Angola Juvenile Awareness Program (JAP), an administrative-backed operation that reaches out to troubled youths by educating them about the reality of coming to prison. "Some kids we talk to don't listen, like I didn't, and they'll probably end up here, like I have," Hill told the *Angolite*. "But some do listen, I can tell."

JAP has entered the loop of other intervention and diversion services that focus on curbing juvenile crime. It offers a wake-up call for teens making the wrong choices in life. "Most kids don't understand they can be incarcerated in a state prison at the age of 15, 16 years old," said inmate Checo Yancy, JAP's administrative liaison. "And that if they keep making bad choices they'll end up here." Yancy routinely warns groups of youngsters: "While you're on the street," he tells them, "you're the predator. But when you come to prison, you become the prey."

The "Scared Straight" Model

The program is not a first. East Jersey State Prison (formerly Rahway Prison) is cited for the first prisoner-involved juvenile program. That program, profiled in the Oscar-winning documentary *Scared Straight,* started in the mid-1970s. Over twenty years later it is still going strong, with tours booked five days a week. But it has changed to fit the times. Program administrator Lt. Randy Sandkuhl told the *New York Times* earlier this year that the scared-straight tactic doesn't work that well anymore. Kids are harder today and don't scare as easy, Sandkuhl pointed out. While keeping some tough talk and harassing attitudes intact, Jersey's program now incorporates more factual information and statistics.

Before Rahway's nationally recognized Scared Straight performance, the Louisiana State Penitentiary made an attempt in the early '70s to scare juveniles from ending up in prison. The effort was unsuccessful due to lack of outside support.

Problems in Getting a Program Started

Then in 1977, and with the Rahway program setting the pace as a model of efficiency, a second attempt was made. At the request of New Orleans city officials, who sought help with the juvenile crime problem of the '70s, a juvenile program was implemented. Bill Hunter, appointed to the Mayor's Criminal Justice Coordinating Council, contacted *Angolite* editor Wilbert Rideau. Rideau introduced Hunter to Lifers' Association officers Bobby Snead and Monroe Green. Several meetings took place between prison officials, city officials and prisoners. Details were ironed out and a format laid. Afterwards, tours of teenagers were escorted through the prison, insulted, threatened and scared half out of their wits by seasoned convicts. Because the youths made the tour only once, the strategy worked. The acting performances by the prisoners captured the kids' total attention and they could not get on the bus fast enough to leave Angola. "Even the guards were in on it," remembered Rideau. "The whole crew could have won an Academy Award."

The prison diversion program lasted only a few years before it came to an abrupt halt. According to Rideau, the news media sniffed it out. "Reporters and media personalities did stories on the program, and that killed it." Newscasters ex-

plained in their reports that most of what the kids saw was an act. The gig was up. The news stories quickly filtered through the juvenile grapevine, and youngsters who came on tours started to scoff at the threats and insults. Eventually, the program was abolished and a long hiatus occurred where Angola had no administrative-backed program for juveniles.

In 1991, the Lifers' Association and United Methodist Men's Fellowship of Angola decided to resurrect the idea of a program to help juveniles. Prisoners from the two organizations volunteered as members and tossed around ideas. They came up with a two-hour program—one that delivered more information and reality and less scare tactics. External Lifer sponsor, Margaret Chaney, Director of St. Dymphna in Baton Rouge, helped the program get off its feet by bringing one group of Baton Rouge teens to the performance. Although the program went well, Chaney was unable to generate further community interest. Again, lack of outside support crippled the program. But this time JAP was down, but not out.

"After Ms. Chaney brought her group up, we struggled, waiting on other tours of children," said Jewel Spotville, JAP assistant coordinator. "We were hoping that somebody would come see our program. We kept practicing, kept on waiting, kept on praying." JAP's determination and persistence paid off.

In 1992, Governor Edwin Edwards appointed Ronald Bonvillian as parole board chairman. With an eagerness to help prevent crime, Bonvillian spearheaded a project in his parish (St. Martin) to help deal with problem youth. He brought black and white community leaders together to form CAD—Communities Against Drugs. Yet, while CAD was patrolling schools, counseling teens and offering after-school activities, it was missing something. So Bonvillian suggested they bring kids into Angola, to see and feel the reality of prison life.

He approached inmate members of Angola's Alcoholics Anonymous Sober Group (AA). They tried to get something going, but prison politics quickly entered the picture. "There was some animosity between the two clubs," Bonvillian recalled, speaking of AA and the Lifers' Association. "I understood it and tried to work with AA, but the warden said, 'I'm going to allow this and not that.' I had to leave it up to Warden John P. Whitley, who was over Angola at the time."

"The Administration would not allow AA to start a juvenile program because the Lifers already had one," said Rideau. Rideau, who had been working with Bonvillian in his efforts to get kids into Angola, then introduced him to Checo Yancy. "He had no alternative. The Lifers' JAP program was the only game in town," explained Rideau. Yancy, then vice president of the Lifers, came back from his meeting with the parole board chairman and told JAP members to fine-tune their program, that tours were on the way.

The Juvenile Awareness Program

Internal Lifer sponsor and classification officer Tyler Strickland and Legal Programs employee Sergeant "Slim" Rogers helped arrange Bonvillian's first tour. "I'll tell you what, you couldn't hear a pin drop for the whole two hours," recalled Bonvillian. "I was amazed, and so were the adults I brought with me." That first tour in 1993 included more adults than kids. Present were a state senator, state representative, law enforcement officials, city officials, school officials, parents and a few teenagers. "We needed to get the community leaders impressed with JAP," said Bonvillian. "That's why we invited so many adults." The strategy worked. JAP members pulled off a successful program. "What really impressed me," continued Bonvillian, "is after that first tour two or three of the parents came into my business and told me their children said, 'Dad, that's not the place I want to be.' That's when you can say something really happened." According to Bonvillian, over the following year he sent about 2,000 people—adults and kids—to see the program.

After a year of interacting with Bonvillian and CAD, JAP wound up back at square one. CAD weakened from community leaders losing interest, and Bonvillian focused on an unsuccessful campaign for political office.

During the lull, JAP took on another inmate organization sponsor—the Full Gospel Businessmen Fellowship (FGBF). Some FGBF members volunteered to be part of the program, and with more people in JAP came more ideas. Before long, the program extended to four hours.

For nearly a year JAP members worked hard at skits, testimonial presentations and mock question and answer periods. Meanwhile, JAP leaders wrote letters on top of letters to public officials, making them aware of the program. JAP was all dressed up with no one to talk to.

Then in August 1995, and with a new prison administration in control, the polished program was unveiled at an all-day JAP seminar held inside Angola. The adult audience included judges, politicians, law enforcement, social workers, criminal justice experts, assistant district attorneys and members from the attorney general's office. Prior to the seminar, Assistant Warden Sheryl Ranatza made a deal with Yancy: If the seminar was a success JAP would receive the full support of administration and she would encourage and supervise tours. Ranatza liked what she saw and immediately took a strong interest. Warden Burl Cain was also impressed. He told the audience of professionals at the seminar he viewed JAP as a Christian ministry that had his blessings and support. "We have to start caring," Cain said from the podium. "You coming here today, you give these men hope [with their program]. Your presence here shows you care." Because of that seminar, JAP fell into the loop of viable intervention programs working to reach troubled youth.

Targeting Juveniles for the Program

New Orleans federal district court Judge Ginger Berrigan attended the seminar. Afterwards she gave JAP the other needed impetus. "I went back to New Orleans to find out how to target juveniles to come up here for the program," she said. Berrigan went to the Chief Judge of Juvenile Court in New Orleans, who directed her to the Marine Institute, a successful and recognized juvenile intervention program that has 42 bases in several states. "This is a perfect group of kids," she told the *Angolite* on the day of a tour, three months after the seminar. "I was told that these kids have been in trouble more than once, and that this is their last step before LTI (Louisiana Training Institute—now known as Jetson Correction Center for Youth), or before they will be treated as an adult. They are an ideal group for JAP to deal with.

"It cost $500 to charter a bus to bring a group up here," explained Berrigan. "We are going to get the Louisiana Bar Association involved, and different law firms to financially sponsor tours of kids. But for this tour, which we wanted to get off the ground right after the seminar, my husband's law firm donated $250, and I donated the other $250."

Kenneth Brown, Director of Operations for the New Orleans Marine Institute, supervised the teens on the tour. "The main thing I'm dealing with is peer pressure," said Brown, an ex-NFL player for the Buffalo Bills, and former South Carolina prison employee. "These kids get so much negative peer pressure from the streets. They see all these materialistic things drug money can buy, as opposed to working at McDonald's or Burger King." He feels the positive peer pressure offered by JAP members is a plus. He also noticed how his kids were impacted by the sight and sound of men who have been locked up for 20 years or more, or by a young man just beginning a life sentence.

Brown said he knows prisoners; knows when they're running a game and when they're serious about producing a positive program. "As a corrections officer I've done everything from working in living quarters, supervising inmates and officers, and working with the extraction team. I was also a senior member of the riot team and worked 15–20 riots in my ten-year period. So I'm pretty much down with the way everything functions inside. . . . JAP is a good program."

In May of 1996 New Orleans Councilman Roy Glapion brought a group of inner-city youngsters to JAP. "One of the main reasons I'm here today with these children is to educate them," Glapion told the *Angolite*, "and to provide them with information about incarceration. Most of them don't believe what actually exists. Today we have

the opportunity to share with the Juvenile Awareness Program what the prison is truly about, and not hear it on the street."

Working with the Ouachita Parish District Attorney's Office, parole board member Verdegra Scott routinely uses JAP as an intervention tool for troubled youth in her community. Another parole board member, Ralph Stassi, is getting his parish involved. "We have about 150 kids in the whole parish who are disruptive to other children," said Stassi. "So we just passed a new tax for alternative schools for problem juveniles in Iberville. We're going to style them after the boot camp impact program, but not as intense. Part of the deal will be to use JAP. We are looking forward to that.". . .

The Program's Content

JAP programs consist of personal testimonies by members who talk about how they ended up in prison, dramatic skits that portray real-life situations, talking one-on-one to the kids while eating lunch together, and a group question and answer period. "Ours is not a Scared Straight program," explained Lifer President Nolan James. "We try hard to reach them on an individual basis by talking *to* them, instead of *at* them. JAP tries to show the kids that this tough, hostile, getting high, slinging drugs, wannabe gangsta crap is going to get them killed or a life sentence in Angola. I think we do open many eyes and put some hard cold facts in their minds."

"I feel that JAP is having a positive result on the kids because they begin to look at different conflicts and problems they be having in more than one way," added Ray Henry, inmate pastor of the Full Gospel Businessmen's Fellowship. "I believe they come here with more or less a one-track mind, but the program gives them a general idea of looking at their problems from more than one angle."

One particular skit has youngsters sit up and take notice. Entitled *It Can Happen to You*, the performance portrays a young man, played by JAP member Jeffery Lewis, who is a drug dealer making fast money, wearing fine clothes and jewelry. He gets busted and thinks he can buy his way to freedom. But his fancy lawyer sells him out and he's sentenced to 30 years at hard labor. While selling drugs he had it all—a pretty woman, fancy car, prestige, and a big bank account. Once in Angola his life is reduced to a white jump suit and a six-by-nine-foot cell. His girlfriend doesn't visit him and his friends forget he is even alive. He's all alone. The scenario is all too real, and the kids sense it.

Other JAP skits include *Babies Having Babies, Materialistic Bondage* and *Have You Neglected Your Child Today*. A rap song is also performed. Written and sung by Ronald 'DC' Reynolds, the vibrant words carry a positive message of the violent consequences of packing a gun.

"I'm a living testimony of what can happen if you don't improve your lives," JAP member Joe Woods tells a group of youngsters from the Jefferson Parish Correctional Options program. He pulls a picture from his pocket and gives it to the kids to pass around. The picture shows Woods when he first arrived at Angola, 25 years ago, at the age of 15. The impact hits the youngsters like a freight train. "Think before you act," pleads Woods, "because you can see what happens when you don't. I'm a living witness."

JAP's administrative co-sponsor, Cathy Jett, plays an integral role in the program. She meets each group at the prison front gate, then tours them around the 18,000 acre prison before the program begins. "In my opinion," Jett said, "the one thing that has the biggest effect on the kids is the images that they see while touring the facility: razor-ribbon fences, the sound of the gates closing behind them, the never ending fields scattered with inmates working under armed guards, the lack of space in the cellblocks, the lack of privacy in the dormitories, and the fresh graves at the Point Lookout Annex (prison cemetery). The inmates involved with the program do an outstanding job of answering the kids' questions and reemphasizing that what they have seen on the tour is the result of a life of crime."

"When you toured the prison grounds with Mrs. Jett, I hope you noticed the prison graveyard," inmate Joe Stevenson told a group of teenagers from Jackson, Louisiana. "When you come to Angola, that's where you end up. . . . We don't want you to be scared," continued Stevenson, president of the United Methodist Men's Fellowship. "We want you to relax and be wise. Be attentive and find out what's really happening here." In the group Stevenson spoke to were four juveniles suspected of participating in a gang killing.

A Link in the Loop

"The program works," JAP coordinator Keith Alexander told the *Angolite*. "Not only are we able to touch kids in their lives and stimulate a desire to change, but the kids are willing to take what they learn back to their own communities. They become educators to their peers."

In recognition for the dedicated work and successful programs, Wardens Cain and Ranatza . . . rewarded JAP members with an all-day barbecue. "This is nice and we appreciate it," smiled Kenneth Hill. "But we don't do what we do for the kids and look to be rewarded. We just want to help them not come to prison."

Society is fed up with juvenile crime and has resorted to adult prosecution (in Louisiana a 14-year-old can now be tried as an adult) and harsher sentencing. Yet, prisons have never been the solution to crime. Early intervention has—early intervention and education. JAP offers education on the hard reality of prison life and how easy it is to take the dead-end road. Youngsters feel, see and hear that it can happen to them.

Jett's assistant, Major Damon Branstuder, spoke briefly at a recent tour and opened some eyes: "There was a youngster your age who toured the prison a few years ago. He didn't listen, he didn't care. Now he's sitting on death row, waiting to be executed."

"When each tour arrives, I have the opportunity to board the bus and have first contact with the kids," said Jett. "At the end of each tour, I am fortunate to accompany the group to the front gate. When a kid looks up from his seat and says, 'Thanks for the tour. You'll never see me back here,' I get a great feeling of accomplishment."

JAP is not the single solution by any means, but it is a valuable link in the loop.

READING 29

DELINQUENCY IN OTHER COUNTRIES

Josine Junger-Tas

Josine Junger-Tas compares delinquency rates among Western nations and finds a number of striking similarities (and some marked differences). Junger-Tas is visiting professor of criminology at the University of Lausanne (Switzerland) and visiting research fellow at the University of Leyden (the Netherlands).

Involvement by young people in crime is more similar in Western countries than is commonly recognized. The recent International Self-report Delinquency Study in twelve countries, despite significant methodological differences in various countries, showed that boys in all countries are 2-to-4 times more likely than girls to commit violent offenses, and 1.5-to-2 times as likely to commit property offenses. The peak ages at which offenses are most common are similar in most countries—14–15 for vandalism, 16–17 for property crimes, 18–20 for violent crimes. There are many other similarities (and some marked differences). This article describes the International Survey and summarizes its key findings.

The problems in comparing official crime statistics in different countries are enormous: countries differ in legal definitions of crimes, in how they categorize crimes, in how crime reports are collected, counted, and recorded, and in how police and courts are organized and operate.

Reprinted from Josine Junger-Tas, "Delinquency Similar in Western Countries," *Overcrowded Times*, February 1996, by permission of *Overcrowded Times*.

Valid comparisons cannot be made without uniform crime definitions, a common measuring instrument, and a common research method. This has now been done for victims' reports of crimes they have suffered, in the International Victimization Survey (van Dijk, Mayhew, and Killias 1990: van Dijk and Mayhew 1992) and for self-reported delinquency in the International Self-report Delinquency Study (Junger-Tas, Terlouw, and Klein 1994). . . .

Victimization and Self-Report Studies Compared

There are important differences between the victimization and self-reported offending surveys. First, target groups differ: victimization surveys are typically based on adult random—often national—samples, while self-reports are usually based on youth samples. Victimization surveys only measure personal crimes, while self-reports measure a more extensive range of acts, including so-called victimless crimes. Self-reports give more information on characteristics of offenders. Moreover, self-reports measure both the proportions of people who commit crimes ("prevalence") and the frequency with which individual offenders do so ("frequency"). In this way they improve understanding both of delinquency and its causes.

Victimization surveys, by contrast, probably produce more valid crime rates, so that surveys conducted on a regular basis, such as in the United States, England, and the Netherlands, are valuable barometers of crime trends. The two types of research instruments thus complement both police data and each other.

The International Self-report Delinquency Study (ISRD) began in 1990 with development of a common measuring instrument. The Research and Documentation Centre of the Dutch Ministry of Justice coordinated the effort. Twelve countries participated: Finland, England and Wales, Northern Ireland, the Netherlands, Belgium, Germany, Switzerland, Portugal, Spain, Italy, Greece, the United States, and New Zealand.

The study had three main objectives: to achieve comparability of measures of prevalence and frequency of different types of delinquency; to contribute to understanding of similarities and differences in delinquency; and to contribute to the solution of methodological problems.

Sampling Initially the aim was to obtain national random samples of 14-to-21-year-olds in all twelve countries. Only four obtained sufficient funding to do this: Switzerland, the Netherlands, Portugal, England and Wales. Spain used a large, stratified urban sample. The other participants opted for city samples. The comparisons of national rates are possible only for countries using national random samples.

Several participants—Italy (Genoa, Messina, and Siena), Belgium (Liège), the United States (Omaha, Nebraska) and Finland—worked with school populations. Access is easy and questionnaires can be distributed to groups of students, but school populations suffer from a number of drawbacks. First, the age range is restricted to the age of compulsory education; in most cases this implied an age range of 14–18. Moreover, truants and dropouts, often more delinquent than the average student, are generally not included. Although efforts were made to achieve random selection of schools, there is no way to know how much the absence of dropouts or truants biased the results.

Because, however, participation in surveys is voluntary, such bias also exists in random samples: marginal youth groups are underrepresented in all self-report surveys. Different procedures

are used to solve this problem. Hindelang and his colleagues (1981) combined a random sample and a stratified one. Another possibility is to add specific youth groups to the sample, such as students in special vocational schools and attendants of youth clubs, which was done in Omaha, or subsamples of ethnic minority youth, which was done in the Netherlands and England.

Response The school surveys generally had high response rates—in Belgium, for example, 98 percent. The Finnish study encountered high absenteeism due to exceptionally fine weather when the survey was conducted, resulting in a response rate of 75 percent. Response rates for the random samples were lower. In the Netherlands, response was related to city size: higher in middle-sized (57 percent) and small cities (66 percent) than in the four largest urban centers (52 percent). Overall, the unusually good summer in Europe lowered response rates, because youngsters did not show up at meetings. All in all, however, the response rates were satisfactory.

Data Collection Interviewers were trained and received elaborate written instructions. Except for school samples, where the questionnaires were self-administered, data were collected in face-to-face interviews. In some cases a combination of methods was used, with part of the questionnaire, which covered the list of offenses, being self-administered. As most interviews took place at the respondent's home, this was done to avoid the influence of the presence of others—generally the mother—at the interview.

Survey Instrument The common instrument resulted from negotiations among the participants. A number of compromises were made. For example, a number of offenses in the United States, such as alcohol use and purchase and "status offenses" are not considered offenses in Europe. Other infractions are seldom prosecuted in most countries, such as cannabis use. The decision was taken that only acts considered to be offenses in all participating countries, if committed by an adult, would be part of the definition of delinquency.

The common core instrument covered five groups of variables:

Prevalence and frequency were measured in

several ways. The questions about delinquent acts began "did you *ever . . .*" (lifetime prevalence), followed by "did you do this *last year*" (current prevalence), and *"how many times"* (frequency)?

Circumstances were also measured: did the offender act on his or her own, where did the offense happen, who was the victim?

Social reactions included discovery and reactions by parents or others.

Social and *demographic variables* included age, sex, socioeconomic status, education, family composition, ethnicity, school attendance, and employment.

Theoretical variables related mostly to social control theory. They covered relations with parents, parental supervision, school involvement and performance, attitudes towards school or job, and leisure occupations.

Validity and Reliability Several participants performed reliability tests. They found that reliability—the extent to which the questions adequately represented the behaviors of interest—was quite satisfactory.

Validity, the accuracy and completeness of answers, was a more serious problem. Because the surveys were anonymous, answers could not be checked against official records. Several techniques were used to solve this problem. First, a common delinquency definition was used, excluding status offenses and treating these behaviors as "problem behaviors." Second, filtering questions were asked before going into details of the committed act. Great care was also given to specificity: for example, did the boy "steal the car or did he merely use it for joyriding," or what exactly is meant by "threatening a person." To lessen problems related to lapses or confusion of memory, questions only concerned acts in the preceding twelve months.

Partial validity controls were introduced by several participants. The Dutch and American studies checked results with comparable studies conducted in their respective countries. They found striking similarities in the relative rank-ordering of offenses. The Finnish survey used a qualitative study on self-reported criminal behavior as a comparison.

Preliminary Results

Four studies were based on national random samples and one on a large stratified urban sample. Two studies—Mannheim, Germany, and Belfast, Northern Ireland—used random city samples, and the Athens study was based on a stratified urban sample. Three studies were based on school samples in particular cities—Omaha, Nebraska, Helsinki, Finland, and three Italian cities. Liège, Belgium, used a mixed approach.

Differences in sampling limit the confidence with which conclusions can be drawn. Thus we must be cautious in interpreting the findings. Nonetheless, it is tempting to see what similarities and differences in the volume, nature, and background of delinquency of young people can be shown in all or most of the studies.

Delinquent Behavior Table 1 shows percentages of respondents who reported committing property, violent, and drug crimes. It should be recalled that the delinquency rates do not include status offenses.

A number of patterns stand out. First, rates in the Netherlands and Switzerland—two prosper-

Table 1: Percentage of Respondents Self-Reporting Property, Violent, and Drug Crimes in Preceding 12 Months

National Samples:	Property	Violence	Drugs
Netherlands	29.5%	29.5%	15.5%
England and Wales	16.0	16.0	26.0
Portugal	21.5	29.5	11.5
Switzerland	33.5	29.0	21.0
Spain	20.0	34.5	15.5
City Samples:			
Mannheim, Germany	20.5	21.5	7.0
Belfast, Northern Ireland	25.5	24.0	20.0
Liège, Belgium	27.5	30.0	8.0
Athens, Greece	35.0	52.0	9.0
Omaha, USA*	37.0	35.0	17.5
Genoa, Messina, and Siena, Italy*	16.5	14.0	6.5
Helsinki, Finland*	38.5	34.5	13.0

*School samples

Source: Junger-Tas, Terlouw, and Klein, 1994.

ous countries—are similar. This is also true of Portugal and Spain, countries that share many similarities, although at a somewhat lower level. England is an exception in that the Home Office modified the common core list, changing the wording of some questions and excluding minor thefts from the questionnaire.

Second, the rates do not differ tremendously whatever the sampling method. Mannheim and the Italian cities have somewhat lower rates, while Helsinki and Omaha have higher rates, but the differences are not extreme.

The category of "violence" is somewhat confusing as it covers violence against objects, such as vandalism, and violence against persons. Table 2 shows the prevalence rates of some violent offenses in more detail. The more distinctions one makes, the more variations appear.

Concerning vandalism, the rates do not differ a great deal except for England where young people seem hardly to commit acts of vandalism at all. According to the rates for carrying some sort of weapon—for example, a knife or a baseball bat—this seems to have become a common thing to do for many youths when going to a café or to a disco, with the exception of Belfast and the Italian cities. Group fights seem most frequent in Spain, Omaha, and Helsinki and less so in England, Mannheim, and Belfast. However, beating up someone not belonging to one's family is rare nearly everywhere, with the possible exception of Athens and Omaha. There was also a question on hurting someone with a weapon and these rates are even lower, with England having the highest (1.5 percent) and the Netherlands and Switzerland the lowest (0.5 percent).

England and Switzerland have higher rates of drug use than Portugal, Spain, and Holland. Drug use also seems to be more frequent in Belfast and

Table 2: Percentage of Respondents Self-Reporting Violent Acts in Preceding 12 Months

National Samples:	Vandalism	Carrying Weapon	Group Fights	Beating Up Nonfamily
Netherlands	12.5%	15.5%	10.0%	2.5%
England and Wales	3.5	9.5	6.5	1.5
Portugal	16.0	11.0	11.0	2.5
Switzerland	17.0	11.0	9.0	1.0
Spain	16.5	8.5	17.0	2.5
City Samples:				
Mannheim, Germany	4.5	13.5	4.5	.5
Belfast, Northern Ireland	12.5	6.5	6.0	2.5
Liège, Belgium	13.5	13.5	7.5	3.0
Athens, Greece	54.5	12.5	20.0	6.0
Omaha, USA*	13.5	18.0	15.0	4.5
Genoa, Messina, and Siena, Italy*	7.5	3.5	10.5	2.0
Helsinki, Finland*	19.5	12.5	12.5	1.0

* School samples

Source: Junger-Tas, Terlouw, and Klein, 1994.

in Omaha than in the other cities. In all participating countries, drug use is mainly limited to cannabis, although in England youngsters more often also mention other drugs. There is much similarity in the most frequently reported offenses. These are vandalism, fare evasion, buying or selling stolen goods, driving without a license, fights and riots, carrying a weapon, and cannabis use.

Background Variables and Delinquency

In all countries boys commit more offenses than girls, varying from 1.5-to-2 times as many property offenses and as much drug use to 2-to-4 times as many violent offenses. Shoplifting and fare evasion are committed by as many girls as boys. The more serious and violent the offense, the larger the sex difference.

The findings confirm claims about the universality of the relationship between age and crime. However, there is some variation by crime type: peak age of property crime was 16–17, but it was 14–15 for vandalism and 18–20 for violence. Drug use started later and continued well after adolescence.

Although there was little relationship between education and delinquency, there were indications that the lower the education level the more violent offenses were reported.

Socioeconomic status was not related to reported delinquency in most of the studies. However, the Belfast study found more serious reported offenses in the lower socioeconomic groups. Moreover, delinquency seemed related to income source: youngsters on welfare reported more violent acts and drug use than did employed young people.

All studies showed less delinquent behavior when the relationship with parents was close, finding that both parents are important in this respect. The English survey found that the likelihood of running away from home was four times higher than the norm when there was a disturbed relationship with the mother, but nine times as high when the relationship with the father was disturbed.

Parental supervision is generally a strong predictor of delinquency. The ISRD surveys are no exception: the less supervision, the more delinquent behavior, including alcohol and drug use and status offenses.

Implications

These results are not yet based on comparative analyses—which will be done after combination of the data in one dataset—so any conclusions must be offered with caution. However, common findings lead to the following observations.

1. Among the participants in the ISRD study, considerable similarity was found in delinquency rates and in the nature of the most frequently reported offenses.

2. Drug use is an exception as it does not seem yet to have penetrated as deeply in southern Europe as in western Europe and the United States.

3. There is little difference between the sexes with respect to shoplifting, fare evasion, and status offenses, but serious and violent delinquent acts show large discrepancies.

4. The peak age for property offenses is 16–17, for vandalism 14–15, for violence against the person 18–20. Drug use typically starts late and does not stop at age 21.

5. In several studies, drug use seems related to early school leaving and unemployment.

6. Both the relationship with the mother and with the father appear to be important with respect to delinquent behavior.

7. Parental supervision is a powerful predictor of delinquency in all participating countries.

An important finding is that the similarity of prevalence rates seems independent of the samples drawn. We had not expected such an outcome, which may be explained in two ways. It might suggest that self-report measures are robust, despite differences in sampling, method of administration, and perhaps other not yet measured variables. However, it may also be possible that the method is insensitive to differences in culture or in socioeconomic settings.

Another conclusion is that the "ever" prevalences are quite high, suggesting that committing delinquent acts is part of growing up for Western children. However, "last year" prevalences are much lower. What they indicate is that half to two-thirds of youths aged 14–21 occasionally commit an offense of a not too serious nature in a one-year period.

REFERENCES

Hindelang, M., T. Hirschi, and J. Weis. 1981. *Measuring Delinquency*. Beverly Hills, Calif.: Sage.

Junger-Tas, J., G-J Terlouw, and M.W. Klein. 1994. *Delinquent Behavior Among Young People in the Western World*. Amsterdam/New York: Kugler.

Van Dijk, J.J.M., P. Mayhew, and M. Killias. 1990. *Experiences of Crime in the Western World*. Boston, Mass. and Deventer: Kluwer Law & Taxation.

Van Dijk, J.J.M., and P. Mayhew. 1992. *Criminal Victimization in the Industrialized World*. The Hague: Ministry of Justice.

DISCUSSION QUESTIONS

1. In the Fox Butterfield reading, we are told that the juvenile court was set up to be a surrogate parent and to understand the social conditions that led the child astray. But later in the article we read about a thirteen-year-old defendant in court by himself because his father is dead and his mother is in a prison boot camp. Near the reading's end we hear a probation officer lamenting that "these kids have had nothing but chaos in their lives." Have times and problems confronting juveniles really changed since the juvenile court's origin, or have public attitudes toward juvenile offenders changed?

2. Interestingly, Butterfield notes that it isn't only conservatives who believe juveniles should go before an adult court rather than juvenile court. Some liberals believe that juveniles are better off in adult court because they have more secure legal rights there than they have in juvenile court. Discuss the issue of which court is "best" for the juvenile offender.

3. Discuss whether Angola's Juvenile Awareness Program is likely to change the behavior of its young participants. What aspects of the program do you think would be most effective? How could the program be changed to "reach" those kids who are apparently unaffected?

4. If the research reported by Josine Junger-Tas is valid, does it suggest delinquency is related more to biological development (i.e., it's just part of growing up for humans) than to social situation (i.e., it is influenced by cultural attitudes and environment)? If the study had included juveniles in places like Africa, Latin America, and Asia, would there still have been as much similarity in the occurrence and characteristics of delinquency?

WEBSITES

www.ncjrs.org/ojjhome.htm

The Office of Juvenile Justice and Delinquency Prevention is the premier source of information on all aspects of juvenile justice.

TQD.advanced.org/2640

This is the site for the Teen Court organization in Knox County, Illinois. It includes statistics on cases from that court, hints on establishing a teen court, and interviews with participants.

www.iir.com/nygc.htm

At this site the National Youth Gang Center provides information about gangs and their effect on society.

CHAPTER 14: CRIMINAL JUSTICE IN THE FUTURE

As John Crank points out in the first reading, it is preposterous to suggest that one can predict the future of a social institution like policing—but, as he also says, therein lies the fun! Crank's reading is especially apt in a chapter on the future since he begins with an explanation of what factors should be considered when making predictions. He lists five themes that orient his story about policing in 2010. Particularly interesting is the idea that single and apparently random acts have a far-reaching impact on a system. Does reading of instances of police brutality against citizens make you more supportive of restrictions on the power officers have? Does reading about acts of terrorism or seemingly random violence in public places make you more supportive of increases in the powers of police? Another theme in Crank's selection is that innovation in one era may result in something quite unintended as time passes. He uses the example of community policing to make this point. As you read the article, pay attention to how the original idea of community policing could result in a very different kind of police force than what may have been intended by its proponents in the 1990s.

Crank's reading suggests possible organizational and attitudinal changes in the future. Since the future will undoubtedly bring technological changes as well, the selection from Gabrielle deGroot provides an opportunity to see what is already occurring in that arena. Although she focuses on the uses of new technology in prison settings, several items she mentions may apply to law enforcement and the courts as well. Before reading deGroot's article, take time to come up with your own ideas about how technology can be used or improved. For example, how could technology help prevent prison escapes? How could we better track the location of persons on probation or parole? How could prison officials use technology to find contraband in prison and on prisoners?

POLICING IN THE 21ST CENTURY

John Crank

John Crank's view of the future touches on many vital issues in policing today—among them, community policing, inner city crime, police training, and the war on drugs. Crank, who teaches at Boise State University, has published many articles on the nature and functioning of policing. His primary research area is on the organization and management of police systems.

This essay is on the future of policing. Any such effort is self-evidently preposterous, and therein lies the sheer delight of it. The notion that anyone can hope to predict the future of his or her own life for even the proximate moment, let alone the future of a social institution over the next eighteen years, is pretentious. What I have written here is a story, crafted from what I believe to be current events that may affect the future of policing, but a story nevertheless. My goal has not been to divine the future—I will leave that task for police psychics of the twenty-second century. I have instead attempted to provide the reader with an entertaining and semiplausible story of what might be: a trip through the looking glass of time, as it were.

There are particular themes in this essay. The first one is historical. Thorstein Veblen described history as "mass blind causation." This suggests a process of incremental although unpredictable

Reprinted from John Crank, "The Community-Policing Movement of the Early Twenty-first Century," in *Crime and Justice in the Year 2010*, edited by John Klofas and Stan Stojkovic, by permission of Wadsworth Publishing Company, 1995.

change. In this essay, I have presented education as continuing its current evolution in the policing sector and culminating in a highly esteemed "doctor cop" who does "community wellness."

The second theme is that there are shocks to systems that may change those systems forever. These are one-time events that appear random when they occur and yet have a far-reaching and systemic effect. The riots of the 1960s and the ensuing Crime and Kerner Commissions marked the decline of the police professionalism movement and the beginning of the community-policing movement; they also changed the way in which many people thought about the role of police in society (Mastrofski, 1991). In this essay, two major shocks to the system are introduced as random events that change policing: the Madison Nuke Fizzle and the Ox-Bow Assassinations. The point in introducing these shocks to the system is not simply to provide entertainment, though that is the goal of this essay, but also to suggest the sheer impossibility of divining a future made unpredictable by unanticipated shocks to the system.

The essay provided here is not, however, a purely episodic accounting of a blind future adrift. Human agency affects the course of events, even at the institutional level, though outcomes may not be quite those anticipated or sought by original agents of change. In this essay, the third theme is that particular ideas of community-based policing sought by influential reformers become institutionalized by the year 2010. Yet the impact of these ideas on police organization and behavior occurs in a particular historical matrix, and the results do not come out quite the way intended. Ideas of police-community reciprocity, reorientation of patrol, and area decentralization of command are presented in this regard.

The fourth theme is context. According to this notion, the enterprise of policing occurs in a broader crime-control context, which in turn occurs within a broader political context, and on and on. These are all systems within systems, all turning on their particular historical axis and all affecting one another. The organization or behavior of the police is affected by its broad institutional environment, and analyses of police organization and behavior should take that institutional context into account, whether that context is local and is described by actors in the municipal arena or includes the whole of the institutional environment of policing. Changes in these contexts over the next eighteen years, I believe, will affect police work. This essay thus develops a variety of interesting contexts (edge ghettos, national crime-control mandates) that interact with and affect the police institutional environment.

A final theme is, simply put, that politics really does make for strange bedfellows. Liberal and conservative crime agendas are presented as subtly different, with unanticipated players and stages.

In all, I have presented an image of policing in 2010 that simply could not have been foreseen and that makes perfect sense when viewed in retrospect. If any of this story is borne out with the passage of time, I am sure it will be with different twists and spins from those described here. I hope you enjoy the tale.

"The Community-Policing Movement of the Early Twenty-First Century: What We Learned"*

The return to law and order on the part of the police in this year 2010 is being hailed as a new era of policing in America. This surprising movement, in sharp contrast in legitimacy and role to

*Keynote address at the 2010 annual meeting of the Academy of Criminal Justice Sciences

the community-policing era of the turn of the twenty-first century, is gaining momentum nationally. Reformers recall nostalgically the policing professionalism movement of a century ago as the golden age when police did something about "bad guys, not social problems." Advocates of police reform today, calling the movement the "police neoprofessionalization movement," are hailing the return to the "pure mandate" of law enforcement.

The neoprofessionalism movement is resisted by traditional, highly educated line officers steeped in community-policing (commonly called "com-pol") training and what they call the intuitive, commonsensical com-pol nature of their work. These officers argue that police officers have to be street-level community managers who understand the fundamental social, racial, and ethnic ecologies of their beats, the network of formal and informal community resources available to them, and how to solve complex social and order-maintenance problems on the streets. However, contemporary reformers are, with increasing political support, articulating a more focused law-enforcement police mission than the service and order-maintenance mandate that is practiced by com-pol organizations today.

Before we as an academy jump too fast on the neoprofessionalism bandwagon, I would like to take this time to reflect on policing's past in the hopes that we might gain insight from the mistakes of earlier eras of police reform. What I wish to avoid is the natural tendency toward a reaffirmation of a catechism of police history that presents a sort of internally driven, evolutionary history of policing and instead critically consider the broad context that affected the development of policing into the com-pol style and organization of policing we tend to take for granted today. We need to remember that neoprofessionalism is the latest in a series of reform movements, none of which had much effect on crime or on how street-level officers did their work on a day-to-day basis. Further, the current era of community policing, considered by many to be highly institutionalized today, was itself in its infancy in 1970, only forty years ago. What I wish to do is examine the history of com-pol policing until the present time, from its infancy to 2010, in the hopes that we can gain some sense of where policing has been and the implications of that history for the emerging neoprofessionalism policing movement.

The Era of Community Policing

We are emerging from an era of reform commonly referred to as the "community-policing era." This era emerged from what were perceived to be broad crime-control problems of the 1960s. These problems—big-city riots from 1963 to 1967, public perceptions of sharply increasing crime since the 1930s, and political turmoil brought about by the Vietnam War—were perceived by the public as symptomatic of a fundamental breakdown in social control in general and big-city crime control in particular. The police had failed by many accounts to do much in the way of controlling street crime and disorder associated with these events and, moreover, were implicated as more than a spark factor by the Kerner Commission in the most violent of the 1960s' urban riots.

The Kerner Commission (1967) and the President's Crime Commission (1968) recommend sweeping changes in police-service delivery, changes that oriented police work toward precisely what professionalized departments disdained—reciprocal communication and involvement in the affairs of the community. In these commission reports were sown the seed of the com-pol movement.

Community-based policing emerged as a new theory of police organization and activity, not only for its potential for crime prevention, but also for its seeming potential to alleviate a broad range of social and moral dilemmas overwhelming contemporary urban society. In other words, community policing was an effort by police organizations to regain the legitimacy ceremonially revoked by the Kerner and Crime Commissions. The focus of the community-based policing mandate was in the area of order-maintenance activity, and it provided a new legitimating theory for police organization and activity when traditional justifications

in terms of enforcement-oriented professionalism no longer were seen as legitimate by the public, the courts, and the police themselves.

Community-based policing diffused across the municipal landscape with as much energy as the neoprofessional movement today. The state of Washington, for example, explored a strategy to convert more than fifty municipal and county police agencies in the state to a community-based policing model. Similar support for community-based policing was provided by the National Institute of Justice, with its allocation of a special granting category for research and experimentation on community-based policing. Textbooks and readers on policing in the United States today universally contain sections on community-based policing. Experiments containing community-based elements were conducted in many major cities in the United States by 1995, and by 2000 virtually every municipal department in the United States was "com-poled"—that is, converted to structures, activities, and mandates that made the department look like what community policing was expected to look like. In short, community-based policing rapidly became institutionalized at the end of the last century and during the incipient years of this one.

Astute observers raised many questions about the community-policing movement. As early as the late 1980s, many scholars challenged the image of the watchman and his work, community-based policing. Some challenged the linkage between aggressive order-maintenance patrol practices and the quality of urban life. Others questioned the existence of institutions that represented the interests of or acted as informal systems of control for communities. Positive, rather than negative, relationships were noted between aggressive order-maintenance behavior and victimization. Still others charged that the community-policing movement was a circumlocution whose purpose was to obscure the principal role of police as a mechanism for the distribution of non-negotiable coercive force. Thus, a large body of literature emerged to challenge many facets of community policing. Yet the vigor with which the movement gained momentum through the 1980s made all the dark clouds of criticism seem like will-o'-the-wisps, until the real problems with community-based policing began to emerge.

The Ox-Bow Assassinations

Retrospect often provides a sense of historical inevitability to events that, when they occur, seem like savage and unpredictable shocks to the system. So it was with the critical blow to the community-policing movement, which was called, for obscure historical reasons, the "Ox-Bow Assassinations." A series of execution-style murders of known criminals occurred in Jefferson City over a six-year period, from 2002 to 2008. What confounded many observers was that many of the murdered criminals, apparently aware of their own danger, were traveling with bodyguards when they were killed. A leak to the press revealed, amid a great deal of public controversy, that a special squad within the Jefferson City Police Department was acting as an assassination squad to, in its members' words, "make Jefferson as safe to live in as any rural American community." Jefferson was exceptionally violent, and they argued that they were simply reinforcing the informal norms that governed the city anyway.

At their trial, the officers charged with the assassinations contended that aggressive order maintenance was a part of their training protocol. The use of training protocol was carefully presented by defense counsel using videotapes that officers themselves had made of some of the assassinations. The shocker, as you of course recall, was when the jury found them innocent. Announcing her outrage, the President in 2009 called for a full-blown investigation and appointed the President's Commission on the Investigation of Police Misuse of Community-Based Authority. The commission called for a sweeping reconsideration of police training, oversight, mission, and role. The role of the police, the commission contended, must be law enforcement. Training should not emphasize service and order-maintenance frills, especially in this third consecutive decade of budgetary crises. It is the conclusions of this commission that are providing the impetus for the neoprofessionalism movement today.

The Madison Nuke Fizzle

The second shock to the system was, of course, what we call today the "Madison Nuke Fizzle." In 2004, a caller to the Madison Police Department announced that a terrorist group had hidden a nuclear device in downtown Madison that would detonate in twenty-four hours. Ransom was not mentioned, and efforts to negotiate were not reciprocated by the terrorists. A massive search by the Madison Police Department located a ten-kiloton nuclear device at the last minute, just sitting in the open between two parked cars, but concealed by the deep shadows of the elevated railway overhead. The priming device exploded, killing fourteen police officers and three National Guardsmen. The nuclear device itself had, it turned out, been vandalized and just fizzled out, although some leaking radiation caused a great deal of public fear.

In the next month, the police stopped and searched those automobiles on major roads in the Madison vicinity "that had suspicious people inside," as they said. One of the terrorists was caught and subsequently appealed the search of her vehicle. The Circuit Court established what is now called the "community safety standard"— that is, due-process protections could be superseded in the event that the police were taking into custody any person whom they believed presented a perceived present or potential danger to the community order and safety. The circuit court case provided the basis for the Stocklin Supreme Court decision, in which the Court ruled by a narrow margin that com-pol trained officers could use arrest as a "tool to maintain the community safety and order even if there was not at the time evidence that an arrestee had technically broken the law." The current debate, of course, is whether arrestees for extralegal violations have to be Mirandized, since they technically did not violate any law.

Internal Dynamics

In addition to random shocks to the system, there were inherent problems in community-based policing. The movement, a stepchild of the

1960s urban riots, always had identity problems. At the outset, it was incomprehensible to the average police officer. Like the poem "Jabberwocky" in *Alice in Wonderland*, there were lots of words that created a nice poem, but none of the words had any denotative meaning. Beyond putting a mechanical hand on the side of the squad car or bike that automatically waved to people on the street, officers spent most of their time doing what they had since the turn of the previous century—covering their asses and dealing with people's everyday problems.

Four areas of innovation in police organizations served as a rallying cry for the com-pol movement. These were *police-community reciprocity* (the idea that the police must communicate a general feeling that the public has something to contribute to the enterprise of policing), *area decentralization of command* (a phrase loosely referring to geographical decentralization of decision-making authority), *reorientation of patrol* (a movement to foot patrol), and *civilianization*, that is, using civilians to perform tasks traditionally reserved for sworn officers. The first three of these goals were realized, but only with twists unexpected by community-policing advocates at the outset of the com-pol movement.

Reorientation of Patrol

During this era, police officers changed their style of service delivery. They returned to walking the beat. This was accompanied by a great deal of public fanfare and often led to celebrated events. Municipal governments were glad for any method of offsetting the tremendous expense of automobiles, especially after the gas tax was put into place and gasoline prices rose to four dollars a gallon. Moreover, citizens enjoyed the easy banter and the visible presence of police officers, especially the relatively prestigious doctor cops. Return to a walking beat thus was a natural move for big city police.

A latent consequence of the return to walking beats was a change in the relationship between police and gangs. Initially, when police were assigned to neighborhoods frequented by gangs, they feared victimization and tended to band together in gang neighborhoods and to overreact to perceived threats. And gang members were quick to capitalize on this fear by intimidating and threatening police officers. Yet a surprising thing occurred—"police rap." Police and gang members began to exchange verbal spars as contests of wit, and these sparring contests served to establish a sort of grudging mutual respect between police and gangs. Then a group of police officers called "Boz-man 'n' the Hogs" became famous as rap music stars in 1999. They toured from city to city, rapping to the accompaniment of local gangs. This changed the police-gang relationship. Gangs began to work with police to maintain social control in neighborhoods, facilitating the community-policing mission (though, it should be noted, at the expense of other gangs). In this way, one of the components of police innovation sought by reformers, police-community reciprocity, came about, although not in quite the way intended.

Today, a concern expressed by critics of the neoprofessionalism movement is that current levels of community control, aided and assisted by gangs, might disappear with the return of police with a "pure" (law-and-order) mandate. A second area of patrol innovation was the reorientation to cycle patrols. Bicycle patrols were especially popular in business areas, and the colorfully dressed cycle patrol officers were a hit among the business elite. Many big-city departments initiated or dramatically expanded bicycle patrols with cycle races. By 2010, the idea of a motorized vehicle patrol in high-population-density areas was obsolete.

Rapid Response Penalty Fees

The reorientation of patrol toward foot and bicycle patrol was facilitated by the shift away from the heavy use of rapid-response (911) systems in urban departments. By the mid-1990s, departments were so overwhelmed with pressure to respond to calls for emergency assistance that efforts to reorient patrols into other, potentially more effective crime-control practices initiated in the late 1970s and mid-1980s were abandoned. A few big-city departments at this time put in place a user-fee structure: 911 callers were assessed a nominal user fee, with the charge in proportion to the priority assigned to the call. Needless to say, the idea of a user fee for emergency public calls for assistance was not well received by the public. Opponents contended that they were already paying taxes for the use of municipal services, and that the police were giving callers from wealthy neighborhoods, who could afford to pay higher user fees, a higher priority, thereby providing the wealthy with more and better police protection. The idea of a user fee was subsequently abandoned, but it was replaced by a "penalty fee" whereby individuals who made bogus emergency calls were charged the estimated cost of the police response together with an additional fine. With police departments using their powers derived from the drug wars of the 1990s to confiscate the property of those who failed to pay penalties for 911 misuse, calls for emergency response finally began to drop. By the turn of the century, they were half of what they were in 1990.

Decentralization of Command

Efforts to decentralize the police command structure also had unexpected consequences. No one realized the enormous growth in organizational complexity that would accompany geographical decentralization. The idea of decentralizing police organizations did not reduce the size of bureaucracy, they simply added the dimension of geographic complexity. After Kansas City shifted its command to substations, the entire command structure previously in place in the headquarters was replicated at each substation. In effect, there were fourteen independent Kansas City police organizations complete with organizational chart, personnel system, and command hierarchy. Kansas City replaced three chiefs in four years trying to find someone who had the sheer tenacity and tough-headedness to take over the police organization. Who would have thought in 1992 that Darryl Gates, the bloodied chief of the Los Angeles Police Department, would ever again assume the leadership of a major police organization? Yet he directed that organization so well that he became the darling of the com-pol reformers and later presidential advisor for the "Keep It Down" campaign.

Civilianization as an element of com-pol reform did not occur. The attraction of civilianization had always been cost savings: Why hire relatively expensive gun-toting officers when civilians can be hired to perform tasks that do not require guns? Well, civilians unionized and became expensive. But that was not the worst of it. Probably the death knell to civilianization was the famous public employee strike in 2003. After a prolonged contract dispute, the public employees' union ordered all civilians in police organizations on strike in New Jersey. When the governor ordered the National Guard to take over the work done by the civilians, the union called for a general shutdown of state municipal services. For three weeks, the ability of the state to deliver fundamental services was effectively blocked. Ultimately, under a general order from the governor, all of the striking civilians were fired and replaced by National Guardsmen and auxiliary police until regular sworn officers could be found to replace them. Civilianization as a goal of com-pol reform was effectively abandoned after the strike.

Crime Trends

The community-based policing movement failed to take into account historical and institutional features of the broader context in which policing occurred, and that context had profound effects on police organization and activity. One of the great conundrums of criminal justice history is witnessed here. It will be recalled that, from the 1970s through 1990, crime went steadily down across virtually all offense classifications, yet political leaders from the local to the national level sold a bill of goods called the "crime wave" to the American public. Who can ever forget that poor criminal justice teacher being savagely beaten by his students in 1993 for failing to change their test grade when they all got the question "Is crime going up or down?" wrong?

The reverse situation occurred after 1990, when community policing was in a period of intense institutionalization. At the core of the community-policing mandate was order maintenance and service. Com-pol leadership argued that, according to research over the previous twenty years, crime was going down, and police organizations needed to engage in crime-prevention programs that would keep it down, instead of archaic law-enforcement strategies that had served their purpose in lowering crime through the '70s and '80s but were inappropriate for the current period. "Keep It Down" became the slogan of the day. I still remember the jokes made about the President when she wore a "Keep It Down" button. The federal government, seeking any excuse to cut into service programs in big cities, willingly abandoned the severe social problems to the police. Yet, especially in inner cities, crime was beginning to rise and sharply so for violent crime offense. Thus, like the law-and-order era before it, the community-policing era justified its flawed policies on perfectly misunderstood crime trends.

Big-City Economic Retrenchment

Another contextual element that profoundly affected police activity was the continuing stagnation of big cities. In 1975, who would have foreseen how bad inner cities would become? Few heeded the warning presented by conditions in East St. Louis in the 1980s, where garbage had been piling up on city streets for years for lack of services and where some streets were literally closed to transportation because of huge piles of garbage. The situation was so bad that the city was placed into receivership to pay the fine for litigation resulting from the beating of a jailed inmate by another inmate. Yet there it was. By the year 2000, at least thirty cities and three states were in severe retrenchment. Curiously, this had an anomalous effect on the collection of crime data. UCR data collected in these cities revealed relatively low levels of crime, contributing to the turn-of-the-century myth that crime was going down. Police services were so sharply curtailed in these cities that an image of dramatic reductions in crime was fostered. We now know that crime was, in fact, increasing rapidly in those areas after the 1990s. Of course, victimization data revealed the sharp rise in crime in these areas even though official statistics did not, but no one outside academia ever took victimization data seriously anyway.

The continuing stagnation of the economy contributed to the "edge-slum" phenomenon. A number of writers in the late 1980s were writing about "edge cities," or the shopping and community-service delivery centers that emerged in areas peripheral to city centers. They prospered in areas where bedroom communities grew in the 1950s and 1960s, and they provided all the functional needs for those areas, including centers for city-service delivery. The entrenched recession of the 1990s turned many of these areas into "edge slums," full of largely abandoned buildings, which were occupied primarily by cigarette junkies, and dispensaries for municipal services. Police organizations, decentralizing geographically so that they could "look like" com-pol organizations, found in these edge slums natural communities for community-policing work. They were in areas of concentrated populations, and thus were amenable to foot and bicycle patrol. Property values tended to be low, and departments could frequently acquire free rent for substation space in exchange for keeping a watchful eye on the property. Moreover, crime concentrated in these areas, so police officers won public support when they established beats in these areas. Thus, the edge-slum phenomenon provided a natural sort of geographic dispersal that facilitated the community-police movement.

Percorders

The camcorder revolution of the early 1990s was quickly followed by the "percorder" (personal recorder) revolution. Following a now-obscure event regarding police brutality in Los Angeles in 1991, by 1995 every major department in the United States had added roof-mounted camcorders to their vehicles. However, toward the turn of the century, departments were converting en masse into walking and cycling beats, and the roof-mounted camcorder became obsolete. Its function, recording officer-citizen interactions, was performed by the percorder. The percorder was a video recording device, placed in police officers' tie clips, that provided a visual recording of all interactions involving citizens. Percorder files were kept and periodically monitored by the police dispatcher (with union authorization). When a small multiple-band radio device with its bands modulated by voice command was added to the percorder, the automobile-based two-way radio was virtually eliminated as a communications technology for the police.

Crime-Control Politics

It is said that politics makes for strange bed-fellows. The turn of the century was marked by a shift in the liberal crime-control perspective that would have been incomprehensible a decade previously. Liberals argued that the conservative crime-control argument, that criminality was located in the criminal, was actually a condemnation of the conservative crime-control agenda. Liberals, in a crime-control about-face, contended that the problem with contemporary policy aimed at rehabilitation did not work in large part because many criminals could not be rehabilitated—there were indeed many very bad people out there. This was a profound indictment of conservatives, they contended. Because the conservatives refused to recognize that a hostile social environment breeds criminality, they had allowed a class of criminals to come into being in the inner cities who were extraordinarily dangerous and who could not rehabilitated. The only solution was incapacitation. The indictment of the conservatives was that their policies had been a powerful stimulus to crime, and the only viable policy, incapacitation, was an enormous expense to the system. Thus, the turn of the century saw liberal crime-control advocates espousing incapacitation, and, in doing so, being embraced by that icon of crime control, James Q. Wilson.

Education

Probably the most significant changes in policing during the com-pol era were in the area of police education. The doctor cops, the shift of postgraduate criminal justice education to colleges of education, extension of Peace Officer State Training (POST) into four-year college programs, and the Stocklin decision previously discussed represent profound changes in education during the current era of policing.

The first change of interest was the appearance of street-level police with doctorate degrees. This was a continuation of a historical trend of education among police officers. Surprising, however, was the dramatic improvement in the status of college-educated police associated with the doctor cop. The idea of a doctor cop, because of its metaphorical resonance with the idea of community wellness, provided those with doctoral degrees high status among both community leaders and com-pol reformers.

Historically, college cops were accorded peripheral status, were cited for their cynicism, and were scorned by other police officers. However, this changed dramatically by the turn of the twenty-first century. As in the 1930s, a sustained period of economic hard times had made an increasing number of well-educated persons seek employment with police organizations. The near disappearance of the middle-class job market during the 1980s and 1990s had resulted in a pool of highly educated individuals available for police work. This era, however, differed from the 1930s in that the literate word, in the form of tests, extensive paperwork, POST, computer terminal use, and the sheer quantity of electronic or hard copy information routing invoked by police bureaucracies, was now integral to the performance and recording of police work. Interestingly, "CYA" in this era became the art of paperwork. Noncollege employees simply could not compete. The new elite of the police core became the highly educated. Especially in the era of community policing, when no one had a clear idea of what they were doing, highly educated police—especially doctor cops—were seen as those who could "give good community" (i.e., provide community wellness).

Postgraduate Police Education in Schools of Education

The doctor cop was only one of the ways in which the linkage between the police and educational sectors affected police change during the heyday of the com-pol era, 1990 to 2010. Related institutional development occurred in higher education in many centers of graduate and undergraduate education. The proliferation of M.A.-degree criminal justice programs in the 1970s and 1980s was paralleled by growth in the number of doctoral programs in the next two decades. What could not be foreseen in 1980 but appears inexorable from the vantage of historical retrospect was the shift of graduate-degree criminal justice programs out of liberal arts schools and into colleges of education. By 1988, there were twelve institutions that provided Ph.D.s in criminal justice and two that provided Ed.D.s. By 2010, there were only five Ph.D. programs in criminal justice, but there were eighteen Ed.D. programs in criminal justice.

What marked the shift toward advanced education in colleges of education? The answer was surprisingly simple. Liberal arts has always been an uncomfortable home for application-oriented criminal justice programs. Criminal justice programs were uneasy bedfellows with the liberal arts and humanities components of liberal arts schools, who typically thought of criminal justice programs as the intrusion of politically oriented crime-control activity into the core academic enterprise of freedom to engage in the pursuit of knowledge, even if that pursuit placed one in questionable relationship with the law. Simply, most liberal artisans thought of criminal justice faculty as academic Neanderthals intellectually ill-equipped to understand the foundations and goals of higher education. On the other hand, those criminal justice programs that espoused the pure pursuit of knowledge and sought academic prestige through traditional channels of research and publication were viewed by the criminal justice community as sterile: They contributed nothing to the preparation of individuals for their future work in the field of criminal justice.

The model for service was found in schools of education. A model was already in place in these schools that linked research and publication in higher-education training preparation for practitioner fields and did so in a way that was well received by the professional nonacademic audience in the criminal justice field and was esteemed by colleagues in the university environment. Simply, the purpose of higher education was to train teachers and prepare programs for credentialing, and emphasis in those programs was on heavy service commitment, but it was not as important as in liberal arts colleges that simply had no other way to gauge the relative merit of their faculty. Criminal justice faculty, in these schools, could commit to community, regional, or national service and receive academic recognition by other faculty in the school in which they participated. Thus, it was not surprising that many programs in the early twenty-first century initiated graduate development in criminal justice in colleges of education.

POST Training and Community Policing

Another development in higher education was the continued expansion of Peace Officer State Training (POST) preservice and in-service programs. The enterprise of POST training received a powerful stimulus at the 1997 annual meeting of the Academy of Criminal Justice Sciences, which formally incorporated into a mission statement support for preservice and in-service peace officer training and established a Board of Educators to coordinate national information regarding developments in POST training. By the turn of the century, with this and the parallel development of the doctor cop, many POST training academies were actively recruiting Ed.D.s (in preference to Ph.D.s, who were seen as temperamental) to provide leadership in com-pol training.

By 2010, the advances in education resulted in the most highly educated police force in the world and highly articulated relationships among universities, police training academies, and community-based criminal justice organizations that employed police officers.

In the professionalism era in the early and mid-twentieth century, the police perceived their mandate in terms of law enforcement. In this regard, the police were creatures of the law, and the idea that arrest could occur when the law had not been broken was unthinkable. However, the shift to community policing redefined the legitimacy of the police in terms of community needs rather than in terms of legal code. As police, in the name of order maintenance, operated more and more outside the parameters of the legal code, they were increasingly likely to engage in behavior that was not strictly legal.

The dilemma was this: How could the police do aggressive order-maintenance, community-based policing, especially make arrests to resolve order-maintenance problems, if every time they did so they became the object of expensive litigation? The answer was in legitimizing extralegal enforcement to the courts. This was done ceremonially, through educational credentialing. The police expanded pre- and in-service training in the area of criminal, civil, and constitutional law; in theory and principles of community-based policing; in criminological perspective, cultural awareness, and local, regional, and national history; and in many other related classes. These were called "com-pol" programs, and by being incorporated into a formal training protocol, these programs ceremonially demonstrated to the courts and judges that police officers had the necessary credentials for extralegal aggressive order-maintenance policing. The Supreme Court, in the Stocklin decision, cited the extensive com-pol training of police as the basis for its decision.

As formal com-pol curricula expanded, pre-service training increasingly resembled undergraduate education offered at four-year institutions of higher learning. From 2005 to the present time, an increasing number of police departments have recognized a four-year degree in a criminal justice program as equivalent to com-pol training. Thus, in many states, POST training and a four-year education became the minimum requirements for entry into police work.

The A-Cig Wars

The drug war finally ended shortly after the turn of the century, not because there were any winners or losers, but because the American public was weary of hearing about it. It all ended with a press conference and announcement of victory. Besides, the police were being reluctantly drawn into the new anticrime effort: the cigarette wars. In 1998, formally acknowledging the severe health risk and staggering death toll asso-ciated with the smoking of cigarettes, the Congress of the United States passed a law banning "the importation, manufacture, sale, and use of any tobacco product or tobacco substitute containing tobacco tars or nicotine."

Fortunately, already in place were models for the anticigarette wars—the strategies and tactics used in the drug wars. Unfortunately, they were not very good models and were no more successful in keeping cigarettes away from the American public than they were regarding marijuana, heroin, and cocaine. Although the cigarette czar plied the media with impassioned speeches on the evils of smoking and "a-cig" (anticigarette) units regularly released to the media footage of high-profile multiple-carton busts, cigarette use continued unabated. Some blame the resurgence of organized crime in the United States during this era to the anticigarette laws and the resulting highly prosperous black market. However, the cigarette wars had their excesses. Even the strongest supporters of the anticigarette laws thought the government was going too far when it ordered mandatory drug testing for the presence of nicotine in the blood of all lung cancer patients. Today, many of the neoprofessionalist reformers in this year 2010 are calling for an abandonment or decriminalization of cigarette laws to, as they say, "refocus our efforts on real law-and-order issues."

Lessons of the Com-Pol Era

What is the lesson of this brief overview of the history of policing from 1990 to the present? Police movements come and go, but the real shapers of police organizational behavior are largely beyond the control of the police. Even when fundamental change sought by reformers occurs, it is deflected by historical shocks to the system and modulated by the influence of other institutions at both the local and national level. There is no way that advocates of community-based policing could have foreseen the end result of their reform efforts, even where, in principle, elements of those reform efforts were successful.

There is one final theme in this essay. It is said that the best predictor of the future is the past. So it is here. For all the reform, for all the change in police structure, for all the education, for all the change in criminal code and in technology, line officers are doing basically what they did forty and even one hundred years ago. They act like street-level bureaucrats, they cover their asses from the command hierarchy, they try to protect other officers from public and departmental oversight, and they just generally try to do what they think is right in hostile and potentially dangerous situations. They are well educated today, so they tend to do those things better than they did one hundred years ago. But they still make arrests where nothing else works or where it helps their career, they provide service if it does not take a lot of on-line time, and they generally maintain order as best they can. The institution of policing swirls around them in constant change and variation, yet what they do on a day-to-day basis on the street is largely unaffected.

NEW TECHNOLOGIES FOR CORRECTIONS

Gabrielle de Groot

As the military downsizes, private technology firms have begun catering to the corrections industry. Their products, designed to make it easier to monitor offenders' activities, are becoming more affordable and numerous. Gabrielle de Groot is managing editor of Corrections Today, *a journal for corrections professionals.*

In 1993, prison administrators in California heard rumors of an impending inmate outbreak. The word was out that a handful of inmates had built a tunnel underneath the Lompoc Federal Correctional Institution, and were planning to make a break for freedom.

Special Technologies Laboratories (STL) was called in to investigate. A team from the Santa Barbara–based company arrived on the scene the next day with equipment in hand, and using a new technology called ground penetrating radar (GPR), was able to locate the elusive tunnel, as well as several other escape routes used by inmates in the past.

GPR works much the way the old Geiger counters did, held in the hand and swept across the ground by an operator. Only instead of detecting metal, the GPR system detects changes in ground composition, including voids, such as those created by a tunnel.

If it sounds a bit like science fiction, that may

Reprinted from Gabrielle de Groot, "Hot New Technologies," *Corrections Today*, July 1997, by permission of *Corrections Today*.

be because it is—at least, in part. Officials at Lompoc didn't really have an imminent outbreak at hand. Instead, they had invited STL to the facility to test out their new pulsed radar technology. And it worked well, demonstrating that GPR could be used in a real-life scenario should the occasion ever arise.

In fact, GPR is just one of many hot new technologies being deployed or tested in the corrections field today. Satellite monitoring, heartbeat monitoring, body cavity scanning, the use of smart cards—these are just a few of the applications of the cutting-edge technology under development.

"Ten years ago, there were very few companies that specialized in technology for prisons. We were the forgotten industry," says Larry Cothran, executive officer of the California Department of Corrections' Technology Transfer Committee. "But then the Cold War ended, and all of a sudden, you had a lot of companies trying to convert their military hardware to corrections and law enforcement."

Today, many of these technologies are coming to market—technologies that can save taxpayers millions and improve the safety of inmates and officers.

Perimeter Fencing

Back in 1992, California began installing the first electric fences around its prisons. The fences are lethal, killing anything and anyone that comes into contact with them. At the time, skeptical industry observers said the system would never work, and would never be widely accepted in the field. Today, all of California's 33 prisons are surrounded by electric fencing, and six other states are planning to install them.

The reason is simple: Electric perimeter fences work extraordinarily well. Not only has no one escaped over the fences since they were installed in California, but the fences eliminate the need for 24-hour watchtower surveillance, saving countless man hours. "When you take the men out of the towers, that's five positions per tower and about 12 towers per prison. You can see this is a tremendous savings," Cothran says. "We estimate that we're saving taxpayers $32 million per year, about $1 million per prison."

Heartbeat Monitoring

The weakest security link in any prison has always been the sally port, where trucks unload their supplies and where trash and laundry is taken out of the facility. Over the years, inmates have hidden in loads of trash, old produce, laundry—any possible container that might be exiting the facility.

Today, a company run by former Texas Gov. Mark White is marketing a new technology that can detect the heartbeat of a person hidden in a vehicle. The Advanced Vehicle Interrogation and Notification System (AVIAN)—being marketed by Geo Vox Security—works by identifying the shock wave generated by the beating heart, which couples to any surface the body touches.

"Regardless of the size of the vehicle, if a person is in it, it is moving to the tune of that person's heartbeat," explains Leo LeBaj, program manager of the National Security Program Office at Oakridge National Laboratory, where the system was developed. "The system takes all the frequencies of movement, such as the expansion and contraction of the engine, and rain hitting the roof, and determines if there is a pattern similar to a human heartbeat."

According to the AVIAN web site (http://www.beicomm.com/avian), a potential escapee can be identified less than two minutes after two specialized AVIAN sensors are placed on the vehicle. Prisons can buy the system for $50,000, or lease it for $1,000 per month. If this seems high, LeBaj notes that the average cost of locating and capturing an escaped inmate is estimated at $750,000.

Satellite Monitoring

It's relatively easy to keep track of offenders when they're behind bars, but correctional officers have always had difficulty monitoring offenders placed on home detention, especially those barred from contacting their victims. That's because electronic monitoring works only insofar as the offender follows the rules, reporting in at the designated times and giving the computer the correct codes when called. If an offender leaves home unexpectedly, his ankle bracelet will sound an alarm, but law enforcement officers often have no further way of tracking him.

Until now. Pro Tech Monitoring Inc. of Palm Harbor, Fla., has developed a system to monitor offenders by satellite using cellular technology combined with the federal government's global positioning system of satellites. As with the regular electronic monitoring system, each offender wears an ankle bracelet, but he or she also carries a three-pound portable tracking device (smart box), programmed with information on his or her geographical restrictions. For instance, a sex offender may be forbidden to come within five miles of his victim's home or workplace, or a pedophile may be barred from getting close to a school. A satellite monitors the geographic movements of the offender, either in real time or by transmitting the information to the smart box, for later retrieval. If an offender violates his or her boundaries, the information can be transmitted directly to the police, along with the offender's geographic location. The smart box and the ankle bracelet also squawk loudly when boundaries are breached, alerting potential victims.

"This will put teeth in a judgment, particularly for sex offenders and pedophiles," says Bob Martinez, former Florida governor and president of Pro Tech.

Already, the system is being tested in Lackawanna County, Pa., for domestic violence and sex offender cases. In addition, the Florida Department of Corrections in 1997 awarded Pro Tech a five-year contract to use the system in Florida.

The cost of the program runs from the mid-teens to the low-20s per offender per day. Martinez points out that this cost is still far lower than keeping the offender behind bars.

Smart Cards

If there's anything that correctional administrators hate most, it's the paperwork that goes along with keeping track of each inmate. Every time an inmate receives an aspirin for a headache, or buys toothpaste from the commissary, a prison clerk must record the transaction and file it away.

Now comes the smart card, a plastic card embedded with a computer chip that will store all types of information about an inmate: his or her movements, medical care, commissary purchases, treatment needs, meals eaten—any information at all that pertains to the inmate. Smart card developer Battelle Inc., of Columbus, Ohio, [planned] to test the technology at the Ohio Women's Reformatory in Marion [in 1997], as part of a grant from NIJ, says Steve Morrison, program manager and deputy director of corrections for the National Law Enforcement and Corrections Technology Center in Charleston, S.C. "This is one of the biggest new innovations in corrections technology today," Morrison says. "When it's implemented, this will really reduce the paperwork in prisons—the paperwork and the manpower."

Pulsed Radar

Special Technologies Laboratories is calling its new technology GPR-X—with GPR standing for ground penetrating radar, and X indicating the new generation of technology that GPR represents. GPR transmits energy into the ground, and by measuring the time it takes for that energy to be reflected, it can detect changes in ground material, according to Patricia Lewallen, science supervisor for Special Technologies.

GPR can detect contraband buried in the recreation yard, for instance, or a tunnel being built under the prison. While it hasn't officially been used for these purposes, it was tested at the Lompoc Federal Correctional Institution, and has been used on archaeological digs and to detect hazardous waste.

Because the technology was developed in conjunction with the Department of Energy, it is not for commercial sale. However, prison systems can "borrow" the GPR system, in exchange for paying the travel and labor expenses of the Special Technologies personnel deployed to operate the system, Lewallen says.

More to Come

Still other hot new technologies under development include:
- X-ray body scanners, which test for concealed weapons and contraband hidden in body cavities;
- Non-invasive drug testing, using eye scans and patches placed on the skin;
- A smart gun, which is computer coded so it cannot be fired by anyone other than the registered user (this technology, under development by Sandia Labs, links the gun's trigger mechanism to a bracelet or ring worn by the officer);
- A language translator, for use by law enforcement and correctional officers to communicate with non-native inmates; and
- Walk-through metal detectors that can pinpoint exactly where the metal is.

The development of corrections-specific technology is proceeding at break-neck pace, with new technologies coming online every few months. And as companies compete for corrections business, the cost of the new technology will continue to decline, even as the technology improves. That's good news for corrections.

"The costs are starting to go down," Morrison says. "With the downsizing of the U.S. government, everyone is looking at law enforcement and corrections as the golden goose."

DISCUSSION QUESTIONS

1. Of the many fascinating questions raised by John Crank's reading, those generated by the fictitious Ox-Bow Assassinations and the Madison Nuke Fizzle are good starting points. If your community experienced extremely high rates of crime, is it plausible that it would support the enforcement of "informal norms" by the police as in the Ox-Bow Assassinations? Why or why not? At what point, if it exists, does a community choose to forfeit some of its due-process rights in the interest of safety and stability?

2. Discuss the likelihood that "police-rap," a penalty fee for bogus 911 calls, and doctor cops might actually occur. What would be the impact of each?

3. Discuss Crank's closing comment: "Police movements come and go, but the real shapers of police organizational behavior are largely beyond the control of the police."

4. Gabrielle deGroot's article most accurately falls into the "future is now" category since the technologies she reviews are already possible, though not necessarily in full operation. Which of the technologies she mentions do you believe has the greatest potential for making dramatic changes in corrections? Which are applicable to law enforcement efforts?

5. Elaborate on the technological advancements mentioned by deGroot by suggesting your own "gadgets" for the future.

WEBSITES

www.nlectc.org

This home page of the National Law Enforcement and Corrections Technology Center includes information and links to all kinds of justice technology. You might find current technology to be more elaborate than you had imagined future technology would be.

www.prisons.com

For a look at technology specifically geared toward corrections, check this very interesting site with the motto "Moving Corrections into the 21st Century" proudly displayed on the home page.

CHAPTER 15: CRIMINAL JUSTICE: A GLOBAL PERSPECTIVE

Both crime and criminals increasingly ignore national boundaries. Some people believe that the countries of the world are quickly approaching a time when cooperation among law enforcement, judicial, and corrections agencies will be essential. Can any country afford, for example, to limit police pursuit and investigation to its borders when criminals increasingly have free movement among countries? At present, a network of police, judiciary, and corrections with global jurisdiction is unlikely, but coordinated effort, or harmonization, of the separate agencies of each country is plausible. The readings in this chapter look at several issues linked to global efforts in criminal justice.

The reading by Gary Marx highlights the importance of a global perspective by explaining how geographic borders are less and less relevant to crime. But just because crime is borderless doesn't mean social control is likewise. Before reading Marx's selection think about the kinds of cross-border social control we already have (e.g., border police monitoring people and goods as they come and go across borders), and what types of problems are presented when social control efforts cross national borders.

One can argue that any cooperation among the world's countries on issues of crime control will require each nation to understand the legal system and agencies operating in the other countries. The last two articles show some ways that information can be compiled and shared. Ugljesa Zvekic reports on the use of probation in many countries around the world. What features of American probation do you anticipate will be present in other countries as well?

The reading from Human Rights Watch was chosen from among many problem areas covered in the organization's comprehensive report. This selection, on disciplinary measures in prisons, is not necessarily the most important of all the topics highlighted by Human Rights Watch, but it does provide a good overview of problems in many countries—including the United States.

SOCIAL CONTROL ACROSS BORDERS

Gary T. Marx

The globalization of crime has meant that controlling crime must now take place across borders, and not just within them. This shift in social control may lead to conflicts and complications among governments, cultures, and other organizations. Gary T. Marx is chair of the department of sociology at the University of Colorado, Boulder. He is the author of Undercover: Police Surveillance in America *and co-editor of* Undercover: Police Surveillance in Comparative Perspective.

For understandable reasons, most research on crime and social control focuses on particular geographical areas defined by national, state, and local juridical boundaries. Borders have not been an issue in most studies of police and crime. In the United States, crime, like politics, has traditionally been experienced and defined as a local phenomenon. Until well into the twentieth century, the United States did not even have a significant national police presence and state police were weak as well. Increased nationalization and the strengthening of police was dependent on the growth of large cities and the development of modern means of communication, transportation and commerce. The latter factors continue to further the nationalization, internationalization and even globalization of crime and its control.

In recent decades the topic has become increasingly important and new elements are present. Traditionally if we asked about geographical place and violation, there was usually no distinction between (1) where an offense was carried out; (2) where the damage or harm from it occurred; (3) who had jurisdiction to investigate and prosecute; and (4) the citizenship of the investigator, offender, and victim. These were territorially, not extraterritorially, based and relatively more fixed and clearly defined than they are today. Borders were relevant to crime because of efforts to smuggle goods or persons from one area to another, or because of the movement of fugitives from the area of crime commission to an area where they sought immunity (e.g., Bonnie and Clyde with fast cars that carried them across state lines or the supposed move of Butch Cassidy and the Sundance Kid to South America). But the assumed links between place, crime, control, and national identity have become more complicated.[1] To a greater extent than ever before, crime and control are uncoupled from a common national territory. The interdependent nature of regional and world systems for domestic criminality has become more evident.

In the case of drug trafficking, for example, international interactions are part of a chain that eventually makes possible local violations. Focusing only on the sale of drugs once they arrive in the United States is a partial and narrow response. The internationalization of terrorism has led the United States to pass laws protecting Americans and their property from assault, regardless of where that occurs. The arrival of cyberspace brings the potential for the separation of violation and physical space to new heights. Changes in communication make it possible to silently, invisibly and effortlessly cross physical borders. This is the case for international electronic funds transfers that may involve fraud or money laundering and for a variety of remote computer violations from malicious hacking and the destruction of data via "electronic mail bombs" to the theft, alteration, or sending of prohibited data across borders.[2]

New on-line forms of harassment, defamation, threat, and blackmail are possible when sent through "anonymous remailers." Such actions may not be crimes in both the receiving and sending country. For example, as of 1993 Russia had no laws against money laundering, fraud, or organized crime. Some activities considered illegal in the U.S. are standard legal banking practices elsewhere. In 1994 the United States was a party to 103 bilateral extradition treaties and 13 mutual legal assistance treaties for the exchange of evidence. This number is increasing as is the number of cases. From 1984 to 1992 the total number of extradition and mutual assistance cases handled by the Office of International Affairs of the Justice Department increased from 535 to 2,238 (Snow, [1997]).

National legislation takes greater account of these changes as well. For example, contrary to the modern universalistic emphasis and equal protection of the law, which tends to assume equivalent punishment for equivalent acts, the 1994 Crime Act makes distinctions based on the national status of the victim or offender and the place of the crime. It contains special penalties for crimes against foreign nationals traveling in the United States and the international trafficking in child pornography, prohibits commercial transactions involving stolen firearms that have moved in foreign commerce, and penalizes the use of proceeds from a kidnapping in foreign commerce. There are efforts to prohibit citizens from traveling to other countries to engage in activity that would be a crime if done at home (McDonald, 1995: fn. 3).[3]

As more inclusive political and economic units appear such as the European Economic Community, violations in the poorer countries (for example of farm subsidies in Greece or Portugal) are viewed as an offense against the entire European Community, even if not viewed that way by many of those in the country in question where the offense occurs.

Apart from unilateral efforts by a given country to extend its social control definitions and activities to transnational and even global scales (as with the United States' efforts to internationalize the war on drugs) and increased multilateral (often regional) cooperative efforts, there are also new and strengthened supranational efforts concerned with human rights, the environment, drugs, and terrorism. Within the modern nation-state there is at least a juridical monopoly over whose rules should prevail and who has the right to use force (in both cases, the state). Yet when national borders are crossed (whether through unilateral, joint or supranational means), the answer to these questions is initially unclear and must (if the action is not to be done in secret with the risks attending this) be negotiated.

The new developments noted above accentuate ambiguities involving place of an offense, nationality, and jurisdiction that have been present since the creation of geographical and national borders. They are not dependent upon cyberspace or increased migration. They are highlighted in traditional colonial and disputed border situations (e.g., as between the U.S. government and Native American tribal courts or Israel and the Palestinian authority in Gaza and Jericho). This article is concerned with the changing relations between place, violation, victim, violators, and social control. It offers a broad sociological introduction to the study of social control across borders. It does so by . . . identifying some new elements that may be present when social control crosses borders. . . .

Some Functions and Structures of Cross-Border Social Control

Social control can be viewed as both an activity or function and as an organization. Among the most frequently occurring forms of cross-border social control activity are described below.

"Border policing" that seeks to monitor and control the entrance and exit of persons, goods, and resources from one system to another. Customs agents do this at national borders and points of arrival. But local police often watch at airport, train, and bus stations to see who is arriving and departing. During the dust bowl in the late 1930s when migrants from Oklahoma and Arkansas came west, Los Angeles police were stationed 300 miles away at the California-Arizona state border seeking to exclude persons without sufficient cash.

Unilateral, cross-border interventions on another system's turf for offenders suspected of violating a system's rules, or for victims, witnesses, and evidence relevant to this. This may happen informally (with or without notification), through formal notification and request for permission to act, and/or for cooperation (as with formal arrest and extradition requests).[4]

Border crossings as protective services in which security agents accompany leaders to other areas, or in which police extend the domestic social control function, sometimes in an undercover capacity, by accompanying their citizens across borders to international sporting, political and entertainment events.[5] The emphasis is on the protection, or policing of system members when they are physically beyond the system's geographical territory.

Multilateral (joint) patrols or investigations in which agents of several systems work together. Their activities may take place across their systems or in other unrelated systems. Violations may involve the laws of only one country, be transnational in violating the laws of several (or more) countries, or be broad violations of international law. Whose laws are violated and where the violations occur is somewhat independent of which country or countries investigates. This may involve general policing of contiguous border regions, or cases defined by a particular type of offense (e.g., drugs, weapons, or money laundering).[6] Agents of one system may operate in another with only minimal, or no, notification and cooperation with the host system.

A well-known example in the United States is the "pizza connection" case that involved extensive cooperation between the United States and Italy with arrests and trials in both countries. Such investigations may be *ad hoc* or routinized and involve formal treaties and agreements, or merely informal cooperation.

Operational, supranational organizations that are not simply a cooperative accommodation or blending of distinct systems of control, but which are new organizations with a distinctive mandate to enforce a system of rules which crosses systems. The European Economic Community's anti-fraud unit is an example. Such units may become ever more important through regional and world organizations, as the mobility of violators and the interdependence among systems becomes ever more important. However, they meet much more suspicion and resistance than in the other forms. Global and regional efforts at prohibiting or mandating/facilitating behavior raise many interesting questions and in some ways reflect the pacification, integrating, and legal homogenization processes that accompanied nation building. This phenomena gives a new meaning to the idea of a "the new world order" (Nadelmann, 1993).

Police liaison officials who are formally assigned to another social control system.

Non-operational multinational organizations, such as Interpol and Europol whose purpose it is to exchange information such as on wanted and suspected persons or stolen property (Anderson, 1997 and 1993). This may occur on an informal basis as with contacts among persons in different countries who are acquainted. It may involve requests for surveillance of locations, telephone intercepts and the examination of financial and other records.

Multinational private policing organizations with operational and information exchange functions.

Joint training and sharing of technologies, communications systems, and information among countries having common investigatory goals.

Direction, training, and resources offered by a dominant system to others. In this century the

United States has given extensive aid to police in South (and more recently Central) American countries. In recent years it set up a national police force in Panama and has helped to revamp the police in Haiti. After World War II it helped to rebuild the police of Germany and Japan. The United States' Justice Department has an International Criminal Investigative Training Assistance Program. Equivalent organizations exist in several countries. South African police have given training and resources to various police forces in Africa, and France has a worldwide program of police assistance. While not quite an international arms race, important elements of national competition are present here with respect to both the economic and political interests of the competing countries.

Not surprisingly these efforts may mix with national hegemonic goals and may conflict with the goals of those who receive the assistance. An important goal of some U.S. efforts has been intelligence gathering and the perpetuation of stable anti-communist regimes. The line between domestic policing and national security has been blurred in many such exchanges and assistance has gone to the military rather than to civilian police, or there may both be a meaningful distinction between these. The CIA and military have played an important role in foreign police training. Domestic crime may be labeled political subversion and criminal investigative means used against political dissenters. While it is certainly not the avowed purpose of contemporary U.S. policy to aid repressive dictators in more effectively penetrating civil society, once the training and resources have been delivered, the donor loses control over how they will be used.

While the forms and functions discussed above are analytically distinct, they are often joined in different empirical configurations. For example members of an elite Colombian police commando unit located and killed drug czar Pablo Escobar in an internal operation. Yet they were screened and trained by the CIA and DEA. A CIA tactical analysis team provided them with intelligence information and NSA spy satellites and C-130 reconnaissance planes participated in the search (*Newsweek,* Dec. 12, 1993).

We see in the above example not only the crossing of geographical and national boundaries but the blending of the police, military, and national security functions. In a democratic society such as the United States these have traditionally been kept distinct, and with good reason! Yet with recent changes in technology and strategy and with the weakening of borders they are, if not merging, at least closer than ever before, and in particular contexts overlapping and even integrated into the same system of control. This has been aided by the demise of the Cold War. As good protectors of bureaucratic turf, national security and intelligence agencies have sought to redefine their mission from spies and political intelligence to criminals and criminal intelligence (Turner, 1991). As the overlap between agencies concerned with national security and policing grows, the term re-inventing government takes on an additional meaning.[7]

This shift in intelligence resources in many Western countries may be one factor in the increased attention and concern over international organized crime. Intelligence agency "enforcement entrepreneurs" are generating data on violations and potential violations (e.g., the smuggling of nuclear materials) that mobilize public concern and law enforcement efforts (Marx, 1981, 1988; McDonald, 1995). In this labeling sense authorities may be unwitting causes of the phenomena they are concerned with combating. When anticipatory preventive actions are taken (as with a recent questionable German undercover case involving an effort to purchase nuclear materials) they may also generate the problem.

What's Different When Social Control Crosses Borders?

Social control across borders has some distinctive features, yet it is still social control. From the most general sociological standpoint, rule violation and enforcement raise common questions, regardless of where they occur. Thus whether we are dealing with car theft in Cleveland or international drug trafficking we need to ask questions such as:

• Who makes the rules and through what procedures?

- How much consensus is there on their legitimacy and desirability?
- How are violations and violators identified?
- What sanctions are applied to violators and through what process?
- What rules are intended to direct the actions of those who enforce the rules?
- What formal and informal means are used in law enforcement?
- Who is law enforcement accountable to?

When social control crosses system borders, regardless of whether this involves families, organizations, or states, we confront issues involving internal and external authority (Katz, 1977). These issues clearly go beyond territorial borders as such, although that is our focus here. One characteristic of the modern democratic state is the presence of a secular legal system that applies to all within its confines. In Western democratic societies law enforcement activity within particular jurisdictions is in principle relatively unitary and monolithic. It is subject to the rule of law and to formally defined procedures expressed through bureaucratic organization. Absent special steps, social control across borders is on the average less likely to be as regulated or to show the same degree of rationalization and standardization. It is often more *ad hoc* and episodic in nature. Much cross border control is *de facto* rather than *de jure*. A legal, social, moral, and organizational framework and common policies to regulate law enforcement behavior beyond system boundaries may be lacking, as is even the means for creating this. This absence can of course offer flexibility; but also confusion, inconsistency, inefficiency and abuse. When the ability to use coercion and deception and to deprive citizens of their liberty is at stake, questions of accountability are of the utmost importance.

At a sufficiently abstract level any human system will show commonalities by virtue of being human and being a system. Yet when borders are crossed, new academic and policy issues appear. While social systems are leaky and interdependent, they also are based on boundaries. When a boundary has a legal basis those within it are likely to face common rules with respect to both

what constitutes a violation and what enforcement means are appropriate.[8] While differences are of degree, as we cross the borders of distinctive units, regardless of whether this involves cities, counties, states, special jurisdictions such as those of Native American tribes, or single focus regulatory agencies such as Port Authorities, regions, or nations, new social control issues appear. These may involve conflicts over what the rules should be and how they should be prioritized, what enforcement means are appropriate, and conflicts over culture and resources and between enforcement and other goals. Some of the most important issues present when social control crosses borders that may be present include:

There is likely to be less consensus across borders on what a violation is and on how the law should be interpreted. Apart from a small number of blatantly coercive or deceptive, self-interested actions such as murder or bank robbery, there may be disagreement across borders about whether a given form of behavior is in fact a crime and if so, how serious it is. For example, the Netherlands, which tolerates the use and possession of small amounts of marijuana, differs from surrounding countries such as Germany with no such tolerance.

What one country defines as terrorism, another may define as resistance, or countries may disagree on which groups offer the greatest threat and even what a threat is. For example a Pakistani religious party recently requested that American rock stars be brought to Pakistan for a trial as terrorists. It said, "Michael Jackson and Madonna are the torch bearers of American society, their cultural and social values . . . are destroying humanity" (*Boulder Daily Camera,* February 13, 1995).

National laws may conflict with each other or with international laws (e.g., lack of agreement over how far national boundaries extend into the ocean generate conflicts over fishing rights). Differences in laws and legal culture need to be accommodated or they simply are transgressed.

A nice example of the latter are international child custody disputes. Each year the U.S. State Department works on about 1,000 cases in which a foreign-born parent returns with an American child to his or her homeland. What is kidnapping in the U.S. may be seen as a religious and patriotic act in the country returned to. Not surprisingly countries tend to protect their own nationals and a parent's desire to raise their child at home. The long arm of the law often doesn't reach. This can lead to secret unilateral actions in which kidnapping is met with kidnapping, as an aggrieved parent hires a private agency to do what the state cannot legally do (*New York Times,* September 5, 1994).

The enforcement of rules across geographical borders that are a crime in one country and not another shares much with the crossing of cultural borders within a heterogeneous country. Both sides may experience moral outrage—authorities at the behavior, and the subjects of enforcement at being arrested for doing something that their culture does not define as wrong. One source of this conflict within and between countries is immigration (McDonald, 1997).[9] Of course culture conflicts do not develop only from immigration. Much of the study of deviance has been based on indigenous groups who simply view things differently (e.g., disagreements over drug use, homosexuality, and prostitution). Here the system borders crossed are cultural not geographical. Saudi Arabia and Singapore with their strong emphasis on the needs of the community as against the individual differ markedly from Western democratic nations in that regard.

There is likely to be less consensus across borders on law enforcement priorities and on how and when the law should be applied. For example, in the 1980s the United States' war against drugs focused on cocaine and not on heroin. The enforcement activities the U.S. encouraged in countries such as Belgium reflect that priority, even though in Belgium the problem with addiction was almost exclusively heroin (van Outrive & Cappelle, 1995). The plea bargaining and deals with informers that are common in the U.S. may be seen as illegal, or at least inappropriate, elsewhere. For example, promises of immunity made to transnational violators in return for their cooperation may not be honored by other countries eager to prosecute them for violations done on their territory.

There is likely to be less consensus across borders on what constitutes legal and appropriate enforcement procedures. Standards of evidence may vary as may the degree of discretion and power permitted law enforcement. Wiretap information may be used only with great difficulty, if at all, in some countries. Until recently, undercover means as used in the United States were illegal in many European countries (Fijnaut & Marx, 1995; Nadelmann, 1993). When the situation involves luring a foreign national into an undercover trap for behavior that would not even be a crime in his own country, using means that are prohibited in his country, it is not surprising that the reaction is negative.

A Dutch police official, wary of certain cross-border operations, views the German police as over-eager: "The sense of values of the Dutch police is very different from the German police. And I put it very mildly. With them, the ends justify the means. I have very bad experiences with that, and that's the reason to keep back on certain cases" (Klerks, 1995). With joint investigations there may be competition over who has jurisdiction, who gets the credit for the investigation, who makes the arrests, and who does the prosecution. Agreements that hold in one country, may not be honored in another.

As borders are crossed the likelihood of cultural conflicts and misunderstandings increases. Beyond the law, differences in culture, customs, language, organization, training, and operation and being in unfamiliar contexts may engender problems ranging from misunderstandings, to inefficiency, danger, and conflict. There may be differences in competence and experience and the way that violence and corruption are viewed. It appears for example that French police have more latitude in their use of force than do American police. A concern of U.S. police, particularly in their dealing with police in developing or rapidly changing countries is corruption and the danger of compromising investigations. For example, consider the problem when police or government officials are the target of the investigation, whether as major actors or as their protectors.

Cross-border control is less likely to see a

single governing entity capable of (and interested in) creating and enforcing rules. This absence of coordination as borders are crossed may mean increased logistical needs with respect to protection of agents, communication, and the need for other resources. There is a research need to understand how the ways in which different types of cross-border social control units create mechanisms for setting priorities, determining and coordinating actions and resolving disputes.

The sophistication of some cross-border crime requires multi-agency and multinational task forces. Yet the more complex the investigation, the more that can go wrong and the greater the need to plan for contingencies and the greater the difficulty in doing this. For example operation C-Chase aimed at Colombian drug trafficking and money laundering networks involved a joint investigating team including Customs, IRS, FBI, DEA, plus agencies in other countries. These problems are accentuated when covert means are used (Passas & Goskin, 1995).

The unilateral crossing of geographical borders may introduce conflicts between law enforcement and other goals such as foreign policy. Thus diplomacy and statecraft may value not creating an international incident or avoiding embarrassment to an ally, or tolerate rule breaking as an anti-communist strategy while police see violations that they want to stop and are likely to be offended by being unable to take action against serious violators. Police may also be in conflict with their own and foreign intelligence agencies. Police may seek to see arrests made, while the latter may be against intervention for fear of revealing sources and methods in a trial.

NOTES

1. Of course things are not that simple. Thus, even with the previous high degree of geographical consistency, there are complications, as with those granted immunity or rival jurisdictions. Police may be given permission to break the law in order to enforce it, and diplomatic immunity which is granted under international law, exempts members of diplomatic services from many laws. The tendency to apply a countries' laws to its foreign embassies and military bases, in spite of local law, is another territorially confounding example. In this sense, susceptibility to jurisdiction is something persons carry with them regardless of whether they are within the geographical boundaries of their own country, much as those subject to religious law do not escape it when traveling. In some countries, theological courts exist alongside of those of government, and federal, state, and local laws may of course conflict. Yet within countries there are more likely to be means for resolving these, such as giving priority to federal laws and court appeals to decide jurisdiction.

2. For example, the case of the hackers in Hanover, Germany, who broke into a variety of U.S. systems described in Stoll (1989). Within the U.S., there are cases such as a couple who was found guilty of selling pornography over the Internet from California to a postal inspector in Tennessee, even though the material could be legally sold in California. The pictures existed only as data on a hard drive in a community where they were not illegal, until they were voluntarily taken by the inspector. In another interesting case, a lieutenant in Kentucky received an e-mail tip from Switzerland regarding a child pornography ring in England. After three months of investigation over the Internet (never leaving Kentucky), he sent his results to police in England who arrested the distributor (*U.S. News & World Report,* January 23, 1995).

3. In 1994, Australia was considering criminalizing travel to the Philippines and Thailand for the purposes of sex with minors.

4. A recent example of the informal was the DEA's involvement in the kidnapping of a doctor from Mexico suspected in the killing of DEA agents. In a private deal the agency apparently paid Mexican police to deliver the doctor to them at the border. Formal permission was not requested but there was some cooperation, although it was with the Mexican police acting in a private fashion. This suggests four types worthy of study (informal cooperation; no cooperation; formal cooperation; formal no cooperation).

5. For a description of this by British police concerned with soccer violence, *see* Armstrong & Hobbs (1995).

6. As we move from the interaction of control agents at contiguous borders and those in the field, to the level of formal national contacts, the dynamics change significantly. Some recent international agreements simply formalize informal practice. It is important to view the link between the formal and informal as distinct, somewhat independent levels. Cooperative treaties may never result in actions and the social control across borders has hardly required formal agreements.

7. An interesting comparison is with domestic law enforcement's shifts back and forth between the political and the criminal. In contrast to the CIA's moving into criminal matters, a Senate inquiry into domestic law enforcement reports that through the early 1970s, there was a "relentless expansion of domestic intelligence activity beyond investigation of criminal conduct toward the collection of political intelligence and the launching of secret offensive actions against Americans" (U.S. Congress Select

Committee, 1976:21). Resources were diverted from conventional crime to political intelligence and the policing of politics in response to the civil rights and anti-war movements. As these movements subsided, partly in response to the civil control efforts, new resources and covert capabilities were directed at conventional crime. There was a significant expansion in the use of covert means (informers, infiltrations, electronic surveillance) that are well-suited to political intelligence and to conventional crime. Interesting contrasts are also suggested by the FBI's reform move out of political policing under J. Edgar Hoover in the 1920s to its return to it in the late 1930s and its emphasis upon domestic communism following World War II.

8. This is of course an oversimplification since even within the same country and geographical region, there is likely to be overlap and conflicts between geographical units (cities and counties) or functional units (regulatory agencies). In countries such as the U.S., with its federal system and the endless dialogue and dialectic between local, state, and federal enforcement agencies, border issues have greater salience than in centralized national systems such as France. The clearer the boundaries and the more homogeneous the population, the less relevant are the factors discussed in the subsequent paragraphs.

9. Some examples from a study of police and immigrants in England include conflicts over killing of chickens and the sacrifice of a lamb; a tradition of street life and neighborhood parties to which all are welcome and liquor is sold by the cup without a license; and disciplining children with force. This study also reports elements of a parallel, if informal, legal system which appeared to reproduce parts of the social structure of some Pakistani villages within England. In one case police intervened on behalf of a man who had received a sentence of 50 lashes from a village council in England. We were told of one English policeman who could speak Hindi and was given the power of tribal judge (Marx & Morton, 1978).

REFERENCES

Anderson, Malcolm (1997). "Interpol and the Developing System of International Police Cooperation." In William F. McDonald (ed.) *Crime and Law Enforcement in the Global Village*. Cincinnati, OH: Anderson.

Anderson, M. & M. den Boer (eds.) (1993). *Policing Across National Boundaries*. London: Pinter.

Armstrong, G. & D. Hoobs (1995). "High Tackles and Professional Fouls: The Policing of Soccer Hooliganism." In C. Fijnaut & G. Marx (eds.) *Undercover: Police Surveillance in Comparative Perspective*. The Hague: Kluwer.

Fijnaut, C. & G.T. Marx (eds.) (1995). *Undercover: Police Surveillance in Comparative Perspective*. The Hague: Kluwer.

Katz, J. (1977, Oct.). "Cover-Up and Collective Integrity: On the Natural Antagonisms of Authority Internal and External to Organizations." *Social Problems,* 25(1):3-17.

Klerks, P. (1995). Covert Policing in the Netherlands. In C. Fijnaut & G.T. Marx (eds.) *Undercover: Police Surveillance in Comparative Perspective*. The Hague: Kluwer.

Marx, G.T. (1988). *Undercover: Police Surveillance in America*. Berkeley, CA: University of California.

Marx, G.T. (1981). "Ironies of Social Control." *Social Problems,* 28(3):221–36.

Marx, G.T. & M. Morton (1978). "Police and Minorities in England." *International Annals of Criminology,* 17.

McDonald, W. (1995, Spring). "The Globalization of Criminology: The New Frontier Is the Frontier." *Transnational Organized Crime,* 1(1):1-22.

McDonald, William F. (1997). "Crime and Justice in the Global Village: Towards Global Criminology." In William F. McDonald (ed.) *Crime and Law Enforcement in the Global Village*. Cincinnati, OH: Anderson.

Nadelmann, E.A. (1993). *Cops Across Borders: The Internationalization of U.S. Criminal Law Enforcement*. University Park, PA: Pennsylvania State University Press.

Passas, N. & R. Goskin (1995). In C. Fijnaut & G. Marx (eds.) *Undercover: Police Surveillance in Comparative Perspective*. The Hague: Kluwer.

Snow, Thomas G. (1997). "Competing National and Ethical Interests in the Fight Against Transnational Crime: A U.S. Practitioner's Perspective." In William F. McDonald (ed.) *Crime and Law Enforcement in the Global Village*. Cincinnati, OH: Anderson.

Stoll, C. (1989). *The Cuckoo's Egg: Tracking a Spy Through the Maze of Computer Espionage*. New York, NY: Doubleday.

Turner, S. (1991, Fall). "Intelligence for a New World Order." *Foreign Affairs,* 150-66.

U.S. Congress. Select Committee to Study Governmental Operations with Respect to Intelligence (1976). *Final Report* [Books 1-6]. Washington, DC: U.S. Government Printing Office.

van Outrive, L. & J. Cappelle (1995). "Twenty Years of Undercover Policing in Belgium: The Regulation of a Risky Police Practice." In C. Fijnaut & G.T. Marx (eds.) *Undercover: Police Surveillance in Comparative Perspective*. The Hague: Kluwer.

READING 33
PROBATION IN INTERNATIONAL PERSPECTIVE

Ugljesa Zvekic

A comparison of probation systems around the world reveals variations in the use of probation due to differences in culture, economics, politics, and criminal justice philosophy. Ugljesa Zvekic is deputy director of the United Nations Interregional Crime and Justice Research Institute (UNICRI) in Rome. He is author and editor of many volumes, articles, and UN reports on topics such as alternative policing styles, development and crime, and informal crime control.

Among noncustodial sanctions that involve supervision and control of the offender, the most common is probation. Its history places it in a category of "traditional noncustodial sanctions." Many countries' legal systems recognize probation in one form or another, yet not so many use it. Despite its long history and growing interest in it, probation has been surprisingly under-investigated at the international comparative level, particularly in the developing and non-Western countries (Zvekic 1994).

The dearth of comparative research prompted the Home Office Research and Planning Unit of England and Wales and the United Nations Interregional Crime and Justice Research Institute ("UNICRI") to collaborate on a comparative project. The main part of the project was an empirical study of probation systems in Australia,

Reprinted from Ugljesa Zvekic, "Probation in International Perspective," *Overcrowded Times*, April 1996, by permission of *Overcrowded Times*.

Canada, England and Wales, Hungary, Israel, Japan, Papua New Guinea, the Philippines, Sweden, and Scotland.

Probation round the world has its origin in two distinct legal traditions—the common law systems of the English-speaking countries and the civil law systems that originated in Western Europe—although it is much more established within the common law heritage. The convergence of these two traditions since World War II resulted in the softening of formalism in the civil law tradition and, conversely, the elaboration of statutory bases of probation in the common law tradition. In addition, two other factors influenced the expansion of probation: the widespread acceptance of supervision in juvenile justice systems and the development of positivism in criminology.

The common law/civil law convergence and the interventionist philosophy influenced the world-wide expansion of probation. The limits of the influence of these three processes are evident when one examines the geographical distribution of probation: common law countries, Nordic and Western Europe, and Asia (high formal and operational presence); Africa and recently Eastern Europe (formal but no operational presence); Arab countries and Latin America (low formal and no operational presence).

One fundamental requirement for a noncustodial sanction is its public acceptance. While direct measures of the extent of public approval of probation are not available, the results of the In-

Figure 1: Proportionate Use of Probation Orders and Imprisonment, Selected Countries, 1990

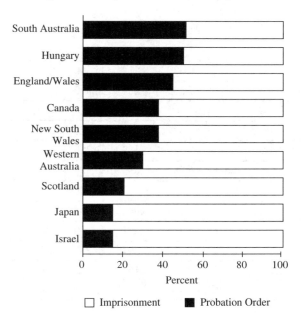

Source: Hamai, K., et al. 1995.

ternational Crime (Victim) Survey regarding attitudes to punishment illustrate certain worldwide trends. Because probation is not found in all of the countries participating in the survey, attitudes towards probation were not directly measured. The most equivalent measures are community service and the suspended sentence, although they should not be taken as direct substitutes for probation (van Dijk, Mayhew, and Killias 1990; van Dijk and Mayhew 1992; Zvekic and Alvazzi del Frate 1995). . . .

The Use of Probation

Table 1 shows numbers of persons sentenced to probation in selected countries in 1980–92. Although comparison of statistics of different countries' criminal justice systems is a hazardous enterprise, in the majority of countries that participated in the probation project, the use of probation is increasing steadily, but not spectacularly. The exception is Papua New Guinea but that is because the probation service began only in 1985 and absolute numbers remain small. Of more significance is Canada where probation numbers, after fluctuat-

ing around 70,000 between 1986 and 1989, rose to 93,000 in 1992. This increase has coincided with economic recession, political sensitivity to prison costs, and a decline in the prison population. In 1991, there were 32,000 fewer probationers than prison sentences but there were 18,000 more in 1992. Japan experienced declines of 43 percent in probation and 30 percent in imprisonment in the decade 1980–1990.

Figure 1 shows proportionate use of probation orders and imprisonment in seven countries (including three Australian states) in 1990. South Australia, England and Wales, and Hungary balance the use of the two, while Japan, Israel, and Scotland make greater use of imprisonment. Notwithstanding the Japanese ideology of "informalism" in dispute processing, the ratio of imprisonment to probation in Japan is higher than one would expect. The 4:1 ratio between prison and probation sits uncomfortably with a view of Japan as a country with a social orientation of nonpunitive character.

The Probation Work Force

Another measure of the potential use of probation is related to the size of the probation system.

Table 2 provides data on probation work forces in 12 countries. Hungary and Papua New Guinea have the smallest probation work forces and Hungary the least favorable rate of population service coverage. Workload is mediated by the types of tasks performed and use of volunteers.

The use of volunteers cannot be divorced from the broader norms and relations of a given social, political, economic, historical, and ideological environment. Expertise-driven probation tends to reveal tensions in the volunteer's role and use in the system. In many countries, volunteers are viewed with suspicion. Canada and England and Wales have no statutory basis for the use of volunteers and no central policies for training, developing, supporting, supervising, or managing them. The situation is different in Japan, Papua New Guinea, and the Philippines, although all differ in terms of volunteers' duties, formal position, and relations with professionals. The largest volunteer work force is in Japan with some 50,000.

Table 1: Numbers of Persons Sentenced to Probation, Selected Countries, 1980–1992

	New South Wales	South Australia	Western Australia	Canada	Hungary	Israel	Japan	Papua New Guinea	The Philippines	Sweden	England/ Wales	Scotland
1980	—	1,411	—	—	—	—	7,989	—	5,577	6,387	33,600	—
1981	—	1,412	—	—	—	1,033	8,197	—	6,629	6,919	35,850	2,573
1982	—	1,354	—	—	—	—	8,101	—	7,883	7,285	36,810	2,573
1983	—	1,430	—	—	—	—	7,709	—	7,469	6,657	37,950	2,601
1984	—	1,505	—	—	—	—	7,487	—	7,627	6,090	40,080	2,813
1985	—	1,354	—	—	—	1,310	7,095	—	7,728	6,183	41,750	2,947
1986	—	1,124	1,836	72,249	3,565	—	6,218	668	6,985	6,535	39,690	2,746
1987	—	1,089	1,936	67,133	4,037	—	6,433	918	5,476	6,497	41,540	2,971
1988	—	1,182	2,086	66,105	7,574	—	5,978	1,262	5,234	6,544	42,440	2,978
1989	—	1,015	1,979	68,475	8,861	—	5,111	1,676	6,317	6,501	43,280	3,435
1990	3,951	1,146	2,255	72,893	7,126	1,505	4,686	1,304	6,670	6,694	46,282	3,771
1991	4,049	1,277	2,475	82,796	8,987	1,566	4,587	1,882	6,517	7,161	45,593	4,086
1992	—	1,295	2,415	93,070	11,908	—	—	2,076	6,927	—	41,369	—

Source: Hamai, K., et al. 1995.

Functions of Probation

Table 3 shows the functions of probation services in various countries. All the probation systems dealt with include, by definition, some form of supervision. Most also have other functions. With the exceptions of Japan and the Philippines, which strictly follow the principle of probation's role starting only after the imposition of sentence, the other systems provide courts with some form of pretrial report. Pretrial investigation gives discretion in the selection and application of eligibility criteria. A certain degree of arbitrariness inevitably is present in social inquiry reports.

At the custody stage, nine of twelve systems use probation officers either to make prerelease assessments or to work with offenders preceding their release from prison. In some systems, as in New South Wales, parole is separate from probation. In others, the two are combined (most recently in Papua New Guinea).

All systems explicitly use supervision after release and in some, such as Australia, Papua New Guinea, and the United Kingdom, it is mandatory.

Trends in Probation

In supervision, the main task of probation officers, three trends appear: from therapy to punishment, from casework to management, and towards social resource management.

The first trend reflects concerns with probation as a soft punishment; by adding punitive elements it is thought that probation will win increased acceptance by the public at large and by decision makers and administrators, and thereby increase its comparative penal value. While there is some overlap in drifts towards punishment and towards management, social resource management is an area in which marked differences in emphasis are evident.

In English-speaking countries, the trend is away from a system of monopoly public service to a contract-based approach: searching for appropriate organizations to fulfill an identified need and directing the clients to other agencies' programs. Analogies can be made to referrals to private prisons and to the growing private security industry.

In the Philippines, a developing country with a

Table 2: Size of Probation Systems in Selected Countries

Country	Size of probation workforce	Population per probation employee
New South Wales	532	11,200
South Australia	184	7,900
Western Australia	224	7,600
Canada	2,750	9,900
Hungary	100	103,100
Israel	170	31,300
Japan	1,440	86,400
Papua New Guinea	88	43,700
The Philippines	1,272	51,600
Sweden	697	12,500
England and Wales	18,500	2,800
Scotland	950	5,400

Source: Hamai, K., et al. 1995.

strong ideology of national development, probation is oriented both to crime and to development. Offenders may accordingly be required to participate in activities geared towards social and environmental improvement. Those guilty of illegally clearing forests or agriculture may be directed to forest conservation work, or those convicted of illegal fishing or coral reef destruction may be trained in sea conservation. Thus not only are jurisdictions' politics and economics relevant to probation activities (e.g., the ex-socialist probation at the workplace), but so are their goals and immediate contexts (commercial contracting on one side and the development of nationhood and civic consciousness on the other).

Conclusions

The complexity of the probation task is such that a unified notion of what constitutes probation is not possible. In much probation around the world, the blurring of care and control is complicated by a zeal to achieve a number of goals including professionalization of the probation service and increasing community involvement. Changes in probation relate to developments of time and place in terms of culture, economics, politics, and criminal justice philosophy. Likewise, probation is affected by efforts to preserve key features as it originated in a jurisdiction and to maintain the professional identity of the probation officer.

One aim of this comparative study was to stress that probation is not a thing to take or leave but a set of ideas and practices, possibilities, and

Table 3: Functions of Probation Services, Selected Countries

	New South Wales	South Australia	Western Australia	Canada	Hungary	Israel	Japan	Papua New Guinea	The Philippines	Sweden	England/ Wales	Scotland
Probation supervision	x	x	x	x	x	x	x	x	x	x	x	x
Pretrial:												
social inquiry report	x	x	x	x	x	x		x		x	x	x
prebail assessment	x	x				x					x	x
bail supervision	x		x	x				x				
pretrial counselling								x				
During custody:												
prerelease assessment		x		x		x	x		x		x	x
preparation for release		x	x		x		x				x	x
Postrelease:												
supervision of offenders after release	x	x	x		x	x	x	x	x	x	x	x

Source: Hamai, K., et al. 1995.

requirements, to be used creatively and strategically for feasible and desirable solutions. Probation is not an external solution to internal problems of criminal justice. Neither probation nor criminal justice can be divorced from international and local developments. Identifying local beliefs, knowledge, and experiences through comparative analyses is the job of a comparativist; provision of a blueprint for all places and times is not.

REFERENCES

Hamai, K., R. Ville, R. Harris, M. Hough, and U. Zvekic, eds. 1995. *Probation Round the World*. London: Routledge.

van Dijk, J.J.M. 1994. "Who Is Afraid of the Crime Victim." Keynote lecture at the VII Symposium of the World Society of Victimology, Adelaide, Australia, August 21–26.

van Dijk, J.J.M., and P. Mayhew. 1992. *Criminal Victimisation in the Industrialized World*. The Hague: Ministry of Justice of the Netherlands.

van Dijk, J.J.M., P. Mayhew, and M. Killias. 1990. *Experiences of Crime Across the World*. Deventer: Kluwer.

Zvekic, U., ed. 1994. *Alternatives to Imprisonment in Comparative Perspective*. Chicago: Nelson-Hall.

Zvekic, U., and A. Alvazzi del Frate, eds. 1995. *Criminal Victimisation in the Developing World*. Rome: United Nations Interregional Crime and Justice Research Institute.

DISCIPLINE IN PRISONS AROUND THE WORLD

Human Rights Watch

Discipline in prisons is justified as a sanction for violating the rules, but as Human Rights Watch documents, cruel and unusual discipline is taking place around the world and is unwarranted, and often unauthorized. In this reading, Human Rights Watch—an independent, international human rights group—summarizes its findings on prison conditions around the world and makes recommendations to help eradicate abuse.

Disciplinary measures are punishment on top of punishment. In total institutions such as prisons, where every aspect of an inmate's life is controlled, many measures affecting the everyday life of a prisoner can be punishments and the list of punishments used in prisons all over the world is almost endless. Disturbingly, Human Rights Watch discovered that in country after country, punishments meted out within the prisons are cruel, humiliating, and frequently applied in an arbitrary fashion without the slightest vestige of due process.

Punishments may range from a verbal reprimand, or a written notation in a prisoner's record, to the denial of certain privileges—such as access to television, being allowed to smoke, the opportunity to participate in social events or purchase goods from a commissary—to forfeiture of good time (a way of gaining earlier release), transfer to

Reprinted from chapter 12, "Discipline," of *The Human Rights Watch Global Report on Prisons*, by permission of Human Rights Watch. Copyright 1993 by Human Rights Watch.

a higher security institution, confinement in segregation or punishment cells, or restraint in fetters or shackles.

As Human Rights Watch investigated disciplinary measures in prisons, we examined the country's prison regulations to see what measures were legally authorized. Often, we found that there were two sets of punishments: authorized and unauthorized. Both were used. The latter usually involved physical violence.

We also studied the range of offenses—it is often revealing to discover what constitutes an infraction in a particular prison system—and the corresponding penalties. In addition, we examined the degree of due process in determining penalties, and whether prisoners were afforded any possibility of appeal.

Types of Offenses

Disciplinary measures are necessary because inmates often violate the rules and sometimes commit serious offenses. Though penalties should be imposed when an inmate attempts to escape, destroys property, inflicts violence on his fellow prisoners or staff, smuggles drugs into the prison, or otherwise disrupts order in the institution in a serious way, the offenses for which some prison systems in fact impose penalties go far beyond such matters.

In communist Czechoslovakia it was against the rules, and thus punishable, to listen to the radio; to own a book or writing pad; to receive more than one letter from one's family; not to take off one's cap when talking to a guard; to call someone "comrade" in an ironical fashion; to finish work early; or to lie on the bed during the day; study; or write letters for illiterate fellow prisoners. At the time of our 1990 visit, following the democratic transformation in Czechoslovakia, pre-trial detainees in Slovakia were still forbidden to exercise in their cells or to wear watches, or to sit or lie on the beds during the daytime.

In China inmates may be punished for not remembering all the words of the regulations; not admitting guilt; standing by the window; speaking loudly; or not arranging one's bedroll properly.

In Romania prisoners may be punished, usually by beatings on the palms of their hands, for lying on the bed during the day or taking too long while using the bathroom. Inmates are required to stand with their faces toward the wall, usually in the cell corner or at the end of a hallway, whenever a stranger enters the area.

In Turkey prisoners are prohibited to write, draw, or put up a picture on a cell wall. It can also be an offense to fail to prevent crimes or disciplinary infractions by other prisoners or else to fail to notify the administration of such matters.

Corporal Punishment

Among the countries where we investigated prison conditions, only two authorized corporal punishment in their prison-related laws. South Africa's Correctional Services Act 8 of 1959 authorizes the use of corporal punishment "not exceeding six strokes, if the prisoner is a convicted prisoner apparently under the age of forty years." During our 1992 visit, a Human Rights Watch delegation was told that such punishment was being used less and less often. The Minister of Correctional Services told Parliament that corporal punishment was used 120 times in 1989; 102 times in 1990 and just 44 times in 1991.[1]

Egyptian Law No. 396 of 1956 authorizes the beating of juveniles and the whipping of adult prisoners as a disciplinary penalty, in specific violation of Egypt's Constitution, which prohibits inflicting physical or mental harm on prisoners. Prisoners under seventeen years of age may be beaten ten times with a thin stick, and adults may receive up to thirty-six lashes with a specially designed whip. According to prison officials, whipping is used to punish major offenses such as striking a guard or attempting to escape.

But various forms of physical violence are used in retaliatory fashion in almost all the prison systems we investigated; moreover, violence is employed in Egypt and South Africa far in excess of what is envisioned by the law. A prisoner in Egypt was whipped for writing a letter of complaint to the country's president. Another prisoner, who had written to the president denouncing that whipping, told our delegation that a few days later he was also beaten on sensitive parts of his body by security officers and then placed in a punishment cell.

A Palestinian prisoner told us that he and some eight other prisoners went on a hunger strike in July 1991 to protest their continuing detention without charge in Egypt's Abu Za'bal prison. "We were taken out separately and beaten with sticks and with hands," he told the Human Rights Watch delegation.[2]

A Somali citizen, Mohammed Mahmud Shak, died on November 29, 1991 in an Egyptian prison after he was severely beaten following an attempted escape the previous July. About a hundred guards had taken turns beating him.

In November 1992 two prisoners in the Boniato prison in Cuba were beaten for conducting a hunger strike. The previous February another Cuban prisoner, Francisco Díaz Mesa, died from a beating he had sustained for banging on the bars of his cell to protest the denial of medical attention he needed, reportedly for pneumonia.

In China, according to one recently released political prisoner, inmates were beaten if they refused to work. Beatings in Chinese prisons have been frequent, by all accounts. Another recently released prisoner reported that guards sometimes beat inmates simply because they did not like their physical appearance.

In Czechoslovakia in June 1990—after the Velvet Revolution—a female prisoner was beaten by some six guards for looking out the window and calling out to her boyfriend.

In Kenya, a prisoner released from a maximum security prison in 1989, offered the following testimony: "Take, for example, a case when prisoner is found with half a cigarette; when he is taken to the duty officer all the prison guards in the office will be hitting the prisoner with their batons. The most horrifying aspect of this beating is that the guards normally have as their target some of the most sensitive parts of the body, mainly the knee and hand joints, and at the end of this the prisoner can hardly walk."[3]

In a lockup in Romania we encountered a young man whose hands were swollen from beatings with a rubber truncheon for offenses such as taking too much time while in the bathroom and sleeping during the day. Many inmates reported being beaten on the palms of their hands, and several more reported witnessing such incidents.

In Puerto Rico we interviewed an inmate who described an incident in which guards kicked an inmate in his genitals in retaliation for making a complaint.

Punitive Segregation

Solitary Confinement I hold this slow and daily tampering with the mysteries of the brain to be immeasurably worse than any torture of the body; and because its ghastly signs and tokens are not so palpable to the eye and sense of touch as scars upon the flesh; because its wounds are not upon the surface, and it extorts few cries that human ears can hear; therefore I the more denounce it, as a secret punishment which slumbering humanity is not roused up to stay.[4]

Thus wrote Charles Dickens after visiting the Eastern Penitentiary in Philadelphia in 1842. At the time, solitary confinement lasted for the duration of the sentence in this prison. The cell walls were thick; each had a small yard; and each cell had a double door—one of solid oak, the other of iron grating. Hence, prisoners never saw each other and their only human contact was with the guards. Typically, they had looms in their cells, or a workbench with tools, so even work was solitary.

But Dickens could have written that passage today referring to China. Xu Wenli, an editor of a *samizdat* magazine, was arrested in April 1981. He was placed in a solitary cell, and was put to work there, attaching ornamental buckles to shoes. In 1985, in a document he managed to smuggle out, he recorded:

I have always had a north-facing cell and have been kept in solitary confinement throughout. Since I have been able to exchange a few words each day with the prison orderlies, however, along the lines of "Lovely weather, isn't it," I have not yet been reduced to losing my ability to speak.

That smuggled document, several hundred pages long and detailing conditions of his imprisonment, earned Xu a transfer to a "special regime cell" where he spent the next several years under yet worse conditions (see below).

The duration of solitary confinement applied as punishment is usually limited by a country's law. But law and practice are all too often two entirely separate matters. In China, Article 62 of the *secret* "Detailed Rules for the Disciplinary Work of Prisons and Labor Reform Detachments" of 1982 stipulates: "Except in the case of condemned prisoners for whom final approval of execution is still pending and also the case of prisoners currently undergoing trial, the period of solitary confinement is in general not to exceed a period of seven to ten days. The maximum permissible period is fifteen days."

In Cuba a 1988 delegation that included a representative of Human Rights Watch was told that prisoners could not be kept in a punishment cell for more than twenty-one days. But one prisoner, serving twenty years for espionage, told the delegation that he had been held in solitary confinement from 1981 to 1985.

In South Africa solitary confinement may last for up to forty-two days if authorized by a magistrate.[5] Yet Breyten Breytenbach, one of the country's foremost writers, arrested for returning to the country illegally from exile in Paris and trying to set up a mixed-race democratic organization, was held in solitary confinement for two of the seven years of his imprisonment.[6]

In Poland an inmate interviewed in a punishment cell during our 1989 visit talked to us of his fears about "losing his mind." Another said, "I get depressed very easily, and stupid thoughts come to mind, like suicide."[7] The maximum time in isolation was then six months. It was subsequently reduced to one month.

In addition to concerns over the length of time inmates spend in solitary confinement, we were also distressed by how easily this supposedly most serious of sanctions is meted out to prisoners.

In Russia almost any violation of the rules—including cursing at or showing disrespect for the guards, refusing to work, arguing with other inmates, or not meeting a production quota—can result in a term in a punishment cell.

In Cuba an inmate was punished with forty-five days in solitary confinement for writing a letter to the Nicaraguan leader, Violeta Chamorro, congratulating her on winning the presidential election.

Vaclav Havel, now the President of the Czech Republic, was put in solitary confinement once for drafting letters for an illiterate gypsy.

Isolation in Conjunction with Other Measures

Even though isolation is usually considered the most severe disciplinary measure, in several countries Human Rights Watch found that it was applied in combination with additional sanctions.

An inmate in Poland told us, "I'm beginning to feel crazy; I get no mail, no cigarettes, no visits."[8]

In South Africa inmates in disciplinary segregation are often further punished through reduced diet. Similarly, in Cuba, prisoners in punishment cells are fed only twice a day and one of those "meals" barely qualifies as such.

In Romania inmates in isolation are required to get up at 5 A.M. and to stand in their cells until 10 P.M. During that time, beds are folded up against the wall. The light is kept on day and night.

In the United States, inmates in segregation in the women's jail in Los Angeles may be additionally punished with a special diet, consisting of fully nutritional but utterly tasteless balls of a specially-prepared blend of nutritive substances.

In Russia during solitary confinement prisoners are forbidden to have possessions with them and are denied almost all other rights, including the right to exercise.

In several countries, physical restraints are used as an additional punishment in isolation cells.

Punishment Cells Punishment cells, in addition to separating some inmates from the rest of the prison population, are frequently designed specifically to inflict physical hardships on their occupants.

In Indonesia a former prisoner held in Besi prison in Java described the punishment cell there as one meter square—too small to lie down.

In Russia punishment cells—where up to three prisoners at a time may be segregated from the rest of the population—are very small (about eleven feet by ten feet), have stucco walls (which are painful to lean against), often have no windows, and have very dirty toilets. Beds in punishment cells have no mattresses.

In South Africa punishment cells are bare except for a mat on the floor for a prisoner to sleep on and a sink and a toilet. We were also told of the use of so called "dark cells," with no windows and barely enough space to lie down.

In Cuba punishment cells in the notorious "rectangle of death" in the Combinado del Este prison in Havana, where many of the most prominent political prisoners served their sentences, were about ten feet long and four feet wide. Up to two people were held in each, although there were triple concrete bunks—with no bedding—indicating that three could be housed there as well. The toilet was a hole in the floor that often becomes clogged, spilling into the cell. Every cell was separated from the hallway by two doors: a barred one, partially covered by sheet metal, and a wooden one that completely shuts out ventilation and light from the hallway and was arbitrarily opened or closed by prison guards. Just inside the wooden door was a very dim light bulb, by which one could not even see one's hands. Similar cells are used in punishment wings of three other men's prisons that we saw.

In Zaire punishment cells have no windows and no ventilation; prisoners may be held in them for up to forty-five days.

In the U.S. cells in the punishment Q-wing at

the Florida State Prison had no windows and very poor ventilation.

In China, the "strict regime" cell to which Xu Wenli was transferred after publicizing the conditions of his earlier imprisonment (see above), was a windowless, damp vault in which a light bulb shone relentlessly day and night. The cell was too small to stand up straight. It crawled with insects. There was a strip of matting on the concrete floor to sleep on and a bucket placed in a corner served as a toilet. Xu spent no less than three-and-a-half years in this cell.

In a Romanian lockup, our delegation saw two windowless cells measuring two-and-a-half by two feet, approximately half the size of a telephone booth. There was no source of light and no possibility to sit comfortably. In several interviews with inmates, we were told that these cells were used frequently, often for a few hours at a time. Such cells are known as *chiquitas* in Nicaragua where they were used in pre-trial detention facilities during the Sandanista period, also for a few hours at a time.

In Brazil we documented a particularly horrific example of the use of a punishment cell. In February 1989, Military Police called to São Paulo's Police Precinct 42 in response to a disturbance that erupted in the lockup, forced fifty-one men into a cell measuring less than fifty square feet, with a heavy metal door and no windows, and held them there for more than an hour. When the door was opened, eighteen prisoners were found to have suffocated to death.

The Use of Physical Restraints

Chains, leg irons, fetters, and shackles are prison-related artifacts one might associate with medieval times rather than the end of the twentieth century. Yet, in several countries, Human Rights Watch found various types of physical restraints are used today to punish prisoners. We want to stress a clear distinction between the legitimate use of physical restraints employed temporarily to subdue a frenzied prisoner, or as a security precaution for particularly violent or dangerous prisoners during transfers or on similar occasions, and the punitive use of physical restraints.

Leg irons and handcuffs are commonly used as a means of punishment in Romania. During our delegation's 1991 visit, we observed numerous prisoners who were shackled in leg chains and/or handcuffs for extended periods. One prisoner told us he had spent eight months in chains in Section Two of the Poarta Alba prison. At Gehrla prison, eight prisoners who had participated in the August 1990 revolt at this prison were still in leg irons and handcuffs when our delegation visited in October of the following year. We spoke to one prisoner who had been sentenced to an extra three years in prison for participation in that revolt. In addition he had been kept in restraints for fourteen months. He was unable to lift his arms above his chest and had calluses where the handcuffs rubbed his wrists.

Nor had things changed much in Romania the following year (1992) when our next delegation received repeated reports of the use of chains, handcuffs (including handcuffing an inmate to the wall in one case) and leg irons as punishment in the lockups.

In China prison rules, which all cadres and inmates are supposed to learn by heart, authorize the use of chains and fetters for those who violate the regulations "in more serious cases."[9] A wide variety of implements are in use, including handcuffs, ankle fetters, and chains. Under the law, the time limit for the use of physical restraints (with the exception of prisoners condemned to death) is fifteen days; in practice, however, such time limits are ignored.

In South Africa restraints are used as an additional means to punish those in isolation. During a 1993 visit by a Human Rights Watch delegation, we saw one inmate in an isolation cell with a chain about a foot-and-a-half long around his ankles.

In India physical restraints—fetters, shackles and handcuffs—are employed more commonly than punishment cells to deal with those who commit infractions. The use of these restraints is prescribed by the Jail Manuals, which spell out in great detail the specific manner in which prisoners should be treated. The Punjab Jail Manual, for example, provides for three kinds of handcuffs. An iron bar variety may not weigh more than twenty-one pounds. As for the leg fetters, one variety that is specified and whose use in practice was reported to us in interviews, has a bar that holds the legs apart. Though the manual says that the bar may be no more than sixteen inches in length, a former inmate gave us a description of a much longer bar that holds the legs apart in such a manner as to cause great pain after the legs have been kept in this position for an extended period. The manual allows the sixteen-inch bar to be used for up to ten days at a time, and other leg fetters may be used for up to three months at a time.

In Zaire, leg chains and metal spans are used in many prisons, mostly in the interior of the country. The restraints often cause severe burns to the skin and require a hacksaw to be removed.

Punishments Related to Contacts with Relatives

Reduced contacts with relatives are often used as a disciplinary measure and are a matter of serious concern. Any such measure to penalize a prisoner for some infraction also penalizes his or her family.

In some countries inmates who commit infractions are transferred to a different institution as a punishment. This often makes family visits more difficult or impossible. It is a particularly serious problem in countries that span great distances.

In Puerto Rico inmates "who cause trouble" are sometimes transferred to a prison in the continental United States. This usually ends visits because air travel is both time-consuming and expensive.

In Spain inmates are sometimes transferred from one end of the country to another as punishment. This measure is used particularly against riot leaders, real or suspected.

In the United Kingdom we were told of a practice nicknamed "ghosting," for particularly disruptive prisoners. This consists of moving such an inmate frequently throughout the prison system, presumably to make it impossible to establish ties within any prison population. It also makes it difficult for relatives to visit such a prisoner. One prisoner reported he had been held in more than thirty institutions during a four-year period.

In addition, as mentioned earlier, a ban on correspondence and visits is frequently used in conjunction with punitive segregation.

Unusual Forms of Punishment

Prison administrations are inventive not only in defining offenses but in designing punishments. In addition to the sanctions described above which are used in many prison systems, Human Rights Watch encountered a few that are peculiar to a single system.

In China prisoners reported that guards would sometimes make an inmate stand naked in the middle of his cell for such offenses as talking to a neighbor during the night.[10] Also in China, inmates are sometimes made to sit motionless for hours every day, staring at a wall, so that they "repent their sins."[11]

In Egypt an inmate's clothes may be shredded as a punishment in addition to placement in a punishment cell.

In the U.S., 1990 court records describe a punishment called "strip status."[12] An inmate was stripped of all clothing, bedding and personal possessions. He was then expected to "earn" back items piece-by-piece through good behavior. The Oregon correctional authorities, under whose jurisdiction this practice was applied, claim this punishment is no longer in use.

A prisoner in Indonesia was punished for playing music by a requirement to walk stooped for two hours. Another form of punishment in Indonesia was to force an inmate to kick rocks with his feet. And a particularly cruel form of punishment for political prisoners in Cuba has been the denial of medical attention.

The Punitive Use of a "Privilege" System In South African prisons, almost everything that is not prohibited is declared to be a "privilege": possessions, letters, visits, access to reading material, permission to write literary pieces, authorization to have a TV set in one's cell and more. Inmates are divided into "privilege" groups A, B, C, and D, regardless of their security classification and the type of institution they are in. All prisoners start in group C; their classification is reviewed at half-year intervals, by an "Institutional Committee" (composed of prison staff members), which upgrades or downgrades prisoners according to their behavior. Under this system a prisoner has to gain the most basic rights—such as contact visits with relatives—through a spotless disciplinary record. Even then, it takes at least one year to move from the entry, or C level, to A group, the only one permitted contact visits.

Collective Punishment

In several countries, we heard complaints that prisoners are often punished as a group without respect to whether they were individually involved in committing an infraction. Collective punishment is, of course, a serious violation of due process; it also adds to a prisoner's feeling that he or she has lost individuality and become a pawn in a large system.

When we visited the Barbetron maximum security prison in South Africa, we found that one whole section was then deprived of access to sports and recreation as punishment for a gang fight several weeks earlier.

In the U.S., at the time of our visit to the Immigration and Naturalization Service (INS) detention center at Krome, Florida (where illegal aliens were held), we were told that all the women in the institution were being punished for a protest by some of them that consisted of messing up the bathroom.

Collective punishment is most frequent in the aftermath of prison protests and disturbances. . . .

Due Process in Disciplinary Procedure

Every prison should have a disciplinary procedure and prisoners should be informed of the offenses for which they are punished and the extent of that punishment. They should also be given an opportunity to defend themselves and to appeal. Even though such a procedure usually exists on the books in most countries Human Rights Watch visited, more often than not it was violated in practice.

In particular, we are concerned that in most countries, punishments are meted out arbitrarily by prison officials without external oversight and that there is no effective mechanism for appeal. This often leads to the application of sanctions that are disproportionately harsh for the offenses committed, and affords the staff opportunities to exercise undue pressure or to avenge personal grievances.

Undeclared Punishment

In countries where law is respected and where disciplinary sanctions in prisons require due process, a problem nevertheless arises when measures are taken that are declared not to be punishment but, in fact, are punitive. Such measures may be imposed arbitrarily by the prison staff, without the possibility of an appeal, and with no time limit on their duration.

In England and Wales, under Prison Rule 43, the prison director may decide to separate some prisoners from the general population for the maintenance of the "good order and discipline" of the institution. Prisoners in England and Wales are generally entitled to a disciplinary hearing if they are charged with a disciplinary offense, but the invocation of Rule 43 circumvents this right. No specific offense is needed to mark a prisoner for segregation and Rule 43 does not specify duration.[13]

In the United States, many prison systems—including the federal, more than thirty state systems and some local jails—have recently designated separate institutions or parts of institutions for the confinement of prisoners under particularly harsh conditions and exceptionally strict security. Such assignment often amounts to solitary confinement for years on end. In the Florida State Prison at Starke, some inmates are held in windowless cells from which they are allowed out only three times a week, for ten minutes, to shower. Otherwise, they are alone in the cell. Such confinement may last for extended periods; some of the inmates Human Rights Watch interviewed in that prison had not been outdoors for several years. In the Maximum Control Complex in Westville, Indiana, inmates are locked in their cells for between twenty-two-and-a-half and twenty-four hours a day, never see anyone except their guards, and are often punished through the loss of access to reading materials, among other measures.

In Marion, Illinois, the harshest prison within

the U.S. federal system and the model for these particularly punitive prisons, where an average stay lasts three years, prisoners are locked in their cells around the clock, except for recreation (between seven and eleven hours a week, depending on classification). Yet placement there is technically not considered a disciplinary measure; it is administrative, and as such is not preceded by a hearing. As a result an inmate is afforded no possibility of appeal, and this sanction is open-ended. The decision to confine an inmate in such an institution is made by prison administrators alone and is often based on the mere prediction that an inmate will be dangerous or predatory rather than on any actual infraction.

In Israel conditions in the modern ultra-maximum security wing of Nitzan prison are the strictest in the system and are the cause of grave concern. According to officials, prisoners are assigned to the wing on the grounds that they pose a physical danger to guards or other prisoners. However, assignment to Nitzan is clearly used as a means of punishment, particularly against Islamists whose original crimes are considered exceptionally heinous or whom the authorities wish to punish for other reasons. Inmates, all of them Palestinians from Israel or the occupied territories, are confined to their one-man cells twenty-three hours a day, and may never go out unless handcuffed. They must wear legcuffs during visits by relatives and lawyers. Conditions at Nitzan's Ward Eight are harsher than at other facilities in ways that have little to do with protecting others. The cells are partly below street level and have poor ventilation and little natural light; access to reading materials is more restricted than at other prisons; and beatings by guards are reported to be more common than at other facilities of the Israeli Prison Service.

Recommendations

Sanctions for violating the rules are necessary in prisons, as they are in any society or community if it is to function properly. But, as the examples cited in this [article] demonstrate, a fundamental right—freedom from cruel and unusual punishment—is often ignored when it comes to punishing prisoners. To eradicate cruelty inflicted on prisoners by prison staff is not a matter of huge investments. What is needed most of all is a policy decision at the central level of the country's prison administration and the will to enforce this policy. Human Rights Watch believes that disciplinary measures, whether authorized or not, should be closely scrutinized by all those monitoring prison conditions: official prison inspectors, judges, nongovernmental organizations, and international bodies. In addition Human Rights Watch specifically recommends that:

- disciplinary measures should be standardized countrywide and set at the central administration level;
- prisons should keep a log of all punishments meted out;
- every prison system should have a means of monitoring the use of disciplinary measures in prisons, independent of the penal administration; the results of such monitoring should be a matter of public record;
- prison officials who employ extralegal disciplinary measures should themselves be disciplined;
- a disciplinary sanction may only be applied when the offense for which it is meted out has been specified in advance and the prisoner has been informed that such conduct is prohibited;
- upon their arrival in an institution, prisoners must be informed what constitutes an offense and the corresponding penalty;
- prisoners must be given an opportunity to appeal a disciplinary sanction to an independent decision-maker;
- no disciplinary sanction may be imposed indefinitely (i.e., "pending review");
- corporal punishment may never be imposed;
- denial of medical care may never be imposed as punishment;
- deprivation of food or deliberately distasteful food should never be used as punishment;
- deprivation of bedding and clothing should never be used as punishment;
- physical restraints may never be used for disciplinary purposes. When used to restrain

a distraught or violent prisoner, they may only be used temporarily, and care must be taken not to cause physical injuries;

- prisoners should not be required to "gain" their basic rights with good behavior; punishments consisting of loss of privileges should be clearly defined and limited in time;
- collective punishment may never be imposed;
- disciplinary measures restricting contacts with relatives should be used as punishment solely for infractions related to those contacts (smuggling contraband, for example). Punitive transfer to distant institutions should never be imposed;
- solitary confinement should be used sparingly and never for longer than a few days;
- punishment cells, whether solitary or collective, should have toilet facilities and such basic furniture as a bed with bedding as well as proper light and ventilation. Cells that are intended to cause physical hardship (because they are too small, very stuffy or dark, for example) should never be used.

NOTES

1. *S.A. Barometer*, vol. 6, no. 19 (September 25, 1992).

2. Middle East Watch, *Prison Conditions in Egypt* (New York: Human Rights Watch, 1993), p. 91.

3. Africa Watch, *Kenya: Taking Liberties* (New York: Human Rights Watch, 1991), p. 167.

4. Charles Dickens, *American Notes.*

5. Dirk van Zyl Smit, *South African Prison Law and Practice* (Durban: Butterworth, 1992).

6. Breytenbach describes his prison experience in *The True Confessions of an Albino Terrorist* (New York: Farrar, Straus & Giroux, 1985).

7. Helsinki Watch, *Prison Conditions in Poland* (New York: Human Rights Watch, 1991), p. 30.

8. Helsinki Watch, *Prison Conditions in Poland. An Update* (New York: Human Rights Watch, 1991), p. 30.

9. Asia Watch, *Anthems of Defeat: Crackdown in Hunan Province 1989–1992* (New York: Human Rights Watch, 1992), p. 77.

10. Human Rights Watch interview, December 1992.

11. Asia Watch, *Anthems of Defeat*, p. 94.

12. *Honed v. Maass*, 745 F. Supp. 623 (D.Or. 1990), cited in Human Rights Watch, *Prison Conditions in the United States* (New York: 1991), p. 47.

13. Prison Rule 43 states: "Where it appears desirable, for the maintenance of the good order and discipline or in his own interests, that a prisoner should not associate with other prisoners, either generally or for particular purposes, the prison director may arrange for the prisoner's removal from association accordingly." Helsinki Watch, *Prison Conditions in the United Kingdom* (New York: Human Rights Watch, 1992), p. 17.

DISCUSSION QUESTIONS

1. Gary Marx notes that today in the United States we find examples of a blending of social control agencies that have traditionally been clearly separate (e.g., the cooperation of police, military, and national security agencies working with foreign agents to execute Pablo Escobar). Discuss both the problems and the benefits of increased mingling.

2. Increased cooperation among the world's social control agencies will likely require increased consensus about what needs to be controlled. Discuss the potential for any significant level of harmonization of efforts when countries such as Pakistan view Michael Jackson and Madonna as terrorists while the United States reserves that label for people like those responsible for the bombing of the World Trade Center.

3. Why is probation popular in so many countries? Alternatively, what might explain Israel's and Japan's low use of probation in comparison with imprisonment, while South Australia and Hungary use the two sanctions in about equal proportion (see Fig. 1 in Ugljesa Zvekic's article)?

4. In the 1990s some prisons in the United States have moved to bring back prison chain gangs, humiliate prisoners by making them wear pink outfits or the old "prison stripes," take away presumed privileges like weight lifting and watching television, and employ other techniques to stop what critics say is the coddling of prisoners. Although relevant statistics do not exist, we can assume that some prisoners (including those in the United States) commit crimes that return them to prisons that have treated them harshly. Given the dangerous, degrading, harsh, and punitive conditions found in many prisons around the world as described by Human Rights Watch, why do people risk being returned to those prisons by committing new crimes after their release?

5. Discuss which, if any, disciplinary procedures described in the reading are reasonable. Which might be considered so outrageous that they violate natural human rights even if they don't violate the laws of a particular country? With which recommendations listed at the end of the Human Rights Watch reading do you agree?

WEBSITES

www.ncjrs.org/unojust

Criminal justice research institutes around the world are linked under the sponsorship of the United Nations Crime Prevention and Criminal Justice Division in Vienna.

newark.rutgers.edu/~wcjlen/WCJLEN!.html

This home page of the World Criminal Justice Library Network offers a variety of information about the justice system and process in countries around the world.

www.hrw.org/home.html

Human Rights Watch provides this website for persons interested in the group's activities and publications.

INDEX